The Life Of Frederick Maehle

From His Memoirs

Edited and Adapted by
Gerda Freedheim

Translated by Hilde Maehle
& Ursula Korneitchouk

The Life Of Frederick Maehle
From His Memoirs

Edited and Adapted by
Gerda Freedheim

Translated by Hilde Maehle
& Ursula Korneitchouk

ISBN — 9781626132290
LCCN — 2020943695

Copyright 2020
Published by ATBOSH Media ltd.

Cleveland, Ohio, USA
http://www.ATBOSH.com

Table of Contents

Preface 5

Forward 13

I — The Ancestors 17

II — Frederick Maehle-His Youth 53

III — School in Reval and Military Service 101

IV — Fritz Joins the Railroad 135

V — The University Years, 1895-1900 159

VI — The Early Years of Marriage 183

VII — The Family Grows, Dynamics Change ... 229

VII — World War I Years 263

IX — Post War Recovery Years 325

X — The Great Depression 357

XI — World War II 403

Epilogue 417

Appendix A — The Island of Dago 423

Appendix B — A Brief History of Estonia 427

Photos 437

References 445

About the Author 447

Preface

This is a story of a family, my family, or at least a part of it. It is based on the memoirs of my grandfather, Frederick Maehle. It was customary in the 19th and early 20th Centuries for people to keep a diary or journal. They wrote their activities of the day as well as their most personal and intimate thoughts. In 1904, grandfather, who was called Fritz, began compiling his memoirs. During WWI, the city of Lodz, where he and his family lived, was under siege; the schools were closed, his work was erratic so he would tell his children stories about his ancestors, his childhood, and his youth. He began his memoirs in 1913.

Although he ended writing the memoirs in 1938, his son, Kola, continued them from notes and journal entries he found after the war. The last journal entry was May 20, 1940. Kola brought the manuscript to Canada in 1950 when he immigrated. I was aware of its existence when I was a teen and, in fact, saw it; Kola had sent it to my mother. I'm quite sure that she read it, although she would never discuss it with us. When I asked her about it, she either brushed it off or told me she didn't have time to translate it into English. When Kola was settled in Canada she sent it back to him. And that was the last I saw of or thought about it until the early 1990s, when Hilde, Kola's widow, sent it to my brother who made a copy for me. Meanwhile Hilde was translating it into English. And so the story you are about to read was born.

Frederick Maehle, nicknamed Fritz, was an Estonian, born in 1871 on the island of Dago, now called Hiiumaa in Estonian, in the Bay of Finland.[1] His mother was a Swede, as was his grandmother. The Swedes settled as free farmers; they were never serfs. Historians think most originated with Scandinavian Vikings, except for the Swedish nobility who were awarded lands or estates by the Swedish government when Sweden controlled Estonia.

How long Fritz's family had been on Dago is not known, but one can presume for many generations, as the island was quite isolated and people, especially the peasant class, didn't move much. According to Fritz, the Maehles were Estonian serfs and peasants. Fritz stated that his brother Hermann, a pastor in Reval, undertook an extensive search for family records. He found church records, which document Maehle births from as early as 1645. Unfortunately, most were lost during WWI. The only remaining few are from the 19th Century and are attached to the original German manuscript. Prior to the 17th Century, there were no written records of his family. They didn't even have sir names until the beginning of the 19th Century. He wrote in his memoirs that his grandmother told him many stories of the family and its history. However, it doesn't appear that he wrote many of them down. The only information we have of his ancestral origins is from his memoirs, as told to him by his parents and grandmother.

There is substantial agreement among archaeologists that ancestors of this culture were Balto-Finns, likely associated with Finno-Urgian

---

[1] See Appendix A for a description of Dago.

nomads who settled down to become peasants with small farms. In 1227 Germany conquered Livonia and vassalages were established. In return for military service these German vassals received estates of land. Gradually the peasants' freedoms were eroded until the mid-16th Century when serfdom became official.[2] Peasants were taken into bondage and became attached to land owned by nobles. They never veered more than a few miles from their homes, which were in hamlets, also attached to and owned by the estate. They were literally tied to their place of birth and responsible for fixed taxes, usually born by several peasant hamlets all owned by the same estate. The estate owners on the island of Dago as well as the mainland were principally German, with some Swedish. Although they had lived in the Baltic for many generations, they never gave up their original identity. German had become the language of the aristocracy in the Baltic.

Russia emancipated serfs in the Governorate of Estonia in 1816 but there were no significant change in the peasants' basic relationships to the landowner or state until 1861 with the Emancipation Reform of 1861. No longer tied to landowners, they were allowed to buy land marry freely and live independently. Reform took many years to be substantially realized as most serfs were poor and uneducated. My great-great-great-grandfather, named Michael, was the first to leave the island for the mainland, where he learned German and apprenticed as a carpenter. We don't know if he left of his own free will or was sent by Baron Stackelberg, whose family owned Keinis, an estate on Dago and also Riesenberg, another on the mainland for

---

[2] They were *de facto* serfs long before that time.

generations.³ Michael became very skilled, and returned to Dago where he oversaw the building of a new textile mill, also owned by the Stackelbergs. My grandfather's generation was the first to be what we would call white collar middle class and professional, although Andreas, my great grandfather's youngest brother became a teacher and principal of a school on the mainland.

While many Estonians were converted to Catholicism, both my grandfather and grandmother's families were Lutherans.⁴ Religion played a dominant role in their lives, principally for social reasons. People were identified by their religion, as well as their nationality. Both the Russian Orthodox and Lutheran Churches had political responsibilities in the Russian Empire. The Baltic States had more Lutherans and Roman Catholics, while Russia proper was predominantly Russian Orthodox. In the late 19th Century, Estonians were beginning to become pastors, a class just below estate owners and a profession closed to them up until that time. They had responsibility for overseeing districts, similar to a parish but with state granted powers. My grandfather expressed great pride in his brother Hermann, who became a pastor in Reval, now Tallinn. Throughout his memoirs, friendships are made with other Lutherans and in Lodz, where he settled in 1900, most of his friends seem to have been Baltic Lutherans. He also socialized with German and French colleagues from his work. He does not mention socializing with any Poles and in fact, never learned to speak Polish

---

³ The Maehles were indentured to Keinis and in the 1820s there was still *de facto* serfdom.
⁴ The Stackelbergs were Lutheran and so the peasants on their estates would have been also. Serfs were converted to Christianity from paganism in the early 16th Century.

fluently; it was always a second language. Social life was so defined.[5]

I have to say at the onset that this story is not one of happiness and prosperity. More, it is a story of survival of a family devastated and fragmented by World War I, then the Great Depression, and finally WWII. Grandfather's writings are painfully intimate. He revealed his heart and his soul. He expressed his joys and his sorrows, his conflicts and his friendships. As already noted, the manuscript is long and somewhat tedious in places, with numerous references to people, places and events that had little or no meaning to me and would not have meaning to today's reader. Also, the translation, which is very good, is sometimes awkward as it is verbatim. After reading it through several times I decided to edit it. Nevertheless, I have tried to retained his full story, often in his own words. I have also retained many direct quotes. I deliberated deleting some of his comments, which were particularly painful to read but decided not to. They are all there — including his growing anti-Semitism around the time of the Bolshevik Revolution. I wouldn't presume to apologize for him or to somehow justify his feelings. But, without apologizing, we must recognize that times then were different. As I've noted, people were separated by their religions, and Jews were a totally isolated group, living in ghettos and interacting with the majority population infrequently and then only for business. When business didn't go well, if Jews were involved, they were blamed. At the same time, as you will see, when there was an altercation with someone else, nationality was blamed if the person was not a Baltic Lutheran. Having said this, I never heard my mother say a single anti-Semitic remark. Most difficult for me in reading this text was thinking

---

[5] For an excellent history of Estonia see Raun.

of my mother as the story unwinds. On balance, she had a very difficult life. Grandfather's story tells why.

I found that I could not write in the first person singular as my grandfather had done, so I changed my text to the third person. I am the narrator. For clarity's sake I am not calling him grandfather, but Fritz. My grandmother was called Maria and sometimes Mamme. I have written the place names and first names of family members as they appear in the memoirs. Some of the names have strange spellings such as Miska (which I got from a letter in her own hand) and Jurgensen, also from a letter to my mother from Fritz as well as the manuscript. The original of more than 600 pages was written in small cursive German script. Hilde translated all but about the last 50 or so pages which Ursula Korneitchouk translated. I have copies of both the original manuscript and the English translations for anyone interested. Amy Freedheim will be custodian of them. I did take the liberty of researching events, mostly political, which Fritz referenced but did not explain. I also added footnotes to give meaning to customs, people and events, which may not be familiar to today's readers.

I am profoundly grateful to Hilde for a true labor of love. How she managed to translate more than 500 pages and bring this story to life amazes me. Ursula, too, deserves a great thank you. Just from the last 50 pages she she became very moved by the story. The translation was not easy, and they did magnificent jobs. I'm also immensely grateful to Jared Bendis, who helped me with layout, pictures and publishing; indeed, he did it for me. You would not be reading this if it were not for Hilde, Ursula and Jared.

And last but never least, I thank Donald, my life partner, the quintessential editor par excellence. He cleaned up all the messes I made and advised me when I had questions about including some events, ideas, opinions or thoughts. He also advised me on clarification when Fritz wrote about political events.

I hope that my children, grandchildren, nieces and nephew will learn something about the lives of their ancestors from this book. It certainly gives a picture of the evolution of a family through generations, from lows, to highs, to lows, and back, like the motion of the oceans as their waves hit the shores.

Gerda K. Freedheim
November 2011[6]

---

[6] Publisher's Note: Gerda spent many years working on this book and back in 2011 we produced an edition of the book purely for her family and friends. After years of coaxing, we managed to convine Gerda that it deserved a wider release and we thank her for letting us publish it.

Foreword
My Family Chronicle
By Frederick Maehle

Lodz, Summer 1913

When I wrote on the first page of these diary collections the proud words, My Family Chronicle, I was aware that this might be a bit presumption. You will find no happenings of worldwide importance; no high and esteemed person is mentioned; and from this point of view, the book might as well never have been written.

If I still undertake the writing, then it is for several other reasons. Firstly, I am of the conviction that our mental as well as our physical existence are strongly influenced by genetic inheritance and find this belief is becoming more and more publicly acknowledged. If one desires to understand oneself better, one should really know his ancestors as thoroughly as possible, even if it is just to estimate how long one's life could be, to understand some of the illness recurring within the family and, last but not least, to know one's own strengths and weaknesses.

Furthermore, we all have a certain interest in history. If nowadays we are inclined to dig literally through half of Europe to find fossils of homo sapiens, then is it not natural to show an even greater interest in our own ancestors — their fate, nationality, professions and places of residence? Our interest should grow and become more intense the further back in time we venture. We are growing our roots deeper into the past. In a certain sense we see ourselves in our ancestors just as we are bound to project ourselves into the future by watching our offspring.

Whether one of my family members in the future will have a deep interest in this book I will not know but I, myself, am deeply interested in these matters, and that is why I am starting to gather all the thoughts I collected on loose sheets so they will not escape my memory. Maybe one of these days, one of the children will enjoy reading these yellowing pages.

My homeland is the island of Dago in the Baltic Sea, Bay of Finland. And as documented, my ancestors were living there 500 years ago. It is therefore only natural that I would like to talk about this piece of land on our globe in detail. Then I will attempt to write about the fate of my immediate family, as well as I know how.

Lodz, Fall 1922

The small booklet, started nine years ago, has grown to several quite large volumes. In the early days of WWI, during which the normal activities were very limited, the booklets grew into war diaries. Since that period was dark and frightening, I often entertained the children with stories from my own childhood and again, I started to collect a lot of loose sheets filled with little short stories and memories which, as such, are probably insignificant. The cut the war and the immediate period afterwards made in our lives was so deep and had such an impact that the time before it, at least to older people, became almost the "good old days." Who could blame us that we took refuge from the present in the past?

Lodz, Summer 1938

The aforementioned big book was still not big enough for all the stories on the loose pages I had collected. The chapters concerning the war years and the years after were transferred from very early diaries. Whenever I had the time and was in the mood, I went over these booklets and transferred these into a big book I started in 1922. Now, in 1938, I am finally at the period after the war. I hope to finish this chapter during this year and will then be up to date.

Chapter I:
The Ancestors

Estonia was under the domination of other powerful neighbors until the end of WWI. Much of its early history was plagued by wars and famines. The 16th century where Fritz began his story was no different. In 1561, Estonia was divided among Russia, Denmark and Sweden. By 1570, Ivan the Terrible succeeded in gaining control of all Northern Estonia, except the city of Reval and the surrounding area, which remained a Swedish Duchy. At that time it was called Estland. The island of Osel, just south of Dago, and Dago remained under Danish control until 1645.

Fritz's Estonian ancestors were peasants, serfs and farmers. Serfs were tied to the land and thereby to the landowner, almost always members of the German but occasionally of Swedish nobility. Although they were allowed to "till the lord's land" for themselves, they could be bought and sold as the land changed hands. Serfs were in effect, slaves. By the end of the 17th century it was estimated that 50-80% of their output was divided between the lord (80%) and the government (20%). Serfs were only formally emancipated in the early 19th century by Russia. Because of the ethnic and class-fixed social structure, Estonians were kept from upward mobility until the late 19th century, leaving the higher classes to Germans and Swedes. Those who did rise on the social ladder could only do so by adopting the language, customs and values of the German elites. Fritz and his brothers were the first of their family one could classify as middle class. And it was a constant struggle, which Fritz plunged into headfirst.

Estonian peasants were not well converted to Christianity and remained a mixture of pagan and Christian well into the 17th Century. For only two generations before him, Fritz's family was Lutheran, probably as a result of the strong German Lutheran influence in Estonia and certainly Dago. Religion was not just something one did on Sunday. It was a social and cultural way of life. It would never have occurred to him to marry anyone but a Lutheran. His friends were all Lutherans — even those with whom he associated in Lodz, Poland. Catholicism, the only other Christian religion of any note, was not even a remote consideration. Jews were always set apart with no social interaction whatsoever.

Fritz wrote a note in the ancestor's chapter regarding sources of dates. He noted that as a child he had little information about them except for stories his parents and his Swedish grandmother, Kersti, had told him. There were a few documents and a few gravestones that he was able to trace back to 1800. When Hermann, Fritz's brother became a pastor in Reval (now Tallinn) in 1908, he was able to obtain old church chronicles and ledgers in the Central Archive. At one point he even employed the help of the city's archivist named Mr. Von Gernet. In 1911, he completed his work, which traced, with documents, the Maehle side of the family to the middle of the 17th Century to Mats of Maeltse, the first ancestor whose name was recorded in church records. The work was affixed with affidavits and the official seal of the city.[7] Unfortunately, Fritz never

---

[7] The few remaining are attached to the original MS.

obtained the whole body of work from his brother, which disappeared sometime after WWI. Thus some information is lost to us. But he did receive a copy of the family tree, now lost, which he used to estimate dates, which were not obtained in records. For example, usually children started appearing the year after marriage and came 1-3 years apart. Also, if there was a wedding date, he estimated birth 30 years before. Thus some incomplete dates are reasoned estimates.

The Oldest Trace of Ancestors (after 1570)

The first person thought to be an ancestor was a peasant of Estonian origin whose name we do not know, but who, as a young man had most likely lived through the devastations wielded by the Tartars under Ivan the Terrible from 1575 to 1580. His existence and time of life have been drawn from some conclusions and oral traditions. It is impossible to say if he was a native of the Island of Dago, for in those days the feudal landlords regularly moved and transplanted their peasants from one of their estates to another. But because the islands were less vulnerable to Tartar attacks than the continent, it may be surmised that he was a born islander. He had three sons born sometime shortly before or during the first decade after 1600, probably after the famine years of 1602 and 1603.

Founders of the Village of Maeltsepere (ca. 1600-1650)

These three sons, whose names are unknown, in all likelihood became the founders of the peasant village of Maeltsepere, Maeltseküla or Maeltse on the southeast coast of Dago. What was said about their father applies equally to them, namely that we cannot be sure where they were born, especially if we consider that after the 1602-3 famine, the peasant population was decimated and survivors were constantly being sent from one place to another. But Fritz noted that that they may well have been people who had been living on Dago for generations since at that time Sweden controlled the continental lands, while Denmark still controlled the islands and the two kingdoms were enemies. At the same time the landed aristocracy didn't really care to which kingdom they belonged politically, and at this time there was already a heavy Swedish influence on Dago although it was only officially ceded to Sweden in 1645.

At approximately the time of the Thirty Year War (1618-48), there were three brothers living in the village of Maeltse. At that time peasants were not given sir names, but they were Estonians and as such, they were bound men, or serfs. We do not know who their master was. Fritz noted that he read someplace that all the land belonged to the de la Gardie family, which is quite possible. The peasants of that period had lived through terrible times; barely 60 years since the Tartar hordes led by Joan Grozny plundered the land followed by plague and then famine. At this time Dago belonged to Denmark. Nevertheless, there was already a heavy Swedish influence on Osel, the large island south of Dago and Dago, both of which were officially ceded to Sweden in 1645. The extensive peasant reformation of the Swedish rulers had not begun and in any case, it did not affect the Estonian peasants. Therefore the three brothers might very well have been the last people who had a very limited idea about culture and Christianity.[8] Of course, Fritz noted, there is a possibility that they were a bit more enlightened if they were serfs to a Swedish landowner.

---

[8] Estonians were not well converted to Christianity and many remained pagans through the 17th century.

Mats of Maeltse

One of the brothers had a son. Born about 1645 or 1648, he was entered into the church register with the name Mats (Matthias, Matthis or Matheus) of Maeltse. This indicates that at this point the family may have become Christian. At about 30, Mats married. He was a serf-farmer in the village of Maeltse. All land probably belonged to the Swedish family de la Gardie. Mats' children were Juri (1677), Kert (1679), Ann (1680), Peter (1682), and Mare (1684). His first wife died during the famine of 1695-7 and he married again. He had one son Mart (1698 or 1699) with her. He died a Swedish subject in 1711, probably of the plague of that year.

Maeltse Matsi Juri (Juri, son of Mats from Maeltse)

Juri, the eldest son of Mats, was born about 1677. He married about 1707. Quite possibly he had children between 1707 and 1712 who died of the plague in 1711. On March 19, 1713 he had a son, Juri, later followed by a son, Thomas, whose year of birth cannot be found. We do not know his wife's name either. Swedish dominance ended in 1721 after 21 years of war with Russia and Juri died a Russian subject on February 12, 1740.

Maeltse Juri Juri (Juri, son of Juri from Maeltse)

Juri's eldest son, Juri, was born March 19, 1713, a Russian subject. He was married around 1751 to a woman named Mare. They had at least three children, Jaak (1752), Simo (1763), and Andrus (birth unavailable). Mare died November 26, 1781 and Juri May 13, 1788. Catherine the Great ruled Russia at this time.

Maeltse Juri Jaak (Jaak, Juri's son from Maeltse)

Again, the eldest son of his father, Jaak was born in 1752.[9] At age 35, he married Kersti, a Swedish farmer's daughter, on December 12, 1787. They had one son Michael. Jaak lived through Napoleon's venture into Russia and died in 1820.

He is the last of the Maehle forefathers who was a serf-farmer. His son left the village and farming, which, through a new social structure, had changed greatly. Under the influence of the French Revolution and in the wake of the Napoleonic War, a growing activism dominated state policy leading to gradual emancipation of Estonian serfs by the mid 19th century.

Michael Maele/Maehle (Maeltse Jaggi Mihkel)

Fritz's great-grandfather was the eldest son of Jaak. At this point there are stories about the person, told to Fritz by his grandmother who had known him. Michael was born August 16, 1790 and in 1815, married a farm girl, Els, born July 28, 1790. In 1816 they had a son, Hans. Twins Simon and Lisa were born in 1819. In that same year the bondage of people finally came to an end. The landowner was no longer the possessor of the farmer. The farmer was now free but he did not have any land of his own. Even the land on which he lived belonged to the lord. To work the land and live in the house the farmer had to pay "working days" which were calculated according to the size of the land. He also had to pay "horse or oxen days" at certain times, especially at harvest. The farmer could appeal disputes with the landowner to the authorities. Yet, while he still had to accept some burdens, he was no longer a thing,

---

[9] Some of the dates are not clear, apparently because Church documents were lost or illegible. Since his parents were married in 1751, it is thought that he, like most children was born a year later.

belonging to the estate and who the land owner could give away or sell. He could also change landowners, take up a trade or immigrate to the city.

One thing was clear; Michael made use of the new laws rather early. According to family stories, between 1820 and 1830, he was in Riesenberg, a farm on the mainland where he worked as a carpenter. Whether he went there on his own or was sent by the landowner is not known. Most likely, the latter since Riesenberg belonged to the Baron Stackelberg as did the estate, Keinis, and the village, Maeltse, where Michael and his family had been serfs and farmers[10]. But remarkably, Michael turned away from farming.

A very important change in the way of life of peasants — name giving — occurred at this time. This too was connected with the termination of the personal ownership. The serf had a first name, which was given to him when he was baptized but he did not have a family name. Now a family name became a necessity. The selection of the name was done by the Lutheran pastor (usually a German) of the district, and the landowner or his administrator. This was done to keep the list of all the people in the congregation in order.[11]

It was also done with little thought or consultation with the family. Often they used the name of the father for the person to be named which resulted in the son's name as son or sohn. Thus Maelte Jaader Michael (literally Michael the son of Jaak from Meltse) became Michael Jaakson or

---

[10] Fritz did not explain what happened to the de la Garda family who originally owned the estate but I think that when Sweden lost control of Dago, it was sold to a German landowner.
[11] Lutheran pastors had somewhat of an official position. They were like a county mayor or administrator. They were responsible for the populous. The congregation was more like a Catholic parish (note in Louisiana, counties are called parishes based on this structure).

Jakobson or Jacksen or if the father's name was Juri it would have been Juriensen or Juergenson. Many Estonian names were fabricated in this way by German Lutheran pastors and thus sound very German or Swedish. Another family name was the village or the congregation from which the person originated.

That was the case with the Maehle name.[12] Apparently the pastor wanted to change the village name into a family name. But because he did not know the Estonian language he created Maele. Michael, Fritz stated, certainly had a lot of trouble with his name since no Estonian could figure out that it was an Estonian name. Since the name Maele looked absolutely ridiculous, "a combination of letters with a lost meaning", Michael sneaked an h into the word arriving at the name we have today according to Fritz. Fritz noted that an Estonian would never suspect an Estonian behind this name and in Riga (Latvia) he was often asked if he were from Lithuania since mehle means tongue in that language.

Another development in 1830 was the building of a textile plant in Kertell, a former Swedish village in the northeast of Dago. It is difficult to contemplate an industrial enterprise at such an early time in such a poor and isolated area. Suddenly the village was no longer a Swedish farming village. Steam boilers, looms and spinning machinery appeared. Foreigners arrived to live in Kertell to administer the plant and supervise its operations. A connection between the island and the mainland began to grow. The sale of manufactured goods to the mainland and the arrival of raw materials opened up the world. Farmers'

---

[12] At his point Fritz goes into a long discussion of Estonian grammar. Suffice to say, the German pastor created a surname for Michael which was incomprehensible in Estonian.

children changed into factory workers and new income possibilities were created. This was especially important for the Maehle family.

Michael returned to Dago in 1830 to become the foreman of the factory. It is not known whether he moved on his own accord or whether he was ordered back by Baron Stackelberg as he owned the estate on the mainland where Michael was employed. The factory was also owned by the Stackelberg family and the Baron knew Michael was a very good carpenter and mason. The young Baron Ernst von Ungern-Sternberg moved from the mainland to Kertell to manage the factory. Fritz met him when he was a very young boy and he was a very old man. His father, Nikolaus, often talked with him about the good old days. Baron Ernst, as he was called also often mentioned that whatever he knew about building he learned from Michael. The plant and all of the surrounding buildings and living quarters were started with wood construction; Michael was the supervisor or master builder.

When Michael moved to Kertell, his family included his wife, Els, his children Hans (b.1816), twins Simon and Lisa (b.1819), Andreas (b.1824), Georg (b.1827) and Lena born in 1832. They lived in an old Swedish frame house on the main street. It is the same place on which the factory erected the general store run by Fritz's father and where the family lived for more than 30 years.

Michael died January 27, 1861 at the age of 70. Towards the end he was confined to his bed and became senile. He also suffered from arteriosclerosis, which seems to have been inherited by his sons and even his grandsons. Els died April 3, 1865. They were buried in the Kertell Roesna cemetery, their graves marked by iron crosses.

Hans Maehle

Fritz's grandfather Hans was Michael's eldest son. He was born on April 7, 1816. He was 15, when his family moved from the estate village to Kertell. Evidence that he was literate is contained in letters that Fritz read written in Estonian and dated from 1840-50. He was trained as a weaver and worked in the factory. On December 6, 1843, at the age of 27, he married Kreet (Greta in Swedish), the 23-year-old daughter of the Swede, Tonis Tacking. Fritz pointed out that while the ancestry on his father's side is strictly Estonian, with the entry of his grandmother, the family became a mixture of Estonian and Swedish.

The Swedish population, as has already been noted, was of a higher class than the Estonians. They were considered "privileged pioneers" and farmers who had never known bondage. Fritz asserts that during the Swedish rule there was an effort to extend freedom to the Estonians but that the Swedish nobility then betrayed the country to Russia.[13] Under Catherine the Great, bondage was at its height. The German Baltic nobility took advantage of the situation by reducing freedoms won under the Swedes.[14] The Swedish people were a thorn in the flesh of the German landowners of Dago and any complaints by the farmers to them fell on deaf ears.[15]

---

[13] 16th and 17th century Estonian history is very complex with constant shifting control between Russia, Denmark, Germany and even Poland. But there were periods when Sweden had enormous control and influence in shaping the population and the culture. For example, Fritz's grandmother spoke only Swedish, no Estonian.

[14] During the Hansiatic League period many German nobles settled in the Baltic States creating large estates, many of which continued until the Baltic independence in 1921.

[15] The story was told that a delegation of Swedish farmers from Dago went to the mainland with complaints for the Russian authorities. They convened in Kertell and because it was a bitterly cold winter, the delegates took a great deal of fuel with them to keep warm. When they arrived on the mainland it was discovered that the bag containing the

The Swedish farms were very appealing to the nobility. Ultimately the Swedish farmers were cheated out of their land. For example, the supposed shareholder-owned textile factory was actually owned and managed by the German Baron Ungern-Sternberg, and was established on Swedish farmland without any compensation to the farmers. The Swedish cemetery was destroyed so that the Baron could have a vegetable garden there. Greta's father's farmland was turned into grazing land for the factory's horses. Farmers who had worked the land for 1000 years then had to pay a lease to work it.

Fritz recalled that during his youth the whole town of Kertell became transformed with new houses for the factory workers, new streets and squares — all belonging to the Baron, except for one old house. Fritz wrote:

> It is tilted and leans. And its straw roof is thatched and grown over by years of moss. From time to time one can spot an old gentleman in the garden. He carries himself slightly bent forward. He has very long silvery hair and dresses in a blue coat, checkered linen pants and a broad brimmed hat. He seldom talks and does not seem to know many people. His Estonian is poor, as if he is trying to express himself in a foreign language. When he sees old Greta on her way to church he stops to talk to her in a language only slightly understood by me.

---

complaints was missing from the sled. Then someone noticed that that the German Baron Grosshoff's scribe was also missing. He had helped a great deal with the warm up in Kertell.

He is "the very last Swede in Kertell, Greta's uncle, the old Christian Tacking," Nikolaus explained. "Why haven't they taken over his house and property?" Fritz asked his grandmother. Greta mysteriously replied, "Because he has the "Right of the Swedes." Fritz continued:

> And once in a while Baron Ungern Sternberg will tease my father, 'Ah yes, you are one of these Tackings with the Rights of the Swedes.' It seems that Greta's uncle still possessed one of the old ownership papers and no one dared to touch him or his property.

From way back, there were four Swedish families in Kertell, all related to one another: Bysa, Tacking, Tarning and Bro. Tonis, Greta's father, who was tall, slim, with long blond hair and a clean-shaven face was a Tacking. He was a miller in the mill, which still stood between the factory and the pub when Fritz was a boy. Tonis married around 1819. His first child, Greta, was born January 2, 1820. Her mother died shortly after her birth and Greta spoke almost only Swedish in her youth. Later on she had an Estonian stepmother and although she learned Estonian, even in her old age, she spoke it with an accent. Tonis was very familiar with the Bible and taught her to read and write in bold Latin lettering.

After their marriage, Greta and Hans moved into her father's roomy house. They had three sons Nikolaus (1844), Karl (1846) and Johannes (1849). In 1847 they were able to lease their own home and 2.47 acres of land for 10 rubles from the nobility who still owned all the land. In addition, they also had to work two full days during the summer on the owner's land. Close to the beach, it was the former quarters for the beach and border guards.

They planted vegetables, hay and kept some cows, sheep and pigs. Since Hans worked on his loom in the factory from morning until night, except Sunday when they went to church, Greta tended the garden and animals. She also worked the extra hours for the lease. She also had to go to Kroog, about 3 km away from Kertell where she had to collect wood in the nearby forest for making tar.[16]

Fritz noted that his grandfather's thriftiness was remarkable, a trait that he passed down to later generations. He remembered well that his parents, like his grandfather, had a long woolen stocking filled with silver rubles. Hans was sober, hard working and literate and had great prospects of becoming a master carpenter in the factory. However, on May 3, 1851, at 35, he died of tuberculosis. This was the only known case of TB in the family.[17] It could have been brought on, wrote Fritz, by a severe case of pneumonia Hans had at the age of 18. Greta was left alone with her three sons, ages 7, 5, and 2. She faced very difficult times since Hans was not able to earn any money during his last years and it was extremely difficult for a woman to earn enough to provide for a family. With three small children she could not work in the factory. But she managed. She worked the fields, kept some animals and worked for other farmers during harvest. She even took in laundry for the factory administrators.

And then some help arrived. One of Hans's younger brothers was a schoolteacher in Reval. He managed to get Nikolaus into a free orphanage on the mainland. After 11 years as a widow, Grete married a carpenter named Michael Orjan. They had no children. Her second son also moved to Reval when

---

[16] Fritz does not say what the tar was for.
[17] Heddy always said that her sister, Gerda, died of TB. Fritz, while describing her illness, never labeled it.

he was a young man while the youngest, Johannes, immigrated to the Caucasus. After her second husband died in 1874, Greta moved in with Nikolaus, who had returned to Dago in 1866. She died in 1906 at the age of 86. Busy from early morning until late at night she took care of her grandsons with a love that only a grandmother is able to give. Being Swedish, she never really felt like an Estonian. She taught Fritz Swedish which he eventually forgot and told many stories about her side of the family. He was so completely taken by this that for years he thought he was Swedish. "Even now," he wrote, "I am never really emotionally involved in Estonian matters, but I cannot deny that I am just half Swedish."

Han's brothers and sister all made something of themselves. Simon became a foreman in the shearing department of the factory. In 1851 he married Anna Marie Peterson, daughter of one of the administrators of the Hohenlohe estate in Dago. They had four children: Wilhelm (1853), Elsie (1857), Alexander (1860) and Christoph (1862). His twin Lisa married a Swede in Kertell; her only son, Wihelm, disappeared as a sailor in America. Georg was a weaver in Kertell. He married Lena Kerjama in 1860 and had four daughters. One married a Baptist preacher, one a Russian and Lena moved to Petersburg and became a housekeeper for a professor. She later married Johann Werrow, a master sergeant. They had a daughter, Sonja.

Han's most influential brother for Fritz and his brothers was Andreas. Neither Fritz nor his brothers ever saw their grandfather, Hans, since he died so young and, Andreas took his place in their minds. He therefore became as granduncle, a person of great respect. He was born August 8, 1824, eight years after Hans. He was a very handsome, intelligent boy. While all of his brothers were employed in the factory, Andreas worked as an office boy for Baron Ungern-Sternberg. Andreas had great interest in everything. His desire for knowledge was nurtured through the close connection his father kept to the gospel hall run by the Herrenhuter.[18] Since he was in the private service of the Baron, he was educated in German. In those days German was the language of the educated people and necessary for entry into the broader educated world.

At 22, Andreas left Kertell and entered the Bauer'sche Erziehungs-Anstalt, a Herrenhuter institution in Reval. Andreas started as a student but soon advanced to a teaching position for the younger students where he stayed until he was 29. He held several other teaching positions over the next several years in various schools and finally became an administrator of a school in Kuda where he remained until 1865 at age 41. At 36 he married 20-year-old Sophie Jannow, daughter of a Nikolai[19] sergeant of Estonian nationality. They had eight children.[20] Andreas had white hair, was very straight forward, serious and God fearing. His appearance commanded respect. He reminded Fritz of an English gentleman. Andreas died on February 4, 1894. Fritz stated that he suffered as did his father, his grandfather, and all of his brothers of the "family disease; they became fragile and very senile."

---

[18] The Hurrenhuter was a combination orphanage and home for young adults established by the Hurrenhuter Brethren strictly along Christian and German lines. Young men and women both lived and were educated with a high school education. The older students were promoted to teaching positions in the elementary schools and the village schools. Some were employed as apprentices by tradesmen.
[19] A member of Tsar Nicholas's army.
[20] Christlieb 1861; Johanna 1864; Aline 1865; Felix 1867; Lydia 1869; Amanda 1871; Erna 1873 and Herta 1882. Andreas' children became very close to Fritz. There are many references to them throughout the journal.

Nikolaus Maehle, Fritz's father

Nikolaus was born November 23, 1844. As already noted, his father died when he was seven and his mother had a very hard time making ends meet. When he was about nine, his great uncle Andreas took him to Pernau on the mainland where Andreas taught school. Andreas enrolled Nikolaus in his classroom and also taught him on his own time. The boy did housework for his uncle, who was still a bachelor. When Andreas returned to Reval in the following year with a teaching position in the Bauer'sch Institute, Nikolaus was entered as an orphan. For one year Andreas was both teacher and boss to him. He was very strict with his nephew. Strapping (hitting with a strap) was still observed and pupils were punished for the smallest mistakes. Needless to say, Nikolaus became quite disciplined. After a year, when his uncle moved to Kuda, the boy remained at the school. He was very gifted, learned quickly and was inquisitive. He learned to speak German fluently (it was the only language spoken in the Institution), developed a very beautiful penmanship and played the piano and organ well. He was a student in Reval during the Crimean War and spoke of the houses around the harbor that, "we set on fire to avoid an attack from the British and French."

His education lasted five years and was the equivalent of a good public school education in Germany.[21] After his graduation, he was confirmed in the German Nikolai Church. Through the good offices of the Institution, he entered an apprenticeship with a master carpenter and craftsman in Narva. Fritz wrote:

---

[21] Fritz noted that his father had a better education than many of the businessmen he associated with in Lodz.

The 15 year old boy had to put up with all the joys and troubles of an apprentice as they were handled in the "old days." He had to endure the pranks, poking, pushing around and teasing from all the other apprentices. After a five year apprenticeship he was required to produce a master piece, a dresser in the Baroque style. He was then required to go before the Guild, Innungs Lad, where he received a letter of credit. He continued to work for the old master further building his skills until 1866 when he received his draft papers. He left Narva for Hapsal via Reval, a trip of several days since train connections were non-existent. The military recruiting committee in Hapsal declared him fit for service and he received his orders to report to the naval station in Kronstadt.

Here Fritz diverted from his narrative to explain that no general military duty existed in Russia. Only farmers were drafted. Since Nikolaus belonged to the Kertell farm community, he was at the mercy of the nobility. The nobility, as well as the community, were obviously interested in protecting the young men who were quietly attending to their duties at home. They tended to "volunteer" people who were troublemakers, orphans, children out of wedlock and other "unwanted elements." The same fate applied to anyone who left the community for the mainland cities. In Kertell, the community, the workers in the factory and the owners of the factory (nobility) were in agreement: Nikolaus, who had been in the city since he was nine years old "living it up" and who was of no use to either the factory or the community must serve.

In those days military service was considered a punishment. At one time a man became a soldier for life. Under Tsar Nikolai I, service lasted 25 years and at the time Nikolaus was drafted, service was 15 years. Life for a soldier was very brutal. They were treated very strictly and roughly. Drinking was prevalent and food was gruesome — once a day some sort of cabbage soup and moldy bread and a bit of meat. There was only one legal escape from service. One could buy his freedom by paying someone else to take his place. As Nikolaus did not have the money to buy his was out, Uncle Andreas found a young farmer willing to take his place for 200 rubles.[22] While these negotiations were going on, Nikolaus was sent to Reval (on foot) and from there to Kronstadt, where he was invested. Since recruits were essentially illiterate, his education and knowledge of languages, especially his fluency in German, was noticed by the officer in charge who decided to give him an office job. When his replacement arrived Nikolaus was discharged. He left Kronstadt on a warship, bound for Reval via Helsingfors. After a beautiful trip through the Finnish gulf he arrived in Helsingfors where he spent another month. He finally arrived in Reval in July, six months after his induction.

Now the question arose, what should he do next? Many former students had become missionaries in Africa and India, a thought Andreas and Nikolaus seriously considered. However, Nikolaus was homesick. He had been away from his home for 13 years, when he was nine years old. The 23-year-old German speaking young man had only a vague memory of his mother and brothers. He had almost forgotten the Estonian language. Meanwhile, when the factory administration in Kertell found out that he had become a skilled mason and carpenter

---

[22] 200 rubles was the equivalent of 2000 working days or about 7 years.

and was free of the draft, they sent a letter to Andreas asking if Nikolaus might be interested in a job in the factory. So Nikolaus returned to the island of his childhood.

There were many changes. His Estonian grandfather, Michael, and his wife, Els, were dead. His mother, Greta, had remarried. His brother Karl had moved to Reval and Johannes, who was a baby when he left, had become a slim young man of 16. There were also changes on his mother's side. His grandfather, Tonis Tacking, had remarried after having been a widower for 30 years. His wife, Anna Rahu, a widow of a seafarer and farmer by the name of Peet Rahu, had a nine-year-old daughter, Kersti. Fritz stated, "When my father (Nikolaus) visited his grandmother and met Kersti, then a lovely young woman of 22, his future was decided." He agreed to a position in the factory, at least until the following spring. However, during the winter a large part of the factory burned down enabling him to accept the position of building supervisor, thus making him a master carpenter. Interestingly, he had the same position as Fritz great grandfather, Michael, who was the first building supervisor of the factory. As an intelligent and educated young man, he soon gained the complete confidence of the management and owner, Baron Ernst von Unger-Sternberg, Jr. In accordance with the tradition of the county, or parish administration, the Baron served as judge for minor offences in the district. He made Nikolaus his secretary. This job and the rebuilding of the factory kept him very busy.

During the time Nikolaus was away from Kertell a fresh wind was blowing. Two schools had been opened, one for boys and one for girls. Newspapers, printed in the Estonian language in Reval and Dorpat were now available and eagerly read. There was a new public library and a new mixed choir in which Nikolaus enthusiastically participated as Kersti also sang in it. His first task was to repay Uncle Andreas the 200 rubles for the military substitute. He then had to find some place to live, so he built an addition to his mother's house.

Unhappily, Uncle Andreas had become a big headache for Nikolaus. Andreas had been more than a father to him and he felt very indebted. At the same time, Andreas had great expectations of Nikolaus and they did not include a return to Dago in an obscure little factory. He and his wife Sophie were also not happy about his thoughts of marriage to Kersti, even though Kersti was the stepdaughter of his and Nikolaus' grandfather and the stepsister of their mother. Andreas' wife, Sophie, had a very pretty younger sister Jette who was also educated in the Bauer'sche Institute. Andreas attempted to subtly explain his wishes to Nikolaus but he did not take the hints. So the family decided to "attack." Sophie announced that she and her sister intended to visit Dago. Nikolaus finally understood what was going on and replied, rather rudely, that "He could only accommodate the ladies in the field between the furrows of the potatoes, since he did not have a spare room of his own and such accommodations would hardly be suitable for visitors from the city." Undaunted, the ladies announced that they were taking a room with brother-in-law, Simon Maehle. Nikolaus remained very stubborn and cool so the ladies retreated. Nikolaus hurriedly announced his engagement to Kersti.

Nikolaus was very much in love with Kersti who was raised in Hiie-saar, meaning Hiie Island in the village of Heiln in the northwest coastal stretch of Dago. The people who lived there were farmers and fishermen. Because of their skill as seamen they made up the Baron's boatmen for his flotilla of sailing ships as well as other coastal ships. One of these seamen was Kersti's father. In 1844 he married a farm girl, Anna. Kersti was born December 7, 1845. When she was five years old her father died of smallpox. At this time the servants, as all these people were, were put under a new bailiff and Anna was moved to another farm 2 km from Kertell. There she married Tonis, already 60 years old; Anna was 40. Fritz wrote:

> The elderly couple must have had the idea that they had to make up for lost time, the old Swede, demonstrating that he was still a "good man" produced four children, Peet, Madli, Mari and John over eight years. Happy to have done his work on earth, old Tonis then lay down and died. The almost 50 year old Anna was left with four toddlers — some fun.

Kersti was employed by a baker named Ruth. She delivered the daily bread in Kertell to the more affluent, and helped in the bakeshop and store, for which she earned one ruble a month. At 17, she decided she wanted to earn more. The only alternative was the factory. So she went to work on a loom in the weaving mill. In addition she always had responsibilities in the home with her four younger siblings. Although she was only able to complete elementary school, she was intellectually very active, read and whenever possible sang in the choir.

Nikolaus realized that Kersti lacked education, especially in German, a measure of all education by most standards in those days. So he started teaching her himself. Also, feeling badly for the distance he caused between himself and Uncle Andreas he decided to send Kersti to Hapsal, on the mainland, to visit his uncle so that his family could see what a wonderful girl she was. He even wanted to have her stay with the family and work in a ladies dress shop, and at the same time learn German. Perhaps, he thought she could even open her own seamstress business when she returned to Dago. These intentions, however, took a very different turn.

Kersti left for Hapsal with great apprehensions. Her feelings were confirmed. Uncle Anreas received her coldly; Sophie and Jette were critical and haughty. Sophie even accused her of running after Nikolaus. Sophie suggests that Nikolaus probably had to marry her and to prove it, took her into the bathroom for a bodily examination. Kersti, humiliated, tried to explain that she never ran after Nikolaus and if he wanted to, he could call the engagement off, but that she would never set foot in Andreas' home again.[23] Nikolaus's reaction was to marry Kersti as quickly as possible. They were married on January 24, 1871. Ten months later on November 26, 1871, Fritz was born. His brothers, Rudolf and Oskar, followed February 23, 1873 and October 16, 1876. Ewald was next in 1878 and Hermann was born in 1880.[24]

The Co-Op

The young family was very busy. Nikolaus finished the new plant building, including the interior furnishings. He served on the municipal council for seven years and continued to be Baron von Ungern-Sternberg's secretary, helping with his jurisdictional affairs. These were the best years for the factory and, in many ways, for the country,

---

[23] Fritz noted that Kersti keep her promise; she never went there again even though the relationship warmed and Andreas and his family visited Dago regularly. Fritz was a teenager when his mother visited Uncle Andreas' brother Karl in Reval. Sophie and her children almost forcibly brought her to see uncle Andreas. He apologized for himself and his wife and for all that had happened in the past. Kersti had finally gained his respect.

[24] There was no exact date of their births in the journal.

especially as Alexander II was enacting liberal reforms. New life was springing up everywhere — buildings, schools, a post office, telegraph office and nice houses for the workers in the plant. The factory was enlarged by 50% and the master builder was Nikolaus.

And then the cooperative was formed which changed their lives.[25] As Dago was completely separated from the mainland for several months during the winter, necessities of everyday life became scarce or nonexistent. The small existing stores did not have the resources to stock goods, especially food supplies. So the management of the plant decided to introduce a cooperative to be owned by the employees but accessible to all people. The workers became shareholders through the sale of shares in the enterprise. This allowed sufficient funds to obtain supplies from Rega and Reval during the navigable months. At the end of the business year, the books were audited by management who maintained control; any profit was distributed to the shareholders.

In 1876, a small building was constructed and Nikolaus was entrusted with its management. Kersti took over the day-to-day sales and management of the store while Nikolaus kept his position in the plant and attended to the bookkeeping in the evening. In 1878, management built a large house for the store, which then included a bakery and butcher shop. The house also contained quarters for the manager and in 1879, the Maehle family moved in. The name of the cooperative became N. Maehle & Co. The demands of the store became too much for Nikolaus to handle two jobs and so he left the factory, much

---

[25] There are lengthy analyses of Nikolaus' finances which I have eliminated. Suffice to say he had serious problems which ultimately led to his bankruptcy and which his grown sons had to solve.

to the chagrin of the management. The building of the new store was the last supervisory job he had in the factory.

Nikolaus and Kersti were both paid by the cooperative. Together they earned 600 rubles annually. While this sum seemed extremely small to Fritz when he wrote his memoirs, his parents were able to support the family on 150 rubles per year.[26] The family lived frugally. And their lodging, adjacent to the store and bakery, consisted of three rooms and a kitchen downstairs and two rooms upstairs. It was free. The bakery had a stove designed to heat the whole house. Firewood was delivered to the store. Goods they purchased from the store were paid for monthly. The family also kept the old house as extra living quarters and as a summer place. That house belonged to Nikolaus except for about two and one half acres that belonged to the factory. Rent was still ten rubles per year. There they grew potatoes, other vegetables, and fruit trees. They had two or three milking cows, pigs and a horse, which really belonged to the store for transporting goods. Kersti managed the farm as well as the bakery. Fritz wrote that his father was always on the job. He was honest, conscientious, sober and hard working. Evenings were spent reading German and Estonian newspapers, science and astronomy, literature, and a wide range of other writings. The family's only social life was church every Sunday, followed by a mid-day meal. Afterwards, the family would read aloud or Nikolaus would play the piano while Kersti and the children sang folk songs. Sometimes they took walks to the harbor or beach. In this way they were able to save 450-500 rubles per year, which

---

[26] At this point Fritz goes into great detail about the money they earned and spent, the goods they purchased and their work responsibilities. See Hilde's English translation beginning on page 39.

went into a savings account at the factory and paid 4% interest per year. By 1890, they had saved 7000-8000 rubles, a small fortune in those days.

And then changes occurred which were to have serious consequences later. The first thing that happened was that some people, all for legitimate reasons (death, moving), took their money out of the co-op. In order to maintain the original capitol, Nikolaus replaced their money with his own, thereby increasing his share to the point where he owned 1/3 of the business. In addition because he could earn more in the business than the savings account at the factory, he took significant sums out of it.

Politically, the control of the country was also changing from German influence to Russian. This was especially true of the administrative structure of businesses. One day the factory management received a notice that the co-op lacked every imaginable basis as a business and should either be closed or apply to the Chamber of Commerce and Trade for certain applications. The management of the factory had its own headaches with the Russians and gave Nikolaus to understand that they did not want any part of this problem. Nikolaus did not know what to do. The shareholders began to loose faith and demanded their money back. But the money was invested in inventory. They finally decided to disband the co-op. Nikolaus gave each shareholder an "I owe you" saying that he borrowed x amount at the rate of 6% per year. The whole matter was looked at by all parties as just a formality to trick the Russians. Nikolaus thus became the sole proprietor of the business, only to find himself in considerable debt. He owed 8000 rubles to the "I owe you" holders. Business however was doing well and no catastrophes were foreseen. He calculated he could buy back all shares over the next ten years thus becoming a sole proprietor. He intended to make Rudolf, his second son, his successor.

He soon realized that circumstances had again changed and his plans were dashed. First, a whole shipment of goods was lost at sea during a storm. Nikolaus called a meeting of the shareholders to inform them that the annual dividends had to be written off. But the shareholders, all workers in the plant, explained that this incident had nothing to do with them. They wanted their 6%. They were not shareholders they said; they were creditors. Fortunately the goods were covered by insurance so the actual damage was minimal. But his eyes were opened. At the annual meeting he informed the shareholders that since they were not a cooperative, he did not owe them any business reports and not even a general meeting. He paid everyone the 6% and sent them home.

The workers launched a complaint with the plant administration, insisting on a general meeting. After much debate the Baron finally forced Nikolaus to treat the business as a profit sharing association, complete with business reports. At the same time, the business was deteriorating. So Nikolaus decided to reinstate the profit sharing concept fully. Both the plant administration and the workers refused, pointing out that lawfully they had invested capital and as holders of credit notes they could care less about the business. They wanted their money back with interest.

Fritz noted that although his father was one of them, he was viewed with considerable jealousy and mistrust — he had four sons who were studying on the mainland, a sure sign of wealth. At one point he was even accused of educating his sons with other people's money. In addition, there was a growing familiarization of socialistic ideas influencing the workers. And ultimately, although he was a very honest man, he was not a businessman and had made some very poor decisions during the course of his co-op management. For example, after Nikolaus had visited with dealers in Riga, selected goods and placed his orders with them, the goods were shipped to Dago. Often some containers held up to 25% of old goods, which were substituted for the goods ordered but were still invoiced for the regular price merchandise. But instead of challenging the merchants, he promptly paid for them as invoiced and the old merchandise remained on the shelves. He also had two employees who stole from the cash register, two or three rubles a day, which amounted to 700-800 per year. When he finally found out he fired them but since he did not have hard proof and the scandal would have created angst among the shareholders who would have blamed him, he did not press charges. Rather, he paid back the losses from his own pocket. One of the thieves soon opened a store in a neighboring town, presumably with Nikolaus's money.

At this point he called Rudolf, who was an apprentice in an enterprise in Riga, to come home. Stricter controls were put on the business. Rudolf found that the casual credit system had gotten out of hand. Some people had "forgotten" to pay; others had moved away or died. Some collections were successful but not popular.

And then Kersti became ill. Her doctor treated her for the "change of life" although she had all the symptoms of a growth on the uterus. She was in great pain and became very nervous, looked anemic, gained a lot of weight and developed heart trouble. She had to give up her job at the bakery, thereby loosing 20 rubles each month. By 1890, finances for the family were strained. By 1893 they had reached the breaking point. As Nikolaus had no money, Fritz and Oskar were forced to interrupt their studies in

Reval. Oskar became an apprentice in a pharmacy and Fritz entered the "voluntary service" for a year. Rudolf was in an apprenticeship and did not cost the family anything. Thus Nikolaus was only responsible for the two youngest boys, Ewald and Hermann who continued to stay in school. Business began to pick up and he decided to invest in the Baron's new sailing ship, which had been in service for quite some time. While things looked better, in fact Nikolaus was spending about 300 rubles more that he was earning. To make ends meet he took more money out of his savings.

In 1896, Kersti traveled to Reval for a medical consultation where she underwent surgery. Rudolf became a partner in the co-op, which was then named N. Maehle & Sons, and in 1898 he married. Nikolaus built a new home for Rudolf beside his home, something he came to regret. It cost him his last 3500 rubles of savings; he was without a penny. In addition, there was a growing competition of shops in the area. Even the Baron had started a competing shop and had taken the butcher shop away from Nikolaus and given it to someone else.[27] Meanwhile Fritz was the only son not dependent on his father as he was already working in Lodz. Ewald was in the polytechnic institute in Reval, Hermann was finishing the gymnasium (high school) and Oskar left his apprenticeship to study in Germany. Nikolaus did not have sufficient income to support the family so he went into debt, which increased annually since he continued to pay the shareholders their 6%.[28]

---

[27] It is evident that although the business was treated as a company owned by Maehle, the Baron and the factory maintained control and thought little of the Maehles' welfare.

[28] Here Fritz laments that he was unaware of his father's financial difficulties. Had he known, he would have postponed his marriage in 1900 for a few years. In many ways he reflects, it would have been better anyway. Maria was too young, and he had little job experience.

In 1905/6 the Revolution came and Estonia was turned upside down. Rudolf wrote Fritz that there were business problems and suggested that he enter the business as a co-owner. The revolutionaries had a hostile attitude towards Nikolaus and the whole family since they were seen as capitalists and "deserters into the camp of the enemy." The business had been boycotted by many working class people who had started another co-op in 1905; many of the shareholders had taken their shares out of the business in fear of things to come. So far the business was making it, thanks to the bakery and the customers from the farming community. Regrettably Rudolf's letter did not show the full extent of the problem. Even he was not fully aware of the situation.[29] Fritz took all of his savings, 1,800 rubles, paid some of the suppliers in Riga and Reval. He also assumed financial support for Ewald who at that time was just finishing his studies.

Finally, in 1908, Nikolaus wrote a very excited letter, followed by desperate letters from Kersti, that they had a deficit of 8,600 rubles and no way to pay it. They were broke. Rudolf had suddenly left Dago for a job in Reval. The store was still under boycott. There were only about 10 customers per day. When the shareholders learned of Rudolf's departure, they went wild, demanding their money back immediately. As a result, Nikolaus was not able to pay his suppliers for goods already ordered and the suppliers who had been somewhat suspicious for several years demanded their money as well. They even turned to the plant administration demanding an explanation.

He was nevertheless irritated that his father had not informed him sooner of his plight.

[29] Fritz comments that Rudolf must have been a worse businessman than his father since he was a partner and had access to all of the books.

Nikolaus became ill, slept little, and had dizzy spells and attacks of paralysis. He was unable to think or act. Kersti did not know the situation well enough to act and her heart began to trouble her again. The sons were shocked. After many cables, letters and running around, Oskar and Fritz decided that the business had to be liquidated and expenses had to be cut to a minimum immediately. Oskar and Fritz borrowed money and, together with their savings, were able to reduce the debt substantially. Nikolaus was instructed to sell the inventory. But in 1909, the sons were informed that despite their efforts, the debt had increased again. Fritz, still thinking that the business was a co-op, wrote the Baron asking for an explanation and assistance. Even Kersti talked to the Baron. His reply to both was polite but unresponsive. The burden was on the Maehles. It became clear to the sons that putting more money into the business would not solve the problem. It had to be liquidated.[30]

Fritz and his brothers had to help immediately, and thankfully they were able to do so. Fritz had changed jobs with an increased income; Ewald had a good job in Novograd (White Russia) as an agricultural engineer; Hermann was an assistant pastor in Reval; Rudolf was situated in Reval; and Oskar's income had also increased considerably — especially since he had been compensated for an accident by his firm with 6000 rubles.

Fritz and Oskar, both living in Lodz, assumed responsibility for managing the liquidation of the business. They could not withhold money from the workers who were blue-collar laborers. So they decided to pay the suppliers only a percentage of the

---

[30] Fritz pondered how desperate his parents were. He was heartbroken for them. They were already in their 60s and in failing health. Kind, gentle and loving, they did not deserve such misery.

debt owed them — 60% of their money immediately or 75% over time. Since Nikolaus had been trading with these merchants for 30 years and many had taken advantage of him, most agreed to the proposal. Here Fritz wrote that he personally met with each supplier in Reval and Riga. Some were polite and even friendly; some were cool and unapproachable and some were simply rude and impudent. The worst were the Jews, whom he claimed, had taken the most advantage of his father over the years, didn't want to hear of any arrangements, talked about crooks and suspected the Maehles of profiteering. However, after talking to them quietly and at length, some, who at first had questioned the arrangement not only accepted it but also offered new deliveries immediately.

When he had completed his negotiations, Fritz went to Dago to visit his parents. He wrote that they looked so pathetic that he had to fight back tears. They had lost everything. They had not been able to save any money. They were ill and alone. They never indulged themselves in anything, but all their lives had sacrificed for their boys and cared for others. They had trusted the Baron, the factory workers; the store assistants and they had only misery and betrayal to show for it. Nikolaus's poor business sense contributed also. He did not understand the systems with which he worked nor the people with whom he dealt. When he ran into a problem, such as the irregularities in his shipments, he let it pass. When his clerk was found cheating he did not report it to the police or demand retribution. And he often let credit accounts continue until it was too late to collect.

Fritz reported to his parents that he and his brothers had managed to settle the accounts and the shareholders would be paid. When he produced a bundle of paid invoices and handed them to his father, he called out in a shaky voice, "Thank God, now I can finally sleep well again at night after all these years," and he burst into tears. Kersti too was very happy and could hardly contain her emotions. On the next day his parents were completely changed. Kersti was happy and Nikolaus was refreshed and well rested. He went directly to the factory where he took 2,300 rubles out of the safe and paid the shareholders. The loud mouth troublemakers from before were embarrassed and some remarks were heard such as, "Well, we never thought that old man Maehle would cheat us." At this point it seemed that everything had been settled. All that remained was to move all of the remaining merchandise to the old house where it could be sold. The store had to be cleared out so that no additional rent was incurred. The parents could now move into the house that they had built for Rudolf since he and his family were now in Riga. The employees were given notice and only one young helper was kept on to help with moving the goods. Kersti kept one maid whom Fritz paid for and when he saw that things were settled, he returned to Lodz. Oskar and Fritz calculated that over the past two years from May 1907 to May 1909, they had paid 10,000 rubles including all travel expenses and all costs.

A few weeks later Oskar and Fritz received a letter from Kersti:

Dear Beloved Oskar and Fritz,

We thank you so much for all you have done for us and all the money you have paid. Thank you a thousand times for you have taken care of us so lovingly and that you have promised also to help us in the future. ...Last week we put the last of our furniture in Rudolf's house and we are living as in heaven now. The house is beautiful. The rooms are large. The garden is all in blossoms. I cannot find the words to express my feelings and emotions when I think about what you two have done for us and how you are looking after us in our old age. I pray for you every day in the morning and in the evening. In the beginning I felt as if I was not at home in this house. I got so used to the living quarters and the store in those 30 years. But you have given us our home back and nobody can hurt us here and throw us out. ...I am very grateful that you enabled me to keep the maid because I am very weak and my heath is not the best. I do have heart trouble and I really felt it this last year when we discovered the discrepancies in the finances. By spring time I felt my heart contracting so much that I became short of breath at times.

I went to the doctor's office. He found that I am not well and that my heart is weak and beats irregularly. He prescribed some pills and told me to walk before dinner daily. When I walk my heart beats heavily and when I sit still it is better but then I cannot breathe normally. That is the way with me. When I am just saying to myself, now you have reached this point when you can relax, something else occurs.

Well, I am hoping for God's grace,
Your loving mother,

Mama

She also wrote:

Dear Fritz and Maria,

I thank you very much for the beautiful bonnet and shawl you gave me. I am a little bit under the weather, as the doctor describes it. It is my heart and sometimes I suffer from a shortness of breath. He hopes that the matter will clear up when I am no longer exposed to excitements. Hermann visited us for two weeks but now he is gone. I was so glad to hear him preach a sermon.
Farewell my dear children, lots of regards to Heddy and Gerda and to all of you, also from papa. He will write to you soon,

As always,
Your loving mama

Fritz then wrote:

A few days later a cable arrived, telling us that her self-sacrificing, caring and loving heart had stopped. She was, one evening, after a bath and in the middle of a conversation with father, overcome by a weak spell. Papa thought that she had fainted and held her up against his chest, while he called for water...but she never woke up. It was a beautiful death — quiet without any real pain and at a time when she was feeling really happy. All her five boys were taken care of. Four of them had studied and were in good positions and she knew that they would help Rudolf. Her favorite wish, to see one of her sons in the pulpit, had also come true. And her own circumstances were all straightened out. The poor, uneducated peasant orphan had completed her work at the age of 64 years.

Maria and Oskar went to Dago and found Nikolaus in an inconsolable state. He had completely broken down and was unable to make any decisions. He was lamenting and crying and had not even ordered a coffin. Maria took over the duties in the household and Oskar, Hermann, and Uncle Karl, who arrived shortly afterward, straightened out all other affairs. Hermann said the eulogies over Kersti's grave. Maria, Hermann and Oskar left and Karl stayed on since Nikolaus was in no state to be left alone. His condition could only be described as a complete breakdown. He was not able to do anything. Karl sold all the remaining stock, which was so old that it realized less than half of its purchase price. Oskar and Fritz had to put up additional rubles but at last all debts were paid and the business finally and completely dissolved. They, along with their brothers Ewald and Hermann, also took over financial support of their father, equivalent to what he had earned in wages before. They sent the same amount to Rudolf.

And then another problem arose. Barely a year after Kersti's death, Nikolaus sent a letter to his boys suggesting that he would like to marry Maria Nowit, the housekeeper who had been hired to look after him after Kersti's death. Fritz wrote, "On account of his 66 years and his otherwise not quite sensible behavior, I could see his wish, with our dear mother in mind, not in any other light than the beginning of senility, our family sickness." The boys discussed the situation and wrote to him that his housekeeper could meet his needs much better if she were not his wife. But he was still thinking about it. When Fritz visited him on returning from a vacation to Norway, Sweden and Finland in the summer of 1911, he brought up the subject again. Fritz returned to Dago the following year to find his father was unable to walk as the result of a stroke. In 1914, with the advent of WWI, all connections with Estonia were severed and it was not until 1917, which Fritz learned that his father had died in the spring of 1915 at the age of 70, five and one half years after Kersti.

Fritz closed the chapter with the following:

> What else should I tell you about my father? I am, in many ways, my father in a rejuvenated edition. I look very much like him, our characteristics, even our faults and our best qualities are almost the same. I think I understood him best of all his sons. I was his favorite although he never showed his preference over the others. And what should I tell my children about my "older self?" Whatever they will say later on about me should apply as a judgment also to my own father.

Chapter II:
Frederick Maehle — His Youth

In 1871, the year that Fritz was born, there were no Baltic States. They had been fought over by Prussia, Poland, Sweden, Denmark and Russia for centuries, never experiencing independence although they were known by the names of Estonia, Livonia, and Lithuania.[31] The vast majority of the indigenous people were farmers and indentured servants, just a rung above serf status. But a middle class was emerging and there was even a small Estonian nobility. Sweden, who had ruled Estonia since 1561 as a result of the 30 Years War, lost it to Russia in 1710 when Peter the Great took the Baltic provinces. In 1721, the Czar guaranteed privileges and local authority to the Baltic German nobility through the Treaty of Nystad. They became the backbone of Russian civil service in the Baltic. By 1820 most of the serfdom in Estonia and Livonia (Latvia) had been abolished by the Baltic German nobility, but without granting land to the peasants.

Fritz seems to have been a gentle, kind and thoughtful person. He was a handsome man and well liked. He was honest, straight forward, intelligent, ambitious, and intellectually curious. He also seems

---

[31] They achieved independence briefly at the end of WWI but lost it with the emergence of the Soviet Union. Again they returned to satellite status until the Union's breakup in the 1990s.

to have been quite acquiescent, a bit naïve, and too trusting. He, like his father, and by his own account, had a very poor sense of business. This becomes evident in his story. He clung to the notion that if he excelled in his job he would do well and people would treat him fairly and honestly, if he treated them fairly and honestly.

He was a sickly baby, suffering from some sort of stomach problem.[32] The doctor at the factory was at his wits end and had actually given up hope, when a natural practitioner, who was a friend of his mother, Kersti, administered some mixture to Fritz saying, "If he dies it did not work, but if it helps he will be in good health and live a long life." Fritz digested the mixture and got well.

He spent his early childhood on Dago. His memories, albeit clouded, go back to his late third year when his grandmother's second husband lay dying in his bed. All the adults were standing around talking of medicine. In Estonian, medicine is *rohi*, derived from the worm plant or weed meaning healing plant. He recalled listening to the adults talking about all the weeds that did not help grandfather. He ran outside found some extra tall grass and weeds and brought them to his grandfather saying, "Good medicine for you." All the adults laughed; he failed to see the humor.

After his grandfather's death his grandmother, Grete, remained in the family's home. When Kersti went to work in the store, his grandmother took over the household. Rudolf was born 14 months after Fritz and Oscar five years later. With three children under six, Kersti hired a nanny of sorts. Actually Leena was an eight-year-old orphan who became a

---

[32] A stomach condition was to follow him for the rest of his life and was probably exacerbated by his diet, which was often very poor, and his smoking.

foster child and playmate for the boys. When she wasn't in school she was supervising and playing with them.

Fritz remembered those early years in which his grandmother always seemed to be outside working in the stable with the cows, in the potato field, or in the forest gathering hay. The children received their daily ration of bread, butter and sour milk (cottage cheese) and were not allowed to venture far from the house. His father, Nikolaus, built the boys wonderful blocks with wood scraps from the factory. Fritz recalled that Leena could build a tower so high that he could not reach the top although Maldi Petr, the eight-year-old boy next door, could climb on a chair and build it almost to the ceiling — and then crash it to the floor with a great sound. The children built farms with stables and fences around them and constructed little cardboard horses and cows, most with only three legs. But Nikolaus came to the rescue and built the children animals with wooden legs as well as sailing ships, cross-bows and beautiful wooden axes, swords and knives with which to play wild Indian battles.[33]

He also remembered his father seated at the table reading to the children from the newspaper about the Russian-Turkish war of 1876 that was taking place. "We," said Nikolaus, "fought brilliantly losing only one Cossack to the Turks thousands." He viewed pictures in vivid colors of the battles and many victories, one in which the Turkish official Osman Pascha was captured in the battle of Plewna, leaving 100 women at home. He handed his saber to the Russian Czar and the war was over (1877). Nikolaus made a transparent billboard of the scene

---

[33] It is interesting that with all the eastern European history, these children, living on an isolated island in the Baltic Sea, would play cowboy and Indians.

— a huge wooden box with a cardboard on top from which the name Plewna was cut out. Candles were put inside the box, which was placed on the street on high posts so that the people going to church could see the victorious battle had happened.

One day Fritz put on his father galoshes, an impressive cap, buckled his axe, knife, and sword to his father's belt and marched off to play Cossack alone. He wandered into a large pond, which was off bounds. Suddenly he heard a sound behind him and turned to see a large snake ready to strike. He did not recall how he made it home but the boots, cap and weapons did not accompany him. He was sick with fear and worry the rest of the day. Grete picked up the discarded items later in the day.

Maldi Petr was a great guy. He told wonderful stories about Ali Baba, (the devil who was always outwitted by the smart farmer), *Till Eulenspiegel*, *Schildburger*, and many other stories. He built beautiful kites and as the boys watched the kites fly toward the sun, they philosophized how far the distance from the kite to the sun might be. Maldi Petr had heard from an older boy at school that the sun was really a huge golden disc, which came out of the sea every morning, and disappeared into the sea again at night, where the boarder of the world was. Nikolaus explained that the earth is really a big ball and the sun is a bigger one and we stick to the earth with our feet as a fly does to the kitchen ceiling, a concept Fritz understood even less. Nikolaus also built a huge swing in the front yard where the children sat, three and four at a time, swinging and fantasizing about the clouds above and of what material they were made; or the factory and its many smoke stacks; or the countries and strange lands across the seas; or to watch the huge sailing ships appearing on the horizon, turn slowly towards shore and lower their sails; or a whole flotilla of fishing boats coming into harbor.

One day Nikolaus came home to say that Dago would receive a telegraph office, and he had to travel over the land to select posts for it. All the neighbors came to ask all sorts of questions about this strange new contraption. Another day a man came to the house with a black box with a hole in it. The family was told to stand very still in front of it while the man covered his head with a black cloth and looked into the box. Many days later a picture arrived from the man showing all of them. Imagine, this picture had come out of that box!

Another time Rudolf and Fritz were wandering through their property which had a creek running though it. The creek became fast and flooded in the spring with the melting snow. The boys were playing near when Rudolf started to slide in through mud, snow and ice. He could not move because of the heavy coat he was wearing. Fritz grabbed him and started shouting at the top of his lungs. The water was up to his chest when Grete finally arrived and pulled them out. He had saved Rudolf's life despite the fact that he was punished for getting Rudolf in trouble. Once Rudolf had very bad eczema on his scalp, so bad that all his hair fell out. The doctor on Dago didn't know how to treat it. So Nikolaus took him to Hapsal on the mainland. When they returned, Rudolf was "wearing a cap" of tar on his head. He was very proud of it. And he also told Fritz of the marvelous city and the many houses and churches with steeples and the steamer they took to get there. Fritz was very envious. Another opportunity to travel over the sea and go to the city was hardly thinkable.

In those days, and actually well into the 20th Century, many items were purchased from door to door salesmen. In isolated villages such as Kertell, peddlers were quite common. They walked from village to village selling the goods they carried in big boxes on their backs.[34] One time a Russian peddler was given sleeping quarters for the night in the family home.[35] In the morning he pinned a picture of a saint to the wall and started saying his prayers. These were the first Russian words Fritz heard. Another door-to-door merchant was the collector of bones and rags who would come every spring. The children would collect all the bones they could find in the fields and happily accepted the kopeks they received in return.

Winter in Dago was brutal. The sea froze, the winds blew, the snow was deep, and the cold was bitter. Days were very, very short and evenings were long and very boring. The children had to stay in and help their grandmother carding wool and even spin it or wind the yarn. Light was in short supply. Grete used chips of pinewood and long dried needles in place of matches which were not available in Dago to light fires. They were placed with one end into slots in the coal-burning oven and then lit on the other end. Sometimes women would run for a long distance to a neighbor's to get fire, returning with a shovel filled with glowing coal, which would be used to start a fire at home. They made their own candles by melting suet over the fire and dipping wool strings into the liquid. They also made petrol lamps — simple tin cans filled with petroleum. A wick was put through a hole in the top for the flame. And then Nikolaus came home with a new device; a beautiful petroleum lamp with a glass cylinder and candles began to be replaced.

---

[34] Kertell, now called Kardla in Estonian, was originally a Swedish town. It is located on the northeast corner of the Dago. With the advent of the factory, Estonians began to move there from the farms.

[35] This was standard as there were no hotels in these small villages.

Fritz's education started in 1876, with home schooling when he was five. His mother got the huge family Bible and taught him to recognize the most conspicuous letters, and his father purchased a slate and chalk. He and his brothers learned three languages: Nikolaus spoke only German at home, Kersti only Estonian, and Grete often Swedish. Grete taught the boys Swedish folk stories and songs, and Kersti taught them to read fairy tales in Estonian.

The co-op was also initiated in 1876, causing Kersti and Nikolaus to be away from the home from early in the morning until late in the evening, leaving Grete in full charge of the children. One day the boys' great uncle Andreas' youngest son Felix, age 11, arrived from Reval to stay with his Uncle Solomon Maehle, the foreman of the shearing plant. Felix introduced Fritz to all sorts of mischief. For example he would gather up little snakes, kill them, cut off their tails, hide them in his hand and then shake hands with his aunts, leaving pieces of the snake in their hands — which led to screaming and fainting. Once he set five year old Fritz on an unruly horse and made the horse break into a wild lope, throwing Fritz to the ground. Fortunately, he was not hurt.[36]

In the fall of 1879 the family, except for new baby Ewald who stayed with Grete, moved to the new house, which was attached to the store. That winter was very cold and as the house was not quite finished, icy wind blew between the joint, which were not yet sealed between the beams of the house.[37] It was so cold that Fritz and Rudolf slept together to keep warm. In fact, the only warm place in the building was the bakery and that is where the family congregated. The boys sat in front of the large bread

---

[36] It seems evident why he was sent to the country — to chill out.
[37] Joints between beams were sealed by using moss and oakum, a blend of fibers coated with tar.

oven and Fritz read aloud the newest Estonian novel or a "creepy" story translated from German. As often as possible, Kersti would come from the cold store to warm herself and listen to the stories.

Christmas time was especially nice.[38] The dough for gingerbread cookies was mixed and stored for weeks to rise. After cutting into various shapes — little men, horses, rabbits and other figures, they were baked and glazed with sugar. The bakery was a great joy at this time of the year. The store was exciting too. Nikolaus pried open big wooden boxes filled with all sorts of toys, books, and musical instruments, dolls, and games for children as well as Christmas tree decorations. And the best was that the boys were allowed to help unpack the goodies and place them on the shelves. In the evening the children would sit in front of the stove at home and tell each other fairy tales and discuss which of these beautiful things might become theirs on Christmas. The Christmas tree had to be extraordinary — floor to ceiling. Kersti gave the children some of the colored paper that came from the city to make decorations — chains, stars, crosses and other colorful ornaments. They also gilded nuts and strung gingerbread cookies for the tree. The big decision was which should be placed on top of the tree a candle or

---

[38] Christmas was hugely important in my family growing up. Reading this part of the memoir shows the roots of the celebration which began weeks in advance with the baking of Christmas cookies. My mother made dozens of varieties. We also decorated the house, inside and out and mother cooked a goose for Christmas dinner. One treat, which I didn't enjoy, was goose grease, adored by the Germans and other northern Europeans as a spread on rye bread. Probably best was the many varieties of marzipan — little potatoes or balls rolled in cocoa, colored fruits and animals, chocolate covered logs with pistachio nuts inside and logs of white marzipan rolled around chocolate marzipan, and of course, stolen. And in the center of it all was a floor to ceiling tree, which was decorated about two weeks before Christmas. I loved to lie on the sofa in the darkened living room and stare at the lighted sparkling tree.

an angel?

Finally, Christmas Eve arrived. At noon the tree was fastened to a stand and decorated. At five the bakery was closed and the family, except for Nikolaus who stayed to close up the store, dressed in their best cloths and went to church. When they came home from church, the holiday started. The children were no longer allowed in the living room. Standing outside they listened as their parents opened drawers, rattled dishes and whispered to each other. And then the doors were opened. The children ran in. The tree was magnificent and the gifts: a big plate for each boy filled with apples, nuts and sweets, and wonderful toys, books, coloring pencils and even new mittens.[39]

In the early spring while the ground was still frozen the sun melted the snow leaving large patches of water in the fields and meadows, which would freeze at night. These became wonderful skating rinks. For one kopek Fritz bought one skate from a boy. It was actually a piece of wood with an old iron blade fastened with string. He slid around, first on one leg and then on the other so no foot would feel left out. In 1880, he got a real pair of skates made from wood with iron blades and tied with leather straps and he began practicing in earnest.

One day Fritz became ill. He was diagnosed with scarlet fever and was immediately quarantined to the old house so that he would not infect his brothers. But Rudolf followed in a few days. They were sick for some time and when they finally were allowed out all the snow was gone and the sun was warm. Soon the gardening began. Potatoes as well as general vegetables were planted. In summer hay was harvested in the forest and close to the beach. The boys were required to help for many full days. But

---

[39] My family also celebrated Christmas in the same fashion.

their help consisted of looking for cranberries and black berries, to disturb snakes and catch lizards and to sit in the hay eating smelts with cold potatoes, bread, butter and sour milk (cottage cheese).

In the fall of 1880, Fritz, at age nine, started school in Kertell. It was connected to the factory and provided elementary courses. Nikolaus bought a new slate, primers in Estonian and German, an arithmetic book, a catechism,[40] and a wooden satchel with a lid. The teacher, a young bachelor from the mainland, hammered time tables into his students' brains so well that Fritz stated even as a man of fifty plus years, he often did arithmetic in Estonian, especially time tables. Misbehavior was punished with a strap across the backside or a ruler across the hands, palms up. Although Fritz never suffered this fate he often had to stay after school, principally because his parents were often tired in the evening and did not check his homework sufficiently. Once, when Fritz had to stay after school Rudolf, in order not to tattle on his brother, snuck into the house and hid under his bed until his brother came home.

On March 1, 1881, it was announced that the monarch, Czar Alexander II, had been assassinated with a bomb in the Russian capital, St. Petersburg. The terrible consequences of this did not register at this time. It was only interesting that there would be a new monarch, Alexander III. All the men had to go to a special mourning service in the church and to take an oath of allegiance to the new Czar.[41] There was a coronation and national flags were hung with

---

[40] Keep in mind that there was one religion, Lutheran, and it was totally integrated into the culture.
[41] Now, Fritz wrote, being an adult, one wonders if things might have been different if Alexander II, a reformer, had survived? Might there not have been a Bolshevik revolution resulting in Bolshevism for the country?

great festivities. Nikolaus made banners and put pictures of the royal family in the store showcases and windows.

That summer Fritz cut his foot in the creek near his home. The barber, not the doctor, was called to bandage it. The boy had to stay in the house for almost a month. But by Johannis he was up and around again.[42] On the first night of the Johannis festival piles of wood were covered with barrels of tar and lighted as men and women jumped over the flames. Folk songs were sung and dancing went on late into the night. The music and dancing continued on the next day, the church choir sang, and races and games were organized for the children.

At the end of the summer there was a celebration of the 50th year of the plant. Free food and drink were consumed all day and an orchestra came from the mainland to entertain. This lasted for two days. In honor of the birthday, the plant donated money to organize a brass band. There were a few men who had played in the military band during their service and several others who joined the group, and from then on one could hear them practicing in the afternoon in the school house. Finally, the plant hired a conductor and they began to sound pretty good. Unfortunately, the conductor drowned during a sailing party when he and some friends had imbibed a bit too much — but the band played on.

During the following winter (1881-2) Kertell citizens formed a theater group. Their first performance was a comedy by Kotzebue, *Confusion-Confusion,* in the schoolhouse. It was performed in Estonian and Fritz did not understand it very well as most of his communication was by then in German. But he loved the magician.

---

[42] John's festival in English is celebrated in midsummer and although Christian, its roots go back to pagan times.

In the summer, Fritz got into a fight with a classmate over a knife his father had given him. The classmate claimed it was his. In the scuffle, Fritz's hand was badly cut, leaving a large scar between his thumb and forefinger. Later in the summer one lovely Sarurday,the Maehles and several other families went with six or seven wagons and lots of food and drink to the village of Koppoe on the long peninsula west of Dago, a trip of 50 km. The peninsula was high with steep descending chalk banks into the sea. On its highest point across the infamous riff, Neckerman's Ground, was a tall lighthouse which the travelers reached just in time to see the sun go down, disappearing into the water towards Sweden. At the same time the lighthouse beacons were turned on, sending bolts of light through all the prisms and lenses of the windows over the sea. On the next day the sea was beautiful and they could see all the way to Osel, the island south of Dago.

The following school year was Fritz's last on Dago. He was eleven and had read the whole Estonian library in the school and his father's collection, from the first to last book. He had graduated from the factory school with a diploma of five, the highest in the school. He was ready, at age 11, to move on, or at least his father thought so. Nikolaus was determined that his boys obtain full educations and become fluent and comfortable in German, the language of the upper classes and the norm for business.

There are times in one's life, which influence all further developments. For Fritz, one such year was 1883. At that time, schools of higher learning were taught only in German; the factory school was taught in Estonian. There was a German school for children of workers from the Reich.[43] There were only seven to ten children enrolled per year. A private teacher came from the Reich and was paid by the plant administration. Nikolaus thought he would put Fritz in this school for one or two years. But he needed permission from Baron Ungern-Sternberg, the "old" Baron. His request was thoroughly rebuffed. He was not a German; his children were not high class (i.e. German children). The Baron was, on principle, against putting Estonians (peasants) into his German school. Nikolaus reminded him that he himself had completed a totally German education, that his family spoke German at home, and that he certainly did not rank as a factory worker but he held a position of a master (i.e., administrator). To no avail! The Baron noted that he, his parents before and his children were members of the Estonian farm community, and for such people the school was not available. When Kersti heard about this she became furious. Fritz quoted her words:

> We are not good enough for that school. That means I am not good enough. Papa is half Swedish by birth; he speaks better German than the masters here. These vagabonds who could not make it in their own country came here without shirts or pants of their own. The Baron had to send used clothing to Reval so that they could be brought over here and he could introduce them as masters. Their jobs? Even those had to be taught to them by the factory workers!

---

[43] The Reich refers to Germany and everything she possessed or influenced. In this case, the estates were owned by people of German ancestry.

But I will tell you this, son. As long as I have a drop of strength left in me you will learn, you and all of my sons. All of you, each and every one. You will show them that you are not slaves and farmhands, that you are able to achieve more than all of these people combined. The farm girl Kersti will show them what she can do! And Fritz, remember, the greatest pain you could ever give me would be the day that these people get the better of you. Promise me that you will never let that happen.

"Well," Fritz noted, "I kept my promise to my mother." When she closed her eyes forever 26 years later, four of her sons had university degrees and her youngest son said the last words over her grave as a Pastor from Reval. But for the sons of the masters, not one had come that far. And how could the Baron at that time suspect that 30 years later a Baroness Erdberg would announce the engagement of her daughter to Kersti's youngest son, and that my sister-in-law married a member of the oldest nobility in the Baltic, the Von Dahms? And that 35 years later all of the Baltic Reich would flee the country and move all over Europe, while former serfs ran the country?

So, as no opportunity existed on Dago, Fritz would be sent to Hapsal on the mainland. Kersti began sewing Fritz's new wardrobe — collars, shirts, pants, jackets, even a coat with a fur collar. Fritz began to prepare for entrance exams, which were conducted in German. Since he already knew all of the material in Estonian, it was just a matter of perfecting his German. For this he used a German Catechism (prayer book) and Bible from which he read one commandment and one story every day during the summer. By coincidence, Andreas, Nikolaus' brother, sent his two daughters, Lydia and Amanda, ages 14 and 12, to Dago. The girls spoke no Estonian and happily for Fritz, he was able to become relatively proficient in German before the fall school year.

School Years in Haspel — Fall 1883-1886

Five AM on the morning of his departure his mother woke him with a soft kiss, "Wake up Fritz — it is time." The wagon was loaded with his luggage; the horse was already hitched for a drive to the town of Helterma, where the steam ship was waiting to take him over the sea to the city, school and a new life away from home. At the door his mother, with tears in her eyes said:

> Fritz, you can't possibly know what this day means to you. This is the last day of your childhood in your parents' house. From now on you will return here only as a guest. Life is going to be more serious now. I cannot watch over you anymore, but someone else will do it for me. Never forget Him, my dear child.

He had a last look at his room, kissed his mother, grandmother and brothers goodbye — and his old dog, Bosi, who seemed to know something was wrong. He went to the store to say goodbye to the baker and long time clerks and then climbed aboard the wagon next to the butcher, Johann, who was driving. His father climbed aboard and they left, over the bridge, around the saw mill, the gas plant which always smelled like tar, the church without a tower, the post office, the customs office, up a hill to the edge of Kertell.

There was a fresh sea breeze from the bay, which was in view. To the horizon he saw the blue with white caps and half a dozen mast boats swaying. Further down there was a steamer laying anchored, and even further he saw the characteristic shape of the signal ship coming in from the Neckerman's

Ground. They passed the windmill on the barren Kertell Mountain, a high hill, called a mountain by the locals. Nikolaus murmured, "Here is where your great grandfather Tacking worked at one time." They passed the inn as more vehicles joined and the road widened. The horse began to trot through the tollgate separating the grazing pastures and hay meadows from the forest of dwarf northern fur trees, short, dense and covered with moss. He wondered how they could exist as the ground was hard limestone; but they came through the rubble and stones, clinging to the sparse topsoil.

The wind picked up and the smell of salt and seaweed were in the air. He saw the trees part for a view of the sea and the faraway coasts of the neighboring island of Worms and Heilse, the village where Kersti was born. They continued over hills, through barren fields with farmhouses with thatched roofs and of course, forests. The road was excellent — and natural. The limestone was so firm that the farmers only had to throw some gravel on it from time to time, especially into the grooves made by the carts. Suddenly the horse turned left and stopped. He knew that this was a resting place. Then horses' tingling bells announce the approach of the postal coach. They all returned to the wagon, as they had to be at the steamer before the postal coach, continuing as before, through forests, past meadows and farms and the village of Pardas. They passed the hayfields of the Grossenhof estate, through another forest and the estate's manor house, stables, silos, windmill, sawmill, church and lovely guesthouse came into view.[44] After a short stop at the estate's inn, they continued. Again the sea came into view and across

---

[44] Estates included manor houses, miles of fields and forests, and complete villages where the servants and farmhands lived. Formerly, of course, these people were serfs.

the sea, Kasjew Island. Further on they came to Keinis, the village where some of his ancestors came from and suddenly the port appeared. Johann took the horse and Nikolaus and Fritz entered the Haelterma Inn, with an immaculate white wooden floor covered with white sand, a wooden sofa, table and some chairs.[45] They sat down for their morning meal, which they had brought with them. It was 10 AM and they had traveled almost three hours.

Finally they drove down to the wharf. Johann carried the luggage aboard the steam ship, Progress. It was full of containers, goods, and animals, as well as passengers. The skipper pulled a rope, the steam whistle blasted, the women and children screamed, and the horses on the wharf shied. Although Fritz was baptized with seawater, grew up by the sea, and had fallen from a sailboat more than once, this was his first time on a steam ship. He was very excited.

Suddenly a two-horse coach arrived. "Better" people alighted — ladies and gentlemen, administrators, young society ladies, students, and a Russian officer. The ship's bell rang again but nothing happened. And there, on the edge of the forest, a carriage, pulled by four horses and followed by a smaller two horse carriage appeared. The skipper jumped down and removed his cap. All of the farmers followed. A tall, slightly bent gentleman with a drooping grey mustache followed by young ladies and gentlemen alighted from the carriages. It was Count Ungern Sternberg, cousin to the Baron in Kertell, and owner of Grossenhof estate. He was also the main shareholder of the factory in Kertell and owned three quarters of Dago. Not far from the landing place on the wharf stood a column, painted

---

[45] Sand was used extensively to cover and clean floors in inns and other public places. Fritz even mentioned the sand cleaned floor of his home in Hapsal.

black, red and gold and crowned by the colorful coat of arms of the Ungern-Sternberg family. It was removed by the Russians a few years later, and with it the symbol that stood for sovereignty.

And so they set sail. An hour later they were in the middle of the strait and the sea began to get rough. The ladies went below. Some passengers got seasick. But Fritz loved it — the wilder, the better. Gradually the mainland coast came into view. He was overwhelmed. For the first time in his life, he saw a city — the gray tower of the old castle from the time of the crusaders, the steeples of the churches, the high silos in the harbor, sailing and steamships at the wharf, and many white sails of smaller boats. On landing there were strange looking coachmen in Russian blue caftans in charge of their two horse carriages, more elegant, it seemed, than those of the Count. A few minutes later Fritz and his father were driving directly behind the Count, whom nobody had come to greet. Apparently, Fritz observed, the Count was not as big as on Dago. He and his dad were almost as elegant as he. The city air made him feel free.

They found rooms in a local pub and the next day Fritz took his entrance exams, which he passed easily with his "farmer's" German. He had become an appointed student at the County School of Hapsal.[46] Next they found a room for Fritz in a little windblown house near the harbor directly at the water's edge. It was so close to the sea that when the waves became rough, the water came up to the door and when the autumn storms blew they had to leave the house and move their belongings to a house on higher ground. It was small and very clean. The floors were scrubbed with white sand and the ceiling was so low that Fritz could almost reach it. Owned by the widow of the

---

[46] It was a Lutheran school and taught in German, not Estonian.

seaman Dampf from Dago, it was Fritz's home for the next 3½ years. He shared a room and bed with another boy, Johannes Joesberg. Nikolaus returned home and Fritz was alone. He was consumed with homesickness and as much as he had longed to see the city, the lonelier he felt. This soon passed. His father wrote often and he regularly went down to the harbor to breathe some Dago air from the Progress when it docked.

Hapsal[47] was a typical Baltic small town of 4,000 inhabitants. It had little trade and commerce. Its main income came from its mud baths, for which it was famous. Even Czar Alexander II had spent summers there from time to time. The town therefore had become fashionable in St. Petersburg. Usually in the early days of May the steamers of the Riga-Petersburg Line started to bring the first guests. The small houses of the town began to fill up. The boardwalk became lively with summer dresses and uniforms and an orchestra appeared. The many bath cabins at the beach and the sanatoriums were filled to capacity. The high season was summer when Fritz was in Dago and by August when school started, the tourist season was almost at an end. The first days of September looked like a "migration of the nations" with steamboats full of departing tourists. By the end of the month few ships docked in Hapsal. Once the stormy weather and fog arrived, navigation into the bay was too dangerous and the steamers stopped altogether; only the Progress continued to sail between Dago and Hapsal until the first drifting ice floats, when it too took to port. Doors and windows on homes were nailed tight and the families moved into the warmest corner of the house for the winter. The few streetlights were dim kerosene and streets were often icy and dangerous. At that time there was

---

[47] Now Haapsalu in Estonian.

no efficient direct land connection between Hapsal and Reval.[48] To travel between them one had to go through rough snow and ice covered land for close to one hundred miles. Hapsal was in hibernation until April when spring brought life to the city again. Houses were opened and scrubbed. Flowerbeds were planted in front of the houses and real estate people arrived from Petersburg to make arrangements for the summer season, which began in May.

The school had been a very fine place for learning in years past but had not yet begun to keep up with the needs of the time when he went there. The curriculum was focused on those who desired a practical profession — shop clerks, office workers, engineers in lower ranks, farmer and farm administrators, etc. The terms were scheduled over 3½ years, two of which were spent in primary classes and the remainder in secondary, finishing around Christmas time, as opposed to summer as most other schools. Subjects included religion, German, Russian, geography, history, biology, elementary physics, very basic chemistry, mathematics, elementary algebra, and plane geometry. The sciences and math were simply taught with applications to certain professions. Art, drafting, music and physical education were also taught, and one could have private lessons in Latin, Greek and French.

The school building had two stories with one schoolroom on each floor, the primary on first and secondary on second. It was very old and in dire need of repairs. Floors and all benches were well worn and covered with hand carved names of their previous occupants. The maps on the walls were old and covered with ink spots larger than some European countries. This was due to leisure activities spent

---

[48] Now Tallinn, the capitol of Estonia.

staging battles using ink soaked paper balls as weapons. There were three closets on the first floor, one which served as a library, another which contained all the drawing equipment, and the third for all physics instruments. Everything had collected dust, and seemed neglected and run down. The library had only half of the books listed in the catalogue, many with pages missing. There was no equipment for physical education.

The school faculty of three teachers was also housed in the school. Except for Mr. Gruenberg, they were mediocre at best. For example, physics was limited to discussions; no equipment was ever used. All classes were taught in German, the official language of the Baltic States at that time. French was a joke — reading from one book — while the teacher, who was usually "under the weather," slept. After three years of French, Fritz was not even able to read it correctly. Biology was not much better. But fortunately, as biology was of more interest to the boys, they became self-taught. Only Mr. Gruenberg who taught history, geography, German and Latin was an efficient teacher. What he taught, the boys did not forget. Fritz said, "He would come over casually and then hit you with the battle of the Catalonian Fields. And if you did not come up with the answer, 451 AD, you received a whack on the ears that clearly helped you remember the next time." Gruenberg was a good teacher and prepared the boys for German better than most students in the gymnasiums. Fritz and he became good friends because Fritz loved history, Latin and German and was very good in all of them. Gruenberg was a very strange man. He was tall, slightly stooped with long black hair and an imposing mustache. He had an ability to fold his forehead in multiple layers of folds of skin and when he was startled, he raised not only his eyebrows, but his whole scalp shot in an upward direction. Fritz practiced the contortion but was never able to achieve the virtuosity of his teacher.

Gruenberg also drank a great deal. There were times when Fritz saw him on the street in a rather foggy condition; but in the classroom, he was always there. Another teacher, Mr. Tichomirow, who taught Russian, also drank too much, although he also was very efficient in the classroom. Unfortunately, he went on a boat trip with some of his drinking companions, the boat capsized and he drowned. He was replaced by a new young teacher who had no control over the class and after a short time moved to Riga. He then was replaced by another teacher who wore dirty clothes and also drank. Years later Fritz saw the young teacher in Riga. He had become a big shot and influential in the Russification movement.

Fritz had to learn how to deal with his homesickness and independence, both challenging. But he enjoyed many good times and many adventures over the 3½ years. One of the first was the September Fair. Booths were erected in the market place for selling sweets, a Punch and Judy Show, magicians, and a juggler dressed as Pagliacci who swallowed his sword, spit fire and pulled eggs from his ears. Russian and Jewish peddlers and second hand dealers arrived by the scores. School was closed on the day of the fair. Hundreds of Estonian farmers, the women in their national costumes, Swedish farmers who came by boat from Nuckoe and Worms were everywhere. The streets smelled of fruit, honey, and smoked and salted fish. The schoolboys were drunk with excitement. They had saved 40-50 kopeks and were just not to be kept down. The juggler, dancing pigs, huge bags of apples and plums, crisp baked cookies with a steaming mug of coffee, the Punch and Judy show; what a wonderful day!

Autumn was a wonderful time. No tourists to crowd the streets. Falling leaves, and white and gray clouds whipping over the sky, and the old castle with the park in front and all its underground paths and nooks in the castle walls were perfect places for young boys to run and yell, hide and seek, and fight to their hearts content. When the snow arrived, the mounds around the castle made perfect slides and even if they did not have a sled, they could use the seat of their pants. Finally the days became shorter and shorter. Interest in the park was waning but as temperatures dropped, the whole 1km of Hapsal Bay froze, as no one who lives in a city with its artificial skating rinks can imagine. Everyone in the town donned skates — women, children, men, young and old. The bay was full of people — hundreds of them. Fritz had received a new pair for his birthday. What a joy! There were even iceboats with sails. When the winter storms covered the ice with snow, the boys cleared a spot directly beneath the wharf wall. Little fir trees were staked in a square and there they practiced figure skating, always in teams.

One day a sailboat way out in the open sea beyond the bay appeared. It wanted to reach the harbor but could not get through the ice. Men with sleds, ropes, axes and iron rods were assembled and teams approached the boat and open water. The sailboat took full wind and raced with all its force against the newly formed ice. The ice bent and after a few heavy thumping sounds, the ship sat solidly on the ice. Teams of men then approached the ship and anchored it to the ice. They sawed the ice to break it in front of the boat and slowly, it was guided into the harbor.

That first winter, Peter, Fritz's landlady Madam Dampfi's oldest son, came to live with them, becoming the fourth person to sleep in the one little room. He loved to read history, make fishing nets, and tell tales about his trips. Early one morning he woke Fritz. "Do you want to go fishing?" he asked. Soon they were on the ice with his dog sled, loaded with a large container, ropes, rods and an iron icebreaker. They sped across the blue ice, he on his sled and Fritz on his skates. It was so cold Fritz could hardly open his eyes. They skated far from the coast where there was a guideline — dozens of birch rods anchored into the ice in a straight line. At the first rod Peter cut a hole into the ice about ½ foot wide. There was a small fish swimming wildly around with a string and long hook protruding from its back. It was the bait. They had to pull very hard. Finally, a huge pike, at least three feet long was raised. They proceeded to the next hole and the next and the next until all had been opened, returning home with about a dozen large pikes, which Peter sold to various customers in the town. The holes would freeze over in the night and the next day Peter could go out again. Meanwhile, he had all night to drink. "A pity," noted Fritz, "Peter was a nice straight forward honest seaman otherwise."

In his first year in Hapsal, Fritz had an amazing experience on his trip home for the Christmas holidays. Written in the first person, it is presented, in its entirety, without editing:

> Christmas is coming closer and I am absolutely sure that no force in the whole wide world will keep me away from home even if I have to travel the distance over the water on the back of a seal. Therefore I start making gifts: for Mama a wooden sewing box with fret work and for Papa a photo frame. From time to time I receive letters from home but soon the bay can no longer be traveled and Dago is totally out of reach. Then the deep freeze sets in at -13° to -16° C for 4-5 days. The sea

screams and thunders, sometimes sounding like cannon fire. That is the ice contracting and breaking again in kilometer long channels as it freezes.

And then the town begins to fill with troikas, sleighs and sledges.[49] We have letters again and school becomes very unimportant. We start packing our skates, mittens and winter furs ready to be on the first caravan home.

One day a caravan of 30 horse drawn sledges arrives from Dago. They tell us that they will return to Dago the following morning. Our joy is immense. At 6 AM, while it is still pitch dark, we arrive at the meeting place. All belongings are packed on a sledge and fastened with rope and soon we leave. Our caravan moves out, over the crisp snow to Rohnruhla, directly across from Helterma, (a town on Dago). In Rohnruhla we have a large breakfast in the inn and by 8 AM, when the sun is just beginning to rise, we start off again. Close to the shore the ice is bad, heaped in great chunks. The sledges are jostling and swaying and we have to hold on for dear life. But as soon as we are a distance away from the land, the way improves and soon there is nothing ahead of us but a silvery, glistening face of a mirror. One cannot see the other side which is 20 km away for the whiteness. We boys have now taken off our heavy overcoats, although it is -12° C but we have put on our skates and are now having

---

[49] Troikas are small Russian carriages drawn by three horses abreast. Sleighs are also carriages drawn by only one horse. Sledges are wide large wagons with thick runners designed for carrying heavy goods and drawn by one strong fast horse. All have runners and can go over snow or ice.

a race with the horses and sledges. The fast legs of the horses with their special shoes which attack the ice surface, the farmers encouraging all of us with whistling and yelling encourage us to pull ahead. The wind too, is in our favor and we leave the caravan further and further behind. Small fur trees have been stuck into the ice every 100 feet to create a straight road across the bay. Soon we are 7 km. away from the mainland and Hapsal. As we look back we can see the caravan moving on the ice like tiny insects. In front of us the island of Dago comes into view. We almost have an accident then. The leader of our group of students, seven boys in all, almost races into a three meter wide gap in the ice. Steam from it is rising into the cold wintry air. The crack stretches beyond view in both directions. There is no way to go around it and to jump across, even if we did not have the skates on, is just too risky, especially for the smaller people in the group like me with my 12 years.

We have to wait for the caravan. It arrives half an hour later. Every second sledge carries a long wooden board. They are now carefully placed over the open crack. The horses are unharnessed and led carefully to the other side. Much more troublesome, of course, are the heavy sledges over the boards. Finally, after almost one hour of hard work, we can move on. Meanwhile, however, the weather has changed. The sky has grown dark and the sun has disappeared. It is warmer, now only -4° to 5° C. The sky looks dusky and from the northwest above Dago, clouds are beginning to appear. The farmers look worried. *Tuisenturm tulemas* — snow storm advancing. If only the ice will keep and not break up, carrying all of us into the Baltic Sea.

We still have to cover 15 km. across the ice and since wind is now against us we must add 1½ hours. The clouds on the horizon have grown black and cover almost the whole sky. Our leader, who is almost 17 and has made the winter crossing six times, talks from experience. He already smokes a pipe and can spit through his teeth like a genuine captain. He says, if we all crawl into the sledges now as hot and sweaty as we are, they will carry us to the cemetery on New Years for sure. We have to get something hot. And with that he produces a bottle of cognac from his breast pocket and passes it around to his followers. Even the four of us from the primary school help him to empty the bottle. Oh that feels good. Now one of the older boys passes a second bottle around. One of the boys has a third bottle but that will have to keep for later. Now we must eat some bread. It is all frozen but it still it tastes good. It is noon. We left Hapsal 6 hours ago, have been on the ice for 4 hours but because of the bad ice conditions on shore and the crack and wind now against us, we have only covered 11 km — with 15 km to go.

The first sledge of the caravan comes into view. The horses have been driven hard and are steaming. The sledges are very heavily loaded and the driving is getting harder by the minute. In places where the snow does not cling to the ice surface the sledges side-swipe easily and then the horses have to come to a stop. In places where the snow has accumulated, the going is equally rough. The animals have to rest at least for half an hour and have to be fed. We put on our heavy coats with collars up, our scarves around our faces and huddle close together. The first gusts hit us and drive very fine snow like a veil over the ice. A strange sound, low at first and then steadily increasing fills the air above and combines with an eerie sound of creaking from underneath the ice — an unearthly kind of music. We are still skating and fighting against the wind working our way as fast and hard as we can. But the increasing snow now builds into high streaks on the ice, making it very hard for us to skate. One boy falls and hurts his knee badly. Another skates right into a pile of snow and hits the ice with his face and can be seen to crawl on all fours for quite a while. I can only keep up because I am skating behind an older boy with a sturdy frame which blocks the wind for me. But we can hardly keep our eyes open. The sharp hard snow hits us full force. It gets into our noses; our ears are half frozen.

Completely exhausted, we finally arrive at the large semi-circle built by the trees which marks the half-way spot. Because of the snow and the distance, we cannot see the caravan behind us. "Listen guys," says one of the older boys who is our leader, "this is no fun anymore. We cannot skate anymore. We have to sit in the sledges. If only the ice holds out. This is only the half-way point, the current is strongest here and therefore the ice is thinnest at this part. If we were just at Heinland (a small island) we would be over the worst." Soon the caravan appears and we climb into the sledges with the farmers and bundle up.

Now the snow becomes so heavy that we can hardly see the sledge in front of us and we realize the importance of the fir trees staked into the ice. If they were not there, there is no telling where we would end up in this white-out. The creaking and cracking in the ice becomes worse. One can see fine black hairline cracks in the surface where the seawater seeps through wetting the snow. My farmer's face shows worry; he has an ax and a coil of rope ready on top of his sledge. The horses seem to sense the danger also as they try fiercely to keep up with the leading sledge.

"The ice is moving," mumbles the farmer. He means that the ice under us starts to heave in a slow motion as the wind presses on from the still open sea. I do not feel very well at all and believe that I feel the up and down of the waves under the ice. The plain ice surface is now completely covered by snow which at least, helps to make the sledges go faster.

Suddenly there is a cry from the sledges ahead: "*JAAA PRA GUNNEYS* — THE ICE IS BREAKING!" As on command, all sledges spread out in various directions so as not to put all the weight in the same spot. Only two cannot move fast enough around a dark puddle which has appeared and is becoming larger very quickly. The seawater forces itself to the surface. Both horses are becoming frantic and thrashing their hooves wildly. The first of the sledges is keeping on the ice as the farmer jumps down immediately freeing the horse by cutting the harnesses with his ax. Freed, the horse gallops away to safety. The sledge however, seems lost. The crack is between the two runners and the ice walls are sinking lower. But the farmers have prepared for this possibility by attaching a coil of heavy rope to each sled. The farmer grips the end of the rope and now the other men come to his help and pull the endangered sledge to the safer ice.

The second sledge, however, is in a complicated situation. It has followed the first one very closely and is now directly on the crack which appeared under the first sledge. The farmer did not have time to jump clear and the runners have broken through the ice leaving the sledge on the mud guards of its runners. The horse has broken through the ice with his hind legs and is trying desperately to get his front legs, still on the ice, to pull himself up. However, his wild thrashing about breaks the ice more causing large pieces to break apart. The farmer cannot get close to the animal because there is a big hole around it. There seems to be no hope to save the sledge. The farmer tries to save the horse. He gets on his knees in the icy water, cuts the ropes which hold the goods on the sledge. But it is too late. He jumps away. The sledge sinks with the back end first — faster and faster into the gaping hole. Half of the load has vanished already and with a dreadful sound, the sledge disappears, pulling the horse in after it. The animal is almost completely in the water now, only his head is above, the nostrils blowing, neighing and humming, the great eyes looking in horror at us. We are still standing helplessly around the terrible black hole. The animal is trying to swim but he is getting slower and slower. Now the ears are under water. What a pity! He was such a fine young animal. The farmer is tearing his hair in despair.

Then suddenly — a crash! The horse has lifted himself high out of the water and the sledge comes up too. Now that it is empty, it can float. The men spring into action. The farmer fastens a rope to his belt while the other farmers hold on to it. He swings another rope with a noose on the end and carefully approaches the horse to the edge of the ice. He coaxes, "Susken, Susken." The horse swims with all his might to the farmer who throws the noose around his neck. Twenty men pull with all their strength and — "hurrah" — the horse and sledge are pulled onto the ice. The men loosen the noose so the horse can breathe. He jumps to his feet, shaking himself.

My friend, Kaup, who was sitting on the unfortunate sledge, jumped down with the farmer but with his heavy fur coat on, he fell down on the icy water and broke through with his foot. My farmer noticed just in time and, grabbing Kaup's hands, pulled him on the dry ice. Now we are all standing around. We do not know what to do. He is wet to the waist and his boots are full of water. It is at least minus 5°C and the snowstorm is blowing wilder than before. Our clothes have not remained completely dry during this adventure either. Most of us have wet mittens and shoes. We still have 7 km to Dago and we do not know how strong the ice is ahead. Kaup is given the last bottle of cognac and has to swallow at least a quarter of it. The remaining is shared among the rest of us. We put Kaup on a sledge, take off his shoes and socks and tie woolen scarves around his legs. We then give him his father's felt boots, which his father had given him especially for this trip. Since the boots are much too large for him, we take hay from the horses' food bags and stuff it around his legs. Soon Kaup is warm. Meanwhile, the farmers have mended the broken and cut harnesses for the first sledge and fixed the second one. Susken has a blanket around his shivering body and is allowed to feed on some hay.

All that is lost are a few bags of salt and flour which are now resting on the bottom of the sea. Nobody can be blamed for the accident. Everyone knows the risks of crossing the sea on winter ice. In fact, everyone is quite happy for the lives of a farmer and his horse have been saved. The other farmers give enough hay to the wet farmer so that he can cover himself for the rest of the journey and we start up again. Now we are in a greater hurry — and much more careful.

We have lost a whole hour. It is starting to get dark at only 2PM, and the storm is picking up force. The slow and eerie weaving of the ice underneath us is increasing. We cannot drive behind each other anymore but make three columns, parallel to each other with ten sledges each. The lead for the middle column is given to Susken because the sledge is empty and the horse has to speed up to warm himself. Half and hour has passed and we are feeling rather uneasy, even though the snow has stopped falling.

And then the storm picks up again and suddenly we hear a loud crash behind us. "Good Lord!" Where we had the accident, the sea is visible — black, wide open and the ice is breaking off further and further. Now we have to race for our lives. The animals instinctively know the danger and, breathing the air from the coast, they run at top speed. They are encouraged by whistling, screaming and yelling from the farmers who are using their whips. The wind is cutting into our faces; the ice flakes from the sledges in front of us hit us like pins and needles. Our cheeks are frozen and our fingers are stiff. For fifteen minutes we keep up this pace and then we can breathe more easily — we are on bumpy ice at the shore. Closer to land the storm looses its force somewhat. We now rearrange ourselves in one line again because there is only one track and we can reduce our speed.

What an experience for a 12 year old boy who has only been away from home once and then for just four months! We know that children grew up faster then. This seems to support that contention. So the caravan continued for another 15 minutes until it arrived at the Helterswmae Inn. The poor drenched animals were immediately taken to the stables and the men and boys stumbled into the Inn to warm their frozen bodies around the huge oven. The proprietor served them coffee and sandwiches and dried their wet mittens and Kaup's wet socks and boots over the stove. By 4 PM they were all dry and fed so they continued on their journey across Dago, dropping off sledges as they went along. At 7 PM the remaining few arrived in Kertell. Fritz was embraced by everyone in the family and the store as well. Full of happiness he settled down for a grand two week vacation.

First he had to show off his shiny city skates to his former schoolmates. He was the envy of all. And Christmas preparations were very time consuming — making paper chains and stars and gilding nuts for the tree. On Christmas Eve, as usual, Nikolaus closed the store early; the whole family went to church and then home for the exchange of gifts. The children waited outside the living room door with anticipation, listening to activity inside. Then Kersti opened the door. What a sight! Gifts for everyone — mouth organs, tin soldiers, drums, gloves, a new fur hat for Fritz, and plates full of sweets, candy apples and nuts. The following week went quickly with visits to friends and visits from friends. New Years was celebrated with rifle shots and melted lead for good luck. After January 6, when the three wise men are celebrated, Fritz had to return to Hapsal.

During the holidays a deep frost and the ice had formed anew. But the trip back was difficult. Instead of smooth surfaces, they encountered heavy ice floats heaped on top of each other, blocks with sharp edges and pyramids of ice, leaving only a snake like trail for the sledges. Where the holes had been, the surface was slippery and the sledges had to balance precariously causing fear that the runners would break. Going was slow and they arrived in Hapsal, shaken and frozen.

When the bay ice began to break up in March and April, the boys invented a new game. They would stand on broken pieces of ice, floating on the water, wearing high boots and using long sticks would sail merrily around until the ice broke under their weight requiring that they jump to another float. Sometimes they would get a cold bath and people watching said that they were playing a risky game. Quite so. When the ice was gone, Peter set out his nets again and caught eels with a trident. Fritz helped, of course. When the wild flower began to bloom the boys at school collected and dried samples. They were then put into books and labeled in both German and Latin, thus earning them a five in biology.

Although many important people came to Hapsal during the summer spa season, one time when Grand Duke Nikolaus (later to be Czar) stopped while traveling around the Baltic, he planted a tree in the newly created park opened in his honor and named Nikolaus Garden. The day of the park's inauguration, all schools participated in the festivities. To his dismay, Fritz had torn his sleeve. Although Madam Dampfi tried to mend it very fast when he finally arrived at the park, everybody was already marching and he was not allowed to enter the gardens. He was quite unhappy until he learned that nobody from his school had been able to see any of the festivities either as they had been placed behind a whole troop of soldiers and dignitaries. Aside from this and a couple of other Russian dignitaries, the greatest activities in Hapsal were a new voluntary fire brigade and a new German language newspaper.

One day at 3 PM the fire alarm was sounded. There was a fire on one of the estates about 3 km out of town. The school boys were the first to arrive. The thatched roof of a large stable was burning and the people on the farm had lost their heads completely. The animals in the barn were not saved and those that were already outside ran back into the stable. Twenty minutes after the alarm had sounded, the first fire fighter arrived, complete with feathered helmet and all, and took his place — not with fire fighting equipment, but right beside the onlookers. Five minutes later the engine with three more fire fighters and drawn by two horses arrived. After another 10 minutes, three more carriages arrived with the rest of the men. Meanwhile the roof had caved in burying 30 animals under it. After a lot of swearing and running around, they were ready to put some water on the flames. The pumping was mostly done by the school boys while the helmet wearing heroes stood at the sideline sweating. The next day the new newspaper described, with glowing imagination over six pages, the firefighters' heroic performance. The paper doubled it size immediately but soon collapsed for lack of news.

Over the 3½ years, quite a few things, both happy and sad, happened. During two fall storms, severe flooding caused madam Dampfi's house to flood. Peter carried all the furniture to safety and Fritz had to stay with some friends until the water receded again. Each Christmas he made the trip over the ice to Dago, sometimes without trouble, sometimes with it. In the summer of 1886 when Fritz was 14½ years old, Nikolaus decided that he should attend the Real-Gymnasium in Reval for a couple of terms to complete his education. That was easier said than done. Fritz learned that he would have to enter the quinta grade and complete an entrance exam. After 3½ years, he would only complete the secunda grade and his knowledge was seriously lacking in algebra and French. What to do? He consulted some of his teachers. Gruenberg moved his scalp a few times and explained that he could not help in either subject but his sister-in-law could give him French lessons. He was on his own for algebra and would have to find a tutor outside of the school. But, no one in Hapsal seemed to know algebra when suddenly, a friend found a book titled *Algebra* in the library his father had left him. So Fritz studied French with Gruenberg's sister-in-law and algebra and geometry by himself. The French teacher was young, only 17, very pretty and they laughed a lot. Geometry, which he had already had in Hapsal, was quite easy but algebra was a different story. The book was not written for beginners. So he worked hard both in and out of school and received his diploma just in time for the Christmas vacation. He was finished with Hapsal.

But alas, another sea problem; it had not yet frozen. The mail was brought in by boat to Worms and then transferred by sledge across the island onto boats again and shipped to Hapsal. Fritz had to try to get to Worms. On the day of departure he and about 20 other passengers climbed into three sail boats filled with mail. The weather was clear and the wind was strong as they set all sails for Worms. They were almost halfway to Worms when someone yelled out, "Ice floats from Hestholm." The whole sea on the wind side was covered with ice which seemed to be closing in fast. If the ice came between the boats and Worms, they could not land. Nor could they return to Hapsal as the ice had already closed in behind them. Once trapped in the ice they might float out to sea since the wind was almost a storm.

"All men to the oars!" The sea was soaring and spray was flying over the boats. They were still about two miles from Worms and their hands were freezing. In addition, the ice was floating dangerously close. It was closing in on the boats. The noise of the cracking, gurgling and hissing ice was thunderous. A young lady, who insisted on coming because, her mother was ill, started to cry. Fritz's boat leaned heavily to one side, took on water and hit the sandy beach. The other two followed — just in time. Floats, roaring, hissing and crashing onto the shore, broke into thousands of pieces, one after another.

Some of the Worms's farmers who saw the landing came to the rescue with sledges which took them on the next leg of their journey to the other side of the island, a crossing of two hours. Midway, they stopped at the village of St. Olai to rest in a Swedish farmer's home. Fritz described these houses as straw covered log houses with inner unplastered walls and exposed beams. Because it was Christmas, the walls and even the ceilings were completely covered with sweet smelling fir twigs and branches. Straw stars and chains were hung from the ceiling branches. There was little communication as the people who lived on this island spoke neither German nor Estonian, only Swedish. The island, he mused, was exactly the way his Swedish ancestors lived hundreds of years ago in Dago.

By one o'clock they were on the other side of the island in the village of Forby, right across from Dago. As it becomes dark about three o'clock they had to hurry, the crossing being almost two hours long. The farmers pushed the boats into the water with all the mail and goods and off they went. At first they were under full sail but then the wind turned, blowing directly from Dago against them and they were forced to row. The Swedish boats, he noted, had four pairs of oars and were very heavy and long. Eight people were needed to row. It was bitter cold with waves beating the sides of the boats and spraying the passengers. The ladies sat huddled together at the mast in their fur hats and coats. The spray froze as soon as it touched their fur coats and hats and the farmers' beards. Soon the ladies began to have icicles growing from their clothes and the farmers looked like Santa Clause. Water was collecting on the floor and everyone who could not row bailed. After almost three hours and in complete darkness, they hit the shore some seven miles from Kertell.

Exhausted and frozen they began to shout for help. Soon farmers came to help them unload the boats. Completely frozen, they were ready to collapse. They had lost most of their provisions to the sea, were very, very hungry but there was nothing to buy. While the sledges were being loaded and the horses were harnessed, they went to a farmhouse to warm themselves. The farmer's wife was cooking a large pot of soup on the stove. The passengers who still had provisions were not sharing and too embarrassed to ask anyone for food, Fritz finally made up his mind to ask the farmer's wife for a plate of her soup for 10 kopeks for himself and his friend who also lost his provisions.

Meanwhile he had put his soaking wet mittens on the edge of a big wooden lid on the pot so that they could dry out a bit. The woman went to the stove to stir her soup and then left. After a while he decided to retrieve his mittens — they were gone! He looked everywhere and then he thought — and there they were, floating in the soup. Since they were dark blue wool, the soup had taken on a definite shade of blue. Quickly he fished them out. When the farmer's wife finally started ladling out the soup, she looked somewhat suspiciously at the fruits of her labor, but after smelling it and shaking her head doubtfully, she served it to the men. Nobody seemed to feel the worse for it but the woman might have asked herself later on why this batch of soup had such a distinctive color.

Fritz arrived home that night about seven o'clock, more dead than alive; and the Christmas holidays proceeded with much activity. Nikolaus was going to Reval with Fritz to attend to all the formalities at the school and make sure his lodging with his brother Karl was in order. While Fritz crammed for his algebra and French entrance exams, Kersti was busy sewing a new suit for him.

All students in Hapsal had worn so-called farmers' clothes and since most of them came from such a background, the hand woven material looked fine. It had even gone through a finishing process in the Kertell plant. And if handled by a good tailor it really looked decent. But this was a tender spot.

Kersti made Fritzes clothes herself to save money. Up to that point it had never bothered him but he was beginning to be noticed by girls, and they noticed what he wore and they commented on it. And as he liked their attention, he had become somewhat vain. At the same time he felt very awkward since girls, to him, coming from an all male environment were extremely foreign. Therefore he was not happy at all with his mother's tailoring. Unfortunately, there was no time to make a new suit so she took one of Nikolaus's old suits and altered it. Fritz had just turned fifteen. Nikolaus was tall and squarely built and his coat did not fit at all. In fact, two people of his size could have fit into the coat.

But Kersti diligently worked on it and when he put it on for the first time he knew what "this doesn't look good on you" meant. The pockets were still around his knees. He could barely get his fingertips into them. Even the pants, which she had taken in and shortened, but not enough, were dreadful. He suddenly realized that all the other suits Kersti had made for him looked the essence of elegance in comparison. But Kersti was very pleased with the outcome. She had even made collars for him (collars were separate from shirts and attached with buttons) that she copied from Nikolaus's. Because Nikolaus wore flat collars which were then in style at the time, and his neck was quite a bit larger than Fritz's, his collars had a low cut look. And to top it all off, he received a gift — a poisonous green tie. He knew then that he would not make a favorable impression in Reval and he began to feel quite inferior. Alas, nothing could be done about it. Fritz was about to embark on a trip to manhood, ill fitting suit or not.

Fritz and Nikolaus started on their voyage to Reval two days after New Year. They had hoped that the bay had been frozen over but it was not, at least the ice was not strong enough to carry the sledges and horses. So they had to go via Worms and Hapsal retracing the route Fritz had travelled only two weeks before. They left at 6 AM and after an hour reached the same village where Fritz had boiled his mittens. They waited in the same farm house until all of the passengers who had booked from Kertell, Grossenhofen farmers who had to go to court in Hapsal, the pastor from Keinis, Naval Academy student from all over Dago and all the fishermen who were taking them had assembled. There were about thirty people in all.

When they left the farm at about 8 AM, still in darkness, it was windy and cloudy. During the night it had snowed quite a bit. The seawater was full of snow which created snow slime and made moving through it easier, as if the boat were lubricated. Things were going very well for the first half an hour and then, another sea adventure began. It started snowing heavily and the wind picked up. Unfortunately, the fishermen did not have any compasses and could only rely on their senses. They were in a total white-out; they could barely see the boat directly in front of them. The air started to howl and scream, the wind gusted, filling the sails and causing the mast to creak. The boat leaned hard to one side. The sky filled with black clouds. The wind was coming from behind, directly from Dago, and there was no ice to be seen in the sea. And then large ice floats appeared dancing on top of the waves which were angry and growing larger and larger. They had no idea where they were going — perhaps to Finland through the open sea when all of the sudden there is a big crash as the mainsail on the Maehles' boat flew wildly around and crashed against the mast. The cross beam was broken. With great difficulty they secured the sail but then had to rely on the jib. The other two boats took down their mainsails also. Progress was greatly slowed and after two hours they saw only gray heavy snow and hail. They should have been in Worms. There was little doubt, confirmed by the huge waves that they were in the Finnish Gulf. The situation was becoming sinister. They were still going with the wind but it had become even darker and the storm was worsening. The fishermen seemed to have lost control.

And then they heard a sizzling and grinding noise from the starboard side. Huge blocks of ice became visible out of the snow squalls and they were coming closer. Behind them loomed a boiling wall of semi-compact fast moving ice. They had to change course to escape it, causing the wind to blow from the front of the boats. The boat leaned over so much that it took on water and side waves were splashing from the windward over the passengers. Everyone was bailing water or rowing. Fritz and a naval student were bailing, calf deep in water. All the adults were rowing. Another two hours passed; the sky continued to darken. All the boats put lanterns on their masts so that they could follow each other in the darkness. One of the skippers stood on the bow with a long pole catching ice floats and pushing them away. The ice began to thin. It was very scary — black roaring water and pieces of ice which passed like ghosts; high waves breaking in front of the boat so that they thought they would bury them any moment. And they had no idea where they were. They only knew that the boat was their life line and death was waiting out there and was very, very close.

Suddenly a wave heaved the boat high on its back. They zoomed into the depth and crash into something hard. Everybody screamed. Nikolaus hung on to the mast while holding Fritz tightly with his other arm. "Fritz, let us say out last prayer together. This must be the end." The storm howled so loud that Fritz could hardly understand his father. He tried to pray but at that moment another wave lifted the boat again and they crashed downward. Fritz closed his eyes and clenched his teeth together and then, a second terrible sound of hitting something hard. More screams. Fritz lost his balance and fell over the seat but Nikolaus pulled him up. Fritz opened his eyes. They were all still alive and the boat was still in one piece. If only they knew where they were!

Those who had fallen off their seats returned to their positions again and again. The waves took over crashing them about. Another fifteen minutes passed. Another loud sound. It was just as fearsome — the surf. They must be close to a beach they thought. But what kind of a beach, with or without rocks? And then a huge wave picked up the boat and flung it on to the beach, filling the boat with water and thoroughly soaking everyone. But they were saved. Still they did not know where they were. It was pitch dark. The snow had stopped but the storm was so strong that they could not hear each other even though they were screaming. The skipper ran up and down the beach swinging his lantern. The other two boats were still out there but all they could see was their lanterns on the masts which were sometimes visible behind the mountainous waves. Finally, the other boats landed.

The skipper went inland a bit to see where they were. They were on Harrilaid, a tiny island about 8 km from Dago. In calmer seas it was half an hour from Dago. And they had been fighting the sea for eight hours! They were completely turned around — but alive. There are no trees or even shrubs on Harriland which is sheer chalk rock. The only inhabitants were a pilot and his wife who lived there year in and year out. His task was to pilot large ships around the many reefs in the surrounding waters. He and his wife had not seen any people for three months and were astonished to see thirty dripping wet ones knocking at their door.

They could not feed all those people as they did not have enough provisions. Some of the students had tea and sugar and one of the other passengers had a large bottle of cognac; all went into a large pot for grog and, together with the food baskets which had not been too badly damaged, everyone was fed and content. For the night, straw was brought in and all were bedded down. The air was questionable but it was warm. The next morning the weather had cleared somewhat. It was very, very cold and the wind was still blowing with the same force but the sea had turned into a weaving white sheet. The floating ice was being driven by the southern storm towards the Finnish Bay. Therefore they could not leave. So they waited, mindful of the fact that they had little food left, and the pilot did not have enough to share. The storm howled and shook the doors of the farm house.

The following morning the weather was clear but bitterly cold. The storm had blown itself out and no ice flows could be spotted. So, cold and hungry, they readied themselves to push on to Worms. The going was very difficult. There was no wind and all the men had to row. By 10 AM they reached Worms's lighthouse only to encounter another problem. Almost half a kilometer from the coast the ice was packed, forcing them to push through, float by float. Finally after an hour of extremely hard physical work, they arrived in Worms. There they learned that

Hapsal Bay was completely frozen over. So they switched to sleighs. They bought bread, butter, smoked lamb, all of which were left over from the New Year's celebration, and boarded sleighs. By evening they were in Hapsal sleeping in clean and warm beds in the Blauber'sche Inn.

The following day they joined a horse drawn caravan of eight sleighs for an overnight trip to Reval. The cold trip was through snow covered forests and villages. In the evening they stopped in an inn where they slept on straw on the parlor floor. It was at this inn that Fritz experienced his first hangover. During supper the adults laced their tea with cognac. Nikolaus put a spoonful of the cognac in Fritz's glass. It was very good. He had not finished his drink when Nikolaus sent him to fetch some more cigars from his luggage. When he returned with the cigars he took another sip of his tea. It seemed to taste quite different and it smelled like cognac. Fully aware that the college students in the party were watching him he drank it down. Soon he began to hear a whistling in his ears and the room started to spin. He left the room and went down to the stables where he was sick — all night.

Interestingly, Nikolaus did not notice his son's condition, and in the morning as Fritz was leaning against one of the sledges, a young seaman came over to him and asked what was troubling him. "Didn't the Seaman's Grog go down well? You look kind of seasick." he continued, "I saw your father give you a spoonful of cognac in your tea so I gave you my glass — ¼ tea and ¾ cognac. I sure hope you feel better soon." Fritz was furious but too sick to respond. When he told his father, he too was very angry, but as there was nothing he could do, Fritz had to suffer through it.

When they reached Reval, Fritz saw something for the first time in his life — his first train, a 40 car freight train. "Imagine," he thought, "is there another boy in all of Europe who at the age of 15 has never seen a train?" It was then that he had to admit to himself that his island life was somewhat backwards. But then he thought, "On the other hand, there must be quite a few 15 year old boys in Europe who have never seen a fishing boat or a steamer. Everything is relative isn't it?" Around noon they arrived at Jakobson Street where Nikolaus's brother Karl lived and with whom Fritz would stay for room and board. His school years in Reval had begun.

Chapter III:
School In Reval
and Military Service

Reval, a city of 70,000 was very different from Hapsal, a small country town. In Reval, one had to go several miles before he could walk in the country. Not only was Reval very different from Hapsal, the school was too. Whereas the Hapsal School had been an example of negligence and laissez faire, the Real School was the opposite.[50] The building, which had been finished quite recently, was large, elegant and comfortable. Fritz was overwhelmed when they went to register and were met by a manservant who took them on a tour of the whole school. Wide stone staircases flanked by busts of Apollo and Minerva, wide halls with colored tiles on the floors, and walls with more busts of Achilles, Zeus, Mars, Hermes, Niobe, Sphrodite, the Laokoon — the whole assembly of Greek and Roman gods. The classrooms sparkled with clean painted floors and large slate black boards, which could be pulled up and down with a special mechanism. There were beautiful maps and even pictures on the walls: American jungles, volcanic mountains, polar scenes and alpine glaciers. In Hapsal they had shared one bench with ten people. Here it was two students to adjacent

---

[50] Real School is equivalent to our High school.

desks made from a highly polished golden colored wood. The gymnasium was a large room with a gallery around the walls. In the front was a huge portrait of Czar Peter the Great studying the city of Reval. On the opposite wall was a pulpit and grand piano. There was also a large hall for physical exercise with a large amount of equipment.

The Physics room was a large amphitheater. On the front desk and in the cupboards around the walls were all sorts of apparatuses. Fritz did not even know their names, let alone their use. The chemistry lab had an equal amount of equipment and looked like a pharmacy. The art room was equipped with adjustable blinds so that the light could be directed appropriately. Along the walls were all sorts of models of flowers, leaves, columns, heads and busts.

The biology room had a human-like model laying on a table. One could remove part of the chest and have a look inside. In fact, one could dismantle the entire body, removing the lungs, liver and other organs. There was also a model of a human eye and a flower which could also be taken apart. There was even a microscope through which one could see the leg of a fly, which looked like a very ugly and hairy horse's leg. The beautiful library had hundreds of books. There was central heating and central ventilation, a large beautiful schoolyard that was covered with fine white sand. Fritz was dizzy with delight. He could never have imagined such a school was possible. And instead of three teachers as in Hapsal, there were fifteen. To him, it was more a palace than a school. He had to go to it — even if he had to go through ten exams!

He felt uneasy when he finally met the Director, Mr. Osse. He was tall with wide shoulders, a long beard and a very deep voice. He looked at Fritz critically:

Hmm, yes, 15 years old — hmm. The report card from Hapsal is good. His knowledge is not too trustworthy and if he goes into the Quinta (he would skip a grade) and cannot make up the missing lectures, he will have to leave the school. The exam is in two days. Bring four sheets of paper and a pen — nothing else — goodbye.

Fritz was already scared of him and he had not even entered school. Would all the teachers be as authoritarian here? He began to wonder if they hit students there.

On the day of the exam Fritz went to the school at 9 AM. The manservant took him upstairs and helped him out of his coat, something new for him too. He then took him to a classroom where another boy was already seated. He later on became his good friend, Kushman. He came from Reval, knew a lot of students at the school, and also some of the teachers. He had taken lessons from some of the older students and seemed much better informed and prepared that Fritz. Fritz suddenly felt very inferior which was increased by just looking at Kushman's clothes — a well fitting city suit, narrow black tie, narrow pants, exactly in fashion, and shoes with buttons and low heels. Compared to his, with jacket pockets almost to the knees, a flat open collar almost resting on his chest, the poisonous green tie and his mother's home made pants which were so wide that one could wrap them around the leg three times. Kushman even had a silver pocket watch, something Fritz did not even dare to dream about.

Soon Pastor Koppel arrived, a very young man with an interesting face, and the exam on religion began. The reverence and envy Fritz had felt for Kushman seemed to disappear after the first few questions. "I am better than he is," he told himself with renewed confidence. And that feeling never left him from then on. After Koppel had examined them for some time he began talking about other things. It turned out that he was a friend of Nikolaus's cousins, Christlieb and Christoph. "Him I have secured," thought Fritz, and his instinct was right. The next man to examine them was Knuepffer, a lively young man with red hair and a mustache. He began his examination with history, a subject that Fritz always enjoyed and knew well. Then came German composition. Fritz had written 2½ pages in half an hour while Kushman was struggling with his first page. Fritz also passed that test easily. Next was Russian translation from Mr. Berg, also quite easy; and finally geography and biology, which went well also.

That took care of six subjects but the main obstacles, namely French and algebra were still to come and Fritz was scared. Soon Mr. Singer, a Frenchman who looked it, arrived. He had black hair and a beard a la Napoleon and wore colorful clothing. He started with a dictation. Fritz was perspiring. Kushman was relaxed; it was his top subject. When the boys had filled a page, Singer began correcting. Kushman's page was perfect but Fritz's was covered with red marks. "Boy, there must have been a lot of mistakes," thought Fritz. Singer's face was threatening. The oral exam was next, followed by grammar, some translation and the reading. Then he knew he was on unsafe ground as Director Osse himself entered to continue the test. He did not seem to be as strict as Fritz had first imagined. His diction was very clear and he spoke slowly so that every word could be understood. He was very patient and repeated questions that the boys did not understand, formulating them in a different manner. He conveyed the message, "You do know this. I am sure you just don't know how to express yourself." Suddenly all of Fritz's fears disappeared.

But then came Algebra, Fritz's self-taught subject. Finally he handed in his answers. Osse checked them very carefully. "They are quite correct," he stated as he left the room to return almost an hour later. Now my dear boys, I can tell you that both of you have passed your exams and you can start school day after tomorrow in the Quinta, room 15. You have to make a very serious effort, especially you, Maehle. You are behind in French and algebra. Who taught you algebra?" "No one, sir." "No one?" his eyes opened wide. "What do you mean no one? Surely you must have had a teacher." Fritz told him that he taught himself from a book. Osse looked at him speechless, "All by yourself? Hmm — well, well, we will see then." So in January 1887, Fritz Maehle became a student at the Petri Real School in Reval.

On the day after his exam, he and Nikolaus went to visit Uncle Andreas. He was then a gentleman of sixty-three, slow and straight forward. His wife Sophie was the opposite. She was gregarious and always seemed to be ready to laugh although she could get very angry, fortunately, very briefly. On their visit they found the house filled with people with many young ones, mostly Andreas' children. Felix was a secunda (last year) student and had already adopted the manners of a university student. Lydia was lively and always ready to tease. Amanda who was Fritz's age and Erna, two years younger, were also there; Fritz had already met both girls when they visited Dago. Last there was Herta, a five year old. Christlieb was a teacher in Petersburg but he always came home for Christmas vacation as did Aline. Only Johanna, who was a governess in Moscow, was not able to come home. There were also friends of the family, especially the Wickmanns and Thomsons.

All of these families belonged to a Christian organization called the Herrenhutter. Fritz never became clear on the goals of the organization but he remembered that the members addressed each other as "Brother in Christ." They held prayer evenings and readings at each other's homes and generally demonstrated a wholesome Christian life style. For example, even during harmless social gatherings, dancing was not allowed. Otherwise they had great fun. The Wickmanns were very well to do. They had farms in Estonia, the largest bakery in Reval and just as Andreas, a large family with eight children. And there were other young friends of the Maehle children at the house. In fact, almost every Sunday during the school holidays, there were at least 20 young people between the ages of fifteen and twenty-three, if not at Andreas' house, at the Thomson's or Wickmann's. The students from both Reval and the university in Dorpat took every chance they could get to attend these soirees. It was a regular Baltic enclave with skating rinks on the Wickmann's pond, birthday parties, games and plays among the students, sing-alongs and even an occasional beer.

At the time of Fritz's first visit to Andreas a great celebration was in progress — two engagements between Fedi Wickmann and Aline Maehle and Costel Thomson and Alice Wickmann. And several others were in the planning stages — all between these three families. Unfamiliar with such socializing and feeling awkward in his old suit, Fritz stayed in the corner. He was even tempted to run away. Even Amanda, to whom he had written regularly since her visit to Dago, must have realized what a country bumpkin her cousin was as she ignored him completely. But Lydia, sensing his embarrassment, and always eager to tease, used the chance to talk to him rather loudly so that suddenly he became the center of attention. Fritz swore he would never go to Andreas' house again and during the first term he hardly ever did.

The following day Nikolaus returned to Dago and Fritz moved into Uncle Karl's home. It was a small cottage with four rooms divided by a hall. The kitchen was also part of the hall. Karl and his family lived in three. The fourth had been divided by a wall to create two tiny rooms. Fritz had half a window in his room, a bed, a small table and a chair. He had hardly enough room to get dressed. The other half of this room was occupied by a strange couple, he worked illegally in the harbor and she was a Taro card reader. Jette, Karl's wife, had no help and did all the housework herself. And then there was their daughter, Lidi, Fritz's eight-year-old cousin. Fritz wrote, "She was unfriendly, a tattle-tale and a miserable brat." Karl was manager of a lumberyard, a stickler for detail and a penny pincher. Since he had only one child from his first marriage and none with Jette, he did not understand boys at all, especially since his own youth had not been happy. He was the personification of morals and a very strict churchman. The family went to church regularly, prayed all the time and he read from the Bible, very badly. He also played the organ — even worse. Jette and Lidi were just as bad. They went through Fritz's belongings all the time, scanning his books for something terrible. Jette became hysterical when he went somewhere with his school friends.

But the worst thing was that they never talked openly to Fritz about his "behavior." Rather they sent letters to his parents, leading them to believe that he had become quite ill bred. Actually Fritz found it very hard to live with this family, and they only came to have a warm relationship after he was married. Because the people in Andreas' group were too elegant and he was unwelcome at Karl's, he shut himself up and worked and read all the time. In addition, the student body was split into two camps as half the students belonged to the nobility of the country and they stuck together. So Fritz studied and learned and in only one month he was the best in the class in math; he wrote very advanced essays, which were usually read aloud by the teacher; and in French he not only made up the missing lessons but also surpassed his classmates. He loved the school library best of all where he read all the travel and adventure stories. At the end of the first term he graduated to Quarta with a very good report card.

Having finished the year, he took the steam ship home to Dago for a two month summer holiday, which he enjoyed more than he ever had before. His brothers, Ewald and Oskar had also grown up, and together the boys had a wonderful vacation, working on the butterfly and insect collections they had started in Hapsal. They also collected fish, animal skeletons, minerals, and fossils. In between their collecting they swam, went on long hikes and worked on the July harvest from early morning until late evening. In late August they picked gooseberries and currents and helped in the wine making. Too soon, vacation was over. When Fritz returned to Karl's he had a very pleasant surprise, two new roomers, Koppelmann and Lucks also students at the Petri Real School. And the dreadful couple was gone. Fritz was especially relieved, as his uncle no longer was able to correct him all the time in front of other people. When he tried, Fritz merely said, "Why don't you tell that to Koppelmann, he did the same thing?"

School was great that year. Fritz soon became first in his class. He still did not feel at ease at Andreas' house and he still wore the same altered clothes and heavy Dago shoes. But in November, his father sent him 20 rubles and his uncle took him to a watchmaker where he bought his first pocket watch. He was so proud that he would stop strangers in the street just to check the time with them. He could not bear the idea of spending Christmas with Uncle Karl so he went home via Haspal and over the bay, without incident. His Christmas present that year was a piece of cloth from the factory, which his mother agreed to have tailor made. Finally, he looked like a student from a better school. All he needed were some ties, modern collars, cuffs and shoes, and he soon found a solution to that problem. When he returned to school, a teacher offered him a job tutoring a seven-year-old boy in the basics of reading, writing and arithmetic. Karl loaned him the money and he immediately bought his accessories. Later on, he even bought a walking stick. He was promoted to tertia looking quite the gentleman. At last, he felt presentable at Andreas' home and he went there often.

In the following year of 1888, Oskar and Ewald entered school in Reval (Rudolf stayed in Haspal.) Koppelmann had moved out of Karl's to take an apprenticeship in a local company and the two little rooms became occupied by the three Maehle boys and Lucks. Karl had given up his lumberyard position and become a cabinetmaker, specializing in coffins. Fritz continued his tutoring with gymnasium students. That Christmas the three Maehle boys stayed in Reval. Karl bought a tree which he trimmed with candles and other decorations and he prepared a festive dinner, all of which he billed to Nikolaus, so typical of Uncle Karl.

During the year, Fritz had become part of Uncle Andreas' social life. His cousin Felix had moved to the university in Dorpat and from then on university students were always part of the partygoers. In November Fritz turned seventeen and started his confirmation classes at the Alia Church. A new suit, tailored in Reval of the best material was made for him. In his words, he was to become a "grown up Christian person." He felt absolutely fit for society, was addressed by the formal Sir in school and was promoted to the sekunda. In May 1899, he again became the first in his class and felt a totally grown up young man.

He started secunda in the fall. It was one of Fritz's most wonderful years in school. Oskar and Ewald had to write exams to enter the Russian Gymnasium as Russification was actively moving through the Baltic. Neither brother knew Russian very well; Oskar barely made it while Ewald failed and had to take lessons for a whole year from one of the older students to be able to enter the following year. Uncle Andreas had resigned from his work during the Russification since he did not understand the language well enough. His place was taken by Christlieb, his son, who resigned his position in Petersburg and came back to Reval. Felix had studied chemistry in Dorpat for one term but had to give up his studies because Andreas did not have enough money so Felix started to work in Petersburg in the director's office of the newspaper, the *Petersburger Harold*.

Costel Thomson, who was engaged to Alice Wickmann, had finished his theological studies and become an assistant pastor in Reval. In an effort to become better known to the congregation he started a children's service. He recruited the entire Maehle-Wickmann-Thomson crowd of young people, in all about 20, to help him teach. Chriestlieb, a very fine singer, formed a group of seven friends, one of whom was Fritz, to sing quartets. They practiced at Christlieb's house and when they had developed a repertoire, they sang at all sorts of events. Their fame grew and they were soon invited to many parties, soirees, and other occasions. Soon they became a main attraction at family gatherings, where, once in a while they even risked a dance when the older generation was not around. Fritz also continued his tutoring. And he also became a member of the church choir where he not only sang in services but also church concerts.

In secunda it was customary for groups of a few students to study together. Fritz, Leo Juergens, Waldemar Werner, Arthur Buschmann, Alfred Kushman, and Leo Gaeuser studied together at each other's homes. Kushman, Buschmann and Fritz were all boarding students so their refreshments were meager but the other boys were local students of wealthy parents. They also had siblings about the same age as the group. Thus a whole new social environment developed. They enjoyed wonderful meals at their elegant homes and frequently their work ended in parties with dancing and lovely refreshments. At eighteen Fritz decided to invest in some dancing lessons as well as learn the social graces. In Reval one went to dancing lessons in either the Plaesterer senior where all nobility went or Plaesterer junior for the upper middle class. Of course, Fritz went to the junior where together with a few students from the gymnasium and several young merchants, he hopped around dutifully to polkas, Rheinlaenders, waltzes, lanciers, and quadrilles. At the end of the course the students met with young ladies who had been taking lessons separately and after a few evenings the whole adventure was crowned with a ball — the gentlemen in tuxedos and the ladies in gowns. A dinner was included in the evening and each young man had to take a lady to the table and entertain her. Mr. and Mrs. Plaesterer saw to it that everything was done in accordance with the rules. The ball cost an extra five rubles so he borrowed a tuxedo from a friend, just as later on in Riga, five young men shared one tuxedo.

An exciting event that year was the Costel Thomson and Alice Wickmann wedding, which her father turned into the wedding of the year. Pastors, directors, business friends, people from Petersburg with decorations over their whole chest, lots of students and the whole Maehle clique were invited. There was no dancing and Mr. Wickmann gave a very pious speech. But then there was all sorts of entertainment: funny plays and musical numbers. And the food and drinks were fantastic. The young couple did not take a honeymoon trip and after the wedding they all went with them to their apartment and the quartet sang a few sentimental songs.

It is evident that Fritz spent very little time at his Uncle Karl's. In fact, Karl became very angry with him and wrote his father that he was playing the big shot, loafed around and did not study at all. He suggested that Nikolaus should take him out of school and find him an apprenticeship with a cobbler rather than let him continue to lead such an "unholy, unchristian life." Fritz received a very excited letter from his father but was able to calm him down when he wrote back that he should wait until the school year ended when he could see his report card. When Fritz received straight fives and was first in his class, Uncle Karl was even angrier. But he kept quiet. And Fritz had taught him not to go behind his back. Strangely, Fritz noted, his brother had a much easier time with Karl.

Fritz loved his school and his school years deeply. He especially loved the personal relationships the boys developed with designated teachers; about 20 boys were assigned to a teacher who stayed with them until graduation as a sort of mentor and advisor. They often met with him in his home, discussing everything from music, art and school subjects to skating, outlook on life, and future plans. They had the same relationship with the school's pastor who taught religion. (This was a Lutheran school.). He noted that young people were confirmed at 17 or 18 and this was the time when "you hear from the "other side" — all the scientific hypotheses which came up with a glittering array of logic...come down in your mind as a confusing concoction."

Every year they had a nice festive break, usually at the end of the spring term. The boys assembled in the schoolyard at 8 AM. The head of the student association carried the school flag in front of the school band and away the student body marched, out of Reval. The student leaders wore blue and white sashes and the greatest honor was to carry the flag, which Fritz did two years as the top student of the prima and secunda classes. They marched to an inn in the forest outside of the city where they spent the day eating, playing ball, and all sorts of games.

At the end of the secunda Fritz and his mother went on a trip together to two towns where she saw some old friends from her youth and then to a health spa.[51] Fritz's brothers were deep in their summer vacation by the time he and his mother returned to Dago. They had many guests that summer, especially their cousins from Reval. The boys also became preoccupied with chemistry. They bought chemicals, vials, tubes, and other containers from the pharmacy and made all sorts of experiments. They made firecrackers, which they exploded for the younger children's entertainment.

One day they decided to celebrate one of the cousin's birthdays with a tremendous firework display. They bought gunpowder and some

---

[52] Spas were, and in many cases still are, very important to the middle and upper class European. Whenever anyone became ill or felt out of sorts he was packed off to a spa. People even went when they felt fine, just to keep from becoming ill. Usually they bathed in special waters, had massages and mud baths, walked in neighboring woods, and drank special waters. Socialization was also very important and often people stayed for months.

chemicals and mixed them all together. The samples were placed on a large table in their room to show the girls when they arrived to go to the party together. Wanting to demonstrate, they lit a little light on a plate but a spark flew into the next dish and then to the next and before they knew it, the whole room exploded in terrifying noise, smoke and light. The girls ran out screaming and the boys had their hands full trying to keep the door closed before their parents could come into the exploding room. When everything quieted down and the smoke cleared Fritz discovered, in the middle of the table, an open container with at least a pound of gunpowder in it. One spark would have blown them and the whole house into the sky. The room was a shambles — nothing but broken glass and big burned out holes on the table and floor. And thus ended their ambitions concerning chemistry and fire works.

The following school year Ewald entered the gymnasium in Reval. At Christmas time Rudolf came for a visit from Hapsal and the four Maehle brothers had their picture taken together (lost). The social life at Andreas continued in full swing although some of the girls had left for jobs elsewhere. Andreas retired from his teaching job and to do something, became the editor of the Estonian Christian Sunday paper. Fritz went to his home weekly to help him fold and bundle the freshly printed newspapers.

At the end of 1890, two important things happened which changed Fritz's social life. Herr Osse, the school director, left and Uncle Andreas broke relations with the Wickmann family. Ossi's downfall had been the "Borki incident." Apparently in October 1888, the Russian Imperial Family was involved in a train accident in the Russian town of Borki. They were not injured and in celebration, all churches held services of thanksgiving all over Russia and Borki day was born. The following year there were celebrations in churches, schools and government buildings. A special Borki chapel was erected at the government building in the Russian market in Reval. A military parade was also planned and all schools were to participate with all students and teachers. But Osse decided to do it differently. He directed his students and teachers to the Lutheran Nikolai Church and sent only 20 delegates of the Russian-speaking students to the Russian celebration. When the festivities started in the presence of the Governor and other high-ranking officials Osse's fate was decided. He was only allowed to remain one more year. So the students decided to throw him a farewell party. Fritz was in charge of assembling a book of group photos. At the party Fritz gave a speech emphasizing the almost ideal relations between students and faculty that had developed under Osse's guidance. He mentioned that the school had become a large family and he, the father. He wished him well and handed him the photo album. Osse had tears in his eyes and was almost unable to talk when he addressed the students for the last time.

The breakup with the Wickmanns came rather suddenly and was, as usual, the fault of both parties. Fedi Wickmann who had been engaged to Andreas' daughter, Aline for four years began writing her letters from Dorpat, where he was studying to become a pastor at the university. He told her that he thought that he had made the wrong choice in careers. Aline, then 27, became rather perturbed. And then gossip reached the Maehle family that he had been seen going in and out of another woman's home. When Fedi came for Christmas vacation, the Maehles told him in no uncertain terms what they had heard and what they thought about it. Fedi returned to Dorpat and wrote to Aline that while he cared for her very much, as a result of the altercation with her family, he did not want to write to her any more. She sent back her engagement ring and the families became bitter enemies. A year later Fedi finished his studies became a pastor in Reval and became engaged to a local girl. Aline never recovered from this disappointment. She became a bitter, prematurely gray old maid. Uncle Andreas was very shaken by all this, had a few strokes, and in a short time became bedridden. He lived three more years.

Thus Andrea's house was very quiet during Fritz's last term of the year. He did note that the old division between nobility and middle class had pretty much disappeared and his study groups, always a social outlet, became mixed with both classes. His personal involvement and duties at the school increased and after the annual school excursion, final exams began. These took a whole week — closed doors, stamped paper on which to write, strict monitoring and later on, oral exams. He graduated first in his class with straight As.

The summer vacation was not very happy. Fritz had the greatest longing to go to Riga to study with his friends. The almost university student-like life he had led during the last years and his excellent scholastic successes had triggered his ambitions. But his parents could not afford to support him any further. They still had three boys in school on the mainland and the youngest, Hermann, would be going to the city the following year. The only solution was, Fritz would have to volunteer for the military. After that he would have to earn his living somehow. He bowed to this decision with no hard feelings, but with heavy heart.

In July 1891, Fritz returned to Reval to apply for the voluntary service. He was anxious to get his name in early as there were three regiments stationed in Reval and many applicants. He went from one government administration office to another and even went to the commanding officer of all three regiments but to no avail. All the regiments were filled to capacity with the quota of Lutheran-Baltic volunteers. There was even a large waiting list. Fritz was desolate. What next? Then he remembered a fellow classmate Winkler, who had not found an opening Reval either but had made it by going to the next post in Narwa. Fritz wrote Winkler about the situation and while he was waiting for a reply another piece of bad news arrived.

Rudolf, his younger brother by two years, who had always had problems as a child, had another one. He was often sick and had suffered badly from serious after affects of scarlet fever with both heart trouble and a hearing loss. As a result he became timid, insecure and depressed. Then the Russification of the Baltic schools started and it really hit him hard. Nikolaus, thinking he would make a fine teacher had planned to send him to an excellent German teachers college when he finished the Hapsal School that Fritz had attended. However, in the middle of his studies, all school lectures were changed to Russian and the course work changed from three to six years. Nikolaus decided that he should stick it out. "What harm could come of being fluent in Russian?" he thought. So Rudolf graduated with six years of Russian and even apprenticed for a year after graduation. And then the news came that the Dorpat Teacher's College had been closed by the government. They did not want any more German-Baltic teachers. If additional teachers were needed, they would come directly from Russia. Meanwhile, Rudolf was becoming more and more withdrawn. He suffered a terrible inferiority complex, lacking the most basic self-confidence. He even became a stranger to his own brothers and they became very distant from him.

While Fritz was still in Reval, Nikolaus arrived with Rudolf, Oskar and Ewald for the beginning of the school year. He then drove to Petersburg with Rudolf to see if he could enter him in a Russian teacher's college there. Rudolf took the entrance exams, was admitted and Nikolaus returned to Reval. But Rudolf, overcome by fear simply ran away from the school. Nikolaus returned to Petersburg not knowing what to do next when he read in a newspaper that there was an agricultural college in Pskow, a far away town that had courses in teaching. So he sent Rudolf to Pskow by train and he returned to Dago. Several days later Rudolf was back in Reval, completely devastated. The college in Pskow was no more than a Russian village school. He wanted to return to Dago where he would be more comfortable. Finally, Nikolaus found him an apprenticeship with a business colleague of his in Riga and he moved there.

Meanwhile, a letter from Winkler arrived stating that there would be no problem in volunteering for the military in Narwa. Although there were quite a few Russian people in the regiment, the Lutheran quota had not been exceeded. The city was small, expenses were low and they could room together. Fritz took the next train to Narwa. He presented himself to the regiment the following morning where he met two of his old friends, Muldau and Tannberg, who were also volunteering. The adjutant was very cordial and explained that their papers looked good and they should hear of their acceptance as One Year Volunteers in about a week. Fritz and the others moved into Winkler's apartment bought their dress and working uniforms, and a few days later learned that they had been accepted into the 2nd Company. The following day they went to the regiment headquarters where they met Colonel Petrowski who was very cordial, and then to the barrack where they reported to Sergeant Cugopolz. Fritz was nineteen years old and a soldier, Number 9120.

Narwa was on the Narowa River, which flowed into the Bay of Finland and which had divided the Baltic provinces from Russia until Peter the Great crossed the Narowa and conquered Narwa. Being on the border, the Russian influence was everywhere although there was still a prominent Estonian element and a dwindling German influence. One could see the four phases in the history of the city of about 15,000 people, first, the old German Baltic Hansa City.[52] It had old stone houses, crooked cobblestone streets, a small Lutheran church, all very medieval. Second was the Russian fortress on the edge of the river with long walls and thick walled towers. Then there was the Russian suburban area of Iwangorrod with poor wooden houses, unpaved streets and a Russian church with onion shaped cupolas. Finally there was the largest suburb, an attractive area called Kroenholm, which consisted mainly of factories, the largest of which were lumber and cotton mills, and living quarters for the workers. It was not a prosperous city and it was not very exciting. In fact, nothing happened in Narwa.

Fritz and Winkler moved into a house on the Estonian side of the river near their battalion station. The family they lived with had a daughter. They were all kind, but with few resources. On Saturdays they would clear out the sewing room, bring out their furniture from better times and entertain. The soldiers were always welcome. Through contacts

---

[52] The larger cities of Estonia were members of the Hanseatic League in the middle ages. Immigrant German merchants developed into a new ruling class, controlling trade and the great guilds, many of which excluded Estonians as members. By the end of the 14th Century, Reval's Estonians were formally excluded from guilds and even their property rights were limited. (Raun, p. 23)

made at these soirees, they met many young people in the town, none of whom were particularly interesting or attractive.

The Russian military volunteers had to serve two years because they did not have the necessary education. They all lived in the barracks and ate in the mess hall. Most of them would be transferred from the regiment as non-commissioned officers to cadet schools and become commissioned officers. They did not mix with the Baltic volunteers who formed their own circle of friends who usually came together in one of their living quarters and chipped in to buy sausages, bread and cognac or beer. The best evenings were at the home of a volunteer whose father was a pharmacist and always served some of his special concoctions — a pharmacist's liquor. Going out was not pleasant as there were many officers roaming about the town and they all expected to be saluted and salutes varied depending on rank. If a volunteer's salute was wrong he would be reprimanded. Even after attending three days of classes on saluting and other formalities, walking the streets was stressful. After a couple of weeks, the volunteers received their rifles, ammunition, began rifle drills and started field maneuvers.

An interesting arrangement was the custom in early fall, that soldiers were rented out to large estates to help in the harvest. One third of the pay went to the soldier, one third to the people who remained in the barracks to work, and one-third to the food administration to improve the food. When the harvest came to an end the field maneuvers intensified. Every volunteer had an orderly, a lower ranking soldier who looked after his rifle and leather gear. Mostly Jews, they received 20 kopecks for their services. Fritz's orderly, named Cyprus Mercedes looked after him very nicely.

Everything seemed to be going along without incident. The commandant was happy with Fritz's performance. And then something happened that disturbed the relationship. Every time Fritz paid his rent, the landlord, Mr. Busch would celebrate with him with 3 or 4 glasses of schnapps. After such celebrations Fritz usually took a nap. One time when he was napping, Mr. Busch forgot wake him. At 2:30 PM he awoke. He was supposed to be in the barracks at 2:00 PM. He jumped out of his bed into his clothes and discovered he had a nose bleed which he finally got under control at 3:00 PM. He ran to the barracks — straight into a guard who said, "Follow me." They went straight to the commandant's office. Fritz explained about the nosebleed. Not good enough. He was sentenced to 7 days in locked detention. "Goodbye officers' exam. Goodbye list of honors." He removed his coat, folded it around his satchel, put on his ammunition belt, picked up his rifle and joined the line.

The commandant followed him like a hawk. He was not standing straight enough. He didn't hold his rifle properly. His chest was out too much. His chest was not out enough. His marching was wrong. His sergeant was called. "How could he put someone like Maehle into the ranks?" This went on for an hour. And then the commandant left. At the end of the afternoon Fritz, sweating from every pore in his body wrote a note to the landlord that he would be in lock-up and to please send his meals there. And then he was ordered to the commandant's office who asked, "Now I want the truth, where were you really this afternoon?" Fritz assured him his story was true. But the commandant replied that he smelled liquor on his breath. Fritz replied that he had a little celebration with the family he boarded with. "Aren't you ashamed then to give an excuse that you had a nose bleed?" So Fritz pulled out the blood handkerchief. The commandant then called the sergeant. "This volunteer will lead the first column in the 2nd platoon so he will be busier from tomorrow morning on." And to Fritz he said, "Now young man, try harder and make sure that there are no more family festivities. You can go now." That was quite a surprise! No only did he not have to go to jail, but he had advanced to Platoon Leader. That night he and Mr. Busch finished off the bottle of schnapps.

November came and the new recruits arrived. There were six people in his platoon, two from Poland, one Estonian, one Jew, one Tartar and one Russian. What a combination that was! The most intelligent, of course," wrote Fritz, was the Jew." He learned his way around very quickly. The Estonian did all right with the exercises but he was stuck on the Russian language. One Polish fellow was very lazy and could not read; he could not get over the fact that Fritz could read his letters for him. The other Pole came from Warsaw and was a pseudo-intellectual, very cunning and insincere. The Tartar spoke a fair Russian and was, as most Tartars were, by far the best soldier. The Russian named Sawan, actually a White Russian, had the build and strength of a bear. He was blissfully and completely illiterate and was plagued by stupidity. It took forever for him to learn maneuvers. The rifle looked like a toy in his immense paws and it took forever until he could move it in one straight motion to his shoulder. And it was virtually impossible for him to learn the ranks and names of the officers and no matter how hard Fritz tried, Sawan could not master the name of the Grand Duke and successor to the throne, as his name and title were lengthy.

One day the Chief of the Regiment came to inspect the new recruits. All went well until he came to Sawan, the Russian. Not even recognition that he understood the question! In a moment he was able to erase the good impression of the whole company. The colonel was furious and ordered extra duty for him until he was instructed sufficiently. This was added to all of Fritz's other duties which essentially required overseeing the workings of the platoon from morning until night, including their meals, their quarter's cleanliness, the guards on duty, checking all passes and visitors, and taps at 9:00 PM. He could be held accountable for any flaw in the routine. At night he had to sit at his desk in the barracks, he was not allowed to remove his coat and consequently he could not sleep. This went on for several days. Fritz was exhausted and Sawan was still not able to retain information. On the fourth night sitting up in his little office listening to 120 snoring men filling the air with their smells he hatched a plan. As soon as the sentry completed his check, Fritz went over Sawan. "Wake up, wake up," he ordered. "Put on your pants. Now!" The Russian complied and they headed for the little office. "Listen here my friend, it is your fault that I have received this punishment and am not allowed to sleep, and as long as I can't sleep, neither will you." He ordered the Russian to kneel and repeat, syllable by syllable, the successor to the throne. On his knees all night, he finally was able to learn the name and Fritz was relieved of extra duty.

Christmas approached and Fritz was granted leave for a week. He went to his Uncle Karl's in Reval. His brothers were also spending their vacation in Reval and his cousin Amanda had arrived from Baltischport to stay with her cousin Johanna and so all had a wonderful time with each other and their Reval friends. He went to a very elegant ball and also saw quite a few friends from his former school. It was the last time he would see so many of them together again.

When he returned to the base he learned that his commanding officer was taking early retirement. His replacement was a social acquaintance of Fritz's and so his life became much easier. This was not true of all the volunteers. One fellow named Tomberg, who was very awkward, timid and anxious, was always in trouble. He had very little understanding of the Russian language and this, added to his clumsiness, put him in the doghouse regularly. Fritz could see him almost daily, standing in the punishment court with his rifle over his shoulder and a knapsack full of bricks on his back in the bitter cold. One day he had severe red spots on his jaws. When Fritz asked, he was informed that his officer did not like the way he held his head and corrected it rather energetically. He never knew when the correction stopped and the physical abuse started. "Now if this was done to a volunteer, how did the simple soldier fare? That in fact, was scandalous." Soldiers received slaps and fists in the face and were known to be knocked about and even pushed and butted with rifles. This was not only done by sergeants and corporals but even officers, especially the older ones. Fritz witnessed a sergeant hit a soldier for a minor fault so hard with his rifle butt in his stomach that he was unconscious for almost ten minutes. The sergeant was momentarily scared and quite relieved when the soldier regained consciousness.

By the same token even the sergeants and corporals were slapped around. Once, Fritz saw a sergeant in charge of a magazine where ammunition was stored, fail to do something. The commander of the battalion ordered him over and while the poor fellow was standing at attention the officer started hitting him in the face right, left, right, left, for about five minutes. Fritz thought, "What to do? You have the right to complain, but, to whom?" The commander hit the fellow. "If you write a complaint it starts at the lowest level with the sergeant and works its way up to, who else, the commander. You can imagine what would happen to a person who would risk doing that."

But the army anticipated this problem. Once a year, a high-ranking officer from Petersburg came to hear complaints. The soldiers were informed in advance that they had an absolute right to complain. But, they better make sure they had a legitimate reason. After cleaning, drilling and polishing, everyone was lined up on the exercise grounds. All the officers were in their dress uniforms. The VIP arrived, reviewed the troops and asked if there were any complaints. "Now," thought Fritz, "would anyone in his right mind complain under these circumstances? Everyone knows that the boss is always right and the little guy would be squashed if he forgot this. He would probably be transferred to one of the disciplinary battalions where he would end his miserable days." But the Russian farmer was used to cruel treatment where he was often beaten and kicked. And through it all, he was able to overcome the situation with his strange sense of humor. "But," wrote Fritz, referring to the Russian revolution, "the revenge came later, and it was terrible."

Once in a while, however, the worst oppressor falls and that happened to the officer who abused Tomberg. One of the Russian farmers ran away from his barracks. He should have known that he would be caught and punished but he was "extremely stupid" and his homesickness and terrible treatment apparently overshadowed all his reasoning. Ten days later he was caught and brought back in chains. A hearing was held befitting a deserter. He received 25 strokes with a rod on the bare behind and back in front of all the men who had to watch. The screams of that unlucky soldier stayed with Fritz for a long time. The deserter's status was changed to previously convicted which meant that he could be hit any time for any infraction, even the smallest. After three weeks he ran away again and was caught again. This time he received 50 strokes and was sent to military jail for four years. But also, the officer in question was relieved of his duties, not because he was so tough, but because he had not been able to keep the man from running away a second time. The oppressor received his just rewards albeit for the wrong reason.

In March, Fritz began studying for the corporal exam. Dozens and dozens of regulations had to be memorized. The commands had to be drilled exactly. Books containing all this wisdom had about 200 pages and they had to be thoroughly learned. Five or six volunteers would study together. Using matchboxes representing various military parts of companies, battalions, platoons, etc. they marched invisible soldiers shouting commands. The exam took place at the end of the month. Everyone, from the commander on down was involved. They had to demonstrate what they were able to teach those beneath them. The entire battalion had to operate like a well-oiled machine. Every commander's future was based on how well his men performed. The exam lasted several days and included proof that they could command and lead a troop and a written exam. Fritz did splendidly. Then came the swearing in ceremony, led by clergy from various denominations. The colonel expressed his satisfaction in an Order to the Regiment and the volunteers became fully accepted soldiers.

One day it was announced that Brigadier General Zappa had decided to make a visit to inspect backpacks. Backpacks had to contain a large number of things — shirts, underwear, socks, towels, needles, thread, shoe polish, boots, thread, etc. and everything had to be in exactly the right place. Everything had to be inspected. Sometimes the soldier had to remove his clothing and even what he was wearing was scrutinized. Weeks had gone into the preparation and naturally every soldier wanted everything to be right. Therefore they stole from each other when they did not have a required garment. In those days, soldiers were not given uniforms but yards of coarse material to make their uniforms. They were also given very hard leather with which to make boots. Nobody wanted to wear uniforms made out of the rough fabric, or boots from that leather, so it was all sold to the Jews who collected from everyone in the company and then sold it back to the military for a good price. And thus the wheels of commerce turned around and around. To have money to buy some boots and clothing, the soldiers sold their bread rations. In case of mobilization there were thousands of boots made from very rough leather, hard as stone, stored in the warehouse. Everyone knew that walking in these boots was impossible. But they were there and available for a backpack inspection.

The formal inspection consisting of about 2,000 men, with the usual command and Zappa at the head, took place on the exercise field. The soldiers were lined up with their backpacks at their feet and the contents on top. A lot of uninvited onlookers had also arrived. It seemed that all the ladies of Narwa had come out to see this show of military display. It was rather easy for them to get on the exercise field as the church for the garrison was on the same field. All one had to do was go to the church and then proceed to the field.

General Zappa stood in front of the soldiers who were all at attention. As he walked in front of the troops, accompanied by several offices he sent hostile looks to the crowd of women. He had the reputation of being an old bachelor who absolutely hated women. Suddenly he gave a signal to the drummer who started a drum roll and then, with a shrill command, ordered "pants down." In 30 seconds, 2,000 men were standing with rather short shirts and bare from waist down to their boots. The women started screaming and running — very, very fast. The soldiers were howling with laughter, the officers were grinning and Zappa was having a ball.

A few weeks later another VIP came to inspect. The barracks were cleaned and polished with splendid white sand on the floor. Since it was spring, the windows were wide open and the air was fresh. The many pictures on the walls showing battle scenes and famous people were cleaned. These were used as historical material during the lessons also. The VIP arrived promptly at 10:00 AM having just completed a good breakfast. All of the soldiers of the barracks were lined up, spick and span. The VIP stepped into their midst. "Well soldiers, who of you can answer a question for me?" His eyes rested on Sawan, the Russian, who really looked splendidly stupid. The VIP pointed to one of the pictures depicting a melee during the Turkish War.

"What does that picture show?" He asked Sawan.

"That's where ours clobbers the others, your Excellency."

"Who are they fighting?"

"The enemy, your Excellency, the Turks."

"Good, my boy. Remember gentlemen, if you come on to the enemy, cut and trample them into the dirt. At ease officers, thank you. I can see that even the slow ones understand what the purpose of being a soldier is about."

The commanding officer's face was like a sun. He never expected such a break from Sawan. It could have gone the opposite way...easily. Fritz concluded that the late night tutoring of Sawan had been successful.

Several weeks later the entire regiment was sent to Kramoje Spelo, an enormous summer camp for the army near Petersburg. It consisted of all the regiments in the Petersburg area, several divisions of infantry, cavalierly, artillery and so forth. There were miles and miles of white tents. Barracks were erected in a small forest hidden from view. The maneuvers were held on a 7by7 km. terrain. A straight gravel road, used only by the Imperial Family and their important associates ran in front of the camp. As soon as a vehicle was spotted on the road the call went out and immediately, all people on duty had to run to the road and stand at attention. Each regiment's colors were mounted in special racks and every person passing them had to salute. High-ranking personnel came and went all day so the call was heard constantly.

Fritz was housed in a wooden barracks with wooden plank beds, straw mattresses and military blankets. His sheet was his own. On the third day he contracted head lice and his battle began. He tried everything from lavender to other old remedies. On top of that, he was almost always hungry. They were fed kasha browned in fat, cabbage soup and lots of bread. But there was just not enough food for twenty year olds who marched and worked all day. In addition, the army was not fed in the morning and by the time they got back to base in the evening; the hunger pains were almost unbearable. It was not possible to buy anything either. Sausage and butter were almost never available. Sometimes Fritz and his friends could not bear it any longer. They would pool their money and buy roasted meat and a bottle of schnapps from the officers' mess, something strictly forbidden. Fritz had very little money. His father sent him ten rubles per month, which he thought would be enough since Fritz was no longer paying room and board. It was not and he was always in a state of nagging hunger.

There was a Finnish regiment of the Czars Rifle guards close to his regiment. Tall, good-looking men, they only spoke Finnish to each other, using Russian only for the commands. Some also spoke Swedish. They had a separate mess hall, which served excellent food and great beer. He and his friends would walk over to their mess as often as possible for a meal. It was terrible to be hungry all the time.

After a few weeks they all began to worry about their next exams to qualify as reserve officers. But first, Fritz decided he should go to Petersburg to visit his cousin Felix who was working at the *Petersburger Herald*. His commanding officer agreed to a pass but insisted he stop in to see him before he left. When Fritz arrived in his best uniform, his officer roared, "You want to show up in Petersburg like that? Remember your first encounter with General Zappa? No way can you dress up like that where the streets are crawling with high ranking officers." So Fritz returned to his barracks where he donned his everyday uniform complete with fur hat, heavy cummerbund, and the very hard boots. Instead of the formal bayonet he had to wear an ax in his belt. He was met with approval and he boarded the train to Petersburg on time. Once there he wandered around the city on foot. He did not have enough money for a carriage and he did not know the streetcar (horse drawn) schedule. It was a beautiful hot sunny summer day. The streets were full of people and an enormous number of military people whom he had to salute — every second step. It was dreadful. He was sweating like a beaver in his heavy uniform as he hammered the pavement with his hard boots. Suddenly he spotted a pub.

"A beer would be great," he thought. He went in.

"What do you want?" asked the waiter.

"A bottle of beer please." He started to sit down.

"Sorry, this restaurant is off limits to military personnel. If I serve you we would both be in trouble," said the waiter.

Fritz was perturbed about that. As a fighter for the country, he could not even get a glass of beer. Finally he saw an old *baba* (old peasant woman) selling soda on the street and he bought one for 5 kopecks. It was noon and he was very hungry. But he could not go into a restaurant. Soon he found himself at the cathedral with a statue of Peter the Great in front of it. He was tired and his feet were hurting so he found a park and sat on a bench. He was there for no more than five minutes when a policeman came over. "Listen soldier, this is not a place for low ranking military persons to loiter. You better move on." On he moved. By 2:00 PM he was at his lowest point. The hunger was painful and he was dreadfully thirsty when he spotted a restaurant. He walked in. "Off limits," yelled the waiter. "God forbid that anybody wearing the uniform of a defender of the Russian fatherland who is dressed in the prisoner's garb of a volunteer or corporal should want to eat in the capital!" Fritz thought.

Finally, Fritz found Felix's office. When Felix saw him he threw his arms in the air and shrieked with laughter. "Man, you look like a woodsman from the backwoods in Wologda (a government detention camp). "Has your chief declared war on the Iroquois? Did he send you on the war path with a battle ax?" Finally Fritz was able to break in and explain his situation. Felix was astonished. He had no idea. And then there was another problem. Felix ate all his meals out and was not equipped to serve meals. What to do? And then Felix said, "I have it." He locked his desk, ordered a coach and they drove to his apartment where Fritz changed into some of Felix's cloths. Soon after they left the apartment, Felix grabbed Fritz's arm. "Are you crazy?" he whispered. Fritz had begun to salute an officer. He would have been in great trouble if he were found out of uniform.

It all ended well. They had a wonderful meal in a fine restaurant and after dinner took a long stroll around the city ending at the ballet. They were in their seats waiting for the performance to start and talking rather loudly with great animation when a young officer turned around in his seat. Fritz recognized him. His heart sank. As the theater darkened, they managed to slip out. They found another restaurant and had just started to eat when another soldier came in who Fritz knew. Fritz pulled his hat as low as he could and as soon as they were finished eating they left. Fritz had had enough of Petersburg and the dress up game. The next morning he returned to camp. He returned to visit Felix a few weeks later and they went to see their Aunt and Sonja, Felix's sister, now living in Petersburg. It was a much more civilized trip.

Most of the time in Kramoje Spelo passed without incident. They marched, ate terrible food and marched. They also held mock battles in the surrounding forests. These often lasted for several days, regardless of the weather. Fritz saw his Imperial Highness Czar Alexander III several times and since Fritz was only 21 years old, it was quite memorable. One time he reviewed the troops, thousands of them. It was a spectacular show of pomp in which regiments all dressed in their best uniforms carrying sabers and shimmering bayonets on their guns, flooded the huge parade field and stood at attention for hours.

When the Czar rode through shouts went up like a great wave, bands played and all sang the national anthem. He was seated on a large horse and seemed to be a giant of a man. He had wide shoulders, was well proportioned in a simple uniform without any decorations. He looked tired, was slightly bent forward and his pale face with his long reddish blond beard was lowered to his chest. He was followed by an entourage of court ladies and gentlemen.

Fritz passed the officers exam with straight As. However, one did not become an officer immediately. The promotion went through the administration offices and indeed, Fritz did not receive his until about half a year later when he was already in the reserves. At the end of his training he returned to Dago, August 1, 1892, with his passport as an officer of the reserves. Now he faced the reoccurring question, what to do next? Further studying at this time was out of the question. Nikolaus' income was not sufficient to support him. He thought of becoming a bookkeeper-secretary, but according to the applicable rules at that time, he was too old (22) for the job. People who wanted to become merchants' assistants and so forth started when they were 16 years old. Furthermore, 1892 was a bad year for Russia. A famine threatened as a result of mismanagement and many businesses and export firms in Reval had to close. Although Nickolas claimed that he did not have any worthwhile connections, Fritz felt that he had other ideas for him.

Chapter IV:
Fritz Joins the Railroad

During his days in the military, the old Baron Ungern-Sternberg had asked Nikolaus about Fritz several times. (Mind you, this was the same man who refused to allow him into his school because he was Estonian, not German.) Nikolaus told him that he completed school with the highest marks and was serving in the military in Narwa. He also told him that he was quite concerned about Fritz's future since the family did not have enough money to provide him with further studies. The Baron replied that he should not worry. One of his cousins was head of the Southern Russian Railways and he would certainly find a job for him as a railway administrator. In fact, the railway was owned by the government and they preferred hiring people with reserve officer passports. In addition, while Russia still had only a few rail routes they were expanding constantly and there would be many opportunities for advancement. Nikolaus could already envision Fritz as the administrator of one of the newly developed areas. He was not very happy when Fritz found a few flaws in his father's plan.[53]

---

[53] It seems that the length and extent of a parent's responsibility for a child's future was extremely long in those days.

It was true that one could advance quickly in the railroad, but only if one had a technical education and a diploma from an engineering institution. This was a point discussed often by Fritz and his colleagues both in the army and in school before. In addition the entrance exams for the Russian technology schools were very difficult and many students tried and failed them. The middle and lower jobs at the railroad did not pay well and the hours were long. The people working in these jobs were not well regarded. But Fritz did not want to upset his parents any further so he applied for a position. His attitude was, since he could not have further education he really did not care what he did. The Baron, upon hearing that Fritz was ready to apply, informed him that he had already received an answer from his cousin and Fritz should start a position at the end of October in Charkow. He had three months to get over his depression.

In the beginning of September he accompanied his father on his annual business trip to Riga on business. He visited with his brother, Rudolf, and became acquainted with the city. While his father was meeting with his merchants, and Rudolf was only available on Sundays, he wandered around the city alone. How he longed to stay and enter the engineering school. By chance one day he met a fellow student from his former school days in Reval who took him to see Buschmann, his old friend from school. Both were studying at the engineering school. Fritz was a little envious until he saw Buschmann. He was dreadfully hung over from partying the night before after a fox hunt. The two students started talking about school — the student duels in fencing fraternities, drinking bouts and so on. Studying was never mentioned. When Fritz raised the subject they admitted that they had registered in the beginning of the year but had only managed to make a few lectures. Since they had both entered the fraternity they did not have time for classes. They suggested to Fritz that he simply register and the rest would take care of itself and that burying himself in Russia was stupid. Fritz thought about the free and easy life of these friends. It seemed like fun — for a while. But he was not about to waste a year in that pursuit. Suddenly the job in Russia took on a new light. It seemed like a good idea to get out in the world and see what life and work was really about. And with that he left his old school friends who were ready to go to continue partying at a "day after the night before breakfast."

After five days Nikolaus and Fritz returned to Dago where Fritz spent the remaining weeks reading books he had purchased in Riga. The only interruptions were the three days in the week when the mail boat arrived with letters and newspapers from Riga and Reval. His cousin Johanna wrote quite frequently trying to talk him out of the southern Russia plan. But by then he had become quite stubborn; only another job would have changed his mind. Finally detailed information from Baron Ungern in Charkow arrived and Fritz was ready to leave. His mother had made him new undergarments and the tailor in Kertell, a new suit. For more serious occasions he still had his confirmation suit. All his belongings and books filled one suitcase and a large wooden crate. In late October he went to Reval with his father on another buying trip. The Baron (in Dago) gave him a letter of recommendation to his cousin in Charkow. He also obtained a letters from Pastor Halm (who had confirmed him) to Pastor Berg in Charkow. Uncle Andreas knew a gentleman, Mr. Hildebrandt, in Charkow and wanted to give Fritz a letter also, but when Fritz got to his home, he was away. Fortunately, Andreas's wife had recently seen the gentleman, and said that a simple greeting from his uncle would suffice.

Nikolaus sent the crate ahead by freight leaving Fritz to carry only a change of clothes. He also bought a one-way ticket and gave him 150 rubles for the first few months. In early November Fritz boarded the train together with his old friend from school Michael Koppelmann who had roomed with him at Uncle Karl's house. Michael had worked in an office of an export company in Reval. But the firm had folded and he was traveling via Berlin to London. Fritz learned later that he had gone to Canada and then to the USA where he became a farmer.

The train went to Petersburg where Fritz had to change trains at a different terminal across town and then several other stops with waits, some as long as a full day. He rode in crowded third class compartments smelling of smoke and sweat and full of rude, unfriendly people. In one of the long stops Fritz studied the railroad administrators and the environment in which they worked — the red cap, signal whistle, Morse code equipment, and baggage they were required to handle. It was not exactly an elegant job to say the least. It was already bitterly cold and snow was on the ground in the forests that the trains passed through. He decided to take a break in Moscow knowing that the job would wait a few more days. Here he saw Russians in their national costumes, in long beards, wearing high boots and wide pants. Waiters were dressed in white Cossack tunics. He went to a hotel and after cleaning up, went searching for Lydia, a friend from the Uncle Andreas days while in school. She was employed by the Nikolski Bazar, one of the most elegant hotels in Moscow. Walking there he encountered more strange street scenes with national costumes, many small chapels with pictures of saints painted on the outside, peddlers everywhere and lots of pedestrians hurrying on in the cold. The Russian language had a different sound from that of Petersburg and there were few military personnel. The streets were not very clean and were slushy with snow. He soon found the hotel where he had dinner with Lydia. The next day he went to see Kushman, also of the Reval circle. He found him in his office. They telephoned Winkler, also from school days and Narwa. Winkler persuaded Fritz to stay with him, which was not difficult as it was free. Together they explored Moscow going from restaurant to restaurant, to cabarets, teahouses and even to a Wintergarten with Gypsy singers. He soon tired of the gay life and opted to inspect the historic sites, especially a walk through the Kremlin.

Finally Fritz boarded the train for the final leg of the journey. It was tedious, long and with many stops. At the stations there were men and women in sheep skin coats all wearing the same large felt boots. The people in the 3rd class were mostly tradesmen and fat women. Not a Jewish person was in sight, as Jews were not given residential permits in this part of Russia. Outside were the monotonous snow covered flat fields, interrupted once in a while by snow covered straw roofed villages and the steeple of a church. Farther south the landscape became a steppe with almost no forest and little snow. Again the Russian language sounded different. Finally he arrived in Charkow, 1,700 miles from home. He was in lower Russia in the northeastern Ukraine. New to him were the ox drawn carts, pulled by ash gray oxen with wide horns.

The first hotel room he found cost four rubles a night so he went on. Finally he found an inn with a room for 1 ruble. It was cold and the bed was hard but he was dead tired. The only food available at the inn was bread and tea but Fritz still had some sausage left, quite enough for the night. The next morning he went to Baron Ungern's office but it was closed. It was one of many Russian holidays. Since the letter of introduction had his private address he walked to his home. He was told by the servant that the Baron would see him at 4:00 PM. So Fritz gave himself a walking tour of the city. It had a pretty cathedral, large government buildings, a theater, an opera house, a university, and a technological institute, veterinary institute and several colleges. There were many students around, all in uniforms. There were also many languages — Greek, Tartar, Armenian, Ukrainian and even German, as there were many German settlers in the area. There were also many people in the national costumes of the Caucuses. After a good meal in a restaurant, he went to the Baron's house where he was informed that the Baron had a previous commitment and he should go to the office the following day.

The following day proved to be one of the blackest days of his life. And it all started so well. He reported to the administration building of the Charkow-Nikolajew Railway and was soon taken to Baron Ungern. He was a rather tall gentleman with brown short hair and a black goatee. He spoke in a singsong Estonian-German. After some small talk he told Fritz that he would have the title of Service Apprentice and would be paid 30 rubles per month. He would also have to take a course in telegraphics immediately. He was instructed to find quarters close to the railway station since the telegraph office was very close to the station. Since Fritz had lived quite well on 25 rubles a month in Narwa he felt he could live quite well in Charkow on 30. He also had 150 rubles of his traveling money left. He found an appropriate small room in a small wooden house, paid five rubles down, and went back to the administration building where Baron Ungern gave him a letter for the chief of the telegraph school, which he easily found. There were several Morse code machines with about half a dozen young men and women working on them. Fritz removed his coat and gave the letter to the chief who ushered him into another room. There, another man in uniform asked him a few questions and ushered him into a third room where he was introduced to a woman who was the telegraph instructor. After an hour of instruction the lesson was over and he returned to the original room to retrieve his coat.

One of the young men dressed in a rather shabby looking officer's uniform seemed to be in a great hurry to leave. Fritz had noticed him before because of his rough and ordinary face. He looked as if he had lost his officer's rank as a result of drinking. His dirty coat had been hanging next to Fritz's who also noticed that he was fumbling for quite some time with it. Instinctively Fritz had looked for his wallet; thank God it was in his pocket. But in returning to the room and seeing the man leaving so quickly, he ran over to his coat. His inside pocket was empty; all his pockets were empty. He remembered having taken the letter of introduction out of his wallet and putting it back — but probably in his excitement, into his coat instead of his suit coat that he was wearing. It was too late to mention his suspicion about the man in the shabby coat, as he was already gone. He had lost four months wages, his passport, a letter of recommendation from Pastor Hansen to Pastor Bergh, and a copy of the freight papers for his baggage, which had not yet arrived. The thief could easily claim all his baggage.

He was desperate. The first thing he did was to tell Baron Ungern about the theft. He looked at Fritz somewhat strangely and shrugged his shoulders. Then he handed him ten rubles. Fritz immediately sent a telegraph to his father. What was he going to do? In those days, one could not telegraph money. Weeks could pass before money arrived and after sending the telegraph all he had left was enough for his room. He could not even move to a cheaper room because to do so he needed a passport. Imagine a person without money or a passport in "Holy Russia" 1700 km from home with only 10 rubles in his pocket. The next morning he paid his landlady. She lent him bedding since his were still in the luggage. She did not mention the passport and he went back to school. At lunchtime he returned home and she asked for his identification. When he explained his circumstances she almost fainted. She could get in trouble if his presence were not reported within 24 hours. "You must go to the police," she insisted. She seemed to think he was a crook or worse, a political adversary. She was very suspicious. But how could he blame her, a relatively well dressed young man with a strange accent tells her a wild story that he came from almost the other end of the world to become a railway administrator — as if there were no such position in his end of the world.

What to do next? All he had were two rubles in his pocket and papers showing that he had graduated from school and was eligible for university. Why would a young man in these circumstances travel so far for such a job? He decided to first see the district supervisor who listened quietly and then stated:

> This is a very difficult and complicated matter. First there must be an investigation. You did contact the police after the theft didn't you? Then notifications will be placed in the daily papers for three days. And you must go to all the police stations and tell them you lost your passport. Then you will have to fill out an application form for a second resident permit which will cost money. It will be sent to the administration at the central headquarters

> because they have all the information on you. If everything is satisfactory, they will send you a new passport.

Fritz decided that before he would go through all that, he would try another approach and he replied:

> I don't think that someone else will be using my passport. I have just finished my volunteer military service and I'm waiting for my papers classifying me as an officer of the reserves. I'm concerned though that if something happens and the military cannot find me in case of a mobilization. Of course, since I reported it to you immediately, it will not be my fault.

The district supervisor changed his position immediately. He excoriated:

> Why didn't you say that in the first place? This changes everything. We still have to investigate and notices of loss are still necessary. But an interim identification paper will be made out for you. It is my responsibility that everything in my district is in order and I insist that you get it right now.

In short, the supervisor saw that there was no money to be made from his predicament. But Fritz would somehow have to make do for the next ten days. However, the following day he received a message from his father that he would receive 60 rubles which should arrive in a week.

After class the following day the teacher kept him after class. She had noticed that something was disturbing him. She also noticed that he had looked all through his pockets as well as his wallet the day before and had taken a large yellow portfolio from his coat. She also remembered that apparently the incident had been observed by the student officer who was very upset with him for making a fuss. He felt that Fritz, an unknown newcomer, could make charges and thereby put suspicion on the whole school. She further noted that the guy was probably a swindler and a crook. Fritz informed the teacher that he had come to this place on the recommendation of Baron Ungern and that he stood under his protection. The teacher realized the seriousness of the situation and suddenly Fritz and the teacher became friends. Subsequently it seemed all the other students came to believe it was the student leader who stole Fritz's wallet.

On Sunday Fritz went to the Baron's home for coffee. He met quite a few people, some younger men interested in the daughters of the house, the oldest of whom was seventeen and very pretty. The other guests included the pastor, his wife, and the owner of a large textile store and his wife. All were of Baltic origin. Fritz told his story to the assembled and while they seemed to exhibit some skepticism, both the pastor and the merchant lent him some money, which he readily accepted. On the following day he went to the main police station to report the theft. Within half an hour he was in possession of an interim resident permit which would be valid until his passport arrived. Five days later his father's money arrived and he paid back the Baron, the pastor and the merchant.

School was going well. Fritz soon mastered the telegraph and the railway tariff system for goods and passengers. His clothes were due to arrive soon and he was concerned that he would have trouble getting them without proper papers. So he went to the station and told the clerk that he had lost the freight letter to claim his belongings. The clerk stated that there were regulations to follow. The boxes would stay in storage for three months and would be handed out to the person coming up with the papers. If no one claimed them they would be auctioned off. Fritz told him that he could describe exactly the contents of each box and that in addition, he had keys to two locked boxes inside. But the man became abusive. "Leave me alone and go to Hell. I told you the regulations and there is nothing in the rules for exceptions so don't try to confuse me," he shouted.

Fritz was furious and immediately went to the Baron. The Baron wrote a few lines on a piece of paper and sent Fritz to the Chief of the Commercial Department. Half an hour later he had a beautifully typed letter addressed to the clerk's office. Fritz returned to the clerk. "What, you again!" he shouted, "What impertinence!" Fritz showed him the letter from his boss instructing him to hand over the goods to Mr. F. Maehle as soon as they arrive and in case they have not arrived to initiate a search on their whereabouts. Anyone else claiming the goods should be immediately apprehended. "You have strange ideas about being polite around here. The Baron was very surprised when I told him how I was treated," Fritz said. The man was overwhelmed and began to make excuses for his lack of courtesy. He then started looking through papers on his desk and lo and behold, the boxes had arrived two days earlier. The poor man would loose his job if Fritz took the complaint further so he let the matter drop, glad to have his possessions again.

The following weeks went quickly. Fritz's quarters were comfortable and the food was good. The landlady had two daughters around Fritz's age; one was quite pretty. Both were working as dressmakers as well as taking extra courses to further their education. In the evenings Fritz and the girls would study together. They also had fun together especially when one of the young men from the railroad school joined them. Fritz also visited the pastor who had received a lovely letter from Fritz's pastor in Dago and the pastor, who had been suspicious of this young man, warmed up considerably. He even invited him to his home when some students returned from the university in Dorpat for the Christmas holidays. Shortly before Christmas Fritz was informed that he had completed his instructions and would be transferred to the Station in Bogoduchow for his practical apprenticeship. So he made his farewells to Charkow and arrived in Bogoduchow on New Years Eve of 1892. He was assigned to the operations department, which was the largest part of the whole organization, had the most employees and paid the lowest wages. Operation inspectors, station masters, their assistants, porters, line switchers, conductors, cashiers and telegraph operators were all employed in this department. Above them were operation chiefs. In smaller stations the stationmaster was also the telegraph operator, sold the tickets and expedited the luggage transfer. Above all of them reined the chief of the railway who was as good as God Almighty.

Fritz obtained a room in the station building for thirty rubles a month, which he shared with the assistant station master, a "low" Russian. The station chief was a German, though now more Russian, with a German wife and two small children. The station was considered one of the better stations despite the fact that Bogoduchow was a small, dirty city of about 10,000 inhabitants and about one kilometer away from the station. The streets were not paved. Carts and wagons would sink in mud to their axles when it rained. Most of the houses were typical Russian mud houses or sheds, almost square in design. The walls were built around a wood skeleton, which was then plastered with mud and straw. The roof was made of straw. Since larger building could not be built in this manner, a farm was made up of 8 to 10 of these little buildings. The reason for this type of structure was there was virtually no wood available in that part of the country, which was principally a steppe. On his first day in town, Fritz took a long walk. He spotted a rather large and imposing building made from stone, which he thought, was the city hall. It turned out to be the district jail. Aside from that building there were only a few more buildings of stone. One belonged to a German sausage maker and baker. The shops were geared to farmers and sold cart grease, birch tar and the like. The two or three churches were not too bad.

The population was composed mostly of "lower Russians," quite different from "upper Russians." They were of medium build and shaved their beards, cultivating instead a thick and long mustache. Generally they were lazy. Even during the spring when farm work was urgently needed, they would sit in front of their huts, smoking their pipes. They regularly criticized the upper Russians, calling them Muscovites, who, in turn called the lower Russians, *Charchol* (peasants).

Fritz took his meals at the station counter, which was run by an Armenian. His job included everything that a stationmaster, his assistant, clerks and porters had to do. He even had to switch trains around sometimes. In March he went to Charkow for his final exam. Everything went well and he became a reserve assistant to a stationmaster. With this venerable title he was allowed to replace stationmasters and their assistants if neither were available. Thus he traveled to other stations in the general area as needed. He also received an extra 75 kopecks (100 kopecks/ruble) a day. Consequently, in some months he earned 50 rubles.[54] He was relieved that he did not have any money problems at this time since his meals were cheap and his savings were growing nicely although, he noted that transfers to smaller stations were not always fun nor were they lucrative. In fact, he noted that one would starve to death on 75 kopecks a day.

One could not count on a lunch counter at the station. In those cases where one was not available, he took food with him or took the train to another station on his day off to buy food, usually white bread, sausage and tea. Sleeping was also a problem and he usually slept on a day bed in the telegraph office. Often he did not change his clothes for days. The gypsy life was getting to him. He had always had a weak stomach and finally it just gave out. He felt sleepy and listless and became extremely depressed and apathetic.

Life in the small Russian city soon became boring. It was also very different from the environment he was used to in the west. On Easter, a priest went around and made crosses on all houses over the front door, no matter if the residents were believers or atheists. And he blessed Easter tables with holy water for which he received at least 50 kopecks. Easter, which lasted three days and nights, was celebrated with a great deal of food and schnapps. As a bachelor Fritz was invited to every house of every administrator. He was also invited to a wedding of one of his railroad colleagues. Fritz wrote that he married a socialite — the pharmacist's

---

[54] While the monetary amounts Fritz talks about have little meaning for us, I have included some of them. Most have not been included. For example in reviewing his father's loss of the store on Dago, he included itemized accounts of the debt and who and how it was paid. He also wrote detailed accounts of his wife's spending which he always seemed to accommodate. Money troubled him a great deal and he was always worrying about how he could make ends meet.

daughter and that for the occasion he had a special uniform made with silver buttons and red piping which he wore with a white ascot and kid gloves. The priest had a very long service during which time Fritz had to hold the crown over the bride's head. His hands were beginning to feel as if they would fall off his arms. Happily the wedding meal was substantial. There was guitar music, folk tunes sung and the younger generation tried their luck in western European dancing without much success. This was the extent of his social life.

Having learned all about his job and seeing the routine that accompanied it he began to worry. What could he expect from the future? The better jobs were only given to engineers. His potential, at best, was a stationmaster in a large station with an income of 150 rubles a month. Was that prospect so intriguing that he should go hungry for days on end? For 30 rubles a month he could work in any better store as a clerk and have a more humane existence. Perhaps he could become an office manager in a large private enterprise. He was diligent, intelligent, knew languages and did not lead a wild life. The whole railroad experience had become a waste of time for him. In fact, he became obsessed with that thought. He had already mentally quit his job.

When he received a letter from the military that he had to report in May of 1893 to Dunaburg for military exercises as an officer of the reserves, the hope that he would not return to southern Russia became overwhelming. The Dunaburg experience turned out to be quite poor. The regiment to which he was assigned was run in an old fashioned way. In addition there were drunken fights in the officer's mess hall regularly. The only bright spot of that experience was that his father had a cousin in the area named Chistel Melle (that is how he spelled the Maehle name). Sadly, all his hopes that he could leave the Gypsy life in southern Russia came to a sudden end. Letters from home were very distressing. Nikolaus had discovered a great discrepancy in his books. One of his employees had systematically stolen from him and he had to make up the difference with his own money. Rudolf had to return from Riga to work in the store. Any plans that Fritz had would have to be put on hold. He did not have enough money to support himself and could not ask for support from home at this time. So he traveled back to Bogoduchow, resigned to his fate.

The year 1893 was the year of the cholera epidemic in southern Russia. A cholera clinic was established in Bogoduchow. A young Russian doctor was in charge and as it turned out he was put in the same room at the station with Fritz and his roommate. He was the first Russian student with whom Fritz had ever had close contact and through him Fritz learned a great deal. To his astonishment he learned that very few Russian students had sufficient funds from home to study. Most gave private lessons or had other jobs on the side. They lived very frugally, completely differently from the student life in the Baltic. Fritz quickly gained a completely new outlook. If he had been a graduate of a classical gymnasium he could have entered law or medical school without any further ado. However he was only a graduate of the secondary school (real gymnasium). He could only enter a technological institute, and he would have to pass entry exams.

But he now had a goal. Engineering was a good profession; many people were going into it and it had many avenues for employment. So Fritz bought books on algebra, geometry, physics, history and philosophy, all written in Russian to practice the language and refresh everything he had learned in Reval in German. From then on the little lost stations became a refuge for study. The railway job existed only as a sideline occupation.

Unfortunately, Fritz stomach trouble grew worse (which would continue for the rest of his life). He developed an inflammation of the bowels and became very run down, but could not go on a healthy diet. Indeed, he was glad if he ate every other day. And the news from home grew worse as well. Nikolaus was in serious financial trouble. Oskar even had to end his schooling at the elementary level and went to Petersburg in the fall to begin an apprenticeship in pharmacy. Only Ewald and Hermann remained in the gymnasium. Kersti was sick and had to give up her work in the bakery, which meant that their income was reduced even more.

As Christmas 1893 approached, Fritz had turned 22 and had completed a full year at the railway. He spent Christmas Eve in a small station, lonely, hungry and cold. He had not eaten in ten hours and his stomach was in great pain. This was not the life he had expected. And then a few days into the New Year he was ordered back to Charkow, where he was given a new job, which entailed identifying and dispatching train-cars as they were needed. He worked under the operation administrator Leiman, the same man who had administered Fritz's exams. Leiman was pleased with his work and kept him on as his assistant. In the spring Baron Ungern called Fritz to his office to tell him he had completed the practical part of his apprenticeship and would be more suited for office work than in the field. So he went to work in the Baron's department and received a raise. But since the cost of living in Charkow was more than Bogoduchow, he actually had a reduction in income with rent to pay and meals to buy. But he had a quiet office. His job was to purchase all wood for any use for the railroad.

He did not visit the pastor or the Hildebrandts as he was self-conscious. His clothes, which he had brought from Dago, were getting shabby and he did not want to buy new ones. He never even went out in his handsome new railroad uniform. Rather he spent most his free time studying. He also came under the spell of the Russian students who were radicals and revolutionaries; a rather Bohemian group he thought. He lived in a room below a pub, probably close to the latrine, as it smelled. It was also damp. His roommate was the first nihilist revolutionary he had ever met.[55] He was a man who would simply say no to anything and everything. One had only to mention a fact of any kind — the earth moves around the sun at 30 km/sec. and he would jump up yelling "nonsense." Fritz soon discovered that he was not very well educated, just very opinionated. But Fritz was fascinated with his thinking. And so they engaged in heated discussions almost every night for about three months. And then their relationship ended abruptly, almost like a marriage.

One morning during the Easter holiday, Fritz was in the room when he heard a knock on the door. A police officer was standing there. He looked over Fritz's papers and interrogated him at length about his roommate. When the roommate returned Fritz told him about the encounter. They had a long conversation and for the first time not in the form of an argument. The roommate came from Poland, had been arrested as an agitator and sent to Siberia where he lived under police supervision. After a few years he was released but could not return to Poland. He was still under police observation. Fritz was rather surprised that he found employment in the

---

[55] Nihilist used here refers to a radical revolutionary who believes that all forms of existing government must be eliminated and the society must start over.

railway administration but that was Russia. Police were fighting the revolutionary elements but outside and apart from them, everyone else was supporting them. At that point Fritz decided that living with a political refugee would not be in his best interest so he moved out. He soon learned that this was a wise decision as he found he had been placed on the black list after only three months of living with a radical when the police made inquiries at his new place of residence shortly after he moved in. But the three months were also good for Fritz. The daily discussions and disputes about social and political matters and the repetition of his school subjects in Russian had proven to be excellent exercises for him. His Baltic accent was almost completely gone and he was absolutely fluent in Russian.

Fritz's new roommate, Katznelson was studying mathematics at the university but had to take a leave of absence because he did not have enough money. He had taken a job with the railway until he earned enough to resume his studies. He was a Jew, about five years older than Fritz. He was unique among all the other assistants in that he overslept every train he was supposed to dispatch. His name was always on the record and there was not a single month that he was paid his full wage. Despite this, he and Fritz were on the same wavelength. They both were students and planned to return to university. They found a very nice room in the home of a widow. The landlady had two daughters one of whom was engaged to a medical student. Consequently, young people often came to the house. The roommates soon made many friends. The landlady arranged frequent social evenings, but because the apartment was so small they had to give up their room. Through these friends Fritz received an invitation to the annual university ball, which he attended, principally so that he could meet the

Russian professors, their ladies and students. Fritz studied harder; sometimes Katznelson drilled him. His plans were shaping up. If he stayed with the railroad one more year he would have enough money for three years of studies. He would take the competitive exam for the Charkow Technological Institute.

In May Katznelson informed Fritz that he wanted another roommate, a female, and that their living together would be terminated. A month later Katznelson informed Fritz that he was marrying the girl and asked him to be his best man. The wedding took place the following week, a real Bohemian wedding. The groom wore a threadbare railway uniform and the bride, a simple housedress. Fritz was the only person among the three others in attendance in a frockcoat and white tie. After the short ceremony they all went to a nice restaurant, each person paying his own bill. Then they all went to the opera where the seats were paid for by the young couple. In the fall Katznelson informed Fritz that their first baby had arrived and towards the end of the year the family moved to Moscow where he resumed his studies.

After Katznelson, Fritz found another room and roommate. His new one seemed to have no political past and his brother was a police officer somewhere in Poland. But he turned out to be one of the most Red people Fritz had ever encountered. In his early twenties, he was a short stocky fellow with short legs and long muscular arms. He had a short neck with a large round head crowned with wild hair sticking out in all directions and an equally disheveled looking beard. Fritz found him somewhat sinister. He often thought he would end on the gallows. Fritz wrote that he probably did him wrong but who can help his own thoughts? By going around with a crowd of his old school friends he was involved in a lot of suspicious activities. Slowly Fritz also became involved, although he could not detect anything treacherous about them. For example, one lovely summer day he attended an event at a farm. There were about 30 people there and they were constantly looking out for police. They served a National Russian Meal consisting of grits with bacon and port, schnapps and tea. Then there was a lecture by a very tall Russian fellow who discussed Darwin and his theories for natural selection. A lengthy discussion followed which Fritz found rather silly. Afterwards the unavoidable theories of Karl Marx were discussed at which time the group again began to check for police. The group of men and women consisted of students, railway workers, administrators and office clerks. Fritz did not know if they were an organized group as he was never asked to join, but there were many get-togethers in his room and the discussions were usually on Darwin and Marx.

There were also discussions and reviews of radical articles and pamphlets, something strictly forbidden in Russia. Finally Fritz had had enough. The debates by these inexperienced kids and emancipated girls about socialism were too much for him, and he also felt that many of these people were involved in forbidden activities. One evening a friend came to the room to say that a search of another friend's room was expected and that the fellow had a Remington typewriter. If it were found the man would be done for and the typewriter would be confiscated. As Fritz's room was clear of suspicion, the friend asked him to hide the typewriter for a few days. That was dangerous! Having a Remington was equal to having an illegal print shop since it was only used to print revolutionary leaflets. If it were found one could prepare himself for a few years in Siberia. Against his best judgment and innermost convictions however

Fritz agreed to hide the typewriter. So for a few nights the typewriter and several boxes of literature were stashed under the beds. Both roommates were very nervous until all was removed.

In October a life changing experience took place. Fritz received a letter from his old school friend, Arnold Buschmann, urging him to come to Riga and enroll in the polytechnicum. Strangely Fritz had never thought about Riga himself. An entrance exam was not even necessary, only a math exam since it had been more than three years since he had been in school. Buschmann wrote that he had worked during the summer months to earn money for the coming school year meaning that studies could be financed as cheaply as in Charkow. Fritz had saved five hundred rubles, enough for one year of school. The rest would take care of itself. He was elated. His plan was coming together better than he had thought possible. A few days later he sent his letter of resignation to the Baron with profound thanks and an explanation of his future plans. He then wrote home and explained what he was doing. And finally he wrote Buschmann that he would arrive on New Years Day; all the necessary steps had been taken except for a letter of recommendation.

In November Czar Alexander III died in Livadia and was transported via Charkow to Petersburg. Under Czar Nikolaus II, the underground intelligence reports grew very uneasy. Petitions were distributed for reforms. The police became very active. Fritz's roommate suddenly moved and shortly after Fritz heard that some of his acquaintances from the previous summer were imprisoned. Fritz was actually a bit worried that he had been put on the black list but since he heard nothing from the authorities, he began to relax, although his stomach gave him considerable discomfort. Two years later in Riga Fritz had a visitor. He was a tall soldier. After a few minutes Fritz recognized him as the student with the Remington. He said that the people in the organization had become more and more subversive until the police got them.

Fritz's new roommate turned out to be a fellow Balt and he stayed with him until he left Charkow for good. They got along famously and Fritz was contented. One day the fellow asked to borrow 50 rubles. Fritz was glad to help him. But when he asked for the money back he was told that it would be sent to Riga. Fritz wrote to him several times from Riga but never received more than 20 rubles. In fact, he became rather impertinent and even angry and Fritz finally gave up. Finally on Christmas Eve of 1894 Fritz left Charkow for Riga. The train was dreadfully crowded and in Orel he left the train for the one to Riga, only to find out that it was not running on the holiday. All he could do was hang around the station for 18 hours until a Riga train arrived. The endless snow covered the fields and thick forests. Three days later he arrived in Riga for a new chapter in his life.

Chapter V:
The University Years 1895-1900

On December 28, 1894 Fritz arrived in Riga (now the capital of Latvia). Giving his luggage to the care of a porter who put it all on a sled and towed it to the corner of Alexander and Gertrude Streets where Buschmann lived; Fritz followed behind. He was glad to get some fresh air and move his limbs after four days on the train. Buschmann was not at home but his roommate, Mueller, was there awaiting Fritz's arrival. For the next few hours they became acquainted over tea and rolls. Finally Mueller put on his student cap and disappeared. Fritz unpacked and wrote his parents informing them of his arrival in Riga. Mueller did not reappear that day and Fritz went to bed early.

About 4 AM he was awakened by a loud noise and in his half sleep saw a large figure looming over him, trying to pull his blankets off. Fritz held tight and the figure stumbled over to Mueller's bed. Loud insults were exchanged and then the room grew quiet. The next morning there was a huge figure lying on the couch in the most contorted way. The couch was small and the head was resting on one corner with long legs draped over the armrest. One boot was off, the other on but a sock was pulled over it. The tie was draped over a chair, but the shirt, still on the body with collar opened in front and buttoned to the back and with one cuff on and one cuff off did not look very clean and certainly quite wrinkled. The gold pince-nez, against all odds, was precariously positioned on the nose of the character. Also a student cap was still on the big head. [56]

The figure turned out to be a fellow student of Mueller's, also from Osel, the large island just south of Dago. They could not make it home for the holidays, as there was too much ice on the sea. The friend had run out of funds and took turns staying with various friends who also fed him, mostly a liquid meal, which he seemed to imbibe liberally. To Fritz, this was living the Bohemian life. He had just come from a place where the students were Russian. They were usually hungry, often did not have rooms, and sometimes were fleeing the police for their radical politics. But they kept on studying. The Baltic students in contrast had completely different ideas about student days. They joined fraternities, drank, fenced, went to theater, skipped school, and drank some more. Looking at this person on the couch, Fritz questioned whether he would be able to work seriously in these surroundings. He tried to find out from Mueller how Buschmann's studies were going. The news was not encouraging. Neither Buschmann, nor for that matter Mueller, had done much of anything in nearly 2½ years of study. The guest on the sofa, who had already spent a whole term at the polytechnicum, had never set foot into the building.

This life had no appeal to Fritz who was prepared to earn his own living and knew how hard that would be, and how long it would take to earn the 500 rubles necessary for a second year. Aside from that he felt too old for that kind of student life. He

---

[56] As noted earlier, collars and cuffs were buttoned on to shirts. Pince-nez are glasses, which are held on by pinching the nose. They were very fashionable well into the 20th Century. Franklin Roosevelt wore them.

was 23 years old and had already spent time in the military and in employment. Those years had passed by and he was not sorry. As it turned out, compared with three other student friends, he was the oldest at the start of his schooling and indeed, the first to graduate. So on January 8, 1895 he wrote the entrance exam, and on January 10 he entered as a student of the Machine Engineering Faculty of Professor Lovis. His dream of the last 6 years had finally come true. He felt as if he had been promoted to a privileged class of society. And in a way that was true. In the Russia of those days, when one had completed higher schooling, one was literally taken out of the ranks of tax paying subjects and did not have to pay taxes anymore. It was similar to being promoted to a special class of nobility. To complete his feeling of well being, he needed a student cap, the absolute distinguishing sign of being a student, of having arrived.

Because he entered school mid-year, it was useless to attend regular classes. He would not have been able to follow. So he studied on his own and attended a few lectures in physics, chemistry, drafting, and architectural forms for the next few months. He was disappointed in the faculty, perhaps because he had spent so much time fantasizing about university. He had expected the professors would be extremely intelligent people, dripping with wisdom. They were not. Despite his disdain of the student life, he managed to spend many lively evenings in the apartment, with old Reval friends, drinking beer and liquor and eating cheese, wieners and rolls. He also spent many evening in a pub adjacent to the Rubonen Fraternity quarters. In fact, he and his Reval friends also spent many evening in the fraternity quarters, despite the fact that none was a member.[57] The fraternity library had a large collection of books from the polytechnicum, which Fritz spent most days reading. He also took books home and soon had formed a sort of reading circle in the apartment.

At Easter Fritz went to Reval to see his three brothers, other family and old friends. His brothers had grown considerably in three years. They were no longer little boys. One day he had a disturbing conversation with his cousin Johanna, who with her sister, Amanda (Great Uncle Andreas' daughters) had visited Fritz in 1883. A few months later he had received a birthday note from Amanda and they had developed a rather regular correspondence. She even came to Dago for a visit when she was 15. They continued to correspond. However, when he arrived in Reval for school Amanda's attitude towards Fritz had cooled. As he achieved more social graces, Amanda's interest perked up, as did many other girls in Reval. But he was not interested in Amanda. In fact, she provoked and irritated him. And she was extremely aggressive, especially with others around. So they fought a great deal and one time he left for Dago without even saying goodbye to her. Nevertheless, many people interpreted the relationship as puppy love. And while the relationship was long standing and intense at times, at least on Fritz's part, it was not love. Apparently, according to Johanna, that was not true for Amanda who had actually told Fritz's mother that she was in love with her son. Kersti concluded that Amanda was too passionate for Fritz and that was the end of the

---

[57] The fraternities in those days in Europe and especially Germany were drinking and partying clubs. Think of the operetta, "The Student Prince" by Sigmund Romber.

subject for Fritz who always had a great respect for his mother's opinions.[58]

It seems that Amanda had a new beau, Rudin, from Petersburg, although in a letter to Johanna she spoke only of Fritz. When Johanna told him of the letter he was shocked. He and Amanda had not been in touch for three years. But, in any case, he made it very clear to Johanna that he could not think of marriage for at least seven or eight years. He suggested that if a good respectable young man wanted to marry Amanda, she should accept. Later Amanda wrote to Fritz that the whole relationship was rather the result of their childhood together; more like a habit and should be remembered as such. Rudin however, was not the one she wanted and she would still continue looking. At the end of the summer Amanda announced her engagement to Rudin.

Towards the end of the term Fritz and Buschmann became tired of the life they were leading and began to look for other quarters so they could work in uninterrupted peace. After a lengthy search, they found real student quarters at Mrs. Markarow's place. This turned out to be a fateful event. If Fritz had never moved to Markarow's, he would never have met Arthur Esser, and if he had not met Esser, he would probably never have met the Jurgensen family and would not have married Maria. And if he had not moved to Markarow's he probably would not have met Reinhold Feldweg and probably would not have gained employment at Allart Co. in Lodz later on. "Now," asked Fritz, "is this coincidence or fate?" He preferred to think it was fate since he believed "that there is a guiding power steering our lives, what name we may apply to it does not matter."

---

[58] At this point Fritz spends two or three pages reminiscing about his relationship with Amanda and his position vis-a-vis love.

In May, Fritz handed in his machine drawings and returned to Dago for summer vacation. He had been absent from his home for three years and wanted to discuss his future plans with his father. Rudolf, he learned, was to become Nikolaus's successor in the business. Education, Nikolaus also stated, was the best use of his money and that upon his death each of his sons would inherit 2000 rubles, which he had set aside. He promised to provide 30 rubles per month from this inheritance and 10 rubles per month from Rudolf's salary, which Fritz would repay to both when he obtained employment. Thus together with his savings from the railway, Fritz had enough money to attend school without working on the side. Meanwhile, his stomach problem had been increasing over the past two years or so, and his meager diets in Russia and Riga did not help, so Kersti spent the summer trying to make him well again. He spent his free time with his younger brothers, Ewald and Hermann, hiking and swimming in the sea. Everything was fine except Kersti's health. She suffered from heavy bleeding, which the doctor in Kertell attributed to change of life. She gained a large amount of weight and became very pale. She was also very nervous and had attacks of cardiac weakness for which the doctor prescribed cold showers.

In August, Fritz returned to Riga to begin his first real year at the polytechnicum. On the boat on the way over he met Johannsen who was also going to study at the polytechnicum, and he agreed to room with Fritz and Buschmann. In fact, over the course of the years roommates came and went and soon the whole pension was filled with Fritz's colleagues. Fritz settled down to serious studies, concentrating on graphic geometry, drafting and drawing. He still found time to frequent the Rubonen Fraternity but declined membership because of finances. And he enjoyed frequent evening gatherings in the pension with all ten of the students, including several girls. They sang student songs, discussed philosophy, ate wieners, herring, potatoes, and drank beer and schnapps. Sometimes after one of these evenings, they would forget their classes and go for long walks with a stop at a pub for a beer to get rid of any hangover. When Nikolaus came to Riga in the fall on annual buying trip, Fritz saw him every night to enjoy a good free dinner. At Christmas time Fritz went to Reval where he partied with his cousins, Christlieb and Johanna, his brothers, Ewald and Oskar and several friends. He also met Amanda's fiancé Mr. Rudin. A great concern continued to be Kersti's health, which seemed to be deteriorating. Finally, it was suggested that she consult a doctor in Reval.

In January Fritz returned to Riga and something significant happened. Arthur Essen, his roommate, had been teaching in Mr. Jurgensen's school.[59] One day Jurgensen asked Esser to invite some of his fellow students to come on a sleigh ride. Several young men including Fritz accepted the invitation. All assembled at the Jurgensen's home where they were introduced to several other families and a whole group of young ladies. At 8:00 PM they left on sleighs for the country where they had a winter picnic and dancing. Around midnight they returned home, singing and happy. Of course Fritz never thought that six years later he would marry Jurgensen's daughter, then a pretty girl of about 13 with a thick blond braid down her back. When the

---

[59] Jurgensen was owner and headmaster of a boys school in Riga. It will be remembered that most education in those days was private. According to Heddy it was a very highly regarded school.
I have seen the family name spelled both Jurgensen and Jurgenson. Because I saw it with an e in one of my grandfather's letters I have chosen to spell it that way.

older girl Hanna turned 15 a few weeks later, they were all invited to the birthday party. There were quite a few 14 and 15 year olds at the party and Fritz and his friends, being 22 to 24 felt rather mature. From then on they were officially accepted in the Jurgensen home and were included in their circle of friends. This remained through all the years of Fritz's studies.

Fritz continued to work hard on his studies and was always the first to turn in his assignments, receiving straight As. At the end of the semester he said good-bye to his friends and the Jurgensens and left for Dago. His mother's illness had taken a turn for the worse. She was in bed, hemorrhaging and with severe pains in the lower abdomen. The Kertell doctor who was treating her, Fritz noted, was as ignorant as he had ever seen a man in his profession. His diagnosis — stomach troubles. That there might be a gynecological problem simply never crossed his mind. For weeks Fritz sat in his mother's room keeping track of her fever while he studied his mathematics. The work he completed that summer, he wrote, "was used for generations as an example for students of mathematics." His mother meanwhile was close to a breakdown. Everything annoyed her, which then made his father irritable and nervous. In July the family received a letter inviting them to Amanda's wedding in Reval. After much discussion it was decided that Fritz should go alone. Amanda, who had not seen him in four years, was very cool and distant. However, all was not lost. He managed to see many of his gymnasium friends.

Upon Returning to Dago he talked his mother into going to Reval to see another doctor. She was admitted to the hospital for observation where tests showed that she had a growth and needed immediate surgery. The surgery went well and Fritz returned to Riga. Kersti remained in Reval until Nikolaus came for her several weeks later to take her home but not before visiting Fritz in Riga for a week.

Right after the beginning of the term Fritz took mechanics I and II, passing with good grades. He had now completed the main courses of the previous term. Only mathematics remained. Social get-togethers continued at the fraternity and in Markarow's house with nine of the gang from the previous spring remaining. They also visited the Jurgensens who had moved. As Mrs. Jurgensen was not very happy with her new apartment however, the boys were not invited back. But they found quite a few other families who were very anxious to have them as guests, especially so that they could meet their single daughters.

Over Christmas Fritz stayed in Markarow's despite an invitation from one of his friends to come home and meet his sisters. But Fritz had had enough of females for a while. Passing his mathematics exam was on his mind. On Christmas Eve he and some friends partied at several homes. Several days later he, along with other young men, were invited to the Jurgensen's who had moved again. It seemed to Fritz that they were having financial problems. It was rumored that Mr. Jurgensen had speculated on horses and lost quite a bit of money. But to the outside world everything seemed fine and a happy mood prevailed. Hanna, the oldest sister, was celebrating her 16th birthday (Jan. 31, 1897).

Parties at various homes, including the Jurgensen's continued through the winter and spring. Fritz noted that it seemed that he did not get out of his tuxedo for days on end. Nevertheless, he passed all his exams with As, and he returned to Dago for a few days before taking a summer job in Reval. He returned to Dago for a nice visit at the end of the summer. His mother's good health had returned and both parents were in good spirits.

The following fall included much of the same socializing with fellow students in the fraternity, in Markarow's, and at homes in the community.[60] The Jurgensens had moved again. Hanna Jurgensen was confirmed in the spring and was now facing her first ball. Fritz and his friends provided her with all the dances of the evening. She could not sit down once. Afterwards they all enjoyed a nice party with her parents. Then during the Christmas break Fritz was invited to the Jurgensen to meet the grandfather. And at it was then that he began to show an interest in Maria. She was only fifteen years old (he was twenty seven) but more developed that her other sisters and much more mature than Hanna, the oldest. Up until this point the students had been coming to the Jurgensens because it was a nice family and Mrs. Jurgensen had a special way of keeping certain decorum amidst all the fun they had. The girls were pretty, they loved to dance and they knew a large group of very nice young ladies. No one paid much attention to anyone yet; it was just childlike flirting. All in all, however, Maria was liked best. She had the nicest personality. Hanna was thought to be capricious; she loved being courted. Maria was just a nice kid and Fritz found himself enjoying Maria's company more and more. He reserved all the main dances such as the quadrille and cotillion for her. She became his exclusive partner at the table and after any party it was he who would take the young Jurgensen ladies home. He did not know if she was beginning to have the same attraction for him but towards the end of one evening

---

[60] Fritz gives the names of the people, families and students, who went to which parties and even what they ate and did. He also talks about their love life and his role in intermediating, or as he says, playing the middleman. Since these people mean nothing to us, I have left most of this out, with the exception of the Jurgensens since their youngest daughter became Fritz's wife.

when it was "ladies choice" he was sure that she would come to him because she had begun to dance as quickly as possible with all the other young men to make sure that she had the last dance with him. As far as he could determine Mrs. Jurgensen did not look unfavorably at this situation but nothing was ever said and nobody paid any attention to them — officially. So Fritz escorted the Jurgensen girls to various parties around town. As all this partying was going on, Fritz's exams and lecture continued vigorously. He played and worked very hard to maintain excellent grades. Unhappily several of his friends were graduating and his group, the Markarow Circle, was breaking up. Fritz was approaching his last year also.

The summer of 1898 was to be his last visit to Dago for six years. Rudolf, who had come back to Dago to work in his father's store, was engaged. He had made strong friends in Kertell and both he and his fiancée were well liked. Early in the summer one of Fritz's friends from Reval came to Kertell as a summer replacement for the town's pharmacist. He was bored to tears in the small village and since he was a born organizer, he had the wild idea of arranging picnics in the nearby Palukal Forest and inviting the whole administrative body of the plant. And they all came and they drank and they partied. Indeed, Fritz noticed that the older gentlemen were drinking beer and chasing it with schnapps — one after another. Not even in Russia had he seen such drinking! Partying continued almost every evening throughout the summer at various gardens and backyards. They all sang student songs, which the older generation quickly learned. They often went to the beach where parties lasted into the wee hours of the morning. A group of partiers thought up some atrocious pranks. For example, they nailed shut the doors and windows of people's homes who did not come partying or they would serenade them with the most atrocious noises in the middle of the night. Dago had never seen such activity.

Fritz made himself useful by helping his brother, Ewald, prepare for his entrance exam into the Polytechnicum. He also prepared himself for several exams he intended to take immediately after vacation time. Oskar, who was also home for the summer, was to report for military service in Hapsal in September. He had hoped that he would be excused from service since he had a hernia but he was not. And he assisted in the preparations for Rudolf's wedding, which, by custom, lasted two days. A week after the festivities Nikolaus held a smaller party. Too soon, the summer ended. It was the last time Fritz would see his parents again until he was already married and had one child.

On his return to Riga he stopped in Hapsal in a hotel with his brothers, Ewald and Hermann, who were also returning to school. One day he visited some old friends and a former teacher from the district school, noting that a reunion after eleven years is an intense thing. They went around to old haunts until 4 AM and by the time Fritz got back to the hotel his brothers were fast asleep. The following day, Ewald and Fritz were on their way to Riga by boat[61]. It was a stormy crossing and there was no hiding his hangover from Ewald who had great fun seeing him in such a miserable state. His arrival in Riga did not improve his state of well-being. He was quite hung over.

His last year of school from August 1898 to June 1899 was very different from the others. The Markarow house was now quite empty. He had promised Kersti that he would complete his studies

---

[61] Although Hapsal is on the mainland, in those days it was far quicker to go from there to Riga and Reval by boat.

in four years, and he still had ten exams to pass two of which, engineering-science and chemistry, he took a few days after his return.[62] Only then could he apply for the final examinations, which included ten subjects. Thus he was looking forward to a total of eighteen exams during the course of the year. And to make matters worse, student unrest was beginning at the university. Everything was in jeopardy. The Polytechnicum had been Russified in 1896. Therefore it had to grant the same rights concerning government positions for its scholars as the technological schools in Petersburg, Charkow, etc. As a result a large number of Russians had entered the Polytechnicum. The growing Russian influence and Russian ideologies were creating hostility among the Baltic students. Fritz wrote that the student body was divided into two camps: one Baltic and the other Russian, most of whom were Jewish.[63] The situation became increasingly aggravated since there was already a never-ending battle in Russia between the government and the students, and soon open clashes ensued. Fritz remembered student unrest only too well from his days at Charkow. But to the Baltic people this was very hard to understand.

During August some scandal had broken out in Kiev. The government had intervened. Reprisals and new laws were initiated and as a result, the Russian Student Council had decided that sympathy strike action had to be taken on all Russian universities including Riga. The Baltic student body,

---

[62] University education was conducted quite differently from what we are used to. One never had to go to class if he was not interested. Lectures were held for those interested. One had only to learn the subject material and pass the exams when he felt he was ready. This is how Fritz could study on his own over the summer and take these exams so early in the school year.

[63] Recall that the Bolshevik revolution was led by Jews who had been repressed for years in Russia. They flocked to universities believing that they could induce real reforms.

which included most of the fraternity crowd, opposed such action strongly. Long haired, dirty looking students from Russia were interrupting lectures, invading classrooms, carrying sticks and disrupting class procedure. Professors were prevented from lecturing. Chaos erupted between the striking students and those who wanted to learn. As a result, at the end of October, everyone had to enroll again. The re-registration was done under strict screening. Even the police were involved. Finally, after several weeks of chaos, classes resumed. But the Baltic students moved from class to class, carrying sticks so as not to be in a disadvantage if attacked.

In the middle of all the strike excitement Fritz received a parcel from Kertell. It contained a beautiful letter case bound in red velvet and embroidered on both sides. It was from his long time friend, Miss Adeline Hosfeldt whom, Fritz recalled, had lost a bet with him years ago. "Aha," he thought, "she is paying her bet." He was shocked when he read the accompanying letter, which stated that she believed by so many little deeds and expressions he must be very fond of her and that she was sending this token to find out. Although flattered, he felt as if he had been hit by lightning. Adeline had participated in almost the entire outing during the summer, but to think that he may have been so drunk as to propose to her was out of the question. He simply was not interested. He immediately wrote a "Dear Adeline" letter that he was very happy with the case, but that her observations were rather dangerous illusions and that he was very much in love with a young lady in Riga. Being a gentleman, she must have noticed that he treated all ladies nicely and if he had overdone it sometimes it should be attributed to the jovial mood of the vacation. He sent a registered letter to make sure it would arrive in time. He had already written to Maria from Dago, congratulating her on her 16th birthday and had visited the Jurgensens as soon as he arrived in Riga.

Parties and social life continued throughout the fall. Around Christmas time Papa Jurgensen celebrated his 25th anniversary as a teacher. He gave a grand ball to which all ladies came in beautiful gowns and gentlemen in tuxedos. Fritz was Maria's escort. And at a New Year's Eve party everyone wrote down their wishes, which they then burned. Fritz wrote his wish for a perfect diploma. Maria told him later, after they were engaged that she had written her wish to become engaged, but she never told him to whom...

After the Jurgensen ball the family somehow retreated. Maria was in her last year of school and was busy preparing for her confirmation. On Palm Sunday Fritz sent her flowers to commemorate the event and later, when he arrived at her house to congratulate her personally, he found a new gentleman, Victor Werther, who had brought an immense bouquet of flowers and seemed quite interested in Maria. They had met at the bicycle club, which Mr. Jurgensen joined after giving the girls bicycles for Christmas. The family had become quite involved in the club — attending meetings and dances and making frequent excursions into the country. Fritz also learned that Jurgensen had sold his private school. In fact, one of his friends' mother who was a gossip, said that he sold it because his affairs were in a bad state because of gambling debts. Fritz had the feeling that she was telling him this with certain viciousness because her own daughter had an eye on him and he favored Maria. By May, Hanna, Maria's older sister, was engaged to Victor Werther, but there were other club members hanging around Maria. One time when Fritz was on one of his visits to the Jurgensen home he saw a picture of Mr. Jurgensen in all his bicycling regalia and standing to the side in a white dress was Maria. He asked for and was given the picture.

Fritz was also very busy with school and exams. By mid June he was ready to graduate with straight fives in all subjects. His exams actually had to be written under police protection because of unrest on the campus. He sent a cable home to his parents, "All completed — straight fives," which resulted in joyous celebration at home. He was no longer called student; he had become a diplomat. All that remained was to complete the thesis, which would be done in the fall term. His thesis subject was the development of a cotton mill consisting of 50,000 fine spindles, a weaving plant with bleaching facilities, construction of all necessary buildings, steam boilers, steam motors, electrical equipment, etc.[64]

During the examinations, two professors asked Fritz to do some work in a newly built plant in Riga. And so, immediately upon graduation he went to work. He was assigned free living quarters on the premises and paid 76 rubles per month. He ate his meals in the canteen of the plant. Soon, Paul Reichert, a colleague from school, moved in with him and they started drawing construction plans, machinery etc. It was a very exciting challenge to draw construction and machinery plans for a new modern factory, which was still in the development process.

On Sundays he went to the Jurgensens' who had not gone to the beach that summer.[65] They were moving again and all were completely absorbed in

---

[64] Students were given a thesis topic; they did not choose one. It was rather like a final exam. Fritz was to spend the rest of his professional life in this field of manufacturing.

[65] This was a tradition the Jurgensen family always had. Later, Mr. Jurgensen got Fritz to buy into a new dacha for the family which he then charged Fritz rent to use.

bicycles and races, as well as other trappings of the club. Two other young men from the club were after Maria, and one Sunday morning, Mr. Jurgensen arrived at Fritz's place, complete with a club bicycle uniform and bicycle, to invite him to the house that afternoon as he was such a good old friend of the family. Maria had accepted a job as a governess in Dorpat[66] and was leaving that day. Of course he went and after dinner all of Maria's belongings were loaded into a coach and everyone went to the station. When the second bell rang the train simply left and that was the end of the scene. Fritz was very confused and did not say much that day. Later on (after they were engaged for some time) Mama Jurgensen said that he had put a lighted cigarette with the wrong end into his mouth.

On the way home from the station Jurgensen told Fritz that he had sold his school and taken employment with a construction company at a job paying 60 rubles a month (this was less than Fritz was making). Fritz was astonished. Knowing the lifestyle in the house, this was not a change for the better. And then it became very quiet at the Jurgensen home. But Fritz was very busy working full steam on the plans for the new factory and he was not feeling well. The work was taxing and the previous exams had taken their toll. Sometimes he was so tired that he fell asleep over the drawing board. He was living in the country and went to bed very early. When Maria turned seventeen, he and Paul Reichert wrote a poem to her so she would not forget her old friends completely. The also drank a bottle of wine to celebrate.

A short time later Fritz received a letter from Feldweg, another Riga friend from school who had already graduated. He had taken a position in

---

[66] A town near Reval.

Warsaw and in his position visited various firms in Lodz.[67] One such firm was Leon Allart & Co. They approached him with a job as plant engineer. After some consideration he declined but recommended Fritz for the position. So Fritz immediately wrote them asking for 100 rubles per month and free living quarters.[68] He received a favorable reply and was told that he should re-apply after he finished his present short-term work. Again, destiny played. If Fritz had not lived at Markarow's he would not have had a friendship with Feldweg and probably never heard of Allart.

By the end of August his work came to an end. Shortly before he moved back into town he received a letter from Johanna, Aline and Erna, his cousins from Reval, saying that they had spent the summer in Osel, the island south of Dago, and were arriving in Riga on the their way to Reval and would like him to meet them at the steamship landing. Mrs. Markarow had left Fritz a key to the house while she was at the beach and the girls stayed there. Fritz went to see them every afternoon and returned to the country in the evening. Before she left, Johanna invited him to visit for 10-12 days until the final term started. So, when his work was completed at the new factory he took his drawing board back to Markarow's and went to Reval to spend time with Johanna, his great aunt and Christlieb. It was wonderful and relaxing. He needed the rest.

In September he returned to Riga to complete his thesis and receive his diploma. His social life came to a virtual standstill. He saw very little of the

---

[67] All the Baltic States and Poland were part of the Russian Empire at this time so that movement among them was like traveling from state to state in the U.S.

[68] It seems that free housing was the norm at this time. In fact, until Fritz became a consultant after WWI, he always lived in homes provided by the company.

Jurgensens and only went out for an occasional Sunday coffee at Reichert's or an occasional party. He received two more job offers, one from an electrical laboratory within the polytechnicum which he refused and one from a company in Budapest who wanted to train a young engineer for their affiliate in Russia. The latter struck him as rather farfetched and very complicated. So he wrote to Allart and was immediately hired. His job would begin in January 1900. He felt very lonely and somewhat irritated since Maria did not correspond. Once in a while he went to Jurgensens' and Mamma Jurgensen told him about a letter from Maria and that she had sent him her regards. Around Christmas as he was deep in finishing his thesis, he heard that Maria had arrived in Riga for the holidays. He did not want to go to her home without an invitation. Also they had moved again for the third time that year.

    One evening he was at home lying down with a headache. Reichert had just moved into the house and was living on the same floor as Markarows. Miss Markarow had told Fritz that Emmi Reichert, Paul's sister, was interested in him. He was annoyed. Why was it always women who were older than he were interested in him? Since he had not heard from Jurgensens although Maria had been home for some time, he was even angrier. He made up his mind not to leave his place at all that week even though there was a birthday party at the Reichert's and all of the Markarow residents were invited. Then one of the students came to tell Fritz that the Jurgensen girls had just arrived at the party with Maria of course. He never shaved and dressed faster in his life than that evening! Maria had blossomed beautifully and looked very grown up for seventeen. She had pink cheeks and a figure that lacked nothing. She was lovely. While they danced he told her that Riga without her was terribly boring, and she admitted that she did not have a very good time in Dorpat. Soon they were in their "old element" again.

When the evening ended, Fritz escorted the Jurgensen girls home as usual, and he told Maria that he urgently needed to talk to her. But during the next two days he was unable to find her anywhere. Finally, on the evening of the third day they met at the skating rink where she was with her middle sister Hedwig.[69] Unaware that the weather had turned very bad, Fritz and Maria continued to skate together. By the time they left the rink, they were engaged. Hedwig appeared very puzzled by what was going on. When the three reached the Jurgensen home, Maria went to her room and Fritz asked Mama Jurgensen if he could call Maria his bride-to-be. Soon Papa Jurgensen, Hanna and Victor arrived and Maria and Fritz were presented as engaged. The joy was genuine. The scene that followed at Markarow's was wild. One friend literally stood on his head on the couch; another performed an Indian dance while another clapped his hands. One was sent out for beer and they all partied.

Fritz wrote, "This then was the second time that my life had been influenced by the guiding fate: without the intimate friendship of Esser, I would have never met the Jurgensens." And so, soon to complete his studies and receive his degree with a new job waiting and engaged to a lovely girl whom he truly loved, the world seemed a wonderful place. "But, he wrote, "everything nice seems to bring something bad." He had planned to keep his engagement quiet until his job situation was 100% confirmed. "But one can hardly be expected to think clearly of all contingencies in one day, especially

---

[69] Although Fritz never refers to her as Hedwig, Heddy was named after her. In fact, when I was a child she used to tell me that her given name was Hedwig but it had been legally changed.

when one is the party involved." The following evening the family had planned to celebrate. Fritz was working hard on his thesis all day. Imagine his surprise when he arrived at the Jurgensen's and learned that they had already purchased rings and ordered the engagement announcements. "What, he wondered, "was the big hurry???" At the very least, Papa Jurgensen should have talked to him about this matter. He was very embarrassed and a little angry when Papa Jurgensen presented him with the rings as he had planned to buy them with his first paycheck in Lodz.

The fact is, the engagement had happened in a state of overexcitement and he had never really thought of all the financial implications in connection with marriage. It was shortly before Christmas and he had ordered a new suit, coat and tuxedo, with a large down payment. He also had not been in correspondence with his family for some time as there were no ships going between Dago and the continent because of the weather. Christmas was before him and he was not able to give his fiancée an appropriate gift. He settled on a book. Also, in the announcement he was given the title engineer while he was still registered as a diplomat. And importantly, he did not know how he would fare in Lodz. He had been planning on at least one or two years before marriage. Maria was just seventeen. "If the engagement is quiet, nobody will bother the bride with silly questions as to when and how, but when the engagement is official everyone will pester the bride at every occasion which can drive anybody to distraction when the date is set so far away."

As the announcements were already ordered it was not possible to protest so he adapted. Now however, every minute was important to him. He had to finish his thesis, but he was compelled to go out and visit people all the time and to think of all the people to whom announcements should be sent. This too did not go off as expected. By some fluke the list with the names of his friends in Dago had been taken care of by Victor and, while he wrote a long letter to his father it turned out that the cards arrived a day before the letter. Nikolaus was very insulted that he had to hear of his son's engagement from "strangers" and his hurt was not softened by Fritz's long letter. Due to the Jurgensens' preemptive action Fritz had not even told his parents before going public! Grand Uncle's family reacted as well. Johanna wrote that it was rather strange that he had not mentioned anything about this when they were just together for a fortnight. She wondered why he had broken their long-standing camaraderie. Aline did not write at all and Amanda sent the card back. Later he learned that she had expected he would "take her away" at the time Rudin was courting her. He could not get over the fact that Aline had been married for five years and had two children. And from that time on Fritz was estranged from Great Uncle's family.

Finally, with lots of help from his study friends all of his drawings were completed and his accompanying notes drafted although not in final form. His professor agreed that because he had to start in Lodz in January, he could complete the thesis there. And on January 23, 1900, Fritz left for Lodz with his friend Bua from Mrs. Markarow house, who had spent the holidays in Riga under the pretense of helping him with his drawings. But he had done almost nothing, while two others, Ewald and Messer, did most of the work. Bua took Fritz to his parents' home and on January 26 he presented himself at Allart. An hour later he became Plant Engineer with Leon Allart & Co.

Meanwhile things had settled down with the Maehle family. Nikolaus and Rudolf were taking care of the store in Dago. Oskar was released from one of three years of military service where he was serving in the medical corps as a pharmacist in Petersburg. Ewald was a fourth term student in Riga and Hermann was in Reval in high school. Papa Jurgensen was a consultant in the firm of Mantel, Maria took an office job, Hanna was at home and Hedwig was still in school. Fritz set off for Lodz, Poland. A new chapter in his life was about to begin.

Chapter VI:
The Early Years of Marriage

The first thing Fritz did when he arrived in Lodz was to finish the last notes on his thesis. Three weeks later the work was completed and he sent the manuscript to Ewald who had it bound. His university years officially ended on May 1 when he received his diploma. The university kept all his drawings and discussion for an exhibition. He never saw this work again. "What a pity" he wrote.

His new employer, Leon Allart & Co., was a cotton-manufacturing mill, an area of engineering Fritz knew very well. After several weeks at the mill it became clear to him that the company did not need an engineer but something they called a *Sitzdirecktor* or administrative director. At first he was very disappointed but then he analyzed the situation as follows: The rapid development of the Russian industry had brought considerable socialist ideas through agitation of radical elements. They fell on fertile grounds since they were supported with vehemence by the liberal intellectual class. During his time in Riga, it will be recalled, the first strikes had already taken place. They were suppressed by the Cossacks.[70] In an effort to fight the workers'

---

[70] Cossacks were members of the Czar's infantry. Most were fighters from southern Russia, Georgia, etc.

movement the government initiated laws that forbid workers from striking. Treated as illegal riots, the leaders risked being sent to Siberia. To counter this, the position of plant inspector, a special government representative to watch that no injustices occurred on the part of the plant owners and management, was created. An intricate new law regulated the relations between employers and employees. In conflicts, the judge was the plant inspector. The idea was good, but most often the inspectors were liberal Russians who went along with the workers' position. In point of fact, working conditions in the plants were almost always in need of reform. Working times were long (usually 11 hours) and negligent work was punished by deducting wages from the workers, which usually ended up in the plant managers' own pockets. In cases of accidents, little or no compensation was paid; the worker was always to blame. And if someone tried to take his grievances to the courts, he was fired. The younger and better looking girls working in the plant were subjected to all kinds of humiliation and usually had to pay for any advancement by giving "favors" to the foreman. In short, it was not a nice picture.

When Fritz came to Allart, the situation was already much better. Working hours were reduced to 10½, terms of notice were given in writing two weeks in advance and any punishments had to be reported and be approved by the inspector. The inspector was also responsible for deciding whose fault an accident was. It became more common to find the plant management at fault, primarily because of faulty machines and insufficient supervision. The inspector was also responsible for determining the amount of compensation. Although he was supposed to be impartial, he usually supported the worker's position and since he wore a government uniform, the idea evolved that plant owners and managers were all leeches and exploiters of the working class. Thus, the plant inspector became a dreaded and unsympathetic figure for the plant owner. He had the full run of the factory, day and night; he could ask any worker any question; complaints and unlawfulness could be turned into written protocols and he could interfere in all sorts of decisions made by plant management when they concerned the workers. No decisions on wages, increases or decreases, could be made without his approval. He even had to sanction increases or decreases in production output. To top it off, if the owner complained too loudly, the inspector could have him jailed; and if he was a foreigner, who many were, he could be deported. To be an owner or manager of a plant, therefore, had become a very unpleasant position.

There was one loophole for plant management. They could install an administrative director and make him responsible for taking care of all the aforementioned. In this way, management got rid of the interference of the government inspector. When the government inspector came for plant visitations, the plant owners and administrators went into hiding. The administrative director led the inspector through the plant, received praise and complaints, had to supply answers to all inquiries, and had to cope with all the protocols. As soon as the inspector left the plant, the administrative director returned to his rather subordinate position.

This, it turned out was to be Fritz's position. The situation in the firm at that time was rather bad. Allart had appointed the commercial director to do this job in his spare time. Not only did he not work with workers, he did not have any spare time. The managing director, Mr. Lamy, was from Alsace Lorraine and was a very commanding and arbitrary person, self righteous and without interest in the new laws. His position was taking its toll on the commercial director. As the result of a serious accident, from which the company was absolved of any negligence, management decided to hire someone new for the administrative director position — someone with a higher education from a Russian institution, who could speak Russian. When Fritz applied for the position, he was totally unaware of the background. He did not know the laws involved, especially the criminal side of the job. But on his first day, Lamy took him around the plant and told him that as an engineer he now had the full responsibility, including criminal matters. Fritz thought it made good sense and, as he had a keen interest in boilers and engines, he immediately began to study the plant and its operations. About a week after he started, the former administrative director called him into his office and told him "the facts of life." He painted the government inspector as a living devil, and his personal enemy, who was out to get him and to put him away. It was now Fritz's job to deal with workers, machines, and inspectors and to take the heat for all problems.

Fritz did not quite know what to make of it. Why, he wondered, would the inspector take a disliking to him when he didn't even know him? He would soon find out what was really going on, as the inspector was due for a visit soon. And on that very day, the inspector arrived. He was an engineer from the institute of Charkow. A rather stout man with hasty movements and very fast speech, he had long dark hair and was of the type you see in southern Russia, almost Tartar. He actually reminded Fritz of the longhaired revolutionary students he had seen by the hundreds in Charkow and lately even in Riga. The inspector looked down his nose at Fritz and addressed him in a very terse way. While he was happy to see a young engineer in the position, he advised Fritz to be very careful. The plant was in a rather neglected state, had insufficient supervision, no protective measures and Lamy was known to be a self-righteous tyrant. So far, Fritz was informed, his predecessor had been covering up for Lamy (implying bribes and bonuses) but that would not continue. He recommended that Fritz acquaint himself with the plant, the machinery, the processes and the laws. Fritz took the advice. He studied the plant, the laws, and even worked in the plant in all sorts of jobs to become well acquainted with the machinery. After six weeks he informed Lamy that he was ready to assume his duties as both administrative director and plant engineer. He reasoned that he was already 28 years old and it was high time he put his theoretical knowledge to practical use. Soon enough, the administrative director position was sidelined as Fritz became more and more engrossed in the engineering of the plant. He conducted heating experiments with the boilers, purchased various indicators and equipment, observed the steam engines during various applications and discovered unbelievable mistakes in applications and regulations which he was able to repair. As he informed plant management of the great number of technical discrepancies, they in turn, began to see the value of a good engineer.

    Fritz lived with two bachelors, Warrikoff, an old friend from Dorpat who was engaged and spent every evening with his fiancée; and Klein, a Frenchman, who partied every night and was of no real interest to Fritz, who spent his evenings (he worked from 5 AM to 7 PM) writing long and detailed letters to Maria. Although they had known each other for five years, they were really little more than social friends. For example, he never knew about her family and their domestic life and problems. When he felt like going out to socialize, it was with Felix, whom he had last seen eight years ago when he visited him in Petersburg from Kramoje Spelo, the military camp nearby. He met several other bachelors, all from the Baltic, Riga and Reval; but, as they partied in very expensive circles, he rarely joined them. His favorite evenings out were with Warrikoff's family where a number of Baltic young people gathered to enjoy good company and excellent food and drink.

After the several Easter celebrations, with wonderful food, drink and friendships, Fritz had to prepare for his required summer military service, and to have a new uniform made. The allowance the army gave for clothing was hardly enough for a good uniform and his old one was worn out. The way he received his service notice was another example of the negligence in all administrative matters in Russia at that time. As an officer in the reserve, it was his duty to report to the military post in the area where he was living. Any change that was not reported was subject to a 100-ruble fine. Of course, he had reported his location as soon as he moved to Lodz. He even reported the change to the Riga post by registered mail. There seemed to be total confusion as his notice to report went to Charkow and then to Reval and Riga. Since he had changed his address several times the notice made the rounds of all his former addresses. Finally it was discovered that he had moved to Lodz. Meanwhile, not having received his notice, he was under the impression that he would not be called. Two days before the deadline for him to report, the police department representative, who was responsible for delivering the notices, came to his home with the notice and a stack of papers collected on their way across Russia. Fritz threw himself into his uniform, said goodbye to Allart, picked up his pay for the month of May, and left by a fast train for the post, which was near Riga. He went directly to the Jurgensens (who had moved again!) where he cleaned up. He then bought a large bouquet of flowers and went to see Maria in her office. The afternoon and evening were spent at the Jurgensens where Ewald joined for the evening. The next morning he went to the post, which was one train station from Riga. And the summer playing soldier began.

With or without a pass, he used every free moment to slip back to Riga to be with Maria. They talked about the future and about their wedding plans. But since he had just started at Allart and had no savings, he could not make definite plans. And by the end of June he was back in Lodz. A short while later Maria informed him that she had left her office job as being a junior chief had become increasingly offensive; she became a governess to a family in Riga.

By 1901, Fritz's job had expanded considerably. As with all the mills in Lodz, Allart was very busy with two shifts (day and night). New construction and repair jobs kept Fritz very busy. Lamy was always asking for new project drawings, cost plans and statistics. In March Fritz took a week to attend Hanna's wedding in Riga, which took place at the Jurgensen home with only a small circle of friends and relatives. Hanna and Victor moved to a small apartment in a neighboring town. Oskar changed his studies from pharmacy to engineering. Maria's sister, Hedwig completed her studies and was sent to a job, in Russia by her father. She only stayed for a short time because she could not stand it. Maria had given up her governess job and moved to the Jurgensen beach house — for financial reasons, Fritz conjectured. His cousin Felix had taken a job in Riga and urged him to apply for an engineering position. He did but never received a reply.

He returned to Lodz and sunk deep into his work. Maria wrote that her father had found a job for

Hedwig at his place of employment, Mantel. She also noted that her father's position at Mantel seemed to be very secure and one of the engineers, whose wife had died a while ago, was very interested in Hedwig. His name was Bernard von Dahm and he was a member of an aristocratic Baltic-German family who owned several estates. After that Maria's letters became anxious. Her father had found another job for her in another office, which she again did not like. It seemed that her father was anxious to get all of the girls out of the house. Hanna was married, Hedwig had a good prospect, and he urged Maria to write to Fritz suggesting that they should marry soon, preferable even before Hedwig. Could Fritz not find an apartment in Lodz for them?

Fritz however, had calculated that they would not marry until he had sufficient funds and a secure stable position, perhaps in four or five years. But questions from friends were getting embarrassing. The engagement fiasco was repeating itself. As much as he wanted to have Maria with him in their own home, it saddened him very much that the reality was so different from his wishes. As a young man with only a year in the firm he was only eligible for a bachelor apartment, which he shared with two other men. He would never qualify for a four to five room apartment with heat and electricity. Warrikoff who had come to the firm three years before had only just married and he had to rent a place at his own expense: two rooms in a farm house which was quite a distance from the plant. Although Fritz's wages had been increased to 120 rubles, that was not enough for the rent, the furniture and the day-to-day cost of living. The plant was located near the city limits and housing in the area was very expensive. In addition, Fritz had debts he was still paying off. Maria was still very young, not yet 19 years old. But the pressure from Riga increased; his hand written arguments went unheeded.

Luckily, Fritz had provided a special service to Mr. Lamy in the previous year. He had fired a foreman because he had stirred up his co-workers to complain about Lamy to the government inspector. The fired worker had then complained to the inspector that he had been robbed of any means of support and could not get another job because Lamy would give him a bad reference. The inspector requested 10,000 rubles from Lamy as compensation. If Lamy refused the inspector threatened to take steps to have him deported from Poland. The request and complaint had already been forwarded to the governor. Fritz borrowed legal papers from a friend who had sued another administrator. He copied that action and with the help of a notary from Lodz, counter charged, contradicting the charges made by the foreman point by point. The foreman was convicted of conspiracy and agitation of workers against plant management. Lamy was delighted and relieved. Fritz felt that Lamy now owed him a favor.

He took a chance and asked Lamy for a transfer into a family apartment. He told him that he had to get married because he had stomach ailments and that he had to have certain foods and simply needed to get married to keep his diet. In actuality, his stomach problems continued to plague him. After some grumbling, Lamy agreed to give him a small apartment in the director's house. It had four rooms and was freshly decorated. He really would have liked to have a year more to furnish the place before bringing Maria to Lodz, since he only had one bed, a wardrobe, a table and two chairs from the bachelor apartment, all provided by the plant. Hanna and Victor, he noted, had been engaged for two years before they were married and he and Maria had not even been engaged 18 months. He wrote to Maria suggesting that he order beds, which he could buy on credit but she wanted to help pick them out. Fritz had the banns read in the Lutheran Church in Lodz and then traveled to Riga at the end of June to talk to Pastor Hellmann.[71] Fritz borrowed 300 rubles from the plant office for the wedding; Maria sent several boxes with her dowry items to Lodz and the wedding was set for September 1, 1901.[72]

The wedding took place in the Jurgensen home. An altar was erected in the living room, Pastor Hellmann read the vows and then they all had dinner. The only people there were the Jurgensens, Cousin Felix and his wife, Ewald, and Esser, a friend from student days. A few of Victor's relatives were also invited. Around 6:00 PM the wedding couple changed into traveling cloths and left for the railway station. Several coaches had been ordered so that the whole wedding party could see them off.

The train was filled to capacity as they squeezed themselves with all their luggage and flowers, into a rather uncomfortable place. But soon the reaction to all the excitement took its toll. Maria went to sleep for six hours with her head on Fritz's shoulder. Around 2:00 AM the train made a stop and Fritz bought some ham sandwiches in the station. Rarely had a meal tasted so good. In the evening they arrived in Warsaw where they changed trains for Lodz. They arrived in Lodz at 5:00 AM, chilled to the bone after two days and nights on the train. Then

---

[71] Banns are customary in many Protestant and the Roman Catholic Church. They consist of a wedding announcement that is read or posted for three Sundays. The purpose is to give anyone who objects an opportunity to make his or her concerns known.
[72] Dowries were the norm up until the middle of the 20th Century. I even had dowry items that friends of my mothers gave to me when I was still a child. Girls had hope chests, which were large chests to be filled with these items; I did not have one, nor do I recall the dowry items except for nine silver spoons with my initials and some linen.

they took a coach to the Allart suburb where scores of factory sirens were whistling, and chimneys were billowing out black smoke. The streets were crawling with people going to work.

There was no friendly maid waiting for them at their apartment that was quite empty. However Fritz's colleagues had sent a bouquet of flowers, bread, sausage and butter with a touching greeting. Although they were exhausted from 48 hours without sleep they could not go to bed. It was broad daylight and the windows had no curtains. The bachelor bed was too narrow to hold the two of them. So Fritz changed his cloths and went to work while Maria tried to unpack some boxes and buy some food. And so began the honeymoon.

Bad news was waiting for Fritz at the plant. The main machinist had met with an untimely death; his body had been found, unexplained as yet, in the cellar of the machine house with a deep head wound. In his capacity as plant engineer and plant administrative director, Fritz had his hands full with all of the gruesome details and interviews. The government inspector, police, and coroner inquiries had to be taken care of. Officially the case was never solved. Everything pointed to homicide and much later it was proven. The man had apparently been killed by his co-workers in a fight.

For lunch that first day Maria surprised Fritz with "flicker-klops" which she prepared herself, and in the afternoon they went downtown to look for furniture.[73] They bought a bed, to be delivered the next day and a few other items. That evening, while cooking together Maria burned her hand on hot grease, and that night they both slept on the bachelor bed, even if it was very uncomfortable. The

---

[73] Flicker-klops was one of our favorite meals when we were children. It consisted of ground beef in brown gravy over mashed potatoes.

next day the furniture arrived and they hired a Polish girl to help Maria. Life began to regulate itself. However, there were some problems. It was customary and polite for directors of the plant and senior administration to conduct introductory visits within the first few weeks. But since Fritz and Maria did not have a decently furnished room to entertain people back, as was also customary, it took them until October before they could start visits. They started with Stefanus, Fritz's cousin and Ferdi and Hugo Warrikoff.[74] Unfortunately, Maria's visiting dress was caught in the coach and had a very bad blotch, which they could not remove. Therefore they had to postpone their visiting again. Later they heard that some people had taken offence.

In November they learned that Maria was pregnant. Fritz mused, "How often do we read in novels that the wife breaks the news to the husband with excited happiness, and the young mother is shown sewing baby clothes? How different real life most often is. The young couple knows that it is a risk for the wife, even with all the progress in hygiene and science, especially with the first child. So this becomes a time of tension; the wife feels more as if she were undergoing an operation." And in the Maehles case, finances were very limited. Fritz's thoughts were swirling. "Will it be a boy or girl; will it be healthy; will it be delivered correctly; is the mother built right? Will she be able to feed the child; what should she wear in pregnancy; what kind of baby clothes should they get?" And Maria was so terribly young and inexperienced. Finally they invested in a sewing machine for 80 rubles on installment. The first Christmas was very sad for Maria. It was her

---

[74] I remember this name from my childhood. The Warrikoffs were very close friends of my grandparents. Ferdi and Hugo were brothers. Stefanus was Fritz's cousin.

first time so far from home. She was living in a very small, plain apartment and had only a little tree in a flowerpot, while at the same time remembering and dwelling upon all the festivities she enjoyed at Christmas time at home. Furthermore, she feared all the new and unknown in this strange foreign city. She was sad that Fritz could not give her a gift — even a small one. She cried and cried. Fritz had already gone through all these emotions when he was 15 and had not had a real Christmas with his family since he was 20. He was really happy with the first tiny tree in "our own home."

In 1902 the work at the plant became more interesting and more demanding. His wages were also increased, and in the spring he received a nice bonus. Maria's condition hindered their social life and they only saw the Stefanus and the Warrikoffs. Hedwig married Van Dahm in April but since Maria was already six months pregnant they stayed in Lodz. Mama and Papa Jurgensen had the satisfaction of knowing that they had married off all three of their girls in one year: Hanna in March 1901, Maria in September 1901 and Hedwig in April 1902.

And so they concentrated on the arrival of their first child. Maria consulted with her doctor and had her questions answered. But she also became extremely nervous and irritable. She developed migraine headaches and weird appetites. Mama Jurgensen arrived in mid-June, as that is when the doctor predicted the birth, but nothing happened. Mama became very irritable and treated them as if they had miscalculated the date on purpose. Finally on July 11, Heddy made her debut, about four weeks late, a very tiny thing with a wrinkled face, large nose, a rather big mouth and dark strong hair. The birth was very smooth. The midwife did not even have to consult with the doctor. And then Mama began to act very strangely. She did not want Maria to stay in bed, as was customary after delivery; the maid could not do anything right and there was always fighting going on. Maria wanted to breast feed Heddy but her breasts were getting very sore. Mama explained that breast feeding was a terribly bad habit and that young women of today were simply not able to do it right.[75] One morning Fritz awoke early to see Maria sitting up in bed with her breasts bound very tightly. Mama triumphantly explained the baby would have to be fed with a special apparatus while little Heddy lay in her crib screaming her head off because she was hungry. So at 6:00 AM Fritz traipsed up to the pharmacy, pulled the pharmacist out of bed and bought an apparatus. That very same day Mama fired the midwife and was so nasty to the maid that she quit. A letter that morning from Papa Jurgensen seemed to make Mama more excited than ever. She announced that Maria should get out of bed or she would become lazy. And with that she packed her bags and left for Riga. And there were the young Maehles, the daughter out of bed, the midwife fired and the maid gone — six days after the birth. Fritz wrote that what she did was neither moral nor normal and he never again had the same respect for her. He also noted that in all the years that followed he never heard of a mother treating her daughter like that. Perhaps Papa was at the root of all this behavior. He was having trouble in his business again and — he wanted to move again.

The results of Mama's behavior became clear soon enough. Although they quickly found help, that summer was warm and wet and the milk turned sour very quickly in the apparatus. One day Heddy needed

---

[75] This thinking began in the late 19th Century and was prevalent until into the 1960s when I had my children. Heddy stated that breast-feeding was barbaric and nurses available to help young mothers in the hospital get started were almost nonexistent.

milk and the new maid did not know the supplier. So Maria left Heddy with the maid and ran more than two km to buy it. Heddy was eight days old.[76] On the way home, a storm broke out and Maria was drenched. When she got home she had to go to bed immediately as she started to hemorrhage. So at last, the doctor was called. He found that Maria had been torn quite badly during the delivery and then had not been properly attended to. He prescribed bed rest, which resulted in Maria taking it easy for almost three months. Finally in August, Heddy was christened with the Warrikoffs and Stefanus serving as godparents.

Meanwhile, Allart needed a chemist (a person who chemically mixes dyes). They tried to hire a foreigner but the government inspector would only give official permission for a domestic chemist. Fritz wrote to several friends about the position and finally found an old friend from Reval whom Allart hired as an assistant chemist. He was engaged to a Riga girl who came with him, so Maria was very happy to have another person from the Baltic area for company. Fritz also noted that during this time he acquired a new assistant from France and his French became remarkably better. At the same time, Fritz's brother Oskar went to Friedberg, Germany to study machine engineering, Hermann finished at the Gymnasium and moved to Dorpat to study Theology and Ewald was still studying in Riga.

In the summer (1902) there was a big fight between Fritz's Cousin Felix, and his siblings concerning looking after their mother, Great Aunt Sophie. Somehow Fritz was dragged into the quarrel as, prior to Felix's marriage to Sofie Buhle, Johanna,

---

[76] In those days women were not expected to recover from childbirth quickly and they didn't. Six weeks was not a long recovery period. But even today, this would be crazy.

Felix's sister, had inquired from Fritz about the bride's family background and appearance. At first Fritz did not respond to her questions but finally, after Johanna promised confidentiality he wrote that the young lady had a good four year education as most Lodz girls do, but her grammar was not good which, he noted, was applicable to almost all the people he had met at that time in Lodz. Otherwise, she was well trained in homemaking and was a pretty girl coming from an old Lodz family. Apparently, Johanna did not keep her word and during the family quarrel, one of the other sisters had repeated to Felix what Fritz had written. Understandably Felix was furious. Although no one mentioned anything about this to Fritz, two years later it came back to haunt him. Meanwhile, Felix went to Southern Russia to become a director in a coal mine.

As the next few years passed, Fritz became confident and secure in his work. His wages continued to increase and he received a bonus every year. Heddy, a very lively child, prospered and showed a strong will of her own. Towards the end of 1903, Maria became pregnant again but had an early miscarriage. According to Fritz, her body had not sufficiently healed from the first pregnancy. She often had migraine headaches and looked rather pale. She had put on weight, which she tried to loose, by taking a drug, which not only didn't help but also had adverse side effects. Her monthly periods were irregular and long, and she became irritable, nervous and sharp. Happily for Fritz and with his help, Ewald got a summer job at the railway in Lodz and moved in with Fritz and Maria.

During this period a small group of engineers and technicians with German backgrounds or speaking German, all working in the large industrial plants in Lodz formed a social group. They had soirees, picnics and outings, both with and without their wives. Over the years the group grew from the original six to 15 to 20 gentlemen and their families. This became the Maehles' primary social life until the start of WW I.[77] During the Christmas of 1903 Hugo Warrikoff gave a "Baltic Evening" in the Mateuffel Hotel. Maria bought her first elegant dress since their marriage. It was a thrilling evening for her and Wanda Warrikoff as they were the only two women at the ball.[78] They danced and danced with all the gentlemen. In fact, Fritz wrote, a gentleman named Mr. Pfaff, whom Fritz had met many years ago at his uncle's home in Reval, seemed to pay particular attention to Maria.

The Maehles were becoming comfortably situated in Lodz. They were part of a socially accepted crowd, something that meant a great deal to both of them. They enjoyed entertaining and being entertained. Then suddenly a dark cloud appeared and before they became aware of it, they were in the middle of an historic event, which created tremendous changes. Fritz wrote, "The whole world was in an upheaval. It gave life new meaning, and I probably will never witness a calm time in my life again."

With the building of the Trans-Siberian Railroad from the Ural Mountains (the western border between western Russia and Siberia) to the Pacific, Russia's interest in the Far East was greatly increased. Port Arthur on the Pacific had been occupied by Russia during the Boer War (1899-1902). The British did not like it but could not give attention to the Russians at that time. So they made a pact with Japan who did not want Russian power

---

[77] Fritz wrote that as he wrote this in 1933, only 4 or 5 including he and his brother, Oskar, who had moved to Lodz later on, were still alive.

[78] One wonders what kind of a ball this was with only two women in attendance.

at their doorstep. Russia began filling Port Arthur with regiments of soldiers until it began to look like an important sea fortress. Russian officers were requesting transfer to the Far East as they expected serious action there and they could advance in ranks much faster on the front. One day Fritz had to travel to Petrokow on business. The train was filled with Russian officers, talking about nothing else but the Far East. He saw men with huge Siberian pelt caps, called *popachi,* who conveyed a very warlike impression. They called the Japanese "yellow faces" and "Makaki Apes" whom they would soon cover with their *popachi* caps. The very afternoon that Fritz returned, there were newsboys in the station shouting the news that the Japanese had attacked Port Arthur with torpedo boats. Suddenly there was war. There was the usual military call up, which primarily affected young men. Fritz was at the end of his 13th year in the reserves and in his opinion felt it was completely out of the question that he would be called.

    At first everyone took little interest in the situation. All were convinced that great Russia could easily defeat Japan, and for months little was heard about any war activities in a theater that was 8000 km from Petersburg. Half a year later the Japanese attack would have been impossible. But, Port Arthur was still only half completed, and only one track of the rail line was useable. And, Russia's Eastern-Asiatic Army was still in a state of formation. Japan, who had started the conflict, knew exactly what she was doing. She landed many troops using "bullet spitter" weapons (an early automatic rifle), which Russia lacked. She also had excellent artillery and well trained soldiers. Russia was severely beaten in the first battle and in the subsequent two; Port Arthur was completely cut off. It was under siege. The Russians began retreating.

Life in Lodz continued uninterrupted. Business was at an all time high; the war brought money into people's hands and Fritz's income went up. He was suddenly able to open a savings account. Ferdi Warrikoff suggested he invest his money somewhere else but he declined. One of Fritz's Baltic colleagues, Gottfried Wieckmann was having trouble adjusting into life at the plant in Lodz. Finally Maria took pity on him and he became a regular at their dinner table. Meanwhile, Maria's health, which had been very poor since Heddy's birth, continued to deteriorate. Sometimes her periods lasted for two weeks and other months she had none. This condition would have been difficult for even the most placid soul. But Maria was very impulsive and high strung. She became more and more irritable and explosive, leaving her mark on the entire household. Harmony in their lives was often disrupted. Finding the Lodz doctors unable to treat her, she wanted to go to her doctor in Riga. As Fritz's parents had never met Maria or Heddy, Fritz decided in May 1904, that this would be a good time to send them to the Baltic for a visit.

Maria's memories of the visit were not good. Her mother was irritable and as Heddy was a very lively child, she was constantly reprimanding her. The Riga doctor prescribed mud baths and glycerin tampons. Since she could obtain these treatments in Dago, she left Riga for the island in the middle of June. In late July Fritz followed. On his way over he visited the Jurgensens at their beach house on the Baltic near Riga. Hanna and Victor were also visiting. He arrived in Dago on Maria's birthday to find her looking well and rested. Obviously the mud baths and therapy had helped. Nikolaus had just turned 60 and looked very distinguished. Kersti was overjoyed to see her son whom she had not seen in six years!

They caught up on the family news. Cousin Felix had become a manager in a lumber exporting firm in Narva, Estonia. Hermann was a theological student, then studying the Greek Bible. Rudolf and Betty, who were in business with Nikolaus, were fine. Oskar was studying in Germany and Ewald was in southern Livland, now Latvia, building bridges. Fritz wrote:

> This vacation was one of the few bright spots in my life. I was healthy, 33 years old; Maria was 23 and Heddy 3. I had a position that was enviable, even by Riga standards, and which looked even more promising for the future. Papa did not seem to have any great problems and if he did, he seemed to be keeping them under control. I had not seen Maria for 2 months and our happiness was great. We enjoyed the free life at my parents to the fullest and called this our honeymoon, since we could not have called our trip from Riga to Lodz that. Heddy was speaking only Estonian and had completely forgotten me which was rather upsetting for her when a strange man came and kissed her mommy.

Everything would have been wonderful — if it had not been for the war. Fritz had a bad premonition just as he would later have about WW I. He could feel the silence before the storm of the political structure of Russia. He wrote:

> The rumors were manifold: unrest and protectionism in the army, insufficient provisions, obsolete and antiquated war techniques, underhanded plotting and constant retreats. The language in the newspapers was very open and stormy; the internal situation seemed to be heading for a

crisis. The extremist parties were exploiting the situation while we, the peaceful population, had no idea that we were sitting on a volcano. Suddenly like lightning, the situation was illuminated. On the day of my arrival in Dago the Minister of the Interior was assassinated. The government still held the belief that the three main supporting columns of the state — the Czar, Autocratic Absolutism, and the Orthodox Church would hold things together.

It was hoped that the birth of a successor to the thrown would bring order to Russia. He was actually born the day Fritz and family left Dago, September 12, 1904. Later on it was discovered that he suffered from hemophilia. This of course, was the reason for the unhealthy influence of Rasputin and the tragic end of the Romanov dynasty. But neither the long awaited prince nor the pictures of the Saints which were sent by carload to the frontier could save the situation. Russia was sick. Everyone who read the newspapers could see the accusing and demonizing literature of the last decade. And who had not observed the ever-increasing subversive activities of the radicals? Catastrophe was coming closer, and Russia was fast loosing ground against the Japanese. The war had taken many lives. The mood of the population was sober and nobody believed in victory; and nobody volunteered for military service any more.

The Maehles returned to Lodz on September 17, and were greeted by their maid, Karola[79] who had already been with them a year. But the situation

---

[79] Karola was their housekeeper and cook for many years. Heddy spoke very fondly of her. Indeed she seems to have been a great influence on her life and a strong mother substitute.

looked ominous for Fritz. More and more older reservists were being called and since his time for the reserves came to an end on September 1, he went to the office of the Lodz Military Command Post and asked to be transferred to the conscripted militia.[80] He was told that during a war nobody would be transferred from the reserves to the militia, and two months later on November 9, he received his notice to report for active duty. What a blow! If he had been single he might have welcomed a trip to the Far East but in his situation now, it was bad.

Should he send Maria and Heddy to Riga? If he were sent to the east they could not remain in Lodz alone. Military cloths had to be bought and they were expensive. The government subsidy was small and he had not had a chance to save much money. And what about his job? Fortunately the officers of the Reserve, all 30 men, were first stationed in Lodz. The firm would not let him go as long as he was in Lodz, and he could keep his apartment and wages. So after he finished his daily military duties he went into the plant and looked after his job as much as possible. But the uncertainty was nerve wracking and almost unbearable for Maria. Again, she became nervous and irritable which, he noted, was no surprise.

One day the men were ordered into the Casino. Eleven officers were to be sent to the front. Tickets were drawn. Fritz's was blank. He was spared this time. This was to be repeated every few weeks until finally, in the summer of 1905, Fritz was called. By this time both Maria and Fritz were at wits end. The unrest was heating up. More and more posters *Long Live the Revolution* and *Away with the Czarists* were going up. This was unheard of in Russia. It was becoming very serious. During the Christmas of

---

[80] This seems to mean some kind of non-combatant status as Fritz used it to get a lesser post than reservist who could go on active duty.

1904, while Fritz was on duty at the railroad station where trains were full of reservists passing through, one of them was almost blown off the tracks by a bomb, which was discovered just in time. The older officers in the regiment blamed the Japanese and the Jews, who were vigorously seeing freedom in a repressive Russian regime. Meanwhile the Japanese were still active in the Far East.

On January 2, 1905, after a brave defense, Port Arthur was taken. Nevertheless, and seemingly for face saving reasons, the government continued to promise the population a victory. They talked about bringing the Russian fleet, which was then in the Baltic Sea, around Africa to continue the fight, perhaps by the following summer. However, discontent mounted all over Russia. A terrible wave of strikes started in St. Petersburg with demonstrations and murders. A priest, it was later to be revealed, was an agent and provocateur of the Government, led a demonstration crowd to the Winter Palace. The guards opened fire into the mob only to learn that they wanted to give a petition to the Czar. Screams of indignation resounded through Russia. The press became threatening and revolutionary. And the restlessness grew. For example, during the annual "Blessing of the Waters," which was traditionally done from ships in the Newa River and to which the Czar and his whole family came, a salute was fired by the military. That time, they loaded the cannons with live ammunition and the Czar's family was almost hit.

The wave of unrest also reached Lodz. In the beginning of February, all factories were still operating full steam when policemen were attacked and killed. District supervisors and workers started to attack hated foremen, directors and manufacturers. People who wanted to work were threatened. As strikes were always prohibited by the government, manufacturers asked logically for government protection. It fell upon the officers and their troops to protect the factories, police stations and civil administration buildings. Fritz was on duty night and day. Most often he slept in full alert positions at the barracks or in the casino, which had been commandeered for the military headquarters. Sometimes his orderly carried mattresses and pillows between his apartment and the place where he was supposed to be when he was "off duty" but still on alert. Maria would not see him for days. His patrols often involved shooting fights, which took their toll. He was announced dead several times and Maria was running between the apartment and the telephone in the plant to find out about him. To top it all off, his personal situation was impossible. A Russian officer had to lead his troops into combat and could be forced to fire on people. And the factory engineer had to protect the interest of the very same people he was challenging. Fritz began to get threatening letters and even death threats. He was called the Moscowitz Officer and told that he was on the black list. Maria read all these letters. No one felt safe.

On March 4th the Grand Duke Serjey was murdered in Moscow. He was a very reactionary soldier, known for his iron will. He had also been Governor General of Moscow. This was a terrible blow and the government tried to make concessions. A meeting was called of all the manufacturers in Lodz. Fritz represented Allart in his officer's uniform. The government decried the situation and implied that the strikes had only happened for economic reasons, while everyone present knew that they were political. But the orders from Petersburg were to calm down the masses; the employers had to grant a 10% increase in wages. The right to strike had been officially sanctioned. And after a standstill of four weeks, Lodz industry started to move again.

This was the first break-through in the wall of the old order, and this first freedom was used arbitrarily from then on. It was apparent that the government was insecure and ready to make concessions. An edict was proclaimed which stated in somewhat general terms that reforms had become necessary. It was very fuzzy and not satisfactory to anybody. Criticism grew louder and when, on March 26th, a huge battle (of Muckden) was lost and Russian troops were forced to withdraw, indignation grew higher and higher.

Despite all this, Fritz received good wages and a good bonus and was even able to save money, for which he and Maria were very grateful. And then an unexpected surprise! They learned that they would welcome a new member to their family in early 1906. Maria's nervousness increased. Fritz anticipated a rough time ahead. His only hope was that the reforms would bring peace and calm. But they would have to go through a lot before that came to pass.

In May the government formed a Duma, an advisory body to the government, which had representation from all segments of society. It was supposed to address freedom of religion, the press etc. Although not a constitutional body it was a first step. Meanwhile the Navy was still on its way from the Baltic Sea to the Sea of Japan, and the Army, even after so many losses, was still hanging on. If only the Navy could have a victory over the Japanese, everything would be right again. Unhappily, on June 14th the Russian fleet was completely devastated. Russia had lost. Conditions of peace were discussed, but Russia would not agree to any of Japan's demands. So Russia continued to arm herself. More troops were dispatched to the Far East. But they were unsuccessful in breaking the Japanese hold.

Meanwhile, the reformers continued their pressure. Fritz believed that this was the time when the government could have put down the insurrection through government force. But by early summer the revolutionaries' resistance became more widespread and violent, with clashes in Petersburg, Odessa, and Moscow. Barricades were erected in the streets; battles erupted and, even in Lodz, there was open fighting in the streets. July 9th and 10th became known as Bloody Wednesday and Thursday in Lodz. There were many dead and the funeral for those demonstrators who died was planned as a large political rally. The police intervened; they buried the dead during the night and nobody knew about it. But demonstrations continued. On Corpus Christi Day, a huge religious parade formed on Petrikowa Street, one of the main avenues in Lodz. This was, in fact, the first time the government had allowed such a parade to take place. As it moved along more and more people joined it. The police, not quite used to parades of a religious kind, noticed only too late that it was not usual for church processions to carry red flags and guns. The police administrator was called. He gave the alarm to a platoon of soldiers stationed at one of the plants in the city. (By this time every plant had a security group stationed on its grounds.) The soldiers raced to the parade and ordered the people to break up. The response was shouting and shooting. The soldiers fired into the air. Everybody raced around panic stricken. Chaos ensued. The next morning barricades were erected on all streets leading into Petrikowa. When Fritz's company returned from guarding a plant, one of the soldiers kicked some barricades aside. His act was answered by gunfire from the houses. That was enough. The soldiers immediately went into battle position. Soon there was shooting into the houses and from the houses. In less than half an hour all the military stationed in Lodz was racing through the streets and in no time the streets became empty. The city was like dead, remaining that way for the next few days.

Before long there were agitators within the military ranks as well. Officers were scarce as most were fighting in the Far East, as were all the well-trained young soldiers. Fritz noted that most of the few officers were guarding the plants with groups of only ten soldiers. The replacements that had been sent to Lodz were bearded workers and farmers many of whom were also revolutionaries. And they refused to take orders, even to eat. Some of the disliked corporals were openly threatened and before the public ever heard about it, Fritz and his regiment was moved to Raducz, a three day march from Lodz. This was a very anxious time for Fritz. He was more needed in the plant than ever. The workers' well being was of great importance and his role as the Plant Inspector was vital to keeping them contented and dissuading them from joining the radical forces everywhere around. But, as he calculated, "At least it was not the Far East." So he left Lodz, putting Maria and Heddy in Karola's capable hands with orders that Maria should get plenty of exercise and fresh air. After all the excitement, threatening letters, restless nights, and being shot at, life in camp seemed like a vacation.

About ten days into his camp experience, Fritz met an old friend on the way home from some strenuous exercises. He was all excited, "Have you heard the great news?" "What? What are you talking about?" asked Fritz. "We just received a telegram from the staff in Warsaw that we — all of the officers in the reserve — are to be transferred to the war theater in a few days. The war is still going strong! Won't that be great fun!!?" Fritz felt weak in the knees. He was in a desperate situation — a sickly wife with a four year old child and four months pregnant with another, only 950 rubles in the bank and some lingering debts with the company who had advanced him money. What to do? How to inform Maria? The excitement could have grave consequences for her health.

Back at camp Fritz spotted two women on Lt. Foester's porch. One woman was Foester's wife who had accompanied him to camp and the other was — Maria — pale, with dark circles under her eyes, her hair in disarray and in a navy maternity dress he had not seen before. Actually, she looked like a stranger to him. What was she doing at camp? Fritz tried to look into her eyes. She had a strange expression, almost haunted and fearful. Had something happened to the baby — to Heddy? Was there bad news from either set of their parents? When Mrs. Foester left, Maria burst out a rather incoherent and confused diatribe that Miss Lang had insulted her terribly and that Mrs. Vaillet had started a terrible rumor about her. She carried on about Bedonk, Andrzejow, Karola and Mr. Pfaff, who had only accompanied her home from the station and about the Foremens' house and Helenhof and on and on. It took some time until he could begin to understand something of what was going on. He was beginning to wonder if she was physically ill, or a mental case.

"Now," he wrote, "I write this down as an older man, writing in 1933, and think back to this time, almost a generation ago. Those things, which seemed so terrible and cost us so much anxiety and pain have become laughable and hardly worth mentioning. But 30 years ago, a young woman could not receive a gentleman alone in her home without qualms; could not travel with a good friend, and could not stay overnight any place she wanted to without notice as she can in the 1930s." As he wrote he realized that today no one would even understand the problem they had had back then; that it was possible to declare a young woman a social outcast and ban her because she had been seen in the company of a man who walked with her, the nursemaid and her child when they came home from the station at 10 PM one evening and then stepped into her home for a cigarette — all while the husband was away.

Fritz and Maria had met Pfaff at one of their Baltic evenings when Wanda and Maria were the only two women at the ball. Later the Maehle's had invited him and one of his friends to their home for tea. He recalled that Pfaff was very attentive to Maria that afternoon, and often popped up out of nowhere to join them when they went on one of their outings to Helenhof or Manteuffel, popular beer gardens in Lodz. They were two places that young people, including the Maehles, frequented. There were no parks in the city and these became the places to socialize and relax. Pfaff and his friend also seemed to show up when Maria went to town for the afternoon to accompany her home safely, and if someone went for a walk, it was often possible to see Maria and Pfaff together.

As with the previous pregnancy, Maria suffered from migraine headaches and was constantly going around as if in a trance. Often one would think that she did not perceive what was going on around her. She had an expression on her face that frightened Fritz. He sometimes had the terrible feeling that she had a great big bone in her forehead! He had therefore emphasized that she should go for long walks and get lots of exercise. She had complied, and on the first Sunday after Fritz left for camp she had taken Karola and Heddy to Helenhof. They walked around and showed Heddy the animals that were kept there and then sat down for coffee. All of Lodz, as usual, was there. She noticed administrators for Allart, and many other people she knew. Soon Pfaff and his friend arrived and asked if they could sit at their table. At 8 PM Maria, Karola and Heddy left.

The next day the entire "Baltic colony" was talking about it. "The husband is scarcely gone when the wife finds young men to entertain her." But it got worse. Every Wednesday a concert was held in Meisterhaus Garden. She was invited to go with some friends. As they were sitting at their table the two young men came along and invited Maria to have a walk around the garden with them — which she did. She then returned to her friends. Soon Pfaff reappeared and asked Maria for another walk around the garden. When she returned to her table her friends had left. Fritz asked how they could have left a young woman alone with young men at a restaurant. Perhaps they had already heard rumors about her and did not want to be involved. In any case, Maria was forced to take a cab home; Pfaff and his friend accompanied her. Meanwhile, of course, the colony was watching behind their curtains. Who was going to accompany "Mrs. Engineer Maehle" home this time? The men walked her to her door, immediately returned to the cab and departed. The colony felt it had something to talk about and it did.

The grand finale came when Karola suggested the next Sunday that they should go out of town to visit with her relatives in Badon, a nearby village. She thought it would be good for Maria and Heddy to spend a day in the country where they would have a lovely meal and fine hiking in the forest. In the evening they returned to Lodz by train. The train was filled with excursionists coming back from their Sunday trips. And who should appear again but Pfaff and his friend. When they arrived in Lodz the train station was unusually quiet because there had been a demonstration in the afternoon and shots had been fired. The streets were also deserted. The young men managed to find Maria a cab. Pfaff accompanied Maria, Heddy and Karola home, while his friend took his girl friend home. They arrived at 10 PM. Heddy had fallen asleep and Pfaff carried her in. He stayed for a cigarette while Karola put Heddy to bed. He then left. Everyone knew that Maria, Heddy and their maid had been away all day and they were waiting by their windows to see with whom she would return this time.

The next day Miss Lamy and Mrs. Baillet were sitting on Lamy's porch when Maria approached, as she often did, to sit with them. As she came up the steps with "Bonjour Mesdames," an icy silence greeted her. Finally Miss Lamy explained to her that they could not have anything to do with her. Maria was shocked and asked to have an explanation. So they explained to her that with her husband away she received night visits from a gentleman. She finally understood that they have misinterpreted her walks and the solicitous behavior of these young men in quite the wrong light. Maria was furious with herself for being so naive and very angry with these people for their spying and suspicions. She left the porch immediately and went straight to Ferdi Warrikoff where she completely broke down. Ferdi decided that the only thing that Maria could do was to go straight to her husband and tell him all this before he heard it from a third party. Maria left immediately.

"Good God," thought Fritz, "this is all I need now!" He was very unhappy with the situation and on top of that he had to tell Maria that in a few days he would have to leave for the Far East. There are moments in everyone's life when it seems as if the whole world will collapse. This was it for Fritz. What could he do? Maria could not remain in the Allart[81] apartmen with him departing into the war somewhere. As long as he was in the Lodz area, camp could be counted as vacation, but once he left for the East his job at Allart's would end. Companies did not pay their employees for fighting in a war. Where would Maria live? And what would she live on?

They went for a long walk. He had to sort the mess out. On the one hand he could not absolve Maria from having shown a certain thoughtlessness and indiscretion. They were not in the Baltic where they were used to unaffected camaraderie between young people. They were in Lodz with an uneducated or worse, semi-educated society. People were often coarse, even in front of ladies, and they gossiped mercilessly and Maria knew this very well. Fritz was convinced that she behaved badly because of the pressure she was under, her nervous condition, and her headaches. But she was seriously insulted which she did not deserve. Her name and reputation should be restored. She deserved an apology, at least from Miss Lamy. The thought of going to court for slander was out of the question. He was going to the front, perhaps in days and by the time a case got to court, Maria would be seven or eight months pregnant. And she was in no frame of mind, under the best of circumstances, to undergo such a trauma. First and foremost, they had to think of Heddy and the unborn baby. That was much more important than the silly gossiping women.

---

[81] The housing was located in a suburban section of Lodz named Widzew. It was founded by the Widzener factory where Fritz was to be employed one day. Fritz lived in a nice apartment at this time and over the years, as his status at Allart's grew, upgraded to more substantial homes. Since most of the mills were in the same area, there were employees from other companies on the same street as the one the Maehles occupied.

Fritz felt extremely sorry for Maria. She would look at him from time to time like a child, trying to figure out what was going on and how all of this had started. She was such a sad sight. Fritz went to the commander to ask for a furlough, which was everyone's right before leaving for the front. Fritz told him that his wife was pregnant, that they had a three-year-old child, were relative newcomers to the Lodz area, and he would like to take his wife to Riga to be with her family. The leave was granted and that night Maria slept peacefully; Fritz did not. He was troubled by the complex state of affairs of his little family.

The next day they returned to Lodz. As they came to their home Mrs. Baillet opened her door and poked her nose out. Maria, seeing this, lost all control and shrieked, "Voila Madame! Aujourdhui vos efforts sont en vain. Je suis avec mon mari!"[82] Mrs. Baillet shot back and slammed the door. A short while later the Warrikoffs arrived. They were rather upset about the impertinence of the "Alsatian French."[83] They urged Fritz to take legal action. But Fritz informed them of his orders to the front and about the necessity to send Maria to Riga and of course, the end of his employment with Allart. They all agreed that there could not be a formal complaint without the accusing party present. But a personal apology was in order and therefore it would be better at this time if there were no mention of the orders. Nevertheless, they had to be prepared for a court action if they did not apologize. Hugo Warrikoff immediately returned to the office to tell everybody that Fritz was preparing to take legal action if an

---

[82] Look here madam. Today your efforts are in vain as I am with my husband.
[83] This is a reference to Alsace Lorraine an area between France and Germany.

apology was not forthcoming since it was a fact that Karola was with Maria the whole time.

Fritz went to Lamy's home since his sister seemed to be the originator of the whole affair. She did not appear but he received Fritz in a rather stiff manner and told him that he personally did not know anything, had only heard about it from his sister, and he had told her not to associate with Mrs. Maehle until the situation was cleared up. Fritz replied that the courts would take care of that. He had come to find out about the name of the person who had reported this gossip to his sister. He, of course, did not know. Fritz replied that the court would ferret it all out and that he would start with his sister's insult to Maria. Further, he noted that Karola, their maid was always with Maria and was a witness. She, he added, was a respected widow with grown children. Fritz stated that the young man mentioned in connection with Maria was a countryman whom Fritz had known since he was eight years old.[84] He would also be a witness in the case and would be very interested in seeing slanderers brought to justice. Lamy was flushed. "Wait! Let me talk to my sister. Don't do anything in haste." He ran out of the room, returning shortly. His sister did not know anything about the matter. She had only heard it from the Baillets. He suggested that Fritz see them. Surely they would have answers. He then added that, of course, his sister felt very badly and would try to make up for the incident and would apologize, especially since it was idle gossip and extremely thoughtless.

So Firtz went to see the Baillets. Mrs. B. had gone into hiding but the old Frenchman was there, red faced from his weekend wine. Fritz told him

---

[84] A huge exaggeration.

about the slanderous remarks his wife had made and that he was inclined to go to court. He also told him that Mr. Lamy had said that it started with Mrs. Baillet. The old gentleman stared at Fritz out of his bloodshot eyes, half angry and half shocked. It was all nothing. His wife, he reported, had seen Maria come home with a gentleman a few days ago and go into her house with her. Nothing more. Fritz noted that if she had prolonged her spying a bit more she would have seen Karola let the gentleman out of the house after a few minutes and he added that Karola's statement under oath would have grave consequences for the originator of these stories.

The old gentleman jumped up and ran out of the room blustering "Court! Witness! Oath! God damn women and their gossip!" Then he turned. "But all that does not give your wife the right to scream at my wife when she is standing in front of her own door!" Fritz replied, "If your wife had not been on the same lookout three days ago, we would not be having this conversation now." Baillet turned and shouted, "Really, do you think so? If you want to stir up dirt and you want to go to court, then go to Mr. Sartore. He is the one who will tell you the name of the guilty party. I don't want to have anything to do with this matter anymore!"

Fritz left. "When you mention the courts, the buck suddenly is passed on to the next gossip," he thought. Sartore lived a few houses down the street but he was not home. As Fritz returned to his apartment he saw Mr. Schapp, the man who left Maria in the beer garden after her second walk with Pfaff approaching. Fritz bellowed at him, "Well, you're a nice neighbor and colleague, first you make a date with my wife to take her to the garden and then you leave without her." To which Schapp responded, "I told her we were leaving but she did not want to go yet." Fritz replied, "Isn't it strange that twenty minutes after you came home she did too?" And again he threatened legal proceedings. Mr. Schapp departed without a word. Mr. Rosenbaum, who was just returning from a walk, came upon the interchange. When Schapp left, Rosenbaum saw that Fritz was very upset and urged him to calm down. "The whole thing is not worth such anger. You are not the first and would not be the last husband whose wife became the subject of idle gossip." He pointed out that if his wife were old and ugly, no one would notice her but she, being young and pretty, attracts attention. He urged that Fritz not blow this matter out of proportion. It seemed to him that the whole matter was one of idle gossip on the one hand and malice on the other.

And then Sartore appeared descending from a cab. Fritz followed him into his apartment. Fritz explained that he had been sent from Lamy to Baillet to him and he would really like to know who started the stories about his wife. Sartore looked at Fritz with malice and hostility. Anticipating this might happen, he stated that he had written everything down. And with that he took out his pocket calendar and started reading. "Sunday at Helenhof — Maria sat at the table with the said gentleman." Fritz replied that this was not accurate, "The gentleman sat at the table with Karola, Heddy and Maria." Sartore cleared his throat and read again, "Wednesday in the Meisterhaus Garden she was sitting with said gentleman at the same table. He accompanied her home at 10 PM." "Wrong again," Fritz pointed out, "She was in the company of the Schapps. This did not prevent her from walking with other people and when the Schapps party left, the gentleman," whom Fritz again noted he had known since he was a young boy, "was gracious enough to escort Maria, Karola and Heddy home." And then Sartore presented his trump card, "On the following Sunday evening the said young man accompanied her home and entered her home with her and," he stated, "I will swear to everything I have just said." Fritz retorted explaining what had actually happened as reported to him by Maria and added, "Where my wife is with her maid and child is nobody's business and my housekeeper is a witness to all of your carefully noted incidents. The young gentleman will be delighted to serve as a witness under oath. You will be a defendant, not a witness. The court does not care what you have written down. In our country (Sartore was from France), only what you have seen is of importance and according to our Russian laws, slander is punishable with prison." Sartore turned red. He had never thought the matter through — he was a foreigner against the wife of a Russian officer in a Russian court! And so began another referral — to Stefanus who was talking about Maria. Sartore had no responsibility in this matter and only started talking after he heard it from Stefanus, a good friend of Fritz's. Perhaps he should go and talk to Stefanus.

Fritz was left in a conundrum. He was being sent from pillar to post and no one was responsible for anything. What had Stefanus to do with Miss Lamy's insolence and Sartore's gossip? Was he in a nuthouse or was he going mad himself? He had to get to the bottom of this mystery. He and Maria had always been very close to Stefanus and his wife. In fact, they were Heddy's Godparents. He returned home exhausted. Maria had been crying and was having another headache. Fritz's eyes were burning from sleeplessness and his head hurt. He tried to sleep but could not find any rest and only dozed on and off.

The next morning he paid a call on Stefanus at his office. When he arrived there was a cab waiting. Stefanus was about to leave the office, carrying a small bag. He told Fritz that he knew that he was coming and that he was in a hurry to pick up his wife and they would be going away for a while and would see him when they returned. He seemed scared. Fritz replied that since he knew what this was about and since Sartore had told him to see Stefanus, before he went to court, would he like to tell him anything at this time?

Good Lord no! What would I know? I only heard some gossip at Allart and I saw your wife sitting at Helenhof with two strange gentlemen whom I had never seen in your house. And I thought that it might be a good idea to see you about this and that your wife might unknowingly be creating a scandal for herself, but this is an embarrassing situation and now you are here in person. I think that since you are going to the front it would be best for your wife to go to Riga. Lodz is in turmoil and is probably going to get worse so that would be the safest thing. And now I must go and pick up my wife.

And with that Stefanus pushed his way out of the office and got into the cab. Fritz was thoroughly confused. What was going on?

On his way to Allart he met Warrikoff and told him about his conversations ending with Stefanus. Warrikoff was enraged, "What a pig Stefanus is! He was engaged in a whispering conversation with Sartore on the Monday morning after Maria was seen in Helenhof. It is quite clear that it all started with him. Sure Stefanus started it all and sure everyone will believe something if it is told by a close friend of the family. Sartore simply didn't want to tell you straight out," Warrikoff stated. Warrikoff seemed to be correct. But why would Stefanus want to do something like that to him and Maria? What had they done to him? Fritz returned home confused. Maria was packing, looking pale and frightened. He told her about Stefanus and Warrikoff's suspicion. Maria was wild. "Stefanus, that old pig! It was quite clear that this all started with him," she cried.

And then she told Fritz that he had been after her on several occasions and was now afraid that his wife would find out. The climax was three weeks ago. Mrs. Stefanus had asked Maria to come over and make some jam for her. She was going out but the maid knew where everything was. Mr. Stefanus was home and at noon a visitor arrived and the maid prepared lunch for them. They were drinking a lot of brandy. At one point they called Maria in and asked her to eat something with them. She ate and returned to the kitchen. The visitor left and Mr. Stefanus came into the kitchen and became crude. Maria left immediately. Now, she felt, he was afraid she would say something to his wife. Fritz couldn't believe what he was hearing. One of his oldest friends! How could this be? He was dumbfounded. And why had Maria waited three weeks to tell him? Maria had little to say. She had not told him, she supposed, because he was such an old friend and this revelation would come as a clash between Stefanus and Fritz. They were their only close friends in Lodz and Heddy's Godparents. Fritz was exasperated. A nagging thought returned — this was all part of a nut-house scene. He immediately took Maria to Lamy's where Miss Lamy apologized and wished her a good trip to Riga. The following day they were on a fast train for Riga. Warrikoff was instructed to close up the apartment and sell the furniture. And so *fini* he thought. This chapter of Lodz was over and the future was a large dark and indefinite question mark.

He dropped Maria off in Riga and immediately returned to camp. Maria would feel much better with her parents and two sisters. However what should become of her, Heddy and the new baby in case he did not return from the war? His heart was aching. As the train pulled into the station all of the reserve officers were standing on the platform in full battle dress. What was going on? One of his comrades came running over to him.

Finally, you are back. A day after you left they sent gendarmes from Warsaw to Riga to get you back into camp in a hurry. Orders were received from headquarters to expedite all of us immediately to the front. It is strange that they could not intercept your trip. Yesterday the medical corps tested us all. All who are fit for action are here. Hurry to camp. They are waiting for you at the regiment.

An hour later Fritz was back in camp reporting for duty. "Thank God you are here," the Colonel said. Fritz was told to report immediately to the adjutant's office and to division headquarters as well to see if the health commissioner was still in camp. He raced back to the adjutant's office where he telephoned division headquarters, but the health commissioner was gone. Fritz was instructed to go back to his quarters and wait for further orders. There he found a letter from Lamy. He had heard that Fritz was leaving for the front and would appreciate his comments as soon as possible since it was apparent that he could no longer count on his services at Allart. Fritz felt like dead. He couldn't even think about Allart, Lamy or any of the rest of Lodz. Everything seemed so futile. He finally fell asleep, more like dead, for 16 hours. During the following day he performed his duties rather mechanically. He was depressed and tormented by a thousand thoughts and the uncertainty of the future. On the third day he was called to the regiment office and handed his orders from the General Staff. He was to remain on special duty at the disposal of the regiment. This meant that he did not have to leave for the front, at least immediately. The adjutant confirmed what Fritz had suspected, that the number of officers in the regiment was now so depleted, each remaining officer had to command two companies and look after administration business as well. In his opinion they were in such a predicament that for the time being there was no danger of Fritz's being sent anywhere. But if he should receive orders to the front, the regiment was not in a position that they could apply for his release from frontier service.

Again fate struck Fritz's life. Most of his comrades were gone for almost a year. This would have happened to him also had they been able to find him in Riga. Even the fact that the cable ordering him back had never reach him was strange. He concluded that he was not destined for service on the front. And what was the reason for his being spared? The stupid gossip!! So Fritz wrote to Lamy that he was not going to the front and would be able to return to Lodz in the near future. He also wrote to Warrikoff to send his wages to camp and he immediately sent 50 rubles to Stefanus by registered mail to settle an outstanding debt and close the book on his friendship. Finally he sent money to Maria and told her the good news.

As it was, Fritz was not able to leave camp until October. But the job at Allart remained intact. Things were hectic at camp. Keeping the new recruits who were wild and unruly kept the few officers' hands full. Officers were never without loaded pistols anymore. There was talk that the Russian foreign minister was going to America to meet with a Japanese delegation. Europe was tired of the war and even England, Japan's quiet ally, wanted to see an end to the conflict.[85] News from Lodz was not good. The

---

[85] England had financially supported Japan against Russia, apparently in revenge for Russia's unfriendly position during the Boar

situation seemed to be deteriorating. There were constant strikes and disruptions in the factories. The foremen were not safe. Working conditions were unsafe. An industrialist was murdered in a streetcar and terror was so great that nobody dared to stop the murderers. Foreigners were fleeing; industrialists and plant directors left Lodz in droves. When Fritz's company finally marched into Lodz on October 10, 1905, Lamy and his sister had returned to France. He was not able to visit the plant since he had to remain in the barracks with his troops.

Finally on October 19, the Peace Manifesto was published. It acknowledged, in mild phrases, that Russia had received a thrashing. Port Arthur, which actually was Chinese property, having been leased to Russia for 99 years, was now in Japanese hands as were other lands in the East. War indemnities were not paid and the international mood had affected this fast peace treaty. The situation was very bad for Russia. The army, which was thousands of kilometers away from Europe, was demoralized, tired and hungry. At home, the leftist opposition, which by now included almost all of the educated Russians, forced the government to agree to a new constitution. As soon as the Peace Manifesto was published, unrest and strikes resumed with renewed energy and on October 29th well coordinated and organized strikes were seen throughout the area. Gas works, mail service, electric stations, communication systems and almost all trains came to a complete stand still. The situation in the government was catastrophic. The army could not even be fed. The government was no match for this show of force. The day after the general strike was called; another

---

War. At this point England did not want to put any more money into the conflict.

manifesto was published, which guaranteed the new constitution.

Fritz wrote to Maria immediately to tell her he would probably be free of military service soon and she should prepare to return to Lodz. He also wrote to Karola that she should come back to work and prepare the apartment. Unfortunately, due to the strike all rail service was interrupted and not safe. Maria and Heddy could not return to Lodz until November 10, when Maria was seven months pregnant. Her brother-in-law Victor (Hanna's husband) who had business in Lodz accompanied her. When they arrived in Warsaw however, they were informed that the trains going to Lodz were still on strike and that Poland was in a state of war. After four days in a hotel they were informed that they could proceed to Lodz. They got as far as Koluski only to learn that the Lodz train was still on strike. In despair they rented a carriage (cars and busses were not available yet) and drove 40 kilometers on hard and frozen streets in very cold weather to Lodz. They arrived cold and tired on November 16. Maria was put to bed immediately; all feared the worst. Luckily, she recovered quickly. Victor returned to Riga after a day but Fritz could not return to Lodz until December 16, exactly one month later. After 13 months of service, he was released from duty.

But violence and unrest were everywhere.[86] In Kiev, Odessa and Sebastopol bloody revolutions were underway. Moscow was literally recaptured by the

---

[86] Fritz wrote a great deal about the political situation in Russia. His comments, by someone who lived through it as more of an observer than a participant, are very interesting. It also seems that he had little sympathy for the protesters. Rather, he seems to have wanted to maintain the status quo, which, by all accounts, was advantageous to him. In fact, throughout his narrative, he seems very put upon by the changing political scene and seems to blame the protesters for much of his suffering later on.

government on Christmas Eve. Even the Baltic was in turmoil. In Kurland, Livland (later to be combined into the State of Latvia) and even in parts of Estonia, Baltic-German farms were being burned down. Pastors[87] and barons were murdered. Families of German ancestry who had lived for generations in the Baltic went to Germany, fearing the worst was yet to come. The Russian military was sent from Petersburg to subdue the violence. Fritz's brother Ewald was almost a victim of it. He had been working in Livland at a narrow-gauge railway construction ever since the Polytechnicum was closed down because of the unrest. He was working on building a railroad bridge when the situation became too dangerous. The work was stopped and he decided to leave for Riga and safer grounds. But all the roads were occupied by revolutionaries and no vehicles were allowed to pass. Finally, he managed to get some sort of paper from one of the revolutionary officer, which entitled him to travel to Kreusberg on the Riga-Danabourg line. But the Kreusberg station had been taken over by government troops. Ewald was mistaken for a revolutionary because of the paper the aforementioned officer had given him. He was arrested and on his way to his execution when a train rolled into the station. A stationmaster emerged who recognized Ewald and, by acting very fast, managed to get him freed. Ewald left on the next train.

And so, the family approached Christmas and New Years with anxiety and sad thoughts. So many things were happening so fast. Century old establishments and systems were collapsing all around and in all corners of Russia. They had witnessed many emotionally upsetting things, even

---

[87] Remember Lutheran clergy had a quasi-official role in government in Russia.

in their private lives; no one could speculate what would happen next. Fritz wondered if this were a bad time to bring up the previous summer's fiasco. Should he go to Stefanus and ask him for an apology? As only half a year had passed the so-called honor from student days would probably have applied. But Maria was already bedridden most of the time and was easily thrown off balance by the least bit of excitement. Fritz could not take any chances. Stefanus was clearly avoiding him. He was still supplying coal to the plant but never came in, and if he saw Fritz on the street he crossed to the other side. Fritz decided not to pursue a confrontation but leave it to "the Gods."[88]

---

[88] Eight years later Stefanus lost all of his savings when WW I broke out. He died during the last year of the war from blood poisoning.

Chapter VII:
The Family Grows and Dynamics Change

1906 began quietly. Maria's pregnancy made her quite incapacitated. Their social contacts had diminished significantly. All the foreigners in the plant, especially since the murder of a German administrator, were keeping a low profile. Only old Mrs. Jung, who was taking care of Maria as if she were her own daughter, and the Warrikoffs came to the apartment.

Fritz's wages at Allart had remained the same since his original employment but he had nice bonuses and of course, a free apartment, thus allowing him to develop his savings. Gerda was born on February 14. The delivery was very long but without complications. And the baby was healthy and calm. Mrs. Jung moved in for two weeks and Maria became more relaxed and settled. In May they celebrated a modest Christening with the Jungs as Godparents, and the Warrikoffs attended. The Engineer Club, their social organization of foreign engineers in Lodz, which Fritz had helped to organize, seemed to officially demonstrate that all the gossip of the previous year was just that, last year's talk. Coach after coach, 20 ladies and gentlemen, arrived at the Maehles' to congratulate them on the birth of their daughter, Gerda.

Around the end of May, Hugo Warrikoff approached Fritz with another project — to invest money in a tannery, which his father-in-law operated. Fritz complied and put his total savings into the enterprise. The business never got off the ground. Fritz considered himself lucky that he was able to get all his money back, even in bits and pieces, by the end of the year.[89] Meanwhile, the fight between the government and the revolutionaries continued on and on. The Duma was formed in May but, because it was so revolutionary, was dissolved in June causing the revolutionaries to increase their efforts. Russian Prime Minister Stolypin showed great strength and managed to survive several assassination attempts.[90]

After the Duma (the congressional assembly with little power) failed, the situation in the factories became desperate. Fighting organizations seemed to be coming out of the woodwork. And all were well equipped with the most modern weapons. The Socialists and the Nationalists seemed to hold their shooting practices openly in the halls of factories. Working conditions were next to impossible. With this kind of terror and indiscriminate violence, anyone in a leading position from foreman to administrator was in constant danger. Monstrous demands for wages were being made. Strikes were called at Allart for two weeks in July, one week in September and one week in October. These impossible working conditions resulted in a lockout and a complete standstill of operations for two weeks. When Allart finally called all workers back, only a few locksmiths and machine operators returned. And so the factory closed indefinitely. Fritz dismantled the

---

[89] Again and again, Fritz exhibits amazingly poor business sense.
[90] In August, he was finally assassinated and the public was so terrorized that nobody intervened.

steam engines and let the water out of the boilers and pipes, constantly under police guard. Then at the request of management, all administrative personnel were asked to take their families on paid vacations. Most of the other plants were doing the same thing and most of the head officers returned to Berlin.

Karola went to her family in the country, and on October 20, Fritz, Maria and the children went to Riga to stay with Hanna and Victor for a month. Although relaxing, especially for Fritz who had been on the go constantly for more than a year, Riga was also suffering from the revolutionary activity. Trade had suffered and everybody was worried about the future of the Baltic States.[91] Papa Jurgensen was knee deep in a new business, selling dry vegetables. Every day members of the family went to help pack them for shipping. Fritz saw many of his old friends from the Polytechnicum — Fischer, Buschmann, Habermann, Bua, Reichert, Wittrock, Johannsen and Feldweg who had since become a professor at the Polytechnicum. He also visited with Mrs. Makarow who had moved to a small apartment. But he was unable to see Esser who had withdrawn from all his former friends. It was said that he was already showing signs of dementia, the result of syphilis, which he had contracted in his last year at the university during a stay in Russia. And of course, he and Maria visited Hedwig, the youngest sister, and Bernhard VonDahm, her husband. Hanna and Victor's marriage was in a sad state. After their son, Wolfi's death and the birth of their daughter, Sigi, the marriage seemed to be hanging on by only a thread. They argued constantly. Hanna was only interested in painting and singing while Victor's interests were outside of the house.

---

[91] Though not independent states yet, they enjoyed substantial independence from Russia.

Exactly one month after leaving Lodz, Fritz received a cable from Allart's to return to meet with several of the other administrations. All were put up in the Grand Hotel and their work began. Fritz began to interview people who had worked at Allart before and who wanted to return under the former conditions. Once done, he started up the machines and boilers and in six days they were ready to rehire workers. Karola returned from the country to open up the apartment and on December 8 the family returned from Riga. Family news was mixed. Oskar had finished his studies in Friedberg, Germany and began a new job with Adler Weke in Frankfurt. Hermann, who had to earn money for his studies by giving lessons, was also approaching the end of school. And Nikolaus was having trouble in his store in Kertell; factory workers were boycotting it. Despite all this, and the fact that conditions in Lodz were very bad for the whole year with factories suffering strikes and unrest, business for the factories was outstanding. The war had brought a lot of money to the people, everyone was investing and it did not look like it would soon stop.

Indeed, 1907 became the most successful year of Fritz's working life. Never again would he be so busy with such love of work and energy in his chosen profession. He had to prepare the factory for new machinery; turbine engines were new and different, requiring new technology, and he had to explore the subject from every angle to prepare the factory for major changes. Since Allart was the first plant in Lodz to develop a turbine system, he had to rely on himself. His regular job as plant engineer had also grown during these troubled times. He worked from 7:00 AM until 8:00 PM and often took work home, where Maria helped him with calculations. The workers had simmered down somewhat after the lockout, but conditions were still far from normal.

Every angle of the tariffs, every condition in the plant requirements gave an excuse for endless discussions, speeches and arguments with the worker delegates. If one of the managers was seen in the plant, he was immediately surrounded with endless questions and arguments. It got to the point where workers started threatening and physically attacking the managers.

Then, in March, a terrible thing happened, the manufacturer Silberstein was attacked by his plant workers. They had been demonstrating all day but he would not give in to their demands. Finally, a worker pulled out a pistol and shot him several times. With his last breath he asked for some water to which a worker urinated into his mouth until he died. He was not the first manufacturer to be murdered by his employees but was the first Jewish one. Previously, not a finger had been lifted in response, but in this case, there was an immediate response. General Kaznakoff arrived from Petersburg with unlimited powers to create order. The factory was surrounded by troops and no one was allowed to leave until the murderer had been identified. However, the people were so terrorized that no one dared to become an informer; all were certain that they would be dead within 24 hours themselves. The government persisted and finally workers began giving names of persons in the opposing party until everyone was named. The parties began to battle each other, and since all had weapons many workers were killed. The violence continued and spread throughout the city. During the second half of 1907 and the first half of 1908, hardly a day went by that people were not found shot to death in dark alleys, in the suburbs and in the surrounding fields of the city.

Despite all this unrest, Fritz had great success in his work with higher wages. He could save money, even though he had taken on the responsibility of paying for Ewald's education, which, he commented, was going at a snails pace.[92] Oskar had terminated his job in Frankfurt and stopped in Lodz for three weeks on his way to Dago to visit their parents. Fritz was heavily engaged in preparing the plant for the new turbine and traveled to Berlin several times to inspect the new machine. On one such occasion he went to see the president of Steinert, another company with a mill in Lodz. Their Lodz plant engineer had resigned and had recommended Oskar for the job. Fritz wanted to put in a good word for his brother. Oskar had no trouble getting the job, and in January 1908, he started in his new position. Hanna and Victor were finally divorced; Hanna was intent on becoming a professional singer.

It was in this year that Fritz heard for the first time that his father was having serious financial problems with his store. He was informed by both his father and Rudolf, who was called a partner in the store. They had been fighting a secret boycott over the previous two years with workers from the Kertell factory who had been taking their money out of the store.[93] Nikolaus wrote Fritz he was short of capital and with 1800 rubles (about 2 month salary), Fritz could become a silent partner, and the store would be saved. Had Fritz seen clearly he mused, he would have insisted on liquidation, but at the time other reports seem positive and he remained optimistic. He sent his father the money so he could pay his

---

[92] Remember, one paid tuition to the university, went to classes and lectures when one felt like it. Only when one felt ready was one examined on the subject. As we have seen, many students spent more time enjoying the party atmosphere than the academic side. The gaiety of student life in *The Student Prince* is not exaggerated.

[93] The store, it will be recalled, was in fact owned by the factory and Nikolaus had, during a time of crisis, sold shares of "ownership" to the workers despite the fact that he was really just the manager. Now, many of the workers called in their shares, which Nikolaus had to pay with his own money.

suppliers. But his own family was not without its crises. In June a terrible incident occurred. Maria still had persistent problems with her internal organs and was given a prescription for Lysol, which she used for douches. The nursemaid accidentally gave Gerda a spoonful of it, thinking it was something else. Gerda's mouth and throat were burned very badly. The doctor had her stomach pumped; for two anxious days it did not look as if she would recover.[94]

The burdens of the last three years with the war, revolutions and continued unrest were beginning to lift. The colony of people from the Baltic had increased quite a bit. Most were employed as administrators and engineers in the many mills in Lodz. Others were employed in banks, insurance, and as managers of businesses. Many of Fritz's old friends from his university days arrived in Lodz, providing the Maehles with a comfortable and busy social life. Business was excellent and life in Lodz was pulsating and more vibrant than ever before. That January, the Austrian Club held a masked ball and the Baltic group decided to attend. Maria, with Fritz's design, made herself an Estonian costume. He, dressed as a gamekeeper, wore a dark green long coat and hat. It was Maria's first great ball and they had a wonderful time. For the first time in several years, they were able to relax and enjoy themselves. Fritz's wages continued to rise. His work on the boiler installation was so outstanding that he had become a well-recognized engineer. "Allart," he noted, "had turned into something like a shrine for all the other companies in Lodz." Engineers and technicians came regularly to look at the machines and consult with him.

---

[94] One wonders if this incident was the root cause of her lung disorder, which turned into TB and eventually took her life in her early 20s.

But the problems with the Dago business did not go away. Nikolaus was only able to pay off part of his debt with the money Fritz and Oskar, who was just starting a new job and had very little, had sent. And the remaining debt was considerable. Nikolaus's letters were totally confused and the legal aspect of the situation seemed to escape him entirely. Maria, Fritz and Oskar were all in a daze. Where were they going to get the money? What was the reality of the situation? By mid 1908, they determined that the business was eating itself up and would need an infusion of more money to get it back on its feet. As his own savings were diminished by the first infusion of money he sent to his father, he had to obtain loans from several sources including Hugo Warrikoff, Oskar, who took money from his initial earnings, the wood supplier and coloring master (dye expert) for the plant, and an advance bonus for the coming year from Allart. With this money they were able to send Nikolaus enough to cover all his debts and maintain solvency for one year. Of course now Fritz was in debt again.

Then, to make matters worse, the children developed whopping cough and the doctor said they should be sent to the beach with their grandparents in Riga. Where was the money going to come from? And then the unexpected happened. Among the pilgrims who came to see the Allart plant and to meet with Fritz was the new general manager, Tigerstadt, of the Widzener Manufacturing Company. During their conversation it turned out that they had both gone to the polytechnicum in Riga. The company was thinking about modernizing and wanted turbines and electricity. Two days later another Widzener employee came to Allart's and asked Fritz in confidence if he would be willing to leave Allart. Wages would be at least twice as much as he was presently making, well beyond what any other plant engineer in Lodz was making. Fritz was dizzy. What timing! He accepted the offer and was hired as a plant engineer, but with the wages of an assistant manager to Tigerstadt. He would take care that the department foremen looked upon Fritz as his deputy. All plant operations pertaining to spinning and weaving became Fritz's responsibility. Wages were 10,000 rubles, an extraordinary amount. Only Baron Tanfani, the president of the company, had to approve the offer. Tigerstadt left for Baden-Baden immediately with confidence that the Baron would be delighted. Fritz was beside himself. If this job came through the most extraordinary jobs would become open to him both in Lodz and in Russia. On June 25, Fritz received a cable to come to Baden-Baden immediately, where he was offered three-year contract of 9,000 rubles plus free housing, electricity and heat to begin October 1.

On July 1 Fritz gave Allart his resignation. It hit like a bomb and although there was some discussion about a competing offer, it was clear that his mind was made up. The very same day Maria and the children left for the beach near Riga. Heddy had recuperated quickly from whooping cough, but Gerda developed pneumonia and had to be sent to the children's hospital. After a month, Maria and the children returned well, healthy and happy. And as a bonus, in September, Ewald finally completed his studies, received his diploma, and started a job as an agricultural engineer in Nowogrundok, Poland. Hermann had also completed his studies and became an assistant pastor in Johannis Church in Reval. And thus, four of Nikolaus's five sons had completed their studies and held good positions. It was also quite clear that the other brothers would now be able to help in paying their father's debts. The first step was to divide the 6000-ruble debt Fritz had incurred equally among the four of them. Sadly,

Rudolf, the unlucky fellow, had somehow been mistreated by fate. Since the collapse of Nikolaus's business, all his hopes to one day take over the business were dashed. He left Dago in the fall and found a position in Riga.

In September Oskar had a terrible accident in the Steinert plant. A steam pipe exploded which not only severely burned him, but also blew hot sand and lime dust into his eyes. He moved in with Fritz and Maria, who cared for him, and for a few weeks it looked as if he would be permanently blind. Miraculously, after about four weeks his sight began to return. He received compensation from the plant and after another six months his eyesight was almost completely normal. In early October the family moved into a new home in Widzew[95] and Fritz started his new job (at 750 rubles vs. 300 rubles per month in the old one). Allart gave him a splendid recommendation and the employees presented him with a beautiful bronze statue of a worker leaning against an anvil, a leather-bound writing case with a gold monogram and a dedication. He was also informed that, because of his extraordinary achievements, he would not have to pay back the advance on his bonus.

And then came some setbacks. In late December, just two months after Fritz had started at Widzener, General Manager Tigerstadt died. Fritz had held great hopes of becoming Assistant General Manager or Vice President. With Tigerstadt's death his greatest supporter was gone and his dreams were dashed. It became clear very quickly that without Tigerstadt's support, the other department heads

---

[95] This is the name of the Lodz suburb adjacent to and founded by the Widzener Manufacturing Company. As already noted, companies provided housing for their management employees and consequently, suburban areas grew around the plants. Widzew is still on Lodz maps.

would never see Fritz as their superior, especially since his agreement with Tigerstadt was semi-private. He was making 1,000-2,000 rubles more than the other department heads. They knew it and they were jealous. He began to feel a quiet but steady opposition and some intrigues, especially from the office manager, Thoelke, who never went into the plant and was almost chained to his desk. He suffered from spinal TB and walked with crutches, but he apparently had the idea that with Tigerstadt's death he would become general manager. Fritz's hopes that he could begin saving more money were also not to be realized.

Maria and Fritz were at wonderful ages; he 36 and she 26. They had always lived a rather simple and frugal life. Maria's clothes were modest; they hardly went to concerts or theater, the Austrian Ball being Maria's first public appearance. In seven years of marriage they had only had one real vacation, the trip to Dago in the summer of 1904. The forced trips to Riga in 1905 when he was supposed to be transferred to the Far East' in 1906 when Allart had a lockout, and when the children had the whooping cough, were not real vacations. He had never joined any organization or club, except for the Engineers Club. Their bookcases were almost empty and now he had a large home with six public rooms[96] and a large garden to care for. New furniture had to be purchased. Life had suddenly become more complicated and much more expensive. All the extra work necessitated that Karola have help. Since Fritz had now become well known in the city, more and more invitations came to their house. They also had to buy tickets to all sorts of entertainment. And their

---

[96] These included rooms such as sitting room, dining room, and parlor for receiving guests, library, living room, and solarium. Bedrooms, kitchen, baths and servants rooms were not included in the count.

circle of friends had become larger. The German theater at that time was excellent; first-rate operas such as *Fledermaus* were performed. Even movies began to be shown in several new movie houses. Money was disappearing too quickly for Fritz's comfort.

Fritz's position had more than doubled at Widzener. At Allart he had been responsible for eight boilers, three steam engines and daily coal consumption of about five railcars. He supervised 1500 workers. At Widzener he had 23 boilers, six steam engines, daily coal consumption of 11 rail cars with 3500 workers under his supervision. In addition he was responsible for the building department where the Widzener buildings, aside from the plant, consisted of an entire suburb of housing for administrators and workers lodging. For all this work he had only one draftsman who was also doing payroll for the technical department. Since the whole system was rather chaotic, he was actually relieved that he had not become a vice president and he jumped with vigor into his work. And happily, he was no longer the general manager for workers. A new general manager, Max Winsche, came on board in the spring of 1909. He was a member of the owning family and well qualified for the position. Unfortunately he was suffering from TB and showed signs of death. Although he was Lutheran, he was trying to learn about the Polish nationals who worked in the plant. In fact, at this time Fritz began to notice some tension arising between the "German Hurrah" administrators and the non-German colleagues in the city, which, he noted, would lead to unpleasantness later on.

In January of 1909, Maria and Fritz attended a German Masked Ball. All their close friends were there. Next they were invited to a Polish Masked Ball. Naturally they went although many of their friends were not invited. By this time all of Fritz's loans had been paid off as had Oskar's. And the other brothers were beginning to assist in the support of their parents, as well as repaying Oskar and Fritz for their share of the store's bailout. Maria, Fritz and Oskar were feeling so good that they decided to take a vacation in Germany at Easter when the plant was closed for the holidays. Maria had never been across the boarder and Fritz only a few times for business. Hanna, who had been divorced from Victor for almost a year had moved to Berlin where she became a stage actress. She met them in Breslau, where she had been performing, and joined them for the trip to Berlin. They had a wonderful time, went sightseeing, got caught up in the holiday bustle and returned to Lodz full of joy and completely exhausted.

By May it became clear that Nikolaus could no longer keep the business. New suppliers and creditors were pressing him for payment. It seemed that as quickly as his sons sent money, new debts arose. The brothers, in collaboration, urged their father to declare bankruptcy as a result of *"force majeure,"* the boycott. Oskar sent Nikolaus his last 3,500 rubles, and in June Fritz traveled to Riga, Reval and Kertell to pay off all the suppliers. He also paid off the few remaining employees. The business was dissolved and Kersti and Nikolaus moved into Rudolf's home. There was still a debt of 1,400 rubles, which would have to come out of the remaining goods from the store. On his return trip home Fritz picked up Hedwig in Riga for a visit with Maria in Lodz. Two months later Fritz received a cable from Dago that Kersti had passed away peacefully after a stroke. Maria and Oskar left immediately for the funeral and made it just in time. Uncle Karl stayed with Nikolaus who had a complete breakdown.

By fall Maria and Fritz were at their wits end. Maria's health was poor. Her female troubles had never subsided and a specialist in Breslau, where Fritz finally sent her, said that she must go to a health spa in Silesia. She left in mid October for six weeks. Oskar joined her in November and they both returned two weeks before Christmas, rested and much better looking. Maria's parents came to Lodz for Christmas with Sigi, Hanna's child, who had lived with them since Hanna had moved to Berlin.

Fritz, too, had never overcome his digestive problems and was also suffering from hemorrhoids. Finally, in the spring of 1910 he had an operation in his home, without anesthesia, to remove them. Meanwhile, Nikolaus had regained some of his strength and was living with a housekeeper, Mrs. Norwid. The brothers sent him 50 rubles a month and 35 to poor brother Rudolf. Fritz wrote, "It is strange that life never seems to give one a chance, a time when you can sit back and enjoy it and what you have achieved." No sooner had he cleaned up his father's affairs, Papa Jurgensen came on the scene. He had bought property in Hinzenberg (the seaside resort on the Baltic near Riga where the family had vacationed for many years) where he wanted to build a house. He felt that Maria's and Hedwig's husbands should give him the money. But Fritz had mounting expenses — trips already taken, his mother's funeral, his operation, some necessities for their home, a piano for Heddy who was already in school. The family's life style had changed also. An engineer in the third largest plant in Lodz was different from being an engineer at Allart. More was expected of him. Fritz felt no remorse for helping his father. After all, had Nikolaus not supported the boys by giving them all his savings for their educations, he would have had sufficient funds to avoid the boycott and would not have lost the store.

But Papa Jurgensen's request was different. He had a good position and had paid very little to educate his daughters. And as soon as they had finished school he had seen to it that they were out of his home and providing for their own upkeep. Aside from some kitchen utensils and a few pieces of linen, Maria had not received a dowry either. Why would they need a house? They had rented a house at the beach for the summer for as long as Marie could remember. But then, Fritz noted, his father-in-law had always been a tyrant and a gambler. He could become extremely abusive and vulgar, and he directed much of his anger at Maria. At the same time, Fritz and Maria had also been talking about their future — that one-day they would like to retire to their homeland in the Baltic. Perhaps it would be a good idea to have interest in some property there. They could go there for vacations in summers with their children, and in the end it would belong to Maria and her sisters. So Fritz agreed to send Papa Jurgensen what he requested.

About this same time, Fritz took up photography. He had a dark room built in his house and on weekends he took pictures. Oskar became just as involved with the hobby. The Maehles' social life was steadily increasing. They had invested in season tickets to the German Theater. Fritz noted that after an eleven-hour day, it was quite difficult to attend theater, which often lasted until 1 AM. They continued to see a great deal of the Warrikoffs but also many other friends. They also entertained frequently and lavishly. A great many teachers from the newly founded German Gymnasium (high school) were from the Baltic and they became social friends with them as well. But how was he going to save money? It seemed to flow out as fast as it came in.

Then, in June 1910, he bought Widzener stock. Mr. Kunitzer, who was one of the founders of the plant in 1876, had been murdered during the Japanese War. He had been very industrious and speculative. Some of his investments failed and his friend Heinzel came to his rescue. He brought new capital into the firm, which from then on was called Heinzel Kunitzer. After Heinzel's death in 1909, his sons Julius and Louis and son-in-law, Baron Tanfani became the owners and shareholders of his portion of the firm only to learn that Kunitzer owed quite a bit of money to the firm. Therefore a large portion of Heinzel's shares had to go into the shareholder company of Heinzel-Kunitzer to cover his debts. Baron Tanfani wanted to avoid an open market sale of shares so he decided to offer them to his top administrators. The nominal value was 10,000 rubles. The firm had taken them over in a critical moment for only 5,600 rubles, the price that they were offered to the administrators with a 6% dividend. The only disadvantage was that the shares were blocked for seven years. Everyone tried to get as many as they could. Fritz, being the newest member of management was only able to purchase two shares. Fritz used his savings of 1,600 rubles as down payment for the shares. He thus owed 9,600 to the company; he applied his dividends to pay this debt.[97]

That June, Maria had to have her appendix removed. She had the operation in their home. Soon after that Karola left to get married. She had been with the family for eight years and all were sad about her leaving. Maria gave her a generous wedding gift. Then in mid-October they realized that Maria was

---

[97] He wrote that, as he was able to add a few rubles every year to his payments, the shares were paid for by the beginning of WWI, although they were blocked until 1917.

pregnant again. Mama Jurgensen predicted doom; it was too close to Maria's surgery. This time however, the pregnancy was not nearly as difficult as the previous ones. Another event was Oskar's engagement to Grand Uncle Andreas' youngest daughter, Herta[98] (Felix, Andreas and Johanna's sister). Fritz lamented that, "Oskar will not be in our house every day anymore once he has has his own home." During the previous three years Fritz, Maria and Oskar had become very close. They shared lots of fun and stuck together during troubled times. Oskar always went to theater or a concert with them and if Fritz was unable to go, Oskar accompanied Maria. He was at the house several nights during the workweek and always on week ends. Heddy and Gerda adored him as, incidentally, they did Karola. All during the fall Oskar and Fritz built a puppet theater for the children's Christmas. The backgrounds and puppets were shipped from Berlin. Then the backgrounds had to be mounted on plywood, the stage had to be built, electric lights and even a bell had to be installed and Maria had to make costumes for the puppets. And so, Oscar was married in Moscow in January of 1911. As expected, when they returned to their own place in Lodz, they were with Fritz and Maria far less frequently.

Since Fritz continued to have trouble saving money in 1911, he bought a life insurance policy costing 500 rubles a year. This proved to be a completely wrong investment. When WW I broke out he had already paid 3,000 rubles, but during the war he was not able to keep up the payments, and even if he could have done so, the insurance company did not operate in the "war sector" of Lodz. Thus, like many other things that had been planned before the war, the investment was lost.

---

[98] A form of Gerda

Fritz recalled a grand time the Engineering Society members had at the German Festival in early 1911. The gentlemen wore tuxedos, the ladies beautiful ball gowns. All the Engineers Society members held very high positions in their respective companies. They had become respected leaders in the community. Years later one of the members would look back on the affair, melancholy reminiscing — "After WWI we were left old and weak, scattered about in all directions and had lost almost everything but our bare existence."

In the spring of 1911, Fritz became nervous again. His three-year contract with Widzener had to be renegotiated and he worried that with all the jealousy in upper management he would be vulnerable. So he wrote to the Baron directly who immediately assured him that he was very valuable and should begin preparatory work for the change over to a turbine system and electricity. He proposed that the contract read, "for an undetermined time" and keep the six-month notice clause. He also gave him a nice raise. Since the change over would take years, Fritz could relax again. Kola (Nikolaus) was born on June 29, 1911. It was an easy delivery and he looked just like his dad. Maria was cared for by the servants and recovered quickly.

Fritz had not seen his father since his mother died and so it was agreed that he would have a vacation and include a trip to Dago. In early August he and the Warrikoffs left via Berlin by steamer for Copenhagen, Oslo, the Fjords and Bergen, then over to Stockholm and Finland; and then, Reval where he visited relatives. Finally he and Hermann went to Dago to see their father. Nikolaus was well but he was talking about marrying his housekeeper, an idea that all of his sons opposed. Upon his return to Lodz he was pleased to find that the girls, Maria and Kola, whom they wanted to christen Nikolaus, were all well. Fritz felt wonderful, physically good, and professionally successful and with a lovely family. He did not have any serious conflicts with Maria, although he acknowledged that they were very different in character. He was 40 years old. His father was well and although his mother was gone, she was at peace. All of his brothers, whom he had helped to educate, were employed and independent; and his job was secure for quite a long time. Now finally, he could start to save in earnest. He had paid for the Widzener shares and he had a new son and two lovely girls.

Then came 1912 which Fritz wrote, "was the most critical year in my life so far and as I look back (written in 1936), even the years of the war and the revolutionary years of 1905/6, compared to this year, seem like child's play." While Maria's pregnancy had gone relatively smoothly and the birth was without problems, Maria developed both physical and psychological symptoms after the birth, which became, over the year, so unbearable that the marriage was almost destroyed, and a shadow was cast over family life for many years thereafter. [99] Fritz said that the most terrifying thing about her condition was he was never quite sure if he was dealing with a well or totally sick person. "One cannot come to any objective view when one is in the middle of what is going on and one is more or less the target of the tragedy that is being played out." Had he, at the time, seen more clearly, he would have sent Maria to Dr. Knorre, the family gynecologist in Riga. Or at least he would have asked Mama Jurgensen to come to Lodz. "Perhaps," he mused, "Mama Jurgensen had been right that the pregnancy had come too soon after the appendectomy." Maria's

---

[99] She seems to have had what we now recognize as a severe case of Post Partum Depression.

condition lasted for a full year and was only brought under control with an operation performed by Dr. Knorre.

The get-togethers of the Engineers Society were also in crisis. "Things," Fritz wrote, "went in a direction which I personally abhorred." Several members were moving in a pro German direction, inventing more and more expensive festivities and extra meetings. Since the male choir had built the clubhouse, the group felt that it had to make the choir a sparkling group, which was very costly for the members. The formerly modest wives of the members became more and more pretentious, each trying to outdo the other and keep up with the very wealthy people in town. An especially bad influence on Maria was Mrs. Elbo. Her husband had made money in engineering. "Probably, Frtiz wrote, "as much as I." Mrs. Elbo began to wear very expensive cloths and elegant coiffed hair. She was becoming a lady of fashion. She was throwing money around right and left, leaving the other women speechless. Since she was very superficial and rather dumb, Fritz was surprised that Maria could get along with her so well. But Maria became her bosom buddy. The sat together almost every morning, lunched together every afternoon and shopped together frequently. Other women in the group also joined the ladies. And there were a series of balls throughout the year, each more elegant than the last and all requiring a new and lavish gown. "When women try to out-do each other there is no end in sight," wrote Fritz.[100]

---

[100] Heddy used to tell me about her mother and her elegant ways, that a hairdresser came to the home almost daily to make her up and she work elegant dresses. That seems to be all she remembered about her mother's appearance or at least talked about.

Maria often told Fritz much lower prices for the clothing she purchased. Consequently, the butcher and grocer had to wait for their money. The situation became out of control. But strangely, his debts grew to an avalanche before he realizes what was happening. And when he questioned Maria, he was told he simply "does not allow her enough spending money." A lack of communication, hostility and a breach of confidence resulted.

Kola's christening was scheduled for the second half of January and because he was the son of an engineer and the Maehles' had a steadily growing circle of friends, a large celebration was planned. Even Ewald came for two weeks. Still the excitement, which Maria normally enjoyed, seemed to have an adverse affect on her. She became more nervous, restless and aggressive. The tension in the home was high. Fritz was suspicious that her behavior had something to do with her female functions and asked her several times to see her gynecologist in Lodz. He did not find anything particularly wrong with her and suggested a trip to the health spa, Bad Kudkowa, in the spring. Since she had a chronic hoarseness (which Fritz felt was caused by her hysterical condition) she went to see other doctors, who also recommended a health spa. Finally, it was decided that she should go to Breslau where she would see a specialist and then travel on to the spa.

During the spring Maria's condition worsened. She became even stranger, short tempered, confused and generally abnormal. She could sit by the window for long periods, motionless, just staring into the street. Or she would walk up and down the path in the park alone. She only came to life when Mr. Winsche, who lived in the neighborhood, accompanied her on her walks, or came to the house for dinner or a visit. Sometimes they played the piano together. The pitiful man, consumed with TB, friendless and unhappy, seemed to arouse her compassion. Yet, Maria managed to continue her frequent visits with the ladies. One of the ladies, Mrs. Jung, was planning to move back to Stuttgart and had "given" Maria her maid, "a jewel of a woman." But Maria clashed with the maid who continually disagreed with how Maria was doing something. "That's not the way we did it at Jungs," she would state. Maria, in her own aggressive way would answer accordingly. It was unpleasant. So the maid went to see Mrs. Jung, who had not left Lodz yet. She told her that Marie thought everything the Jungs did was stupid and wrong. Mrs. Jung wrote a violent letter of insults to Maria, thus ending a friendship, which both Maria and Fritz regretted later on.

Fritz could see that the home was less and less interesting to Maria. Kola was having trouble also. He was a delicate little fellow, always sick from something. He looked anemic, was very lethargic and even had convulsions when he was teething. The children hardly ever saw their mother anymore. In the afternoon she was usually out and often did not return until after their supper. Heddy and Gerda came to their father with their school problems and homework. They were clearly disturbed, especially Heddy, who became more timid and pale. She would practice the piano for hours, just not to be scolded if her mother decided to check up on her or took a sudden interest in her playing.

One day Maria announced to Fritz that she and Mrs. Elbo had decided to take their daughters from the Rothert School for Girls and send them to Mrs. Iwanowa's school. The change had already been made! It might not have been a bad idea since Rothert did not have the right to give qualifying papers, and Iwanowa, as a Russian school, did. But to take such a step without even discussing it with their father hurt Fritz deeply. It was, he said, characteristic of their relationship at that time. As a result of the hasty decision, Heddy lost her vacation that summer. Because her Russian was not sufficient to even get her through the admitting exam, she spent her entire vacation learning Russian. Fritz even had to go to Warsaw to see the Director of Education so that she could be admitted to the school.

By May even the Maehles' acquaintances began to notice Maria's aggressiveness. She became an even greater puzzle for Fritz. Her facial expression was usually indifferent or fixed. But toward him she showed an unconcealed fury and hatred. Finally the situation became unbearable between them. Her disdain towards Fritz had expanded to include the entire household — servants, children, even Oskar whom she had always been so close to. Finally Fritz confronted her. She told him point blank that she could not stay with him anymore because of her aversion to him. She felt that they should separate without any bad feelings. After her trip to the spa she would live with her parents or somewhere else. In any case, she would not return to him. As far as the children were concerned, she would take Heddy; he could keep the other two. She could not stand Kola because he looked so frightfully like Fritz and Gerda was just too fat. The whole conversation was not in the tone of a fight. Rather, it was carried on in a cool manner. Her decisions were offered in a very triumphant and self-assured way.

Fritz was struck by cold terror! Did this trait run in the Jurgensen Family? [101] Hanna, Maria's

---

[101] Her mother had exhibited the same behavior when she came to stay with them during WWI. She would fly off the handle for any little reason, abuse all persons in the household, screaming insults at them, and fly out of the house to look for a job since she could not stand to

sister, had spent some time in a mental clinic when she was Maria's age; she had divorced Victor and had "given" their child, Sigi, to her parents. Fritz also noted that Hanna and Victor fought constantly, even when they were engaged. Victor dealt with the situation by finding other interests, outside of the home. But Fritz was different. He was attentive and loyal. He had protected Maria when she got into trouble. He was generous to the point of recklessness with savings always diminishing rather than growing. He never deprived Maria of anything she wanted. In fact, most of the household money went into her wardrobe and personal care. He was a real homebody. He admitted that some of her behaviors were very irritating — her anger, bad temper, and flightiness. She was extremely self-centered. And then again, she had been very young when she married and assumed responsibilities of homemaking and motherhood. And those moods had increased steadily since Kola was born. She had become an indifferent mother at best.

Aversion for a spouse is usually associated with another love interest and he didn't think she had one. In addition, that should not affect her affection for her children. And the bottom line was that in Poland aversion alone was not sufficient grounds for a divorce. One could obtain a divorce if one's partner suffered from a disease or was unfaithful. In the later case the unfaithful party loses all rights to the children and could never marry anyone from the same faith again. The idea of a peaceful separation and her proposition of sharing the children was impossible under Polish law. In other words, her whole manner was just a rather sick imagination of a hysterical, unbalanced woman.

---

live with her daughter any longer. And recall her behavior when Heddy was born.

If Maria's mother had been there Fritz could have consulted her. Only Oskar was around as Herta had already left for the summer vacation in Estonia.

Fritz went to see Oskar. He was not even surprised. He said that he had noticed the tension for quite some time. In fact, he and Herta had cut their visits to their home for that very reason. They did not want to get involved. He was convinced that Maria was either sick or absolutely hysterical. Perhaps she had a female condition or an inherited factor — or both. Oskar suggested that one should not oppose the wishes of such a sick person to take a trip. Fritz should not try to keep her home as this might lead to enormous repercussions later. A trip away from home might calm Maria down and certainly a check-up with a very good gynecologist would be advisable. Maria's mother should come to Lodz to help with the children or meet with Maria wherever she wanted. Finally, Oskar felt he should tell Fritz that there had been talk in their circle about Maria's flightiness and rumor had it that her behavior was more and more connected with Mr. Winsche (the man with TB), his visits to their home, etc. He personally thought their relationship was a harmless flirt at worst. Fritz felt dizzy. That on top of everything else! Of course, the husband is always the last to know to what extent his house was the center of gossip again. What was he to do?

It seemed too late for Maria's mother to come to Lodz, but Fritz could not oppose her plans to leave. She had already hired the Warrikoffs' sister, Manja, to look after the household. Her departure date was set and she had informed Manja that she did not intend to return. The only thing that Fritz could think of was to inform Maria's mother immediately and ask her to meet Maria abroad and see what could be done about her serious condition. So without telling

Maria, he wrote to her mother who replied that she would do all she could to help.

And so, Maria left, first for Posen where Hanna was working. When Maria told her the news, Hanna also thought she was crazy. From Posen Maria went to Breslau where she saw Dr. Kuehnau. Fritz had written him a long letter explaining what he had noticed and asking for a very thorough exam. He wrote back that he had found nothing physically wrong except for a sight infection in the lungs and a "psychic-depression." He prescribed a treatment in Bad Reinerz rather than Bad Kudkowa.[102] Mama Jurgensen left for Bad Reinerz with Sigi a few days after Maria's departure. Interestingly, Mr. Winsche also went on vacation to Bad Reinerz with his mother although, at the time, Firtz still thought that Maria was going to Bad Kudkowa. When someone at the plant informed him that Winsche was in Bad Reinerz, Fritz had the presence of mind to say that his mail was held up but that his mother-in-law was also in Bad Reinerz with her sick daughter. Most of the northern spas were overrun with people from Lodz and gossip traveled easily and fast. Fortunately Fritz was able to stem off some vicious and cruel gossip.

Mama Jurgensen remained in Bad Reinerz for about two weeks. She came to Lodz in the last week of July. En route to Lodz she met some acquaintances from Lodz whom she informed that she had been staying with her sick daughter, who would have to undergo an operation before she could

---

[102] Bad is German for bath. As already noted, bads were very popular in Europe for cure-alls and probably account for the positive affect they seemed to have on their patrons. Many are very elegant towns with grand bathhouses, fine hotels for the wealthy and less elegant hostels for the middle class. Different spas have different cures and emphases. But in all cases, people have all sorts of massages, mud baths and wraps, sulfur baths and "curative waters" to drink. They are still well loved and respected rituals.

come home. She repeated the story to several other Lodz acquaintances during her stay. When she saw Fritz she was shocked with the way he looked. He had aged by years, was pale with deep lines in his face. He had lost weight and looked worn down. No wonder! He had not been able to eat and walked the floors at night for many weeks. He was glad when he could doze off for a few hours in the morning; he never slept more than 3-4 hour at most. Mama told Fritz that Maria was living in a Lutheran Hostel, was unbelievably nervous and completely unbalanced. She expressed an almost morbid hatred of him, which her mother found very hard to understand. Maria had not talked about home and had shown no interest in the fact that Mama would travel to Lodz on her way home. She did not even bother to send her regards to the children. Only time, it seemed, could help.

During her first week in Bad Reinerz, Maria wrote to Fritz to tell him she wanted to file for a divorce immediately. She stated she hoped to be free in a few weeks. If he would not do it, she wrote, she would start the procedure herself. The letter threw Fritz into new agonies. What was he supposed to do now? She obviously had no idea in her confused state that these things are complicated and cannot be accomplished in a few weeks or even months. She had already stated so many thoughtless things that Fritz trembled in anticipation of what would come next. So he went to the Pastor Dietrich and asked for his advice before Maria could make a bigger mess of things. He listened sympathetically until Fritz talked about her aversion towards him and Kola because he looked so much like him at which time the Pastor stared in wide-eyed disbelief.

"How old is the child?"

"One year."

"How was she after the birth of the child?"

"Loving, as any young mother for the first six months when this aversion started."

The Pastor jumped up and started pacing the floor excitedly. Finally he turned to Fritz:

> Dear God, Mr. Maehle, we are dealing here with a deep psychological breakdown. When the mother's instinct, which is the strongest instinct in the female, becomes dead she must be extremely sick, even if she thinks she is well. You can call it hysteria or whatever you want but there is a physical basis to this behavior. You can trust me, as your pastor, to be a judge of things like that. I see hundreds of marriage problems a year and I urge you not to do anything yet. Even if you had proof of her misconduct, you cannot go to trial with a sick person. Words said and acts committed by a sick person have to be looked on in a different light than when done under sound conditions. Lucky you came to me. Any careless step could ruin the lives of five people forever. Remember what a tragic term, "child without a mother" represents. And what is the unhappy woman to do when the motherly instinct returns and it is too late. You have to give your wife time. When she returns to her children it will be hard enough on her alone for all the idle gossip and this goes for you also. The pain cannot be avoided. But since we are Christians we have to take things like this as a visitation and test. Leave it all to the Power who is steering our fate. You cannot know now but maybe this test is good for something and will deepen and strengthen your lives together. Sometimes we human beings need these punishments, just as a child needs a strap.

Fritz returned home more composed. The pastor had found an explanation in the illness. He wrote to Maria the very same day that he had gone to the church's office regarding the divorce but that the matter was not as easy as all that and that it probably would take many months and a personal appearance from both of them, first in Lodz with the pastor and then before the Church Council in Warsaw. Mama Jurgensen was relieved. She agreed with Fritz and the pastor, both of whom confirmed her own opinion regarding Maria's mental health. A few days later she and Sigi returned to Riga. Fritz looked much better; the tension was gone from his face and he was finally able to eat and sleep.

Six weeks later he received a second letter from Maria. She had written from a women's hospital in Breslau where she had been sent to have a D&C. She felt very ill and asked for 300 rubles as she was being sent to Ulberichshoehe, a sanatorium for nervous disorders. And finally, she asked about the children. The question about the children was definitely a positive sign. But as far as the actual facts were concerned, it was a sad state of affairs. Manja, Ferdi's sister, was a dumb chicken without any experience in running a household; the children's help was a child herself. Heddy, who was 10 years old, looked pale and anemic. She was desperately learning Russian and was very quiet and introverted. She was an intelligent girl and had noticed for quite some time that there was something wrong between her parents and it was eating her up. Gerda was only 6 — too young and happy-go-lucky to think about such problems. But Kola was seriously ill and it grew worse by the day. Did he instinctively miss his mother? The little guy lay in his crib all day with his eyes closed, dozing. He showed signs of headaches and only whimpered sometimes. He did not have a fever but he showed blood in his urine. Fritz was worried sick that he would not survive, all the more since both doctors he consulted were very pessimistic and had not come up with a diagnosis; they were awaiting the results of a urine analysis.[103]

Fritz wrote a short, matter of fact letter to Maria telling her of Kola's condition. Shortly after he mailed it the results of the analysis came back. Kola was anemic. The brain had an insufficient supply of blood thus causing the headaches. It also looked as if his kidneys were infected. And then everything started to happen. Maria must have received Fritz's letter on the last day that she had to remain in bed and the mother's instinct, so long suppressed, broke through. Maria cabled: "Reply immediately Kola's test results." Fritz replied: "Lack of blood supply to the brain." Maria cabled back: "Arriving tomorrow 11:20 train." He picked her up at the station with a factory carriage.

The storm that had blown over them had taken its toll. She looked exhausted, very pale and hollow-eyed. An expression of determination had replaced her fixed expressions and the fighting expression in her eyes had made room for a more haunted one. Besides everything else she must have left the hospital immediately after Fritz's last cable to make the trip home so quickly. "But thank God," he wrote, "the children had their mother back after 7 ½ weeks. That was the most important thing at the time and the children were overjoyed. Kola became visibly healthier." The deep rift somehow seemed to close between Fritz and Maria also and the deep personal aversion she had had for him began to fade.

---

[103] These sound like symptoms of anaclitic depression, a condition found in children who are abandoned or neglected by their maternal figure.

Maria however, was far from a complete recovery. She was still very nervous and became agitated easily. Her short-tempered outbursts appeared at the smallest provocation. She needed a great deal more rest, mental relaxation and a change of scenery. Fritz wrote Mama Jurgensen who had always been under the impression that a long stay at her home would be best for Maria. She also had an unswerving faith in Dr. Knorre in Riga and in addition, there was a well-known sanatorium for nervous illnesses in Thorenberg, a short distance from Riga and Hinzenberg, where the Jurgensens were then living. Fritz thought a trip to Riga would be best for Maria also. Not only would she get the care she needed, she would be free of the gossip, rumors about the divorce and talk going on. Maria however, was not much in favor of the plan. On the contrary she said, "I do not have to play hide and seek. I haven't done anything wrong." But then something, which Fritz had been anticipating for some time, happened. Her great friend Mrs. Elbo, who had traveled all summer from one health spa to the next found it necessary to treat Maria very badly during one of their teas at another lady's home. Maria ran home and cried hysterically for hours. In addition, her physical condition was very poor. She apparently had a painful infection of the ovaries. The Lodz doctors could do nothing but suggest rest. At this point, Fritz reminded her of what the pastor had said and she agreed to go to Riga. Aunt Hanna said she would come to Lodz to look after the children. She arrived in late October and Fritz and Maria left for Riga a few days later.

When they arrived in Riga the first thing they did was to make an appointment with Dr. Knorre. He examined Maria but could not find anything wrong with her. He suggested that she should see someone about her nervous condition first. And after several consultations, she was admitted to the sanatorium. Fritz then went to Dago to see his father. As winter was approaching he was fearful that all the boats would soon be stopped. The crossing to Dago was very cold and stormy and he had to take a sleigh to Kertell as Dago was covered with heavy snow. Nikolaus had visibly aged and Fritz could see that he was displeased that his sons had opposed his marriage to his housekeeper. But he was living comfortably and quietly, smoking his cigars, which his doctor wanted him to give up, and reading a lot. Fritz, of course, had no idea that this would be the last time he would see his father alive and also the last time that he would see the place of his birth. After a week he returned via Rival where he visited colleagues from his student days and relatives. He went to the city hall and found it staffed with a completely Estonian administration — a sign of the times. This would have been unheard of in his student days. He then went to Riga for a week where he visited with his brother, Rudolf, and some friends from student days and, of course, Maria in the sanatorium. Upon his return to Lodz he found Hanna and the children very well.

When he returned to the plant he found a letter from the Director stating that he should apply for a passport so that he could travel in Europe in January to see the newest and most modern developments in the field of turbines and boilers. The administration was finally ready to change over. Fritz was to present the project with complete cost estimates by the fall of 1913. He was overjoyed with the prospect. At least this was a welcome distraction at the end of this unhappy year of 1912, the year which had taken its toll on him. He and Maria had to find a new way of life together and their style of living had to change. In all the years that he was making so much money there had never been a chance to put any into savings. The daily expenses had to be revised and they had to put aside something for emergencies and sickness. Fritz could not even finance a little trip for the holidays from his meager savings. If he wanted to go any place he had to ask for an advance on his salary. Maria came home shortly before Christmas. Fritz met her in Warsaw and they took the train home together. Maria was quieter and seemed more in control; the sanatorium seemed to have done some good and they celebrated a peaceful Christmas with Hanna and the children.

Chapter VIII:
World War I Years

With the coming of 1913, the Maehles seriously began to rebuild their lives together. They retreated from all of the festivities and entertainment. Happily, Maria was even able to make peace with the ladies group and Mrs. Elbo, although she stopped meeting them for the daily luncheons and shopping and declined the many afternoon teas.[104] Fritz continued his dues for the Men's Choir and Engineers Club, but he seldom attended meetings and he cancelled their season tickets for the theater. And when they did go to theater, opera and so forth, they took the streetcar and went directly home after the performance. Their circle of friends was reduced to Oskar, the Warrikoffs and Mrs. Frisch who had shown such sympathy during the critical times in the past year. Johanna stayed in Lodz with Maria during January while Fritz traveled to Berlin, Switzerland, Ausburg, Kolmar, Munich and Nuremburg to talk to people in other plants regarding their equipment. It was a very successful trip lasting a full month and as soon as he returned home, he began to plan for the factory's upgrade to electricity. He was working around the clock.

---

[104] Early in 1913 the ladies group broke up. Mrs. Elbo moved to Moscow and one of the other ladies had a breakdown from which she never fully recovered.

Meanwhile, Hanna announced her engagement to Bodo in Berlin, Fritz had seen them when he was there and knew the engagement was imminent.[105]

In the summer Maria traveled to Hinzenberg to her parents' summerhouse with Johanna who then returned to Riga, as Maria was strong enough to get along without her. But no sooner had Maria settled in, a huge fight erupted with her father. There had been an agreement that Fritz and his family could stay there rent-free in lieu of Jurgensen's payment of interest on Fritz's loan to build the house. Maria's father demanded rent from his daughter and when she reminded him of the agreement, he went wild. Finally she wrote Fritz who determined that there was nothing he could do but pay the rent, especially since Maria's health still left much to be desired and they had agreed that she should see Dr. Knorre again. And finally, the source of all the long years of her suffering became clear to Fritz. She was diagnosed with many polyps, including a very large one on her uterus. "Why," Fritz wondered, "had Dr. Knorre not seen this in the previous winter or in Breslau where they had done a D&C?" In any case, Maria had an operation in Riga, which went very well.

During Maria's absence, Fritz had the house completely redecorated. He was also working long hours, even on Sundays. He even designed an annex to the plant building in which he combined all the mechanical departments and his office. And their new quiet life style and personal savings system began to show results. In addition, his Widzener shares doubled several times and paid 11.5%

---

[105] We heard Bodo's name frequently in our home, especially since my mother had lived with Hanna and Bodo while a student in Berlin. Bodo's last name was Graefe. I don't know precisely what he did for a living, although there is a later reference in this narrative to his purchasing a business from a Jew when the Social Democrats came into power in Germany.

interest. He calculated that between his savings, stock and loan to Papa Jurgensen, he was quite well off and should something happen to him, his family would be left very comfortable. He was feeling very good as he left for Hinzenberg at the end of the summer. Maria was home from the hospital and feeing much better. And then he received the bad news that Nikolaus had had a stroke and was paralyzed on his right side. Fritz sent him a wheelchair so that he could go into his garden. Nikolaus was 69 years old and his health was failing.

The family returned to Lodz for the beginning of school, and Fritz and Maria furnished the house with lovely furniture: leather chairs and sofa in the den and so forth. Everything was going smoothly except Fritz's health, which was poor. His ever-ailing digestive system had been harmed seriously in 1912 when Maria was in Bad Reinerz. He had suffered terrible stomach pains, which were becoming worse. Even on his trip to Germany, and Switzerland he had constant stomach aches and an ever-present nausea. And during the summer they did not let up, but continued to worsen. He knew he had some kind of serious problem so he went to see his doctor, who pumped his stomach and told him that he had a "complete acid plant" in his system. From then on he was on a strict diet, which caused him to loose weight and look old. He felt better for a while and then the pains recurred. And then came 1914, the dreadful year, which led to the great worldwide catastrophe.

The year started out very well for Lodz mills and factories. All industries were working full steam and the immense country of Russia was swallowing up everything they produced. Over production was unknown. Even Germany was exporting everything to Russia. The forthcoming gloom was not visible to the Maehles yet. In January, Fritz traveled to Berlin with his project drawings and cost estimates for the central electrical building. He was accommodated in the elegant Savoy Hotel and upon arrival invited to a gala dinner. The following day he presented his plans to the central administration, where the project was accepted without discussion. Fritz would be responsible for its execution. Fritz wrote:

> A person who does not know and has not lived during the time before WWI cannot possibly imagine what planning went into a large-scale project at that time. Think about it; here is a firm from Lodz, not even the largest in the cotton mill sector, and it decides in one meeting which does not even last a full hour, with the stroke of a pen to spend 1,500,000 gold marks (3,200,000 zloty) to modernize their plant. Today (28 years later when he wrote these memoirs) one would have to think quite some time before spending 200 zloty even for a <u>necessary</u> repair job. And it would only be done as a last straw. That proves how poor we have become over the years.

Before he left Berlin he also visited with Hanna and Bodo who were busy planning their marriage. When he returned to Lodz he began project implementation, which started with discussions with the parts suppliers. "And for the first time in my life," he wrote, "I first felt strong anti-Semitic feelings, which had been increasing more and more over the past few years." It all stemmed from an increase in the power of Jewish businessmen and what Fritz perceived to be unethical business practices. It's not clear why he attributed certain traits that were unsavory or unethical as exhibiting a particularly Jewish characteristic, since he had already had many questionable contacts with Christian businessmen. But one must attribute his feelings, at least in part, to the general level of anti-Semitism prevalent in Europe, and especially Germany and Russia at the time and his lack of personal relationships with Jews. Indeed, he had few personal relationships with Catholics except as servants who were another class. In fact, in later years when he had contact with Catholics through his daughter Gerda's marriage, he showed similar signs of stereotyping and prejudice. His son-in-law was not a plain old louse — he was a Catholic louse.

At this time, Kindler and Winsche, the company president and chief financial officer respectively, and Fritz were having "bloody battles" with their suppliers. Some representatives of the firm came to him in privacy to inform him that a certain Jewish engineer, Margulis, had gotten hold of all his plans for the project, drawings and estimates and was running around town telling all of the suppliers that he had the final decision regarding the supplies, and that he would make his decision according to the kick-backs he received. How did this come about? How did he get Fritz's plans? "And how did he have the audacity to interfere with a project that was not his responsibility? He was not even employed by Widzener!" Fritz had been opening every discussion with the suppliers by pointing out that there were no kickback provisions for anybody; they were out of the question. He immediately went to Kindler and Winsche about this and an express letter was sent to Tanfani, the firm's head, in Berlin. Two days later Tanfani replied that he had written Margulis, demanding that he return the documents he had obtained and explaining to him that he had nothing whatsoever to do with Widzener's business.

The following day the plans were returned to Fritz by messenger. Fritz still could not figure out how Margulis had obtained the documents. Then a long letter arrived from Tanfani explaining that he had given them to Uscher Kohn, Widzener's representative for their Jewish customers in Lodz and the surrounding areas. Following Fritz's meeting in Berlin, Uscher had visited Tanfani and during the course of the visit purchased a great many shares of Widzener stock. Tanfani seemed to think very highly of him.[106] Tanfani gave him the whole package of documents asking him to drop them off at the plant when he returned to Lodz. Uscher mentioned that he had a good friend, Margulis, whom he would like to have look at the plans as he was interested in modern instillations. Tanfani agreed. Margulis felt he was covered by Uscher who was in such good standing with Tanfani as well as being a large shareholder. Thus, Tanfani's letter to Margulis was seen as big slap in his as well as Uscher's face and later on, when Uscher became head of the factory, he did not let Fritz forget it. Fritz wrote that Margulis, made the most of the affair. He was consulting engineer to many Jewish as well as Christian firms and several of them were in the process of modernizing. Most used the same suppliers. So Margulis simply told the suppliers that he should have a bonus from them for the Widzener procurements, or he would not consider them for future orders with his other customers. Some of the suppliers became intimidated enough to promise him the bonus. None of this ever materialized since the deliveries never took place — because of the war.

All of the main suppliers had received Fritz's orders and construction was to be started. Since Fritz's engineering diploma also entitled him to supervise the construction and since, as he stated, he was rather ambitious and determined to supervise his plans in person, he went to Petrocowa to apply

---

[106] Later on, Uscher was to become manager of the whole plant and Tanfani was cut loose as President of the Board.

for the Registration of Authorization. Included with the necessary papers was his diploma. When the papers were returned his diploma was not among them; the company's representative forgot to ask for it when he picked up the papers. Fritz never saw it again. During the war all the archives were evacuated to central Russia and were lost forever. He finally obtained a new diploma after the war by writing to the Polytechnicum in Riga, which had become the capitol of the new state of Latvia. In any case, by June the construction of the new buildings was well underway to the extent that Fritz felt the new equipment could be installed by September or October. So Maria and the children went to Hinzenberg on the Baltic as in previous years while he remained at work. As Oskar and his family also left Lodz for Osel to stay with brother Hermann, who was getting married during the summer, Fritz had little to do but work.

And then the world changed. On June 28, 1914 the Austrian successor to the throne, Archduke Franz Joseph and his wife, were assassinated in Sarajevo by an Austrian citizen of Serbian nationality. The French President was on a peaceful visit in Petersburg and Emperor Wilhelm II was vacationing in the fjords in Norway. Austria, holding Serbia responsible for the murder, even though the assassin was an Austrian citizen, sent an ultimatum to Serbia asking for subjugation of the Serbs under Austrian police and began mobilizing her troops. Serbia accepted almost all of the points of the ultimatum but was mobilizing also. So Russia started mobilizing troops near the Austrian border, since she had a defense agreement with Serbia. All this happened with lightning speed within a few days. The newspapers could hardly keep up to date. Cannons between Serbia and Austria seemed to go off almost on their own. Russia prepared to influence

Serbia if Germany were to do the same with Austria. But Berlin had no intention of stopping Austria as they were in agreement with her. So Austria became aggressive and Russia threatened with a general mobilization of troops.

Fritz read it all, and people talked among themselves, but there was no belief that an actual war was upon them. Had he an inkling that it was war, he would have sent for Maria and the children immediately. So, on July 25, he left for Hinzenberg to be with Maria on her birthday. He planned to stay until the beginning of school in September when construction of the new buildings would be completed. As he had planned everything before he left, he did not have to supervise the final work. All he could think of was that if there were a war, it would be absolutely terrible. But, that was unimaginable.

There was a great deal of tension when he arrived in Hinzenberg two days later. Every half hour or so there were extra bulletins in the news. All of Europe was in a fever. Every country seemed to be looking for a key to the solution. Some believed it lay with Russia; others thought Vienna or Berlin; but nobody actually knew anything. On July 28, Maria's 33rd birthday, red posters were placed everywhere giving orders for mobilization. The situation looked very serious. Fritz and Maria drove back to Riga to be closer to the pulse of happenings. Riga was hectic, although the mobilization was orderly. Every few moments newsboys were seen running around with news bulletins and telegrams. In the afternoon a huge rainstorm hit Riga. Maria and Fritz had dinner in a hotel dining room. They were almost alone. They stayed in Maria's parents' apartment overnight and awoke at 5:00 AM to return to Hinzenberg. They had calmed down during the night. "After all," they reasoned, "a mobilization is not a war." And so thought everyone else. Personally Fritz thought that he had nothing to worry about. He had been out of the service since 1906. And then, as they were entering the railroad station for their train to Hinzenberg, a newsboy came racing around the corner yelling "Extra! Extra! Germany has answered the Russian mobilization by declaring war. The die is cast; the disaster is on its way." Fritz's political assessment of the situation was as follows:

> Again and again and long after the war ended, talk was about Germany's guilt in starting the war. We had believed this truly and even now (1922) it is hard to deny the matter as a lie. Of course many countries were guilty but Germany did not have a small part in the guilt. If Emperor Wilhelm II of Germany would have intervened in Austria, she would have stepped back and not invaded Serbia. But the invasion brought Russia into the picture almost automatically as Russia felt she had to act as protector of the Balkans and Serbia against Austria. Russia against Austria however, required that Germany come to Austria's aid. One cannot help thinking that Austria and Germany had started the war. But another country was not free of responsibility — Great Britain. We do not know the full history and what happened behind the scenes but we do know the German war plan was known a long time before they thought about the real thing; invasion of Belgium to northern France, crushing France and after a complete turnaround, the army would be sent to Russia and a peace would be dictated in Petersburg.

Of course, England knew this plan. If England had informed Berlin, even in the last moments before the war was declared, that a war with Russia and invasion of Belgium also meant war with England, Germany might have thought twice. But England cunningly waited two days so that Wilhelm declared war on France without any provocation and asked Belgium for free passage — which Belgium naturally refused. So Germany declared war on Belgium and two days later England explained that she was the protector of Belgium's neutrality and therefore had to go to the side of Germany's enemies. Belgium had initiated a military pact with France when the German plan was first discovered, and this was known to both England and Germany. So the whole neutrality bit was a farce.

Maria and Fritz stood in the station from 6 AM until 9 PM without food or drink in an unbelievable hubbub. The whole world it seemed was standing on its head. This was, he reminded us, Riga's big tourist season with up to 40,000 vacationers. And they all seemed to be at the station trying to get home. But, there were no passenger trains running. Instead there was an endless stream of freight trains with military equipment and personnel rolling toward the German border. By 10 PM the Maehles were on a train back to Hinzenberg and that night they held a family meeting by candlelight until the wee hours of the morning. All were rather depressed. The normal thing to do at this time would have been to get back to Lodz where Fritz's work was, but under the circumstances, and after seeing the station the day before, traveling with belongings and children was out of the question. So they prepared to wait for calmer days when traveling would be possible again. Fritz immediately wrote to Widzener and asked them to forward some money to his account in Hinzenberg. Days went by and he received neither an acknowledgement of his letter nor money. He sent cables; no answer either. Unbeknownst to him, WW I had begun.

How were they, isolated in a seaside resort, to know that the Russians had evacuated the border cities and all the administrative offices and banks in Lodz, and that the German troops were approaching the front line? With all of the furor and press coverage, the newspapers did not report any of this. After about two weeks of waiting and knowing nothing, they learned that Germany had followed exactly the long known plan to attack Belgium, stopping just short of Paris while Austria overran Serbia. At the same time, the Germans were pushing into Poland. Meanwhile the Russians were destroying the Austrian frontier in the North and East Galicia[107] and the Austrians were retreating via the Carpathian Mountains towards Cracow, Poland. Then the French bombarded the Russians with urgent cables to do something to save Paris; they asked Russia to invade Berlin. So Russia turned her army from Galicia and attacked Germany in Eastern Prussia.[108] It was an extremely clumsy move as there were no train connections and the road connections were very poor. This maneuver, Fritz wrote, threw out the original plan altogether, but France was saved. Hindenberg, the Chancellor of Germany, rounded up

---

[107] Galicia was the northern most province of the Austrian Empire until the end of the WW I when it became part of Poland.

[108] Until the end of WW I, Prussia was the largest and most important of the German states; Berlin was her capital. The chief member of the German Empire and a state of the Weimar Republic until 1933, Prussia occupied more than half of all Germany on the Eastern side and the major part of northern Germany. Before 1919 it consisted of 13 provinces. The Maehle family identified strongly with Prussia and its people who were educated, aristocratic and dominated many German institutions. Prussians also considered themselves the most pure Arian, superior to most if not all others, several hundred years before Hitler.

several battalions and in a terrible battle at Tannenberg, East Prussia, defeated the Russians. But the attack on Paris came to a halt at the Marne River as a result of weakening the German army on the Western front by taking out the troops to fight the Russians. And then the war was everywhere. They were all digging in, from the Swiss border via Verdun, to the beach in Belgium. That was the state of affairs just three weeks after the beginning of the war.

Still in Hinzenberg, Fritz read in the paper that all retired officers up to age 60 were required to report to their military posts. They were needed for service behind the front lines. Fritz was 42 years old. His passport noted that he was an officer in the reserve. If he were to ignore this call up, he would be in trouble the next time his passport was checked. He and Maria immediately went to the military reporting office in Riga to be informed that he was to report to the office in Lodz, as this was his residence and place of work. They were both very disturbed that he had not yet heard from the Lodz office, but he prepared to report to Lodz. They decided that initially he would go alone so that if he had to go into the army again, Maria and the children could stay with her parents in Riga. (At this time the children were Heddy — 12, Gerda — 10, and Kola — 7.) Fritz remained in Hinzenberg until August 22, on which day there was a total eclipse of the sun.

As Hinzenberg lay in the center of the total darkness zone, a scientist from the University of Dorpat had established himself and his telescope a few steps from their house. But as a result of the war, the other scientists from Petersburg, Finland, Sweden, etc. had not arrived and the man was desperate. He asked Fritz, along with some other gentlemen from Hinzenberg, to stay through the day and help him with his recording equipment. The eclipse took place on a beautiful bright sunny day at about noon, and by afternoon Fritz was on the train to Lodz via Riga and Warsaw. In Riga he stopped over for a couple of hours to see his brother, Rudolf, who told him that Oskar had already left to report to his medical unit in Petersburg, and Ewald was assigned to a mobilization camp. Rudolf, who was never drafted because of his health problems, had just been laid off from his job as all the factories were closed. He was very depressed. Fritz felt sorry for him and although he had regularly sent him money, he told his brother that he could no longer count on it as his own resources were limited and he didn't know what was going to happen when he got to Lodz. When they said goodbye at the train station the brothers did not know that this would be the last time they would see one another. Rudolf and his family soon moved to Reval; he died in October 1925 before Fritz ever had a chance to return to his homeland again. He also saw Papa Jurgensen that summer for the last time; he died in August 1918, while Riga was still occupied by the German Army.

The trip from Riga to Warsaw took 18 hours under normal circumstances. This particular trip took four days, as Fritz's train was frequently sidetracked in obscure little stations to make room for military transports. People on his train were literally starving. And all the food in the stations where they stopped was gone. Once in Warsaw Fritz raced across town to the Lodz station and there he heard for the first time that there had been no news from Lodz in two weeks. Apparently the Russian authority had not reached that far and the German troops were advancing into Poland from the German border. At this point Fritz had absolutely no money. He had had only one sandwich in four days and it had cost a fortune. Luckily he met quite a few people from Lodz in Warsaw. Several had fled in advance of the Germans; others, coming home from vacations in Finland, Sweden and Petersburg, were as surprised by the war as was Fritz. All were trying to get back to Lodz. Fortunately he met Mr. Stein from Allart (his old factory) who lent him enough to pay for a hotel room. Finally on August 28th a train left for Lodz. It was jammed with Lodz residents who wanted to put an end to their odyssey and go home.

Fritz arrived in Widzew in the afternoon to be greeted by their anxious maid Anna who had begun to doubt that she would see any of the family ever again. In the Lodz railroad station the district police commander told Fritz that all military administration had been evacuated from Lodz. They were expected to come back as soon as the military situation was clear, but at that point nobody knew anything. Regarding Fritz's reporting for military duty, he said that one should not assume anything just because of a public notice in the newspaper. The government had not even called up the police. He advised Fritz to put his name, address and rank on a postcard and mail it to the military administration. So Fritz did just that and from that day forward he never heard from or had anything to do with the Russian Military again!

When he returned to the factory he found that the telegraph office in Lodz had been dismantled. Fortunately he had sent a cable to Maria from Warsaw and expected to hear from her soon. And meanwhile, what had happened in Lodz? First, the Reichsbank (central bank) had left the city with everything — all money, savings accounts, etc. As a result everyone was out of money since all private banks usually deposited their cash every evening with the Reichsbank. This situation continued for the remainder of the war. The Lodz police had fled and a civilian militia had been established to keep things in order. When the police returned, at the same time Fritz did, they stayed in the background as a support to the militia. A consortium of private banks and industries had issued some emergency money, which would be redeemable three months after the war was over. As a result of the departure of the Reichsbank, the occupation of the coal mines at the German-Russian border by the Germans, and the hasty military mobilization in and around Lodz (population about 60,000), industrial life came to an immediate standstill. On top of this most of the foremen, specialists and managers were either from Germany or Austria and had already been taken prisoner by the Russians. They had been sent to civilian camps in the inner part of Russia and Siberia.

Postal and telegraph service as well as the railway were paralyzed. The German infantry and cavalry (soldiers riding horses) were slowly making their way towards Lodz. There was virtually no Russian resistance. The very day that Fritz had photographed the eclipse, a German infantry battalion had moved through Lodz to Zgierz, a city north of Lodz, although it had to retreat soon after. And while Fritz was in Warsaw, a bloody battle had taken place in Tannenberg and another at Krasnik, both near the area of Lublin, another Polish city in the area. A few days after his return to Lodz, several bags of mail came in from Warsaw. They were more than three weeks old but for the first time, Fritz had word from Dago, Osel, Hinzenberg, and Reval.

Two weeks after his return from Hinzenberg, Fritz received a letter from Maria that she was in the process of returning to Lodz. Since the post office in Lodz did not forward any private messages and since the only repaired telegraph was used for military messages during the day and would only receive private ones during the night, there was no communication available to respond to Maria. Then he received another telegram from her that she had already left Hinzenberg; he took the next train to Warsaw. But since there was no regular train service the family arrived when nobody expected a train from Petersburg and he missed them in Warsaw. While he was running around looking for them in hotels, they were arriving in Lodz. Again he met the ever present Mr. Stein from Allart who told him that Maria was very upset since he had not answered her telegrams and had not shown up in Warsaw, and that she had traveled with a great deal of luggage, which could only be transferred on a different train from Riga to Warsaw. She had given the luggage tickets to Mr. Stein with the request that he look after the luggage, which was supposed to arrive the following day. She felt she could not wait around with the children. Fritz called Maria that evening to let her know that everything was in order and the next day he returned to Widzew with luggage in tow. On September 9, they were finally all together again.

Communication with Warsaw began working again so that the factory was able to receive money. Administrators received, 30% of their wages. This did not change for the duration of the war. Fortunately, because he had free housing and utilities, it was enough to live on. Work at the factory also resumed permitting them to finish the installations and bring the machines on line. But around the end of September the police, who were stationed around the city, became restless and then disappeared, only to return the following day. That evening the Maehles could hear cannons, and the next day Lodz was without its police force again. All government buildings including the post and telegraph offices were closed. And nothing could be seen of the Russian military either. On the morning of October 8, German troops arrived in Lodz. General Siebert, the commanding officer, arrived in the evening and with lightning speed, German order was installed. Lodz became an occupied city. The newsstands, which had only the day before sold Russian papers, sold German ones. The Grand Hotel was confiscated as the headquarters for the German general staff. German troops were everywhere. Large masses of troops were pushing forward towards Cracow. This operation was thought to relieve the Austrians who were getting clobbered in Galicia by the Russians. Most people, including the Maehles, were in the dark as to what was actually going on, but the grapevine was reporting great military transports toward Warsaw.

On October 27, the Germans began blasting everything associated with the Widzew railway system. The station was set on fire, all railway bridges and overpasses were totally destroyed, and all tracks and switches were detonated, even including private tracks to factories. And then overnight General Siebert and his troops left Lodz, followed the next day by an endless stream of new German military — soldiers, artillery, and cavalry — moving into the town. There seemed to be no doubt that the Germans were retreating after an unsuccessful attempt to invade Warsaw. The grapevine had it that there was a huge battle between Lodz and Warsaw and the purpose of the destruction of the rail system was to slow down the Russian troops who were in hot pursuit. German troops were everywhere blanketing the streets of Lodz and Widzew. Maria and Fritz stood at their front windows watching the parade. The soldiers looked exhausted. The horses pulling wagons and cannons looked as if they had been requisitioned from the farms; most were lame and their backs chafed. The cavalry looked like a collection of left over troops. From their uniforms Fritz could distinguish Dragonerswith their peaked helmets, black hussars, Ulan, and some

Austrians.[109] The weather was cool and it was raining and muddy. The soldiers were filthy and covered in mud as were the vehicles. The infantry were dragging their feet, bearing down under the weight of their backpacks. Many looked as if they were in a trance with their eyes half closed. When a column stopped they threw themselves on the ground where they lay like the dead. When they were commanded to attention they picked themselves up with difficulty and plodded on.

Where were they going? Fritz decided to have a look so he went to the high water tower at the factory and climbed to the top. The fields where the Maehles had spent many a Sunday with Oskar were covered with gray figures. Yellow lines began to appear, zigzagging and widening. Trenches were being built. And all this so close to the Maehles' home. After a few hours all the German military began flooding back to Lodz as if they didn't know which way to turn. A platoon of cavalry took shelter in the Maehles' stable for the night, and in the morning before departing they took five horses, but not before the commanding officer handed Fritz a receipt.[110] But by the following morning, the army was back in Widzew and by 11 AM Fritz calculated about 150 cannons and 2-3 divisions of infantry. Then the Maehles' home was confiscated. All the doors were opened wide and a sign appeared on the garden gate reading "Staff, 27th Division." A major, a lieutenant and a medical officer moved in. An orderly was sent to prepare a bath.

---

[109] Dragoners were German military police. The rode motorcycles with those infamous sidecars in WWII. They were heavily armed and considered strong and brutal. I suspect that they had not attained these distinctions until WWI. Nevertheless, they were disciplined and well trained. Ullan were lancers and jussars "elegantly" dressed light cavalry.

[110] People still used horses and carriages in those days and most middle-class had their own liveries.

They were hungry and exhausted. Listening to their conversation Fritz could tell that they had not had a rest for 15 days. But their morale was high because even though they were retreating, they felt they were winning the war. They lay down for an all too brief rest.

Meanwhile Fritz had stationed himself on the water tower again. There he saw the infantry coming out of Widzew in swarms. They were moving between the railroad station and the Storki factory just out of town. He could see a messenger moving between the lines. The artillery was being positioned directly behind the station and the Widzener plant workers' houses. The following afternoon there was a great rumbling of Russian cannons, and immediately the German cannons started up. The duel went on and on. Fritz could see the shrapnel fire across the fields and the flash of the German artillery. When he climbed down from the tower he saw workers and their families running with their belongings to take cover in the factory. The German troops were rushing out of the city and the Maehles' guests had left their beds in a great hurry. When the main troops had finally cleared out, Fritz spotted some deserters taking shelter with some families in Widzen; they were captured by the Russians a few days later.

On October 30, the Russians arrived — first the Cossacks, then the infantry and artillery. The Factory Workers Orchestra of Widzener was playing for them and Maria, along with all the other women on Petrikowa Street where the Maehles lived, gave their whole supply of winter fruit and cigarettes to the soldiers. And again, the Maehles became hosts to a staff. This time it was a Russian colonel and seven other officers. The colonel also used the factory office because of the telephones in it. But again, the next morning this regiment left and another one arrived. This time they were aviators, a completely new branch of the armed forces. They took a position in a field behind the spinning mill of the factory and confiscated Fritz's well-equipped workshop in the factory. A whole section of military engineers was commissioned to repair the bridges and railway. Fritz and a cadre of his people from the plant were assigned to remove the blown up overpass bridge from the highway and to clear the road. In seven days the military trains were running again.

With the arrival of the Russians, Lodz also received mail from Warsaw. Papa Jurgensen was desperate since he had not heard from his daughter. He asked why they did not write. He even wrote a letter to the plant to find out what happened to his family and if they were still alive. Of course he had no way of knowing that Lodz had been occupied by the Germans for almost a month. The Russian newspapers did not report anything about the German advance because they were not allowed to. Papa asked that they send a telegram immediately, forgetting that this was not possible. And they could not write a very detailed letter either because all letters were now censored. Fritz wrote immediately in Russian as writing in German could be interpreted as treason. Fritz was also very worried about his father — alone and partially paralyzed in Dago. Since Fritz sent his father financial aid monthly he usually heard from him regularly. All he could hope was that Hermann, who was then a pastor in Osel, would be able to look after him. But Fritz knew that his father was worried because he probably thought that he and Oskar were in the war and perhaps Fritz was on the front. Oskar was, of course, in the medical corps and stationed in a relatively nearby city. Fritz received a postcard from him asking that he come to visit with him. But how could that be done? The rails were full of the military and military equipment. There was no longer a fear that the Germans would return. The grapevine reports had the Russian cavalry already crossing the border into Germany. Then after two weeks, just as Lodz was getting used to the Russians, things became unclear again.

On Sunday, November 15, a certain unrest and nervousness became apparent in the city and surrounding area. Rumbling could be heard over the fields and around Widzew from the north. Since the Germans had left Widzew in a westerly direction how could this cannon thunder be coming from the north? And then the genius of the German battle plan, designed by Hindenburg and Luddendorff, developed. After the failure of the plan against Warsaw, the army was called back to Germany, pulling the Russians behind it. Once on German soil, the army had time to regroup and then, thanks to the excellent railway and road connections, took a right flank through eastern Poland and the back of the Russians. In order to avoid a catastrophe, and to keep the retreat line open to Warsaw and avoid being encircled, the Russians had to return to Lodz. The tremendous fight lasted more than three weeks and secured, as Fritz wrote, "Our city a place in the world and war history as the Battle of Lodz." [111]

The following narration is quoted exactly as Fritz wrote it and Hilde translated it. It describes his family's life in the middle of a war zone.

---

[111] My mother had her father's memoirs in our home when I was a teen and I cannot believe that she did not read them. But whenever I asked her what they said or to translate them, she said that she did not have the time. She subsequently gave them back to Kola (who had brought them from Germany) but it was not until after he died that Hilde, his wife, translated them into English. It is interesting and noteworthy that my mother never spoke of these experiences despite the fact that she was already 12 years old when Lodz was occupied, and 16 when the War ended. Whether she blocked it, couldn't talk about it, or preferred to let us think that her youth was always idyllic and happy, we cannot know. But until reading her father's memoirs, I was under the impression that she and her family always lived in great comfort, as certainly seemed to be true before the war.

The Battle of Lodz, 1914

To us, it meant 3½ weeks in the center of this gigantic battle field, surrounded by death, horror, destruction, sheer Hell, and completely severed from the rest of the world. I have kept a detailed diary about these times and only repeat here in an abbreviated form what happened.

November 16

Ferdi Warrikoff visits us and tells us that his brother Hugo has died. Hugo left Lodz at the end of September (completely unnecessarily) being afraid that as a Russian veterinary doctor for Lodz and the surrounding area he would have difficulties with the Germans. He and his oldest son were stranded in Kobryn behind Warsaw and he died there on November 13. At this time the road to Warsaw was still open and Mrs. Jenny and Ferdi's wife, Wanda, who was carrying her baby, Sigi, had traveled there. Now as the thunder of the cannons worsens and is getting closer, Ferdi is increasingly worried.

November 17

The cannon thunder is now very close and the windows rattle. Great numbers of the Russian army are flooding back and forth towards the city. Since we are living on the main through street, and since I am the one person who knows about the plant buildings, the workshops and the workers, our doorbell rings at all hours, even in the middle of the night. I have to answer questions, look after quarters and so on. I am terribly anxious and upset and suffering from nervous stomach troubles. I literally sleep in my cloths and doze only for three or four hours at most.

November 18

In the morning the cannon thunder is so strong and loud that the plates on the table are jumping and by 2 PM all Hell breaks loose. For the first time, we lock all the doors of the house and, grabbing everything of importance (documents, money and food), we scramble to the cellar and take shelter. The cellar has an arched ceiling and seems to be fairly safe. We go to my former dark room and we sit on the wooden floor which I had installed. The front line cannot be far — probably at the Stoki Mill — because one can hear the tec-tec-tec of the machine guns very clearly.

By 4 PM it lessens a bit and the noise seems to quiet down, so we crawl out of the basement. The hazy weather has cleared up and the sun has set. The sky is glimmering wintery. Soon the devilish concert starts again, but we have gotten used to the noise, so that the family is coming out now to watch the terrifying scenery from a balcony on the second floor of the house. The cannon balls explode against the evening sky like fireworks. The entire horizon is in a semi-circle — blood red from all the burning villages. In between, one sees the sheet lightening of the rapidly firing cannons. The rolling thunder of the artillery and the short intense cackle of the machine guns mixed with the never ending noise of the rifles of the infantry are constant. The scene is indescribably eerie and the winter air carries the "Hurrah" screaming to us which makes the blood run cold.

We are glad to be back in the house, even if it is not very comfortable. We are not allowed to use fire during the day for cooking as, we are told, the smoke might be a dangerous signal. But now, in the evening, we can cook something. Maria boils potatoes and we eat those with some ham which was smuggled to us by a friend some time ago. And with a cup of tea, this is our meal. We have not seen bread for quite some time.

At 8 PM the doorbell rings. Doctor Skalski, the plant physician, has opened a field hospital in the city's hospital and is treating the stream of hurt and wounded people. He is running out of space and needs other rooms. I rustle up as many workers as I can from our night watchman's office and see to it that four classrooms in the school across from the hospital are cleaned up and heated. Beds are not available; clean straw on the floors has to do.

There are already more than 8,000 causalities in the city and the number is constantly growing. There is an unbelievable number of wounded arriving in trucks, carts and stretchers every day and we are becoming immune to the misery that is constantly passing by our house. Those with slight wounds are limping, half conscious from hunger, cold and loss of blood. There are still streetcars running back and forth carrying wounded to the center of the city. Most of the soldiers seem to be hurt on their left hand; some have head injuries and their faces are bandaged. I gave one soldier a cigarette and it was hard for me to find his mouth under his blood soaked bandages. I have never seen people smoke with such greed. Cigarettes have become a great palliative.

At 10 PM I am having hot tea in the kitchen when a dreadful shelling starts in the immediate neighborhood, so strong that the whole house shakes. I rush the family into the cellar where they bed down on their straw mats on the floor. I then take my coat and run into the street to check out what is happening. It turns out that the artillery has taken up positions very close to our spinning mill and is shooting directly over our house. But that means everything is alright and we can still relax. Maria and the children have fallen asleep in spite of the terrible thunder above. I climb downstairs again and, fully dressed, fall on my bed. At 2 AM I am called out again and before I have a chance to fully wake up, the house is full of officers who have to have some tea at least. This kind of life goes on for almost a month. As our house is situated on the main road, we have a daily influx of visitors. Our family is living in the kitchen and the bedrooms, when we are not in the basement. To clean the dining room, living room, study, halls and so forth would be a silly thing to do as the floors are all covered with straw. We do not even have time to clean up with all the traffic of soldiers running in and out of the house.

I too, am running in and out between the plant and the house. Sometimes a whole regiment wants to come into the plant, and I do my best to find room for the frozen soldiers in the boiler house and machine sheds. It is warm there since the boilers, so far, are kept heated. The hot water must be kept in case of fire, as everything around us is frozen. Later on the army forbids this too, because the smoke from the chimneys could be seen for miles around.

November 21

The worst part for us is that we do not know what is going on in the outside world. Our newspapers are not allowed to print anything about the military situation. The officers who are coming from the frontier do not know any more than we do, and the general staff, of course, does not tell anything either. The rumors that are going around are from one extreme to the other. Finally we begin to interpret from all the information gathered that in the beginning the situation for the Russians around Lodz was very precarious indeed, and the battle that began a few days earlier north of Lodz has progressed in a semi-circle to the south of the city. Therefore we are now encircled and the horizon, with the exception of one small interruption, is a belt of red from the many fires in the outlying villages. Rumor has it that a German official was escorted to the Russian headquarters in the Grand Hotel to ask the Russians to surrender. But they did not and now the cannons have grown quiet. There is talk about a lack of ammunition on both sides.

November 24 and 25

I have been given orders to turn off all the street lights in Widzew and the electric lights in the court of the plant. We can see clearly on the horizon three giant reflectors throwing their light bundles against the sky. This, we think, means an air attack by Zeppelins (a blimp). We now hear a deep and low rumbling of cannons and see the light reflection of cannon fire from the direction of Ozoekow. (Many years later by reading a lot of war literature, it became clear to me that those light bundles were actually signals given by the Russian Army to inform their troops that the long awaited replacement army had arrived and was participating in the battles. What we had actually seen was the sheet lightning.) Now the tide turns against the Germans. A whole German division is surrounded in Brzeziny and the Russians are waiting for their surrender. But the German commander, General Litzmann, takes a great risk and breaks out through Strykow (another town). Without this feat of daring on the nights of November 24 and 25, the whole war might have taken a completely different turn.

The situation for us however, does not change. The daily migration of casualties is instead increasing. Around this time a friend of Maria's pays a visit. She is working in a hospital downtown. She asks us to help out with shirts, pants, shoes, even slippers, sleeping bags and linens. The distress amongst the thousands of wounded people is terrible. Lodz is ill equipped to deal with the onslaught. No beds, no blankets, no bandages and only a few doctors and the number of casualties has risen to 30,000. They are put up in the German Gymnasium and other schools, empty factory halls, etc. Maria joins in the effort and all dispensable linen is taken to the hospital. From now on Maria and Heddy go daily to the hospital to help.[112] Since we have been confined to the house or the cellar almost constantly over the last 10 days, this is actually a welcome change for Maria. She also collects food and wine for the wounded and in this capacity she goes to Allart to ask Mr. Stein and Ferdi Warrikoff for help. Ferdi is desperate. Wanda had left for Warsaw with their daughter, Jenny two weeks ago with plans to return immediately. They are not back and nothing has been heard from them.

From this time on, our house becomes sort of a meeting place where bandages are made from flannel, etc. We hardly notice the thunder of the cannons anymore. Food is a great problem. The farmers cannot come to town anymore and many farms were burned down. Many farmers are afraid to leave because their horses can be confiscated by friend or enemy at any time. Most of the livestock and animals have already been taken. What little food that remains in the city is only available on the black market. We are lucky in so far as we have already stored our winter supply of potatoes, peas and flour. We also have a ham which we smuggled in some time ago. During the night Maria bakes a cake. Bread has not been available for quite some time. Tea and sugar are still in our house but not coffee. We can only guess how the poor people are feeding themselves — probably potatoes, sauerkraut and the meat from

---

[112] Heddy sometimes told us that her mother was trained as a nurse. Undoubtedly she got this idea from this period. If so, it makes one wonder how much more she remembered.

dead horses which are lining the streets. Even the human corpses are often robbed. Many are completely nude and no corpse still has boots.

November 29 and 30

On November 29, casualties and prisoners are transported out of the city by trains as the rails are in Russian hands again. While so far, the war activities have been between the military forces, now the civilians have suddenly become involved by the bombing of Lodz on November 30. The whole city is shelled with grenades, especially around the central city where the Grand Hotel is located. Soon airplanes are over the city and the noise is now coming from all directions. Smoke coming from the plant shows us that the tar storage shed has been hit. The bomb was probably meant to hit the gas or utility plant. I was particularly concerned about Maria today. She was alone at the hospital, without Heddy that is. At about 7 PM she finally returned home all out of breath. She had run the whole way in great fear. She tells us that the central city is in turmoil. She said that a few people who worked in the charity organization had left the hospital a little before her. A few minutes later they were brought back on stretchers. A bomb had exploded right in front of them. Everyone must have been hiding in their basements because the streets were deserted. But she kept on running along the long row of houses until she reached Widzew.

An hour later we are all sitting in the basement. I am writing my diary by candle light, when the noise of detonations starts to come from directly over our heads. The gates of the factory are torn open and people from nearby houses come running in to seek shelter in the lower lying basements under the plant's building. Several houses in Widzew have been hit. It seems that our office building is among them too. We are so used to the war by now that we have learned to distinguish various sounds and phases. I climb upstairs; three shots almost simultaneously, obviously from the line of the enemy; a fast approaching whistling and hissing sound and a three fold bang of the explosion that makes the walls in the house shake. Maria and the children, however, are sleeping in their blankets on the straw mats on the basement floor. The temperature is only 40° F. Even that does not bother them. The bombing lasts all through the night. I cannot sleep at all. My nerves are fluttering while I am moving between the house and the plant like a ghost. Endless columns of military pass the house. At 4 AM orders have been received that all vehicles have to leave the city with wounded and tired soldiers. Some of the civilians leave the city also, hopefully to arrive in Warsaw one of these days.

Finally, around 10 AM we hear the details of what had happened. A German battery had advanced so far ahead from their previous position and had camouflaged themselves so well that they were able to bombard the city for a whole 12 hours before they were discovered by the Russians. This attack took the lives of 200 civilians. Huge craters have embedded themselves in Widzew between our house and the factory. Fragments are embedded in the walls of the office building, the shutters of most of the windows are blown off and there is quite some damage in the offices. Almost all window panes are shattered; the entrance door has not one panel left. The roof on the storage building has a gaping hole and the apartment on the top floor is demolished. Two people who were walking past the building were killed during this attack. The center of Lodz and the northern suburbs are much damaged as well.

We cannot quite understand the military administration. Nothing can be printed in the newspapers. They run reports somewhat like this: Mr. Herzberg, of Nikolai Street, 1st floor, was killed yesterday when the ceiling and a wall fell down in his apartment. He died instantly. His wife, who was in the next room, was miraculously not hurt in this accident while the cook in the kitchen was badly injured by flying metal parts. These idiotic reports were filling column after column, but the bombs were never mentioned. What the administration wanted to achieve is beyond me. It only resulted in increasing the anxiety and panic of the population.

December 1-5

On December 1, we receive word that the Wanda Warrikoff and her daughter had arrived home after some danger to their lives and many adventures. We spend several more nights in the basement and then on December 5 at 8 AM, a general departure of the troops begins. They are heading towards Warsaw — trucks, carts, hundreds of wagons, the infantry followed by the cavalry, artillery and finally motor cars with the general staff. It goes on all night. Quite a few of the wealthy civilians also leave with the army. Maria is inconsolable and in tears, and I am suffering from the worst stomach cramps I have ever encountered. As a last memory of the Russians, a streetcar rolls from the town and comes to a stop in front of our house. It is loaded with freshly baked beautiful smelling Russian bread for the soldiers. The Russian soldier in charge of the bakery obviously had just put the loaves in the oven when the order came to leave. He was not about to leave the bread in the oven and run. It is government property and worth about 200 rubles. So he stayed and waited until the bread was baked and then, since there were no vehicles left, he confiscated the tram thinking that he would catch up with some military vehicle. Now he is standing in front of our house, scratching his head. He is talking to the man in charge of the factory storage rooms who just happens to be the first one on the scene. Since the Germans, who are continuing to advance, cannot be too far behind, it is becoming a rather urgent matter now. Finally we all have a bright idea. We buy the load of bread at the current military price and the baker moves on the catch up with his outfit. If he cannot bring the bread, at least he can bring the money. We even write a short note for him explaining the circumstances. Then we start to unload the bread and soon our storehouse is swarming with people from Widzew who, just like us, have not seen bread for three weeks. Never has a slice of bread tasted better to me than this fresh baked soldier's bread.

By 6 PM the factory is swarming with spiked helmets. Most of the German soldiers are very young. They are covered with mud but otherwise well dressed. They are cold and many are coughing. Small wonder as they have been living for days in the trenches, in dirt, snow and cold. We have to give them the office building and they put straw from our storage rooms into the offices. Then we heat the boilers up and soon we observe a lot of nude men getting rid of their underwear and shaking their clothes over the fires. Then the battle against lice begins. Suddenly I become aware of a group of Russian prisoners. They must have been hiding in the Widzener plant and they are now being marched off by a German sergeant. A young lieutenant is sitting on his horse in from of the plant. "What kind of people are these, sergeant," he bellows! "Seven Russian prisoners, Sir." "Aha, they probably had enough of the war. Do any of those dumbbells know German?" "I understand German," replies one of the prisoners. "Are the Russians heading to Warsaw?"

asks the Lieutenant. "No, they are going into trenches at Kurowice, says the Russian. "What! Just six km from here! God damn it!" And off he gallops down the street, presumable to report the news. Meanwhile I return to my house and join my family for a nice cup of tea.

Soon the doorbell rings and I am confronted by ten German officers. They demand quarters and I let them in where there is still straw on the floor from the Russian occupants. They ask for beds which I cannot provide. Then they ask for cognac and liquor which I do not have either. All I can come up with is some tea and that without sugar. Most of these officers leave again in the morning to be replaced by officers in charge of communication. They put all their equipment on our dining room table and begin to nail the apparatus down. The wires are strung through the windows into the garden. The door to the street is constantly open and orderlies and messengers arrive all the time. A Major von Marshall has taken over the living room and in the front room is another major with a southern German accent and a very young German officer, who speaks a better Russian than I do. It turns out that he is of German parents who live in Petersburg. Being of draft age, he was immediately snatched up by the German army while he was on his summer vacation in Germany when the war broke out. He is very worried about his family in Petersburg. We also talk quite often with the major who has an industrial background and has worked with textile machinery and had business deals with Russia and Poland. In his opinion the war with Russia is as good as over. Peace will be with us at Christmas. "When the leaves fall, you will be home," he proclaims to the young officer. I have grave doubts.

December 7-12

Our good leather furniture is strewn all over Widzew. Most of the pieces are at Lorenz's home where there are also house guests. The guard at our door makes a great fuss whenever we leave the house or come back. And on the following day, December 7, the cannons start up again. However, this time it is the other way around. First the Russians were in the city and the Germans outside. Now it is reversed. On December 11, the front line troops leave Widzew and follow the Russians and our militia returns to the city. The front line troops were arrogant and hard to deal with and there were squabbles and fights. It was a noisy time with shouting and arguments and we are glad to see them go. But there were some reasonable human beings among these people also. One day an officer of the Dragons (German military police) introduced himself as a colleague of the electrical faculty and asked me if I were chief of the plant. He asked if there was any place where he could take a bath. So I took him into the boiler room where our workers had made up a simple but clean bathroom for their own purposes. He was extremely glad and grateful. In our conversation he expressed his regret about the war. He had many friends and colleagues from his university days among the Russians against whom he now had to fight. The war had taken a tremendous toll during the few months since it began and most of his good friends were already in a "better world." His fate was already decided but no one could have predicted what was yet to come.

December 14-Christmas

On December 14, we heard for the last time the sound of the cannons, after we had listened to them for a whole month. As we find out by and by, the Russians retreated to very well prepared trenches to the North and for the next few months, the Germans are attacking these lines over and over again, without ever reaching their goal — Warsaw. On December 17, the major with the southern German accent tells me with a certain satisfaction that they are moving on to Warsaw after all and he leaves. The other major, the officer from Petersburg, and their two comrades leave on December 19, and with them the telegraph people from our dining room. Maria has a great fight with them as they want to take half of our belongings too. We immediately start to clean and by afternoon we have managed to fill three carloads with old straw and dirt from those occupied rooms. Even the bathroom returns to a "fit for humans" condition and that very evening all of us are finally able to take a hot bath.

The next day we clean the rest of the house and collect all of our furniture which is scattered throughout Widzew, and we are at last prepared now to celebrate Christmas in clean surroundings. However, food is a catastrophe and we cannot even think about Christmas gifts. But we have a little Christmas tree in a flower pot which costs as much as a floor to ceiling tree in the pre-war days. Kola is happy with a box of tin soldiers; Gerda has a coloring book and Heddy, a new apron. I have made a jumping jack from cardboard for Kola. Maria has managed, with her surprising economical talents to serve us the traditional Speckkuchen (German Christmas bread, a little like stolen) and she even produces half a bottle of cognac. We are very happy. We have a roof over our heads and warm rooms. Millions of other people are definitely worse off than we are.

We are, of course, still very anxious about the fate of all our loved ones, especially, my parents-in-law and my father. Shortly before the battle of Lodz started we received a postcard from Herta, Oskar's wife, stating that my father had caught a bad cold and had run a high fever. We were questioning if he would still be alive and if so, what was he living on? I was not able to send him any money. But my hope was that Hermann was still close enough to be in contact with him and the clergy, hopefully, would not be financially affected by the war. What has happened to my brothers, Oskar and Ewald, in the army? We would not hear more detailed news until the end of 1917. We do not leave the house between Christmas and New Years. Indeed, where should we have gone?

All of our friends have the same problems and the empty cupboards do not help much. We receive a letter from Frau Lorenz — a German soldier was the courier — from Breslau. She wants badly to return to Lodz and is concerned about her home and the fate of the city. Obviously, according to the papers in Germany there are only a few smoke stacks left in the city of half a million people. The mood of her letter is very depressed. She, being born a German, writes that it is hard to describe and to believe how many sacrifices this war has already asked and how many lives have been taken. What a blessing that none of us has any idea that the war will last another four years. We did not even dare to think one month ahead at that time, let alone speculate what there would be in store for us and what the results and consequences of this war would be for the whole world. But the Battle of Lodz is over.

The family started New Year's 1915, depressed and filled with vague fear. At least they still had a home and health. Maria was recovered from a bad case of shingles she developed as a result of the shock during the bombing. The children were well and even Fritz's stomach had settled down. While Maria played with the children, Fritz relaxed with a glass of Glüehwein (hot red wine) trying to forget the dark future for a moment. Again, a complete surprise — how did Maria get red wine?

When the Russians departed, the immediate danger to the city of Lodz came to an end and although the Germans were still occupying the city, life somehow regulated itself. But the situation was still pretty grim. Fritz wrote:

> We watched our life disintegrate before our eyes piece by piece. Everything which we had considered a basis of our world, our outlook on life and the things which we had been prepared to encounter, and which were familiar to us, the feeling of belonging to this immense complex of countries called Russia — all this was falling apart. When the war finally came to an end we were sitting on the ruins of our lives and discovered that we were treated more or less as a nuisance, as aliens in the young state of Poland in which the national waves of independence surged high.

The feelings of the Poles were understandable, but the Maehles could not completely share in them. They were too new to the country, had lived there too short a time and, last but not least, had grown up under such completely different circumstances that they felt like, and were treated like aliens. In fact, they barely knew the Polish language, German being their first language. However, in the beginning of 1915, nothing of all this was felt. They were still at the beginning of the war, which would clobber all of Europe. It was calm in Lodz and only the German patriots were convinced that the Russians would never return. Their home continued to be occupied, albeit now by German officers and fewer of them. And their lives became more normal, more like the months just before the outbreak of the war. The first issue that had to be solved was school for the children. One term had already been lost when all the schools were closed and Heddy and Gerda's school had left the city altogether. Ferdi Warrikoff began giving private lessons so that the girls would not lose everything they had learned so far. But this was only a temporary solution.

In early February the Reiher family, friends from their Baltic circle, moved back to Lodz making all the remaining Balts happy to have their group enlarged by one more family. Food continued to be a problem. Although the farmers began to return to town in January, it was a short-lived reprieve. Soon German occupying forces cut off all food imports from all directions and severe food shortages resumed. By summer people were issued ration cards for bread and sugar. Meanwhile, the ruble was declining rapidly. By the fall, they were paying three times the normal value for food. In the beginning of the year Fritz received about 30% of his normal wages. But, being paid in rubles, it was only worth 10% of his salary. Fortunately, they had enough cloths, and they still did not pay for their housing so the money could go for food and necessities. By March, when the factory started working again, wages were paid at pre-war levels of 65% so the employees could live a little better.

The plant had a new problem. Uscher Kohn, the fellow with whom Fritz had had a conflict when he gave Fritz's plans to his salesman, began forcing his way into management. At the beginning of the war Kohn had been immensely pro-German, exhibiting great hatred for the Russians. Throughout, he ingratiated himself to his German visitors, lavishing black market wine and delicacies on them. Being convinced that the Russians would never return he became very aggressive at the plant after the Russians left. In January he announced that he had plans to start the factory again and would deliver goods to the German army. Mr. Wuensche, still the technical head of the Company told him that if he wanted to be hanged, go ahead. Wuensche had served in the Russian army and, like Fritz, was an officer in the reserves. So Kohn dropped the idea for a short time but soon began behaving as if he were the owner of the company. The issue was complex. The actual owner, Tanfani was in Germany and could not be reached. And even though Kohn was not on the Board of Directors or an administrator of the company, he had the largest amount of shares. At the end of February, Wuensche had several strokes. He was not expected to recuperate. Kohn used the situation, and supported by Lorentz, also a German patriot, who had returned from Germany where he had been stranded at the outbreak of the war, had begun to work his way into administration. Meanwhile, Maria and Fritz had made no bones about their pro-Russian feelings. On March 22, Wuensche died and Kohn was put in charge of the factory. He produced a letter from Tanfani appointing him CEO and Tanfani's personal representative in the administration. Tanfani only realized what he had done to himself when somewhat later, Kohn got rid of him. Kohn had successfully outmaneuvered him and completely taken over. So Kohn reached the top position without any interference to become the CEO of one of the largest cotton mills and the only one working full time in all Lodz. He was beside himself with self-importance. He trusted the Germans completely. They were even going to make Lodz a harbor by building a channel from Lodz to the Baltic Sea.

  Despite all the chaos surrounding the Maehle family, things began to pick up for them. They were able to celebrate Easter in their home with all their friends because Widzener was the only plant working to capacity. In May, Italy joined the entente with Germany to purchase cotton and metals. And then the occupation forces announced that they would confiscate all cotton and copper in the factory. This included their expensive printing rollers and turning lathes necessary for the enormous quantities of weapons they were making. Kohn became depressed and his enthusiasm for Germany waned. By June everyone, including Fritz had been reduced to two to three days per week. More was impossible as they lacked raw materials and coal.

During the summer the military situation for the Russians became worse. After the battle of Lodz, the frontier was shown as a line from Eastern Prussia to the Carpathian Mountains. All during the year there had been a continuous exodus of German troops from Warsaw. Every half hour or so a heavily loaded military train carrying cannons, rattled over the tracks, through the fields behind Widzew. By the middle of February the Russians had been squeezed out of Eastern Prussia in the Battle of the Masures, and by May the Germans had penetrated the frontier. The Russians had no ammunition left. The front in Galicia began to crumble and the Russians began to retreat. They surrendered Warsaw on August 4, leaving the whole Congress of Poland with immense influence on the mood of the population. Up to this point only a minority of the population was hostile to the Russians. But the mood was changing to complete indifference. The way of thinking was, if the Russians with their army of millions could not keep the enemy out of Warsaw, they might as well stay away.

Agitation by the socialists and radical thinking intelligencia began. The Jewish people, like Kohn, were more in favor of annexation by Germany; the Polish Christians were in favor of independence. To complicate matter even more, there was a split in the

German population. The German colonists on the farms but also in the cities, who had been treated very roughly by the Russians and their sympathizers, could not hide their jubilation. Now, one way or another, they were determined to come under the German government. A number of the Maehles' friends and acquaintances acted in a very unrestrained manner. The more sober Germans however, especially those involved with manufacturing, some administration and sales people who had been traveling abroad and in Russia before the war, stayed loyal and committed to Russia. They believed that breaking away from the giant Russia would be a catastrophe for their industries. It was with this group that the Maehles and their close Baltic friends most sympathized.

After the fall of Warsaw there was a strong movement to Germanize their lives. The militia was dissolved and replaced by a uniformed troop of policemen who were commanded by Dragons, the professional German police. New passports were issued by the German occupation force and Russian passports were destroyed. It was no longer permitted to provide financial assistance to laid off factory workers, which meant that they were tempted to move to Germany for their livelihood. Germany was in dire need of metal workers and many did leave.

The German occupation force was working hard to turn the mood of the Polish people in their favor. They re-opened the University of Warsaw and tried to enlist the Polish army to fight with them against the Russians. But the confiscation of materials continued; chemicals, metals and other products necessary for manufacturing cotton were constantly being taken. Copper was also confiscated from private homes. At the von Reyhers' suggestion, the Maehles hid their copper samovars and casseroles in an empty apartment in a nearby house but somehow the landlord learned about it and gave the goods to the German authorities. "At least," Fritz reported, "they were all healthy." There was a time in January when they were afraid of an epidemic of sorts because of all the dead bodies of people and animals laying in the streets. But somehow they were spared. After the Battle of Lodz, the whole city was cleaned up. Interestingly, the German newspapers stated that the city was cleaned up after years of filth and neglect.

The big question on everyone's mind was "what will happen to us?" Most people were living with anxiety and fear, punctuated by occasional socializing in an effort to forget the difficulties and uncertainties of the times. It was said that no country had been prepared for such a long drawn out war, for such gigantic armies, or for such extreme amounts of ammunition. The war techniques were all new; airplanes, zeppelins, bombers, fast firing cannons, gas attacks, wireless communication systems and submarines. As a result of all the excitement and fears in daily living and his nasty habit of smoking, Fritz's stomach continued to act up.

And how well was Russia equipped? Before the war began Fritz noticed one Russian captive balloon floating at approximately 400 feet in the air. When he arrived in Lodz the Germans flew zeppelins at least 1000 feet high every day while the Cossacks aimlessly fired their rifle and shook their fists. During the Battle of Lodz there were five French single engine planes stationed behind the spinning mill. The Russians tried to fly them a few times but were immediately attacked by German fire. Meanwhile German planes were swarming over the city daily, not only during, but also after the battle. There were only two plants in Russia that produced cannons, rifles and ammunition. That was it!! France and Britain had their large metal industries, which were changed over to war production, and they also had help from the United States. Russia, however, was completely cut off from all traffic with her Allies. She had abandoned Lodz and Warsaw to the enemy including all the machinery etc., which the Germans dismantled and shipped to Germany for their war production. The Germans even engaged the civilians, including Fritz, in assisting them with their production efforts. Many years later, a professor from Warsaw gave a lecture in Lodz concerning this particular situation. According to his findings there was a ratio of one soldier to eight civilians working for Germany while for Russia the ratio was one soldier for less than each civilian.

Fritz thought, "And that was how they expected to win the war?" Even comparing the Russian soldier to the German soldier was an embarrassment. The German forces were well dressed, well trained and well fed. They were seldom seen on the street without their pipes, cigarettes or even cigars. Conversely, the Russian chaps would ask people on the streets for a cigarette, money or even a piece of bread. The Russian soldiers did not even have warm clothing during the Battle of Lodz, although the short fur coat had already been introduced into the Russian army when Fritz served. The poor boys coming into the hospital did not have more than torn shirts and gray wool coats. Many did not have sox or underwear — and they slept at 30°-40° F. on the bare ground. Fritz wondered why they didn't have the same equipment he had 15 years earlier?

There had been no mail delivery for almost two months. The post office building which had been evacuated at the beginning of the war was still not fully functioning; only a few temporary wickets were opened. The soldiers had no mail from their families.

Similarly, there had been no news from Estonia or Riga. Interestingly, when the Germans controlled the city large trucks of mail, including parcels, for the troops arrived regularly. The troops on the German front lines were young, 18 to 30 years old. This was not the case in the Russian army where all ages served in all positions. There were aged patriarch with long beards marching side by side with new 20-year-old recruits, and they all seemed very demoralized. After observing the various differences between the Russian and German troops, Fritz wrote in his diary, "The fantastic organization and their education made the German a terrible and fearsome enemy. They would have been invincible if, after four and one half years of war, the hunger and social disturbance within the county had not forced them to their knees."

That Christmas was much better than the previous one. Heddy and Gerda received Russian and German books and a few other gifts, and Fritz made a cardboard saber, helmet and toy soldiers for Kola. The family even had a large tree and again celebrated the holiday with their friends from the Baltic circle. They also received the good news that Hanna and Bodo had married in October. But Fritz continued to contemplate the future, which to him was still dark and uncertain.

By Easter of 1916, the plant had run out of both raw materials and coal and stopped working altogether, resulting in the termination of all employment contracts. The firm offered to provide loans on a monthly basis, if the employees would keep themselves available and work in the interest of the firm and turn over shares of their stock as security. From then on, the Maehles lived on borrowed money although happily, Fritz continued to work, making up jobs for about 200 employees. They leveled ground between buildings, dug out a basement for the spinning mill, and constructed a larger storehouse for cotton. The Germans had ordered that all material not working should be sent to the war material collection point. But Fritz managed to bury several carloads of copper cables and tubing in the ground under the rubble of the incomplete electrical building, the weaving building, and even the plant water ponds.

Daily life at home continued with a schoolteacher and piano teacher coming to the house to teach the girls during the first semester. All the children were taught French.[113] By Easter, Maria and Fritz were able to return to the German Theater. They also got together with their friends from student days who had moved to Lodz. And in August, Fritz and two friends from the plant steeped themselves in learning English, which lifted their spirits and took their minds off fretting and worrying about the daily annoyances in connection with Kohn. By October Fritz was able to translate little stories by Mark Twain. Meanwhile a second group began a course in conversational English, which Fritz joined. By the second semester the Rothert School was reopened and the girls returned.

Kohn's expectations of making millions were thwarted when the plant was forced to close. But he could not rest. During the Battle of Lodz great amounts of forest were damaged around Lodz. Kohn decided it would be a good idea to buy the wood cheaply and saw it into lumber. So he sent Fritz out to look at a saw mill and buy the necessary equipment to open a mill. Soon loads and loads of

---

[113] Heddy used to tell about the governesses the children had in their home. She said that they taught foreign languages which of course, she knew very well. Obviously this is the time she was referring to, which is interesting in that she remembered or at least talked about this period and her early childhood, but not the previous three years, and certainly not in the actual context of the times.

timber were delivered to the factory and stored in the court in front of the main building. But the evening before the business was to start, the Germans confiscated the lumber. Kohn was furious. "He called them every name in the book," Fritz noted. But it got worse for Kohn. A week later the Germans requisitioned an extra inventory of all manufactured goods — at 1914 prices! (Prices had increased 400%) In addition the Germans demanded taxes be paid on the previous year's wages. And then to make matters worse, it was found out that the owner of the sawmill next door to the plant had told the Germans that Kohn was going to open a saw mill and ruin him. Kohn was beside himself. The Germans, whom he had welcomed with open arms, he now spat upon.

In fact, the pro-German group who had been so enthusiastic in the beginning of the war was cooling. Rumors had it that there were talks about a separate peace between Berlin and Petersburg and that Berlin would keep Poland, which was still part of the Russian Empire. Later on it became clear that the rumors were based on reality. In 1915 the German Chancellor had made it clear during a speech before the German Reichstag (parliament) that they expected peace overtures from the Allies. The time was certainly ripe. Germany had already conquered Belgium, Northern France, Poland, a large part of White Russia (Western) the Ukraine and Serbia. But London and Paris answered with scornful laughter. That was when Germany tried another angle, a separate peace proposal with Russia. Indeed, there was no real disagreement between Germany and Russia except that Germany had supported her ally, Austria, and Russia joined on behalf of Serbia. Aside from that, the Germans had always been welcome in Russia. Russia was one of Germany's greatest trading partners and in fact, the common Russian really didn't know what the war was all about. And to top it all off, Russia was not looking very good in the eyes of her citizens. It was scandalous that they could not manage some 40 million Austrians and 60 million Germans when they had an army of 160 million people under their command and were getting help from Great Britain, France, and Italy as well. But Russia was losing land miserably. There was a catastrophic shortage of ammunition and the skimpy railroad system was not able to support the demands of the frontier.

In addition there was the sad happenstance that the 12 year old heir to the Russia throne had hemophilia and the Czar and Empress, who was intensely interested in mysticism, grew almost morbidly depressed. Her position in court was also a touchy subject since she was a German princess by birth, although she had grown up in England, was raised at the British Court, and felt more British than German. At that time Rasputin, a simple Russian farmer who could hardly read and write, came to Petersburg. His head was filled with confused religious ideas and somehow he became identified as a mystic monk, first to simple farmers and then to the Empress. And, as Fritz noted, "he was never a monk and it became well known that he knew a great deal about alcohol and women." In her despair, the Empress latched on to Rasputin and, strange as it may seem, the child seemed to be getting better. So the trust of the Czar and the Empress held for Rasputin grew out of proportion. He was looked upon as a saintly man and the time came when the Czar would not make any decision in his governing business without asking Rasputin' advice. Now, Rasputin was against the war from the very beginning. He was aware of the deep grumbling in the country and he warned the Court whenever he could. He found a willing listener in the Empress because she was fully aware that if the war were lost, the dynasty and the throne would be lost for her son. Finally he managed to influence two other opponents in the elected government, the Ministers of the Interior and Exterior. Soon after that, the rumors about a separate peace with Germany began to surface. Even the price was mentioned. Russia would give Churland (a part of Latvia) to Prussia and Poland would become independent. The billions in war loans that Russia had lent to France would be taken over by Germany, and they would straighten out the matter later with France. There were some other conditions as well, but Britain and France did everything in their power to make an exit from Russia impossible.

Finally it leaked out that the Germans would not remain in Poland. This was bad news for all the pro-German people in Lodz. One barometer of how unhappy they were was Mr. Lorentz from the mill. He was gung-ho German until the Germans, after entering into the Battle of Verdun in February, accomplished nothing after three months of fighting but a great loss of life. Lorentz and his friends became very despondent. Then on May 3, a Polish diplomat arrived at the German Headquarters in Warsaw and demanded the initiation of a free and independent Poland. General Baeseler, the German commander, waived the proposal aside. If the wishes of the Poles were to be considered, they would have to renounce all rights to Galicia (Austrian East Prussia) and Posen (Poland) and would have to fight the Russians as a German protectorate. Poland rejected the offer and the pro-German people began to raise a lot of questions about Germany. And from that time on, everything seemed to go wrong for Germany.[114]

---

[114] Between 1772 and 1795 the entire territory of the Kingdom of Poland was divided between Prussia, Austria and Russia. Called

On June 8, the German fleet lost a huge naval battle in the Skagerack Sea off Sweden. The Germans could not change the desperate situation in Germany itself. England had accomplished a complete blockade and by the end of August, Rumania entered the war against Germany. Germany reacted with lightning speed and was able to take Bucharest in three months. But again, this conquest did not change Germany's overall situation. On the contrary, the grumbling masses became more and more vocal. The opposition had already voiced its favor of ending the war in March and after Skagerack, the socialists began demanding an end to the war. Germany answered that peace would be dictated by the sword. The death of the Austrian Monarch, Franz Joseph, on November 21, 1916, did not change the situation. It only became more apparent that the Hapsburg Monarchy was coming closer to its end. Meanwhile, France and Britain had been working with Russia. Nikolaus II, who was given to changing his mind frequently, finally fired the two anti-war ministers

---

Partitions of Poland, Prussia acquired the western regions of Poland, esp. those, which were later renamed to West Prussia (formerly Royal Prussia) and the Province of Posen (the area around Poznan or Posen. The southern Polish territories around Kraków and Lwów were incorporated into the Austrian Empire and renamed "Galicia." Even before the Partitions of Poland, Posen had some German population but as it became part of the Kingdom of Prussia, the German colonization increased significantly. Most of the settlers were Lutheran and many Protestant parishes were established. Before WWI about 35% of the inhabitants were German speaking. The majority of them lived in the western and northern districts while the central and southern part of Posen retained its Polish and Catholic identity. After Germany lost WWI, the territory of the Province of Posen was returned to Poland, which became an independent nation in 1921. The majority of the German-speaking inhabitants of the Polish parts of Posen immigrated to Germany after 1920. Galicia, which had various boundaries, was, at this time, the eastern territory of Posen and under Austrian control until 1918. Many of the inhabitants were German speaking also.

and the War Party took over. The criticism and condemnation against the Empress became so vocal and widespread that the War Party threatened to have her brought up on charges of treason. Nevertheless, there was relatively little action on the German-Russian frontier during all the discussions of a separate peace and, as a result, on November 15, an independent Poland as per the German conditions was announced by General Baeseler in Warsaw.

The Polish army was then organized under German leadership. The pro-Germans were filled with anxiety. Mr. Lorenz suddenly discovered that he was really a Russian subject and the whole matter did not concern him in the least. It was clear that Germany was acting under pressure, as it did not have any great love for Poland. But Germany was advancing well into White Russia and could not afford an enemy at its back. It was also clear that Poland would never settle without Galicia, Posen and the rest of Poland. Indeed, there was no flag waving. The clergy would not even read the proclamation from their pulpits. The farmers let it be known that they needed bread, not the "King of Prussia." And almost no one came forward to serve in the new army. Nobody, not the pro-Germans, the Jews who had seemed to favor the Germans, the Balts, nor the Poles were happy. Nobody had anything to gain. Even the sea channel from Lodz to the Baltic was lost. Around Christmas time, Emperor Wilhelm of Germany forwarded a peace proposal and the American President Wilson offered his services as a negotiator. But the allies wanted to wait for a total German collapse, which they thought would be soon.

As they entered 1917, Fritz and Maria began to notice that over the year the deprivations and the anxiety of the war had taken their toll on the family's health. Kola and Heddy came down with measles in January and Gerda became jaundiced. Maria developed boils on her neck and had to undergo surgery. There was an outbreak of Typhus in the city; even some doctors died from it. Fortunately it did not spread to Widzew and the Maehle family. The food situation was also very bad. Even with ration cards there was no more bread after January. In September they received ration cards for potatoes. Fritz was loosing weight and his stomach was very bad. They no longer cared what the outcome of the war would be — just so it would be over. Fritz noticed the same attitude in Mr. Lorenz, who was becoming friendlier with the Maehles, especially when his father-in-law, an officer in the German Army who had some position that took him behind the battle lines to Warsaw, appeared for a visit in the middle of the year. There was even a severe hailstorm in the spring. Many windows were broken all over Lodz and Widzew but there was no glass to replace them. Since the skylight in the Maehles' house was broken, the rain poured in. All efforts to contact relatives using the Spanish Embassy, who was representing the interests of the Russians in Germany, failed and the uncertainty about the fate of their families added to everyone's unrest. However, even that Christmas they managed to have a tree and gifts for the children, including a book, *Max and Morris*[115] One of their Baltic friends, the Reyers, arranged a children's party where the children had to demonstrate their French.

---

[115] This is a German children's book, similar to the *Struvelpater*. We had both in my home when we were children and they terrified me. They show what happens to BAD children in the most ghoulish ways, especially the *Struvelpater*. I simply can't imagine a parent thinking that this would be a nice gift for a child. I was so frightened of the *Struvelpater* that my mother had to keep it on a very high shelf out of sight. I still have the book. And ironically, Donald had the same book in his home when he was a child.

Oskar had been sent to Petersburg at the beginning of the war to be with his medical unit. He had returned once for a few days to pick up some things but he had retained his fully furnished apartment. So, Herta, his wife, wrote to Fritz asking him to vacate the apartment, put everything in storage, and contact his employer, the Steinert Manufacturing Co., to pick up some money owed him. There were neither people nor transportation available to move anything. Fortunately, and as the rent was being paid by Steinert, Oskar's landlord said that it would be all right to leave everything in the apartment for another month or longer, if necessary. However, when the German military arrived in Lodz, they took over the apartment. When they left it, they also left a great deal of damage. Oskar's suits were cut apart and the beds were unbelievable dirty. The household linens and Herta's clothing were stolen. Fritz thought this must have been done by the prostitutes who had been invited by the soldiers occupying the house.

When the Russians controlled Lodz after the Germans left, Fritz had not been able to get into the apartment to clean it and when the Germans returned, they again requisitioned it. It had remained occupied until Steinert called Fritz to say that it was free. Fritz was able to remove all that was left of the linens and Herta's clothing, but the furniture had to remain in the apartment. The following day, Fritz received an order from the German Commander's office informing him to return all linen and other articles to the apartment or they would requisition his linens. Maria exploded. She marched straight to the commanding officer and made such a noise that he decided to take the apartment off their housing list. It was left to Fritz to remove the furniture from the apartment and deposit it at Steinert. Meanwhile, the landlord suddenly demanded rent for the whole time of the war. He was an Austrian citizen and Oskar was a Russian soldier. Fritz went straight to Steinert who straightened out the whole matter and the furniture went into the plant's storage.

During all of 1917, the family again lived on borrowed money against their shares of stock. In January, all transmission belts, including those in the repair shop, were requisitioned. They were all bundled up waiting for pickup the following day but during the night they were stolen. This led to another fight between Fritz and Kohn, who held him responsible for the theft. As a result of this requisition, the plant had to be shut down and all the people still employed were fired. Kohn had the idea that the repair shop could still be utilized to make hand held grinders for grain, something that was forbidden by the Germans since they wanted to avoid any possible way of secretly grinding flour and creating an even worse shortage. Fritz agreed to manufacture the grinders only if Kohn provided a handwritten signed order as the manager of the plant. Since this activity was punishable with jail, Kohn refused. But he hated Fritz even more for not taking this risk for him.

The winter of 1916-1917 was cold and snowy. The family spent a great deal of time skating on a friend's large pond. But Poland and Russia were in turmoil. Poland had just declared independence from Russia, bringing joy to Lorenz and several other acquaintances since recent elections in Lodz, based on Poland's declaration, had resulted in a clear Jewish majority of officials in the city. A few of the pro-German group were still holding their breath hoping that Germany would take over the country. Others of the pro-German group announced that they were just suffering from a kind of "war sickness." Fritz quoted, what he said was a typical Lodz joke:

Two friends meet on the street

A) The Prussians are really smart fellows aren't they?

B) Why do you say that?

A) They have achieved what the Russians have not been able to do in over 150 years. And they have done it in two years.

B) What is that?

A) To make the Polish people into Russians![116]

The independence given to Poland had not achieved what many had hoped for, especially since the German Occupation Administration was completely under the influence of the Jewish elected majority, who had assumed governance of the German Occupation Administration's Raw Material Procurement Office.[117]

In December, rumors began spreading like wildfire that American President Wilson had already spoken of the creation of a total Poland, while Berlin categorically refused to discuss the question. And in Russia, things were developing with breathtaking speed. The efforts at the beginning of the year made by Germany to come to a separate peace treaty with Russia collapsed. The Grand Duke's party, supported by Britain and France was trying

---

[116] This joke is apparently a lament of some of the upper class foreign residents, especially the non-Jewish ones who saw their unique control on the economy in the city eroding.

[117] This office, called the "people robbing office," was responsible for confiscating personal goods from residents of the city, farmers and all sorts of factory materials (as has been already noted). At this point in the narrative Fritz apologized for his anti-Semitism. But stated that this "is how we were raised."

everything to keep this from happening. The Czar was commanded to rule in a democratic-constitutional manner and to call back the DUMA. The Czar had discharged the Military High Commander, sent him to Siberia, and declared himself the High Commander. But nothing was helping. The DUMA viciously attacked the government, especially the German born Empress who was being held responsible for the separate peace talks. Indeed, she was being accused of treason and there was growing talk of a revolution against the Czar. Rasputin was tricked into a trap set up by members of the Czar's family and was shot shortly before New Year's Day, 1917. The Empress, devastated by his death made daily pilgrimages to his grave, thereby contributing more and more to her own downfall.

The Russian government simply could not cope with the extreme stresses of the time. The infrastructure was antiquated. The railway system broke down completely and consequently the supply of ammunition and food to the front, as well as food to supply the cities was in chaos. A Women's Protest for Bread continued through February and March. Workers were on strike all over the country. Meanwhile, the war was not going well. The ruble was slipping rapidly to only ten percent of its former value, and by the end of April it was taken out of Poland and replaced by a Polish Mark with the same value as the German mark. And on February 3, Riga fell to the Germans. The DUMA wanted to meet with the provincial administrations to develop a working relationship with them, but they refused. By February 1917, Russia was in a civil war and tempers were flying. The Czar tried to dissolve the DUMA; they refused. Then insurgents took over the capitol in Petersburg and the military took the side of the DUMA. On March 17, 1917, Nikolaus II abdicated declaring his brother Michael regent for his son. Michael refused. He, in turn, asked for a plebiscite (vote) in the DUMA, and Alexander Kerensky, head of the DUMA, claimed the right to govern. According to Fritz, Kerensky was a "muddle headed fellow whose first order to the military amounted to asking the soldiers if they would formally greet their officers or not? "That," Fritz said, "was equal to destroying the last discipline in the army and from then on there was total decline."

Meanwhile Germany was making the most of the situation by smuggling Lenin from Switzerland in a sealed railway car through Germany all the way to the Russian frontier, hoping that he could organize the Communists to bring Russia to a separate peace with Germany. Although the Russian front line was still holding at this time, food was harder and harder to come by. By spring there were uprisings in Germany as a result of food shortages; Hanna came from Berlin to stay with the Maehles for the summer to recuperate from the famine in Germany and Bodo joined them in August.

Unfortunately, conditions were not much better in Poland. Rationed bread was 24% rye, 26% chestnut flour and the rest dried potatoes. "No wonder," Fritz wrote, "that the result of this food was beginning to show on our health." Maria had several painful boils, one under her arm, which had to be lanced by the factory doctor. Fritz's health was at a low point also. He went to see a doctor who diagnosed heart trouble, sclerosis, and hypertension. He was given some medication containing iodine, some vitamins and told to stop smoking. Kola was not looking well either. He contracted a cold in January which lasted all through the spring. He was running a constant temperature. He even showed some blood when he coughed. The first doctor he saw put this aside as just a little irritation of the lungs. But since it did not subside, Maria took him to another who mentioned tuberculosis. The family was very anxious and immediately had him x-rayed including his leg, which he said was in severe pain. A deformation on the shin was detected which the doctor said might be a tumor or sarcoma. On August 21, Kola underwent surgery at the Anna-Maria Children's Hospital. Part of the infected bone was removed and the remaining pieces were connected by a pencil thin piece of bone. A close inspection of the removed bone material did not show any malignancy and the missing bone part grew back quickly; he was soon back on his bike.

As a result of the revolution, the war situation had changed in Russia, despite the fact that it looked as if the revolution would fail. The allies had finally convinced America to enter the war. The U.S. had already invested a great deal in the war by lending money and supplies and would face a loss of billions of dollars if the Germans were to win. In an effort to prevent the U.S. from physically entering the war, Germany was agitating through Mexico. This of course increased the Americans' hatred of Germans in America even more. Diplomatic relations with Germany were cut off and U.S. forces were dispatched to Europe immediately.

The English and French were doing everything possible in Russia to put life back into the "tired giant." Kerensky and the DUMA were in favor of continuing the war, but the Communists under Lenin and his followers had created a secret secondary government. They had a much better understanding on how to handle the Russian masses, all the while working towards a complete reorganization of the existing order. To gain the confidence of the conservative farmers, they promised them the distribution and appropriation of all estates then owned by the nobility. They promised the workers a complete government by the proletarian and since neither promise could be realized while Russia was at war, a new slogan appeared, "Enough of the War."

After his abdication in March, the Czar and his family were held under house arrest in the Alexandria Palace in the town of Tsarskoe Selo (25 km south of Petersburg) where they had many loyal and devoted followers. The Bolsheviks were worried that they might try to escape or somehow try to regain power, so in August the family was transferred to Siberia. In July there were two Russian offensives in Galicia and Brussilow but under the Bolshevik influence, which had developed a very effective underground, the soldiers began to leave the front for their homes on their own initiative. They did not want to miss out if the nobilities' estates were divided. Chaos reigned. Kerensky and his government were absolutely helpless. The end was nearing.[118]

Bythe end of October Germans had landed on Osel, the island south of Dago. The Russian army was driven to the mainland. The Germans were heading for Reval via Dago and Vick, another island. Fritz wrote, "My homeland is now in the hands of the Germans." At the end of October the postal service reopened and Fritz wrote to a friend in Riga to inquire about Maria's family. Three weeks later he received a reply that they had left Riga shortly before the Germans arrived. They were living with friends in another town. On November 30, he received a letter from Hermann, who had given it to a soldier who was going on furlough and mailed it on his way home. It was a sad letter, all about things that had happened during the last three years.

---

[118] The royal family was moved to Ekaterinburg, east of the Urals. On July 17, 1918, they were all executed. For a firsthand account see Pavel Medvedev, one of the soldier guards at www.eyewitnesstohistory.com.

Nikolaus had died in April 1915 after a lengthy illness and pneumonia. Cousin Christlieb had died of cancer of the throat in the spring of 1916. Rudolf was working in a factory in Reval and living with his family in Uncle Karl's house. He earned very little money. Cousin Johanna was ill and lived with Herta, Oskar's wife who was working in an office and thereby supporting herself and her children. Oskar was still in the army somewhere in the south at the Romanian border. Ewald had advanced to the rank of staff captain, had had appendicitis and was discharged. Nobody seemed to know where he was. Hermann and his family were living in the country and he, being the pastor of the local Lutheran Church, was rather well off. He had a year old son named Gunnar.

There was not much good news from the Widzener Plant, especially for the top management. Kohn had, like the other manufacturers in Lodz, hidden a great deal of merchandise, first to save it from sudden requisition and second, to sell it on the black market at very high profits. He and his son, who had studied law in Warsaw but then had gone to work for the plant, had hatched a clever plan. They had figured out that the German Red Cross was under special protection of the Empress, giving them the right to purchase all sorts of goods and materials for hospitals. They met with the senior medical officer of the Red Cross in Warsaw and offered him several million meters of cotton free of charge. In return, for each free meter, they were allowed three meters to be sold on the market, without getting involved with the German War Office for Raw Materials. They explained to the doctor that all the manufacturers have hidden lots of goods in their warehouses and they knew how to get their cooperation. The doctor seemed to be agreeable and wrote a note of 5-6 lines with an order and signed it — rather illegibly. They returned to the plant and asked Fritz to make a photocopy of the document since he was the only person with the equipment to do so. Armed with copies of the order, Kohn and his son ran around to all the other Lodz manufacturers and merchants. They showed them the order and ordered them to turn over their hidden goods at the lowest price, threatening that if they did not, they would be reported to the German War office for Raw Materials, which meant that the goods would be confiscated without any compensation.

Kohn's goal was to gain a monopoly in the market. But when Kohn returned to Warsaw he found that the good doctor had been transferred to the French front. And during the night the military police had come to Kohn's son with a search warrant, confiscated the list, and put him in jail. The following night the same thing happened to Kohn. The Germans ordered him to hand over the order written by the doctor and all the copies as well as the film. Then, using Kohn's list they searched all the industries listed and all the others as well, finding goods upon goods that were not reported. All were confiscated. Kohn and his son were jailed for several weeks, but since the German administrators felt they had already punished the people of Lodz enough, they were set free — after they paid a hefty fine. As a result of Kohn's spying the other manufacturers in Lodz started a boycott of the plant and he was thrown out of the Merchants Club in the town of Widzew.

Meanwhile the war continued and Russia was in chaos. Soldiers were deserting and running over to the Bolshevics. On November 14, 1917, Lenin was declared victorious. The new government offered an armistice to Germany and on November 18, it was signed. At the frontier, Russian soldiers were selling military equipment, including cannons and machine guns to the Germans, killing their officers, and running home to kill the owners of the estates and take over the farms. Fritz wrote, "What we knew as Russia and what we called Russia ceased to exist."

Elsewhere, other parts of the world as they knew it were collapsing. Riga welcomed the Germans with great enthusiasm. The Rifle Club, which Papa Jurgensen had belonged to, and the nobility of Kurland (later to become part of Latvia) proclaimed German Emperor Wilhelm II, the Duke of Kurland. Estonia formed a National Government and declared its independence and called all Estonian soldiers home from the Russian Army. Fritz thought that all these actions were some sort of war sickness that had befallen them. The world seemed to have been turned upside down in those 3 ½ years. But the worst was the total collapse of Russia. And the tension between the Polish people and the German occupation forces was steadily growing. The University in Warsaw had been closed the previous summer and the city administration dissolved by the Germans.

Fritz was occasionally approached by the Allart firm concerning technical questions since the administrator, Hentschke, a German, had been sent back to Germany. Unfortunately, Allart's administrators had hidden fine wool material in a corner of the factory, which the German occupation forces learned about. So the former acting administrator was sent to jail and the German administrator who was brought in by the Germans to replace him was sent to the front. And so the third Christmas of the war approached. The weather was beautiful, cold with lots of snow, and the local pond became a beautiful skating rink. Heddy and Bubi Lorenz (son of a family friend) were almost the same age and, war or no war, they and their friends wanted to be together. So the young people got together frequently at the Maehles' and the Lorenzs' homes to have coffee and dance. The German commanding officer for Widzew was also a guest at both homes. He even celebrated New Year's Eve with Fritz and his circle of friends. And then the war ended and peace talks began.

Chapter IX:
Post War Years Recovery

The end of the war did not bring financial comfort to the Maehles, whose situation was still dubious. They were living on money borrowed, against their shares of Widzener stock. And the amount taken out by the factory each month was getting very large as a result of the devaluation of the Polish mark. Fritz's account had been adjusted when the mark was introduced, but with the constant devaluation he had no idea what his situation really was. All calculations had become illusions. Nevertheless, their social life began to pick up a bit with new invitations coming in from friends around the city.

The peace talks between Germany and Russia were taking place in Brest-Litowsk and at least on the Russian Polish border, people were able to breathe somewhat more easily. But the talks were going very slowly. The Bolsheviks wanted plebiscites in all former Russian parts — Estonia, Lithuania, Kurland, Finland and the Ukraine. They hoped that the people would vote for Russia, but Germany strongly opposed that move since she felt the Baltic States should be under German influence. After long and agonizing discussions Trotsky declared the war was over. The Germans declared it was not and continued to occupy much of the disputed territory.

Finally, on March 3, 1918, an agreement was reached. Kurland (which became part of Latvia), Lithuania and Poland were severed from Russia. Germany promised to remove troops from the Ukraine, Estonia, Finland and Livland (which became part of Estonia and Latvia) if Russia agreed not to interfere with them. And as a result of the peace, German prisoners of war were released. At the end of April the first living witnesses returned to Lodz from Reval with news of the family. It was Herta's maid who had gone with her husband and daughter to the Baltic at the beginning of the war when Oskar had to report for active duty. Oskar returned to Reval shortly before Christmas, wearing a soldier's coat with no officer's markings. He was very down trodden, had no job, and could not get a travel permit despite all efforts to get back to Lodz and his job. Fritz immediately wrote to tell him that his job was waiting, but that the 800 rubles he had saved would be a much a smaller amount because of the devaluation of the ruble.

In May, Professor Feldweg came from Riga to stay with his aunt for two weeks. The polytechnicum, he said, had been evacuated to Moscow during the war but had just been returned to Riga. Also in May, Bodo moved Mama Jurgensen and Sigi (Hanna's child) to Berlin. Then Kola began to complain about pain in his leg. The family was worried and radiotherapy (perhaps x-ray therapy) was prescribed for about two months. The pain disappeared and never returned; the matter was never clarified. Kola had always been a delicate child; in his early years he had cramps and convulsions while he was teething and during puberty had fainting spells and even a broken rib. So the family decided to spend the summer at a farm in the country. Maria and the children went for two months and Fritz joined them on the weekends. After the terrible three war years the vacation was wonderful and they had lots of company from Lodz.

On August 1, Fritz's wages were straightened out somewhat, and he received back payment from April 1916-August 1918. Interestingly, as the mark and rubble were still decreasing in value, no one was able to figure out how the payments were all worked out and at which rate they were calculated. But at least Fritz did not have any debts with the company, although he was not rolling in riches either. And then, on December 31, he received his notice — if the economy and the overall situation for operating the plant did not improve, the plant would have to close. But, no sooner had he been laid off, when Allart made him a proposal, which sounded rather adventurous: to accompany Mr. Saladin, who represented the firm and would probably become the future general manager, to Moscow. Fritz was to prepare a full report about the degree of destruction in the plant, and at the same time to write to Mr. Lamy in Alsace with a full account of all the technical matters involved. Lamy was still the major shareholder in the company and would be the person deciding whether or not to reopen the Lodz factory. Fritz was a little skeptical about the trip to Moscow, especially since things were still topsy-turvy in Russia. The latest news was that the German Ambassador, Baron Mirbach, had been murdered in Moscow and General Eichhorn had been murdered in the Ukraine. Nevertheless, he wrote to Lamy to find out what his future with Allart would be.

Since Tanfani, the founder and chairman of Widzener, was inclined to hand over the plant to Jewish leadership, Fritz and many of his colleagues at the plant had already been preparing to face a change in their positions. He wrote that during this period he had a number of meetings with Mr. Stein, manager of Widzener, in his home and often they were served coffee, accompanied by beautiful white bread. When he looked questioningly at his host, he smiled, knowing that Christians had to eat a concoction of flour and sawdust called bread. Stein asked, "What do you want? This is Passover and we have to observe the rules and the occupation forces deliver our matzo flour." "Appaently," thought Fritz, "everything can be done in the name of religion." [119]

Fritz and Lamy were corresponding about a proposed position at Allart when the family received news that Papa Jurgensen had died at age 66. He had fallen ill while he and Mama were at the beach house, was hospitalized and passed away in the hospital. Maria was unable to get a travel permit to go to Riga but Bodo, Hanna and Hedwig were able to go to the funeral. In September, Heddy entered her last year of school. She was an excellent student, very talented and much interested in music. According to Fritz, Heddy had a serious rival all during her school years. Apparently the girl, Erna Koenig was jealous of Heddy and, not being very talented, tried to out-do her everywhere. Some years later Fritz felt forced to threaten her father with court action because she had started bad rumors about Heddy. Wanda and Fergi Warrikoff's daughter Jenny was also jealous of Heddy and sensed a strong competitor in music with her. Heddy had suffered under these conditions and the family almost had a fight with the Warrikoffs about the situation.[120]

---

[119] This is either some variation of matzos, or Stein was making a reasonable sounding excuse for getting something others could not. Fritz would not have known the difference. Furthermore it was not Passover so there would have been no reason for Stein to need matzos at Christmas time.

[120] There was no further explanation about either of these statements. It does seem throughout the journal that several interpersonal relationships were very tense.

By the end of September, the powers in Eastern Europe collapsed. The Americans initiated an offensive in Metz (Czechoslovakia), the Bulgarian frontier in Macedonia was severed, and the Turks encountered a disastrous defeat in Palestine. The Austrians departed the Balkans and US President Wilson announced his 14 points, a basis on which a future peace should be founded. The pity, Fritz opinioned, was that these terms were created without any knowledge of European conditions and caused more damage in the long run. In fact, European conditions were not taken into consideration when peace was finally agreed upon. Some of the points were a fair distribution of the colonies, general disarmament of all, return of Belgium to its former independence, the return of Alsace-Lorraine to France, self rule for the people of Austria and Hungary thus ending the Hapsburg Monarchy, the creation of Poland, and the inauguration of the League of Nations.

In the first week of October Prince Max of Baden was elected Chancellor of Germany, Scheindemann and other Socialists became ministers, and they accepted Wilson's 14 points followed by a series of stressful communications. Finally Wilson made it known that the enemies would be more approachable if Kaiser Wilhelm II abdicated, and on November 9, both he and the crown prince abdicated taking refuge in Holland. Chaos reigned in Berlin. A general strike was called and all trains and communications were stopped. Members of the military and civilian workers rebelled. Germany was in a state of revolution when on November 11, the armistice was agreed upon. Germany and Kaiser Wilhelm were destroyed. A year and a half earlier Czar Nikolaus II and the Hapsburg Monarchies had also come to an end.

The German army left Widzew on November 13, marching in the direction of the German border, the captain in front and all the soldiers with red ribbons on their rifles and caps. This was the "hero's act of disarmament" according to Fritz. With the departure of the Germans, all of Lodz was in disarray. There was complete disruption of telephone and telegraph service as well as a breakdown of the police force, which had been running so smoothly under the Germans. It was months before everything was in order again.[121]

Finally, Fritz received a reply from Lamy that he would like to have Fritz back at Allart, and if he wanted to change his position the company would be very pleased to have him do so. The following day Kohn informed the laid off workers and staff that their employment would be reactivated immediately. It was expected that things would get much better very shortly and with the end of the war that seemed logical to Fritz. And then he did something he should not have done. He decided not to go with Allart and remained at Widzener. He was hoping that Tanfani would soon take over administration and the company would function as it had before the war. Also, Allart was badly damaged and normal conditions could not be expected there in the near future. Saladin, who was still in Moscow, was rather unknown in Lodz and all of the Maehles' friends who were employed at Allart complained about the lack of support from the firm during the war. His decision turned out to be a huge mistake. Tanfani had no intention of coming back to Poland and left Kohn in charge. Soon it became clear that Kohn was only interested in getting the plant up and running using old and trusted workers, only to replace them with

---

[121] After WWII, the US instituted the Marshall Plan, thus avoiding the pitfalls after WWI.

his own choices. As it turned out, the head of Allart, who had just returned from a Russian POW camp, had no intention of leaving Allart, and he was a stable responsible person.

Poland had become an independent country. Josef Pilsudski, back from a German prison, formed the first government, which, under influence of her neighbors, was rather "red." The workers in Lodz went wild. They called a meeting at Widzener forcing Kohn to give in to their demands — 25 marks increase salary for each. A commission was formed in Lodz to assess the damage and Fritz was asked to join it. He was running around town registering losses and damage, including Oscar's losses at his house. He even called Oskar's former maid as a witness, but they never saw any compensation.

Peace arrived in 1919 — or at least there was no more death and destruction. But there was no happy and elated mood in the country. Tremendous chaos reigned all over Europe. "This," Fritz wrote, "is hard to describe to anyone who had not lived through the war. All the empires, which for centuries had seemed invincible, had collapsed. States such as Turkey, Bulgaria and Hungary had buried under their ruins, the total foundations of capitalism, their economies and their pseudo-liberal governments, and from the ruins the hungry and poor were desperately looking for a new order and a new way of life. Socialism and Communism seemed to be an answer to their grief-and invariably accompanied with violence. If only, he lamented, the established economic connections had not been so brutally disconnected, the healing process would have been so much faster and better. But under the blind leadership of Clemenceau, Lloyd George, Wilson and Orland, the new Europe was created by the monstrosity of a peace treaty which would remain a disgrace for all times."

The German forces had left the Baltic provinces, and the German Socialist Government declared that they were not interested in protecting the Baltic nobility and landowners. Bolsheviks were popping up and striking terror all over, but especially in Riga. Peace returned only after they were thrown out by the Baltic militia who together with some leftovers from the German army, cleaned up the city. Fritz felt that the new order would not last-not even fifty years. By creating a number of new small states, some of which were just separated from their former large state economically, a high price had to be paid for self-government. They had no armies, no government, no constitution, no income and few markets to support their expenses. Soon huge conflicts began to break out; Poland wrangling with Lithuania, the Ukrane with Czechoslovakia and Poland, and so forth. Estonia and Latvia were wrestling about their border, which ran through the middle of the small city of Walz.

The outcome of the treaty was no surprise to Fritz. He reflected that the theory and basis for Wilson's 14 points had originated in the brain of an idealist, totally unaware and alien to the European problems. Wilson had no idea about the various nationalities, their customs and their histories. He judged from an American perspective and the famous points were not adhered to when the victors thought otherwise. So Germany was torn into all sorts of pieces, taking large amounts of Polish territory away while not allowing Germany and Austria to combine areas where it would have made sense. For example, Sudetenland (Germany) was given to Czechoslovakia because the Allies wanted it to be strong. Especially Clemenceau took a devilish delight in gagging Germany as if he personally wanted to rid the world of the Germans. He often had clashes with the Americans and British. Wilson's child-like approach to all European questions did not provide any serious resistance, and the British were silent because they were also interested in getting rid of Germany, their strongest competitor in the world market. Italy, too, was placed at a disadvantage by the Americans while England said nothing. Germany was not even present at the Versailles peace talks that January. They were only called in later to hear the verdict.

While Germany was trying to cope with her version of the Bolshevik Revolution, the Galician provinces of Posen were turned over to Poland. Ignacy Jan Paderewski, the famous composer, pianist and statesman, became an overnight hero and at the first session of the new Polish government, was chosen to be the first president at the behest of Pilsudski. One Sunday morning, Kohn called all of the management staff to his home to announce he had great plans for the company. He would go on a buying trip to Switzerland, being the only country that had any materials to sell. In preparation, every department was asked to take inventory and make a list of those materials that had previously been requisitioned and which now were missing. The outcome was huge lists of needed and missing materials from all departments. Meanwhile there were mass meetings of the workers who were violently calling for three people to be removed from their positions: the electrician and an administrator, both of whom were Germans, and another administrator for unknown reasons as he was born in Lodz. By the end of February Fritz had completed the war reparation job for Allart and could spend full time at Widzener.

In March, Heddy started confirmation classes with a pastor who did not belong to the church the Maehles attended. Fritz had to fight with his pastor before he granted his permission but she was confirmed May 8, 1919, just shy of her 17th birthday.

It was a quiet and dignified celebration and both Fritz and Maria also received communion.[122] She had only to take her final exams and she would be finished with school, and in June she graduated from Rothert's school. But even then Erna Koenig, who had gotten hold of an essay written in German by Heddy, copied it and claimed that Heddy had copied it from her. A simple test of German knowledge showed who had copied from whom. Heddy was exonerated.

In late April Kohn received all the inventory lists and immediately departed for Switzerland. He also planned to meet with Tanfani and his son-in-law, Marquis Farinola to discuss the financial situation and the possibility of reopening the plant. Meanwhile the few remaining staff (all administrators, no workers) was trying desperately to clean up the ruins. But since they were lacking in almost everything and no workers could be hired, they could accomplish very little and were anxiously waiting for Kohn's return.

In June, while the children were visiting a former maid, Martha Dittman in her village, two German officers were billeted in the Maehles' home. In fact, 300 men and horses occupied the plant, while their officers went to administrators' homes. They remained through June, until the peace treaty was finally signed. Three areas of Germany became part of Poland. Germany had no choice but to accept

---

[122] In most Protestant churches, confirmation is done at a younger age but it seems that in the Lutheran Church confirmation coincided with graduation from high school. It also seems to have been a very important event. We have several pictures of Heddy in her confirmation dress as well as her certificate. Someone, probably Kola or Maria, felt the document was important enough to bring to America. I never saw it in my home growing up. And interestingly, although Heddy was choir director in the Presbyterian Church for 30 years, she always called herself a Lutheran and never took communion in the Presbyterian Church.

all the conditions of the Peace Treaty. Any rejection would have been met with a threat to carry war action into Germany. All of the German naval fleet was destroyed and all waterways through Germany were supervised by an international committee; reparations were astronomical. All the nations of the world were invited to join the League of Nations, which Germany might be able to join later, if she were really good. The League of Nations, according to Fritz, had only one task at that time: to watch and make sure that the Allies remained on top of the situation with Germany. Germany was not even slightly trusted. It was considered the lowest of all nations-ever.

When the troops and their officers left Lodz, the children returned home rather suddenly and much earlier than expected. Martha, whom Fritz had supported during the war, had developed a rather fantastic agility of taking money for every little service and since there did not seem to be any service rendered, he discharged her. Heddy decided to study music and started her studies with Tausig (a teacher) as soon as she returned from vacation, and in September Gerda returned to Rothert Gymnasium. Kola had to start a new prep school because the German Gymnasium, where he had been studying had been occupied by Polish people during the war and still had not been released for educational purposes.

In July, the first shipment of cotton arrived in Lodz but Widzener did not bid on it as Kohn was still abroad. Thoelke, who was in charge while Kohn was away, felt that anything he did, would be wrong in Kohn's eyes. Then a letter from Kohn announced that he would be home shortly with lots of goods and the cleanup should begin immediately. So they started working feverishly. The task was enormous. Much of the equipment and machines were buried underground to save them from the occupying forces. By early August the plant was back in working order. The biggest problem was coal to run the machines. The mines at the new German-Polish border were almost all inoperable and the miners were all on strike anyway. By the end of August, Kohn returned. Expectations were high. Staff was looking at 11 packed wagonloads of beautiful goods parked in the court. The first wagon was opened. All held their breath. They looked. They rubbed their eyes and looked again. The wagon was filled with raw rough cotton, as were all the rest of them. It turned out that this "business man" had used the total credit to buy cotton material, which had been ordered by the Italian Government but was not taken when the peace treaty was signed. It was meant to be used on airplanes. Kohn thought he could be the first one on the Polish market to sell this material at three to four times the price he had paid for it. Only in the last car, did they find anything worthwhile: a few rolls of leather belts for Fritz's machines, some strings, two barrels of grease, but no cables, no motors or parts-none of the things that had been on the infamous lists. They looked at each other in disbelief. What kind of a manager did they have? A junk dealer maybe, but never the head of the largest textile plant in Poland.

They went to Kohn and asked him how they could start manufacturing if they did not have the equipment needed, and which he was supposed to have brought. That, he replied, would arrive next day from the old part of town. A week passed without signs of cables or belts so back they went. Belts, Kohn explained were not used anymore; now everything was operated with ropes. It took a long time before Fritz was able to explain to this "petty-minded soul" that in only a few cases could belts be replaced by ropes. But Fritz promised to do his best to replace belts with ropes wherever feasible. This satisfied Kohn greatly, but after 48 hours he came back to Fritz to see if he had mounted the ropes. When Fritz explained that he needed 80 rope disks which had to be formed and turned in the machine plant, Kohn accused him of sabotaging the project and only simmered down when Fritz told him that he already had ordered the discs and was waiting for confirmation and delivery times. Three days later he came back to Fritz to find out where the disks were, since they were in a great hurry. Fritz explained that he estimated that it would take three months. Kohn had a fit. He hopped around and raced to the telephone to talk to the factory himself. They told him that it would take four months; he threw down the receiver. He went into the old city to see if he could get his disks but came back empty handed. He was a broken man but he finally resigned himself to the fact that he would have to procure belts. That was the way he was, an expert in everything with his fingers in every pie. And when the results did not turn out to his liking, it was always someone else's fault.

But even under such a fool, it was wonderful for Fritz to be back at work after three years of idleness (since March 1916). By the end of October, 700 looms were operating, and by the first of November his wages had been adjusted to the standards. By the end of the year Fritz could feel great pride in the fact that the plant was way ahead of others in their recovery. They were operating at almost full speed, thanks mostly to his "superhuman" effort. Unfortunately, prices of things were exorbitant. Fritz's friend Lorenz was not pleased with his new wage, quit his job, and on November 29, took his own life. It was a terrible blow to the Maehles since he and his family were good social friends and close neighbors. And to top it all off, Mrs. Lorenz and

Gerda found him hanging from a rafter in their house. Mrs. Lorenz had a nervous breakdown.

Over Christmas the play, "English Spoken Here," was performed at Rothert's School, which also received the profits from it. Fritz was the director and Heddy was one of the actors. They had a great time working together, and it gave them reprieve from the sadness of the Lorenz situation. But the country was boiling. Paderewski had had enough of the Presidency of Poland and resigned. Then Poland went against Kiev, which called the Russians into action. The wave of Nationalism was rising higher and higher. Since the Maehles were born as Russian subjects, but were not born Russians, they could not participate in the Polish elections. In fact, they were considered Estonians as Fritz was born there, despite the fact that Estonia was under Russia at that time. So they had to report monthly to the government as foreigners. And then the professional organization for engineers and technicians decided that all foreigners had to either become Polish citizens or resign from their jobs. The trouble was that nobody knew how to go about becoming a Polish citizen. There were no citizenship papers available; in fact, they had not been written yet because no rules had been adopted. These problems, added to the tension with Kohn, gave Fritz great nervous agitation. At one point he feared he was going the way of his friend Lorenz.

At the beginning of January 1920, Fritz heard that Kohn was having discussions with several Polish technicians and engineers for new and replacement jobs he was planning. On January 13, Fritz went to Kohn's home to find out first hand what was going on. A sharp argument ensued and Fritz resigned on the spot, just as Lorenz and a number of other administrators had done. Since he had a six-month notice in his contract he quit as of July 15, 1920. He actually felt rather relieved. Widzener was no longer good for him. He could not get along with Kohn and their mutual dislike, which had existed from the beginning, was unbearable. He knew he could not last there much longer. Fritz also believed that Kohn wanted to get rid of him because he didn't need him any longer. The plant was running well and Kohn was now in a position to hire younger engineers. In addition, coal was to be rationed and Kohn felt if he could buy off people in the government by promising them jobs when the coal was stabilized and the temporary government appointments were terminated, he would get a larger portion of the needed coal. As it worked out Fritz had the satisfaction of knowing that by resigning his job, Kohn had to hire three technicians. And from that day on, Fritz no longer cared about the plant. He became exhausted and physically sick. He was diagnosed with a cardiac insufficiency and his stomach was acting up again.

Shortly after he resigned from Widzener, he received a job offer from a spinning mill in another city, Sasnowice, but the situation was not right for him and his family. Meanwhile it was unclear where the proceeds were from the stock that most of the shareholders had sunk their savings into. Finally the one remaining old-timer, Thielke, the accountant, wrote a letter to Tanfani telling him about Kohn's antics. Two weeks later Thilke was fired. Tanfani had sent the letter to Kohn asking for an explanation. Finally, Tanfani came to Lodz and his eyes were opened-too late. He had provided enough money to reopen the plant but Kohn owned 50% of the stock. He was no longer in control of the factory he founded. Tanfani went to see Thielke and lamented about the situation. Thielke listened for a while and then quietly said, "I wrote to you about this 2 years ago. As a thank you, I was fired and now I am too tired to help you anymore." Tanfani returned to Germany like a whipped dog.

In February Fritz had to get passports for Maria and Heddy, who was going to the conservatory in Berlin. This presented a dilemma. Who were the Maehles? Were they actually registered and what nationality were they? Their Russian passports, which they had until the war started, had been taken away by the Germans during their occupation and had been replaced by something called an Occupation Passport. They were sufficient to remain in Poland, although there was pressure to issue Polish ones. However, the border could not be crossed with them. And to top it all off, Fritz could not even vote in the Polish elections. This, he noted, according to the peace treaty of Versailles, was wrong; the treaty gave them equal status with Polish born people. It read that any occupant of one of the three stated divisions had the right to declare himself a Polish nationalist if he could prove that he lived in Poland for ten years before the WWI. Instead Fritz was directed to contact the new Estonian government, declaring that his family members were Estonian citizens. Apparently the Polish government was not familiar with the specifications of the treaty. Over the years all the people from the Baltic States who wanted to remain in Poland became Polish citizens, but poor Fritz was the first to encounter the question of the passport and no one had any experience with how to deal with it. It was just bad luck that Heddy had to go to Berlin just after the treaty was signed, but before its contents were known to local administrations. So Fritz went to the Estonian Consulate in Warsaw.

The Consulate was in an old hotel up some rickety stairs in a small dirty room filled with cigarette smoke. The room was occupied by two men in military outfits without any rank or decoration. In the corner was a black, blue and white flag, probably representing the new colors of Estonia. Fritz tried to remember all his knowledge of the Estonian language but he had been in Poland for 21 years. It was difficult and his words were mixed with German and Polish as he tried to explain his reason for coming to the Consulate. They were not very understanding or helpful. He showed his passport from before the war in which he was listed as an inhabitant of Hapsal. He also produced his Russian Military Passport from 1906, which showed his birthplace as Dago and his nationality Estonian. After much discussion they finally handed him a typed paper that stated the Maehles were former Estonians. It was not a passport but sort of a certificate. To make a copy, the man in charge put the paper into a book with a piece of copy paper and put the book under the foot of the bed and by sitting on the bed and wiggling his body back and forth delivered a copy. When he returned to Lodz it turned out that nobody but he could decipher what the paper contained. Fortunately, the man responsible for authorizing the document was a friend of Fritz's, and he accepted his word that these were provisional Estonian passports for Maria and Heddy. He put an official stamp on the document and signed it, and with these strange documents, Heddy and Maria crossed the border easily. "And this," Fritz stated, "is how my family officially became Estonian citizens."[123] Subsequently the whole family received valid Estonian citizenship papers and passports.

But the question still remained how Fritz would finance his daughter's studies in Berlin. His only hope was to sell his shares of Widzener stock.

---

[123] When I was a child my mother told me that when she became a U.S. citizen she had to swear (which was done at that time) off allegiance to Estonia, Russia and Poland. And after a bit, the judge said, "You better swear off Germany also." I really never understood this until I read the memoires.

He still did not have another job and even if he had one, his wages would not have been enough to pay for her studies. The currency was rapidly falling and he could barely keep up with routine expenses from month to month. He had 120 shares, which were valued at about 4,500 rubles ($22,500) before the war. But at this time they were trading for $25-$30; nobody was interested in them but Kohn, who bought them through a middleman. All the Maehles' savings had been deflated by 85%. Fritz decided to sell 17 shares and to put the money into long-term interest bonds. Unfortunately, he could not buy them in dollars as holding dollars was against the law. He received about 250,000 Polish Marks, equal to only $500. To protect this money from the fantastic devaluation, he lent it to the millionaire Emil Guenther at 10% per month. It was a rather dark deal in which Guenther purchased dyes for textiles. There were middlemen in the transaction and by the time Fritz got his money back he received only his initial investment and an additional 10%. The balance of the profits had been swallowed up by the middlemen. Meanwhile the initial capitol had lost an additional 40%. Fritz decided not to play that game any more.

    Another problem the family had was housing. Not being an employee of Widzener any longer, they had to leave their home, which was owned by the company. In the years after the war there was a great shortage of housing. Much housing had been destroyed and people were looking for some place to live everywhere. They were even coming in from the country and across old borders, which had changed after the war. Many were fleeing from the Bolsheviks, especially the intelligencia. In addition, hundreds of Polish and Austrian Jews came to Lodz. Lodz had become a regional seat of government, and as the new Polish administration replaced the Germans and

Russian, there was a need for a great deal of additional office space. Rent laws protected inhabitants from eviction and rent increases, but another trade was born out of this necessity. People who had large living quarters sublet as many rooms as possible and in this manner made a fairly good living. But, those who had the misfortune to have to change their living quarters, as the Maehles did, had to pay a tremendous amount of money to even get an apartment. Fritz and Maria spent long hours house hunting without any results. Only one possibility of an administrator's apartment, at Allart, on a short-term lease, emerged.

Meanwhile, Maria took Heddy to Berlin to enter the Sterne Conservatory. Grandma Jurgensen had been living with Hanna in Berlin since 1919, and Heddy also moved into Hanna's place with room and board arrangements. While Maria was away, Feldberg, the friend from Riga whom Fritz had helped when he left Lodz by putting all his furniture in storage, returned to Lodz to straighten out his inheritance. As he was leaving he announced to Fritz that he had given him power of attorney to look after his inheritance. Fritz protested but Feldberg left. Fritz never saw him again. Maria returned to Lodz by the end of April and apartment hunting became a serious matter. They had to move out of their home by July. Luckily, Fritz knew a high administrator at Julius Heinzel Co. and personally knew Baron von Heinzel. Through them he obtained a consulting engineer position, with living quarters costing about the same as the small monthly fixed income he received. This marked his third major textile mill employer in Lodz: Allart, Widzener and now Heinzel.[124] All at Heinzel had reasonable hopes that

---

[124] Lodz was known for its huge textile mills, mostly owned by Germans and other foreigners.

the firm would soon regain the important position it held before the war. One of Fritz's main problems was now solved, and he gladly trained the three men who were to replace him at Widzener; he was anxious to leave the place and forget all that had happened there.

Heddy came home unexpectedly in late June and on July 10th the family moved out of their home of many years. Happily, Fritz received a large severance check. The new quarters, which were terribly dirty from the war and the last inhabitants, took a week to clean but soon became quite comfortable. There was a small courtyard behind it and a very nice park nearby. They were now near the city center of Lodz, and not, as with Allart and Widzener, in the suburb of Widzew which was then beyond city limits.

At last Fritz had feelings of extreme peace and quiet after the nerve-wracking times in Widzener. Although he stated, he was as good as unemployed, it did not bother him.[125] Heddy was studying in Germany, Gerda was in the gymnasium and in the fall Kola would start there also. They had living accommodations, some income, some remaining shares of Widzener stock, and no debts. The possibility existed that the stock might even pick up in value. Finally, Heinzel could not remain inactive forever and Fritz had already begun work on developing new machines for the dye department. Aside from the Heinzel income, new consultations began to come in. He was approached by one company to restart their turbines. He also registered with the Municipal Office as a building inspector for which he had a diploma. Through that effort he took

---

[125] From the time he went to Heinzel he never held a full time job again. He managed to become successful as a consultant, but the depression and WWII both reeked havoc on the normalcy for all of Europe.

on the supervision of smaller projects by firms who could not afford to employ a full time architectural engineer. He was even able to use Heinzel's offices and costly instruments for these jobs. Before the war quite a few engineers, mostly Jewish, had made a good living as free lance consultants, indeed more than full time engineers who were on fixed incomes. His hopes were high.

In less than two months after leaving Widzener he had landed a part time job supervising the technical engineering and start-up of new machinery at the Barsinski plant. His income became sufficient to live on, but far too little to cover the family's expanding needs. Heddy returned to Germany in mid-August and Kola started attending the Gymnasium in early September. Because the actual school building had become a hospital during the war, the lessons were given in the hall of St. John's Church. But Kola was inordinately proud of his uniform and cap. The new school year also made demands on Fritz who had accepted a temporary position at Rothert's to teach two fifth-year physics classes, until a permanent teacher could be found.

The external politics were critical at this time as well. Pilsudski, who was now leading a newly formed Polish army against Kiev to get rid of the Bolsheviks, met with surprising resistance in an astonishing counter-attack. Pilsudski and his forces retreated, and by August, they were about 25 kilometers from Warsaw, with the Russians in hot pursuit! By a great stroke of luck (called the miracle on the Vistula), Pilsudski and the French General Weigand, a strategic consultant the western allies had sent to help Poland, managed to trounce the Bolsheviks, who fled in complete disarray. By September, they were negotiating in Riga. Because of these uncertainties, the Lodz industrial community adopted a wait-and-see attitude. Factory start-ups were either slowed down or cancelled altogether. Heinzel's dye works was cancelled and Fritz had to cut short whatever projects were already in progress and let the workers go. This situation was what caused the unfortunate delay in getting businesses off the ground and, according to Fritz, became one of the main factors that triggered the ensuing recession four years later.

Shortly before Christmas, Haebler, another manufacturer, became Fritz's client. He received a contract in which he was asked to oversee some construction. This made him extremely nervous as he had previously had an accident at a construction site under his supervision when a foreman took it upon himself to give orders that almost caused the death of one of the workers. But despite these consultations and the galloping devaluation of the Polish mark, he was still not making enough to support his family. He had to sell more stock at a pittance of its former price for Heddy's tuition. And food prices were rising daily.

Finally, five years after the outbreak of the war, Fritz's brother Ewald sent detailed news. In the course of the war he had advanced to the rank of staff captain, received several medals, and got appendicitis somewhere in Galici, where he had an appendectomy in a primitive field hospital. The wound from the surgery refused to heal, and continued to fester. He escaped being taken prisoner in the hospital thanks to a Moravian peasant who carted him away to the Russian front lines. At the outburst of the revolution he was in the Ukraine where he was demoted to private, and after the Ukrainian declaration of independence was discharged from the army. Then came a time of adventure! Just like lots of other officers in the same situation, he earned a living by singing and performing theatrical skits, as a waiter and a reel winder in cinemas. He also became a substitute math teacher. When the Germans appointed the Russian officer, Skoropadski, as their man in charge of the Ukraine and Ewald became a German-Russian interpreter in the Ukrainian army. This turned out to be a German debacle and Skoropadski was removed. Ewald became a branded "Ger Pilsudski, manophile." He tried to retreat to distant Estonia, but it became an endless game of hide and seek to obtain a visa and another string of adventures ensued, including spending a month in quarantine, before the half-starved, miserable and totally run down man managed to join his family in Nowogruden.

The year ended when, on New Year's Eve, the family received more bad news from Estonia. As members of the German aristocracy who were being dispossessed of their lands, the Dehns, Bodo's family, had to relinquish their large estate to the State for a mere pittance, being allowed to keep only the central portion, which included some estate buildings, but barely enough for them to eke out a living.

From Nikolaus (Kola) Maehle Wiesbaden, January 1949:[126]

Thus ends the final manuscript draft of my father's "family chronicle." However, I have also been able to find and gather together some original "rough" drafts of the manuscript plus a number of related loose leaf notes, family

---

[126] Kola continued writing the memoires from his father's notes. The remainder of the chronicle was translated into English by Ursula Korneitchouk, a lovely woman and skilled translator whom I employed for the task. As in the previous text, translated by Hilde Maehle, I continue to shorten the text and eliminate references that have no meaning to me — names of places, people, and events that I found vague or out of context. I am also continuing to write in the third person.

documents, etc., all of which had followed my mother to Oberndorf-on-the-Neckar[127] after my father's death, but had remained there when she emigrated to the United States. I discovered the trove in two crates filled with Dad's books that were standing in the attic of the house that now belongs to Miska.

Reading the family chronicle prompted me to sift thought the crates in search of additional documentation, so that I'm now able to fill in certain gaps in the chronicle. I shall remain true to the original text, without adding anything to or subtracting from its content. I reserve the right, however, to integrate certain annotations or telegram-style remarks jotted along the margins of the original pages into the main body of the revised text to assure its smooth flow, in an effort to do Dad's beautiful, elegant style as much justice as possible.

1921

On April 1, Barcinsk, another firm that had contracted with Fritz, let him go after seven months on the job, during which time he got the whole project off the ground. But as soon as the scheduled term expired, he was immediately rehired as their consulting engineer at a 30% salary cut. His previous position went to a Jewish engineer who had graduated from the polytechnium. At the same time Fritz's colleague Hoffmann, who had become a spinner at Podnanski, urged him to apply for the engineering position. He did not find their offer appealing, as they would require him to shut down the locksmith shop, a machinery factory, and lay off

---

[127] A southwestern region in Germany close to Luxembourg where Maria and Miska, lived after they fled Poland during WWII.

the workers whom they had been feeding throughout the war to tide them over. He also did not like the set-up of being in an administrative capacity rather than technical. And finally he feared that his provisional Estonian passport would most likely cause him trouble. In any case, he had finally become used to being a consulting engineer and that work brought him great inner satisfaction.

The hurricane-like inflation was devaluing currency daily. One worked hard to earn 10,000 marks for which he could only buy a piece of cotton ware, and two days later the same item was 13,000 marks. Five days later the mark was down 50% more. One could not save money, and it was illegal to buy foreign gold standard currencies such as the Swiss franc and US dollar. Most people bought items as they received their money and most found the only thing to buy was wool or cotton cloth. And everybody was buying it. There must have been hundreds of cloth shops on Patrikauer Street (a main residential street), at least one or two in every house. Rooms were stuffed with cloth from top to bottom. People also invested in oils, paint, straps, leather, sugar, flour and other commodities. But the right kind of storage was always an issue and cloth was the easiest to store. Speculators were running around buying up entire inventories of this and that article to push up the prices. Once the prices went sufficiently high they sold their supply at the inflated prices and the prices toppled. Copycat speculators, hoping to bring off a bit of profiteering of their own had to pay dearly when they were left with a pile of devalued merchandise. In short, it was horrible.

And as the Maehles were stewing in anguish and fear, Maria hit upon an idea of becoming a breadwinner herself as a seamstress. While in Berlin, Heddy met a Miss Ullrich from Lodz who once had taken a course in pattern making and dress cutting.

When she returned to Lodz, Maria decided to take dressmaking lessons from her, with the goal of opening a dressmaker salon with her. "If other women can make a living that way," thought Maria, "why not I?" The plan was that Miss Ullrich would be in charge of the design studio/workshop and Maria would contribute the start-up capital and sell the clothing. She would mind the cash and the budget but not otherwise get involved. The studio was to be in Miss Ullrich's home. It needed furnishing for a shop, which Fritz did with extra furniture from Oskar Steiner. Fritz also had to sell more stock to invest in the venture. Maria was to take orders for custom designed dresses; Miss Ullrich was to do the fittings. The girls in the workshop were to make these garments, as well as standard sized blouses and children's apparel to keep the shelves stocked. Maria was to pay the salaries and bills and handle all the money, and she and Miss Ullrich were to split the profits.

    The shop was opened for business by Easter of 1921, but by the end of July, a mere three months later, it was all over. For one thing, Miss Ullrich lacked genuine fashion flair so she generated little enthusiasm for the clothes she designed. Also, the customers were very demanding and many refused to pay. Unsold blouses accumulated on the shelves; there were several thefts and Maria spent all day at the salon while her home became increasingly neglected. Finally, because of the relentless currency devaluation, the cost to produce a garment had to be recalculated weekly in order to raise the prices appropriately. However, Miss Ullrich interpreted the price difference each week as a net gain and half of the new price for herself. For instance, there were twenty blouses on the rack that originally cost 40,000 marks to make. None of them sold but by the end of the month they cost 50,000 marks.

Consequently Miss Ullrich claimed half of the 10,000-mark increase for herself; Maria gave it to her-even though the blouses were not sold.

It just wasn't working out. Grandma Jurgensen was even asked to come and look after the house, but she said that Heddy should abandon her studies and come home to mind the household. That, of course, was out of the question. Heddy did come home for summer vacation, got her outfits for the next semester made, and the dressmaking project ended. Fritz had to sell more stock to pay for her new clothing. In addition, Heddy was suffering from some kidney problems and looked extremely miserable. But under Maria's care she recovered in time to return to her studies in Berlin by the end of August. The good news was that in June, Fritz obtained a permanent Estonian passport whereby all members of the family acquired Estonian citizenship.

In mid-September Maria decided to participate in another business venture, this time in association with Miss Alix Warrikoff,[128] Mrs. Rohrer and her daughter, and Mr. Durowski, all friends of the family. The business was opened in a small storefront in the Warrikoffs' apartment building. Maria contributed the left over blouses as her share in the new venture. But this one was even more inconvenient than the former. Finally Grandma Jurgensen offered to come to Lodz, principally because living with Hanna and Bodo began to wear on her. Heddy also moved into a boarding house. And then, while in the process of obtaining her entry permit, Grandma Jurgensen fell and broke her hand. Meanwhile Maria's business was failing. Because of the currency devaluation, the price of the merchandise was rapidly falling to less than 40% of its original purchase price. "The simple

---

[128] Her relationship to the Warrikoffs is not noted.

fact," wrote Fritz, "was that all shops were filled to bursting with merchandise and no one was buying."

Toward the end of the year another shock: Gerda, barely recovered from her appendectomy, was diagnosed with swelling of her bronchial glands. If neglected this condition could lead to tuberculosis; something urgently needed to be done about it. Fritz sold more stock so that Maria could take her to a spa where she was ordered to undergo a cure for at least three months. As Fritz was about to sell his stock, Taufani, who had returned to Lodz, found out about it and told Fritz he would like to buy the stock himself. It turned out that seven years after the outbreak of the war, Taufani had come back to gather enough evidence to become convinced that Kohn was cheating on him. He determined to buy back as much stock as possible. Fritz was, of course, receptive to Taufani, providing he met his asking price. Taufani asked for time to consider it and Fritz went home only to find a buyer (probably a Kohn agent) waiting for him. He offered to pay more than Taufani and Fritz sold. The following day Taufani wrote that he accepted Fritz's price. Fritz informed him that he already sold them to a higher bidder. Taufani was furious and summoned Fritz back to Widzener where they had a great argument. In the end, because Taufain was Baron Julius Heinzel's brother-in-law, and Fritz was loathe to cause an unpleasant dispute, and Taufani had grudgingly agreed to meet the other buyer's price, Fritz sold five of his remaining shares to Taufani, retaining 43 shares for himself.[129] Thirty shares had been completely gobbled up in Maria's ventures and that was all he managed to achieve in 1921 with his

---

[129] Private company stock was not sold on the public market but privately. Price was negotiated between buyer and seller. In fact, I don't think there was much of a public mark, if any, in Poland then.

meager earnings. He decided not to sell any more shares, but to reserve them for his daughters' dowries. It was fortunate, he noted, that the German mark was falling against the Polish mark, which meant that Heddy's upkeep was costing much less. Also, toward the year's end, Fritz's earnings had increased noticeably. He was involved in consulting jobs that connected the manufacturers of machinery and measuring instrument with the right customer, playing the middleman in all sorts of transactions where technical expertise was of the essence. He was beginning to make a name for himself. Hopefully, that state would continue into the following year. What was so upsetting was that however much money he made on one day, it would loose a great deal of its value the following day. This forced people to spend what they earned immediately.

The Maehles' friends, the Rybers and their children, had spent the summer in Riga and were hatching plans to move there permanently, since the business situation in Lodz was hopeless for him. Christmas was gloomy because two of the Maehle children were missing; Heddy in Berlin and Gerda in the spa Rakopane. Maria, Fritz and Kola spent a quite holiday visiting with the Rybers and Reymonds on New Year's Eve. "In any case," wrote Fritz, "I would be ungrateful toward God and providence if I didn't concede that things are getting better. I feel new hope and am confident that when we celebrate New Year's Eve next time around we shall look more cheerfully to the future than this time-so help us God!"

1922

In February, Gerda returned from the spa in time for her sixteenth birthday on the fourteenth, looking rested. As she seemed to have recuperated, the family's fears were dispelled. Fritz had obtained several new consulting jobs, which earned pretty decent money. He was even offered a position as plant engineer at a factory in Warsaw, which he turned down, as he simply could not see himself moving the whole family at that time. Principally though, he was also reluctant to the move with little guarantee of job security in those difficult times. And, he had come to enjoy the consulting business with its variety of tasks and companies. In fact, he had come to think of himself as a civil engineer and found it much more interesting that a plant engineer. At the same time, Maria's shop was being dismantled with the tax collectors breathing down the Maehles' necks for payments on a failed business.

 Heddy returned home for summer vacation to the joy of her family, but Maria and Wanda Warrikoff, had a falling out, apparently because Wanda seemed to criticize Heddy's piano performance when she was visiting Berlin once. At the end of the summer, Maria returned to Berlin with Heddy for a visit with her sister, Hanna. Fritz's work situation began to improve in the second half of the year. Wages and salaries were finally automatically adjusted to keep pace with inflation in Poland. Fritz wrote that he was making so much money that he could afford to pay for Heddy's new outfits without having to sell any stock. But German inflation was rising so fast that, by the time Maria and Heddy arrive in Berlin the German marks that Fritz bought for them had only half of the anticipated buying power. There was nothing he could about it. These things happen in international currencies.

 In September Mr. Thodke, Chairman of Widzener passed away. Taufani, hearing he was ill went to seem him on his deathbed, whining that Kohn had stolen the factory from him. "Didn't I warn you?" said Thodke. "I wrote to warn you! And because I did that and you then showed my letter to Kohn, he simply removed my desk from the office and kicked me out. If that hadn't happened, perhaps I wouldn't be dying now. You are getting what you asked for." And with that, he turned to the wall.

Oskar's furniture problems were finally settled.[130] Upon receipt of a letter from him in Reval, Fritz sold the dining room pieces. He got so much money for them that he was able to hire a mover to pack up the remaining furniture (parlor, bedroom, clothing, linens, etc.) and send them to him. There was even enough money to remit some cash, which Fritz did in English pounds that he somehow bought (or perhaps pounds were legal). At the end of September Maria returned with Grandma Jurgensen who moved into the spare room in the children's quarters.

In mid-November Fritz's colleague, Frisch suffered a severe stroke, following a serious fight with Scheibler that got him fired. It seems that during the occupation, Scheibler initiated a search for soft coal and began mining in the Wloklawek area. Frisch was directing the project with the help of German specialists. Unfortunately there was too much ground water and the mine was flooded. Once the war ended, digging for soft coal was no longer a priority since hard coal became readily available again, and Poland acquired additional mines with the annexation of Upper Silesia. The money sunk into soft coal had been wasted, and Frisch was blamed for not having anticipated the water danger. As Frisch had staked his entire future on the coal business, he took the misadventure very hard, which is probably what triggered his stroke. He left Lodz in 1923, as an unemployed invalid and it fell to his wife to dissolve his business. He had been making sufficient money for several years but had invested it

---

[130] Recall his furniture has been in storage in Lodz since before the war.

catastrophically in sinking German marks so that he soon became destitute. He returned to his brother's farm in Latvia and died in August 1928. He had been the soul of the English lecture-study group, which continued as long as he lived in Lodz. When he left, Fritz took over the leadership out of loyalty and sense of duty to his friend.

Toward the end of the year Heddy informed her parents that she was no longer attending the conservatory, but was taking private lessons from Professor Kosner. Grandma Jurgensen hired Oskar Ficher to help mediate a problem with the summer villa in Hinzenberg; Latvia had repossessed the land and requisitioned the villa too. And so the year ended for the Maehles. Fritz was back on his feet. He was taking iron pills that Maria had brought from Germany and feeling well. Of course, he wrote, "it's partly due to my financial recovery." Maria, on the other hand was not feeling well: gout, rheumatism, nervous breakdowns, irregular heartbeat, all very worrisome. Gerda and Kola were fine; the boy was growing fast and remained healthy.

Chapter X:
The Great Depression

1923

The financial recovery that Fritz began to sense in 1921, continued throughout 1923 and into 1924. He made valuable contacts in numerous factories and his consultations increased substantially. He became sought after as an engineer who could solve problems including factory examinations, plant supervision, monitoring, purchasing equipment and so forth. Most (about 70%) of his consultations were on monthly retainers, and Heinzel even provided a free home with heating and electricity. He had to travel frequently and became so busy that he had to hire a draftsman to do his drawing work. He was delighted with the way things were going and no longer had the slightest desire to land a full time position with a single firm.

Early in the year he received a letter from his brother, Oskar stating everything Fritz had sent had arrived but for one crate filled with bed and table linens, clothing, photo album, books, correspondence, etc. What arrived instead was a miserable old crate filled with dirty marine uniforms. Fritz contacted the shipping company and several months later was informed that the crate was in London. Upon receipt of an inventory list they would ship the crate to Oskar in Reval. Naturally, Fritz had made a detailed list, which he brought to the company who was utterly embarrassed by the whole thing. One month later, Oskar received his belongings-after 8 ½ years in storage!

In March, Gerda was confirmed at Trinity Lutheran Church. She had taken a job in January with a Swiss cotton thread salesman and seemed to have developed a knack for her work, which she loved. It agreed with her a lot more than school ever did. Unfortunately, noted Fritz, the man she worked for was "uncouth and rough, as the Swiss usually are." Thanks to her job, her social life had intensified, and Fritz and Maria were pleased to see one particular young man, Erwin Sacke, around the house. He was the son of a director at Steiner (one of the mills) and never missed a chance to wait on Gerda hand and foot. But there were several others as well. In May, Gerda quit her job with the Swiss and joined the Mendelssohn shipping agency.

In late May, Fritz went to Germany on business and spent four wonderful days in Berlin with Heddy, where he met Rudolph (Rudy) Kilian, a student at Charlottenbury Academy. Fritz suspected that something was "afoot" between them. When he returned to Lodz, he learned that his entire home was to be redecorated at the company's expense. He also learned that before he died in 1918, Papa Jurgensen had officially given the property in Hinzenberg, which Fritz had purchased in partnership with him, to Bernhard von Dehn, Hedwig's husband, and that the Latvian government had dispossessed him of it, as von Dehn was a member of the aristocracy. The property was confiscated by the government and was thereafter closed to the Maehles.

In late October, Gerda formally announced her engagement to Janusz Dobriski, very much to the disappointment of her parents. They had met Dobriski the previous year at a party at a friend's home. Heddy had been in town and at the party also, and Dobriski was pretty obviously siding up to her. He attempted to pay his respects the very next day at the family home but when he came, Maria and Heddy received him so frostily that he thought it wise not to show up again. Fritz noted that he could not remember why Gerda was not with the family at either event. And then sometime in the fall of 1923, Gerda joined Maria and Fritz at another party and Dobriski, whom she had never seen in her life, started courting her desperately; the two danced together all night and once again he escorted her home and showed up the very next day. A short period of "enforced courtship" followed. The way Fritz saw it, he managed to turn her head completely; she forget Sacke and all the rest. Dobriski promised her the moon. He cast himself as heir to a vast estate in Lublin, pretended to be so rich that his officer's salary meant no more to him that small change. He boasted that he owned large riding stables at a big estate near Swidniczek (near Lodz) and after writing a few melodramatic letters to Gerda, in which he threatened to commit suicide if she refused him, he formally proposed. Fritz wrote:

> We were simply pushed against the wall. What could we say? We learned from our mutual friends that his father was long deceased. He once held an important position in the provinces and was well-respected among his peers. His mother still lives on what is left of the family's former estate near Lublin and has so far, been able to supply him with plenty of money. His elder brother is a plenipotentiary (diplomat) and an executive manager of a Government Minister's wealth and is married to the daughter of a certain Orecki, a Warsaw millionaire, and is leading the life of a grand "seigneur" near Swidniczek, and so on!" Was it

this fancy swindle that hypnotized Gerda? Or was it the "politicalization" with which Gerda had been so brainwashed by her Polish teachers at school that she felt ashamed of her parents' poor command of the Polish language and longed to get away from home? Or was it both? Who knows?

In short, after Dobriski had given his word of honor as a Polish office-and this was something that no one would ever dare doubt in those days-that all this false pretense was actually the honest truth, Fritz and Maria gave in, albeit most reluctantly. Never mind that Dobriski's personality, his Catholicism, and a whole lot more, displeased them enormously.

What followed was an utterly hectic engagement period with nightly receptions at the Maehles' home (and eventually at some of their friends homes), or with Dobriski taking Gerda to the casinos, the races and dances at elegant nightclubs. It was a crazy time that cost Fritz "an unholy amount of money," while going against his and Maria's grain.[131] Fritz wrote, "God only knows where Dobriski found the wherewithal for his outlandish courtship." Fritz was under the impression that he simply wanted to draw out the engagement period to enjoy it to the hilt, without seriously intending to get married. There were many objections and obstacles to overcome with relatives who wouldn't accept a Protestant or a German woman,[132] and with the military authority who wanted to thwart Dobriski's career for the same reason. Even the threat that he might be forced to resign did not faze him in the least

---

[131] Apparently Fritz paid for the courtship.
[132] Throughout, the family strongly identified themselves with and as Germans.

bit. Finally Maria took the fancy fellow to task and gave him only two alternatives: either fix a wedding date immediately or put an end to this ridiculous courtship, whereupon Dobriski consented to set a date for the wedding in late February 1924. Fritz wrote, "My daughter's lengthy engagement is so expensive that my monthly income simply wasn't enough to pay for her dowry as well." Once again he had to sell stock. With Maria's consent, he sold half of his remaining 43 shares. Fortunately, the price had risen to $20 per share. As the Polish zloty to dollar ratio was 1:10, he was able to make 4,000 zlotys available for Gerda's dowry, with which they purchased a beautiful bedroom set, linens, and cloths for her.

Meanwhile they received desperate news from Heddy who reported that because of the unbearable living conditions in Berlin (where a streetcar ticket was said to cost several million marks!) she had contacted TB and was feeling miserable.[133] Fritz wrote back to her to drop her studies and hurry home so that they could care for her properly. Heddy arrived home sick and wretched. She couldn't get over the abundance of food on the table when the Germans had to think in billions each time they went to the grocery store. At that time she and Rudy were corresponding regularly and she informed her parents that they were as good as engaged. Both Maria and Fritz liked him and so were very happy to hear the news. A short time later Rudy wrote Fritz and Maria asking for his little "Peterchen's" hand.[134] Robert Kilian soon followed up with a letter and after

---

[133] Berlin was the hardest hit by the post WWI depression. Inflation was out of sight and many people were starving. However, I think millions and billions seems a bit exaggerated — although I recall reading that the German mark was virtually worthless. Heddy was probably sick with bronchitis but she did not have TB.

[134] Peterchen is an endeering term — actually little Peter.

additional exchanges of letters; Heddy's engagement to Rudy became official in December. She was 21 years old.

1924

January brought once again the endless circus of fancy casino balls, theater evenings, etc. "And all the expenses of it could raise one's hair," stated Fritz. But finally, in late February, Gerda and Janusz Dobriski were married. His brother, Wacek, gave a spectacular dinner in their honor at the Grand Hotel. The wedding itself was a huge bore. The nicest part of it was the traditional party on the night before the wedding, which lasted until well after sunrise. Gerda's former beau Sacke was there, still in stunned disbelief. The church ceremony didn't go very well because Janusz's friends, who were to have arranged it, had done nothing. Then came the wedding banquet at the Maehle's home, and Fritz lamented that he was saddled with the awkward task of addressing, in Polish, the assembled guests, including a bevy of Catholic clerics, who then settled down to play cards until past midnight.

It was about this time that Wacek stepped up and asked Fritz whether his brother had explained to him how he was hoping to earn enough of a living to support Gerda. Fritz and Maria stared at him in amazement and replied that he had assured them of being well enough off to even consider quitting a lucrative military career, which he did not enjoy and did not need financially. At this point a very upset Wacek waved Janusz aside and filled Fritz and Maria in on the reality of his brother's circumstances; he had nothing but debts. Visibly chastised, Janusz grabbed Gerda and left the premises. Fritz and Maria were devastated. What was the fellow thinking? At the time of the engagement Fritz had made it very clear that he could barely provide a dowry; Fritz had no money.

The newlyweds were living in a requisitioned room that the military was obliged to provide for Janusz. He was so poor that he did not even have funds to pay for the required one-month's advance rent. The Maehles' amazement kept growing. For Easter, considering that they now counted a Catholic among their family members, they had to stage a special Catholic party, which turned out to be a gigantic affair. Almost all the locals of some rank had to be invited. Right in the middle of the celebration, Gerda took Fritz aside and desperately implored him to help Janusz get a loan, saying that he temporarily found himself somewhat strapped for money because some debentures he owned had recently depreciated so much that if he sold them he would have to do so for peanuts. She also told him that several people owed him a great deal of money, among them the government minister whom his brother worked for. She said that it would only take three months at the most to straighten everything out. But in the meantime, she and Janusz urgently need to furnish a home for themselves and establish a business office for Janusz. She asked Fritz to pledge Janusz with his remaining shares of stock.

Fritz had earmarked those shares for Heddy's dowry, but Gerda firmly believed in her husband and, simply because Gerda was his child, after talking things over with Maria, he relinquished his remaining shares to Gerda, never to get as much as a penny back. When Heddy got married and Janusz found himself pushed against the wall, he came to Fritz with a mere 500 zloty, saying that this was the exchange rate of the day, when in fact it was ten times higher. But Fritz and Maria didn't want to risk a fight with this awful guy for fear that Gerda would suffer the consequences. And to add to Fritz's grief, in April he learned that Oskar had muscular dystrophy.

The relationship with Janusz continued to deteriorate. His lies became more and more transparent. For instance, he had the nerve to make a scene with Gerda with respect to the piano that was standing in the requisitioned room where they were lodging. He finally managed to persuade Gerda that the piano was actually his. But when he sent movers to transfer the piano to their new apartment, his former landlord, infuriated, threw the movers out the door. Heddy too had had no use for him from the time that she left school to return to Lodz when she was very ill and covered with boils. It seems that Janusz had, in a drunken state, insinuated to his drinking buddies that the suspicious illness of his fiancée's sister might well be a sexually transmitted disease that she had brought home from Berlin. So one fine day in May, all of this anger exploded between Janusz and the Maehles, including Heddy. It ended up in a horrific row in which Heddy chased her brother-in-law out of the house with a horsewhip![135] Gerda, not knowing what to do, ran after her husband. As a result the Maehles had no further contact with either Janusz or Gerda for quite some time. It was also in May that Fritz began to feel a paralyzing slump in the Polish economy, mainly stemming from the introduction of the Polish zloty, a draconian measure by the government. At that time 1-pound sterling cost 6,000,000 zloty.

In early June, Maria and Kola went to a spa, where they followed a liver diet and cold water cure. Fritz joined them in mid-June and all returned rested

---

[135] This is amazing to me. I never saw Heddy lose her temper or become hysterical. She could whine and pout but never fly off the handle. At the same time I know that she disliked Gerda's husband immensely and even blamed him for her death.

and sun tanned, only to be informed that Fritz's regular contracts with Heinzel and Eisert were being terminated. It was a fearsome blow and completely destroyed whatever hopes he had been nursing for the past two years with regard to the development and growth of his own consulting business. He had even lost his contingency reserve, which had been given to Janusz. On top of that, his building permit was about to be withdrawn because they were foreigners, and the growing crisis in the industry made consultations increasingly hard to find. The only little bright light was that Eisert paid Fritz a severance of three months, a very short-term band-aid at best. Although things were very tight, Eisert did not want to let him go but he had a cousin who finally managed to get out of Russia and he had to give him a job. Heinzel, on the other hand, was genuinely going down the drain. In fact, at that point the administration was no longer concentrating on production but was pursuing stock market speculations instead. Because of the government clean-up measures, hundreds of newly formed shareholding corporations were collapsing like so many houses of cards.

And for the Maehles, the worst was yet to come! In early September, an infected thumb on Maria's mother's (she was now living with the Maehles) right hand began to fester dangerously. Fritz felt that she probably had only herself to blame for having tinkered around with a pair of scissors or a needle.[136] Hanna rushed in from Berlin and tried to help but little could be done for her. She was diagnosed with blood poisoning and after a second

---

[136] My mother often told the story of her grandmother's death in an effort to get me not to poke around with needles. I was told that up until the time Grandmother Jurgensen got the infected thumb, she used to walk a mile a day with a stick between her shoulders to keep her back straight.

unsuccessful surgery, died in excruciating pain on September 25. Fritz naturally was responsible for the accumulated costs of her illness, operations, and funeral. Hanna proposed that their sister, Hedwig and her husband, should also be involved. However, both Hedwig's and Hanna's husbands wrote that they were unable to share in the expenses; in fact, Bodo wrote that he did not want to pay for Hanna's train fare and the cost of mourning cloths. In October Heddy left for Berlin to introduce herself to her future in-laws. She stayed for a month and upon her return came down with a nasty inflammation of the ear and was confined to bed where she remained until New Year's.

1925

By January, the Maehles' financial situation had become desperate. They were facing financial ruin. The loss of Heinzel and Eisert, Gerda's wedding, and Mama Jurgensen's death had taken their last reserves. Julie[137] was still living with them and paying a small rent. Fritz still had some consulting contracts, but with Kola's tuition, a family of four plus a maid, who was necessary for such a large house, Fritz was running all over town, knowing full well that there was hardly enough money to keep the family from starving. In addition Raymond could no longer make a profit as Fritz's sale representative in

---

[137] This is the first mention of Julie, although there are quite a few pictures, both in childhood and as an adult. Mother called Julie her foster sister and was very close to her. She told stories about her when they were children. She and Julie were close to the same age and used to give Gerda, two years younger, a hard time. One story was that they convinced Gerda to climb through the small opening in the chicken coop. Gerda, being chubby, was unable to get out. There is little background information on her although there is a later reference that she had family near Lodz. She seemed to have been treated as a daughter and perhaps in later years filled the void in Maria's life left by Gerda's death and Heddy's move to America.

his consulting business and their close collaboration was slowly dissolving whether they liked it or not. Toward the end of 1924 Heinzel had declared bankruptcy, and the bankruptcy administration was parceling out their business to various other Jews as franchises (you will recall that a Jew had acquired the company). In January, Fritz was, once again, hired as a consulting engineer for an amount that barely covered the rent and utilities. And in February one of the new owners named Mr. Makower asked Fritz to accompany him to Bucharest where he intended to move his factory. They stayed for two weeks during which time Fritz bought a steam engine and a kettle. Returning to Lodz, he got the transmission underway and supervised the assembly of the new machines. By May, Fritz had landed several other consulting positions, which allowed him to breathe a little more easily.

Miska, Gerda's daughter, was born on April 1.[138] In such a case, a mother's place is, of course, at her daughter's side and Maria went to the Dobriskis' where she remained for two weeks. Janusz, remorseful and subdued, asked her, on bended knee to forgive him all his lies, saying that it was his overwhelming love for Gerda that motivated him, for he felt certain that the Maehles would never allow her to marry a good-for-nothing. Gerda chimed in and implored Maria to forgive him, saying that his letters of credit were indeed real but had lost their value. She agreed that while his situation had never been as brilliant as he had made the family to believe, they were certainly not common folk. Indeed there were officers who were in much worse shape, and so on. So Fritz and Maria decided to put the whole sordid

---

[138] She spelled her name Miska although it is more commonly seen as Mishka.

affair behind them. Even Heddy managed to get along with her brother-in-law.

In the summer Gerda took Miska to visit her mother-in-law in Janiszow while Janusz stayed home to study for some courses he was taking.[139] In mid-September Heddy returned to Berlin for six weeks. Rudy was busy studying for his diploma in mechanical engineering and working as an intern in an automobile factory. In October Fritz lost another of his consulting positions but was soon offered another permanent consulting position with Hoffrichter, who also had a daughter married to a young officer. In her case, her husband claimed to be an engineer although he lacked all the necessary credentials and skills. When he was hired, Fritz was assigned to do his work, a position he retained, with certain modifications, until 1938. In October Fritz's brother Rudolf, died in Reval, now Tallinn. And a few weeks later the daughter of a good friend from Reval visited the Maehles and filled them in on the details of Rudolf's passing, which are not mentioned in this memoir.

By the year's end the crisis in Poland had reached catastrophic proportions. The government's stringent finance policies had paralyzed everything and ruined the young country.[140] Businesses were closing; unemployment skyrocketed; suicides became epidemic. Fritz wrote that their situation became so desperate that they could no longer afford to buy enough coal to heat the house, and all household members crowded together in three rooms

---

[139] Janiszow is a small village of 2,000 people in southwestern Poland where the Dobriski estate was located. It had been part of the family's estate at one time.

[140] Poland only became an independent country after WWI and only then initiated its own currency. But the crisis had reached epidemic proportions all over Europe. While the government may have been inept, they surely couldn't take full responsibility for the situation.

on the street floor. The Christmas and New Year holidays were sad.

1926

In late January Kola was running an errand on his bike, got dizzy and fell. Had a passerby not rescued him in the nick of time, he would have been run over by a streetcar. The passerby dragged him into a concierge's office, where a paramedic picked him up, dirty and dreadful looking, bike and all, and brought him home. The medic felt that Kola had probably suffered an epileptic seizure. "That's all we need," thought Fritz! As he had never exhibited these symptoms before, Fritz simply refused to believe it. He decided to watch him closely and to send him to a rest home in the country in the summer. Gerda and Miska were still in Janiszow with Janusz's mother. Fritz speculated that it was probably easier to feed the baby there. Then suddenly Janusz's mother died leaving Gerda with no choice but to stay and try as best she could to run the household. Hoping to be of some help, Maria joined her in mid-January and stayed until mid-March. Meanwhile Janusz moved in with the Maehles.

By March Fritz only had three regular consulting jobs left. Consultations were almost impossible to come by because of the dire economic crisis. By mid-month, Maria had only 10 zloty left for household expenses until the end of the month. In May, the so-called "May Revolt" in Warsaw drove the populace to the limits. There was much shooting and violence. Pilsudski, the former Prime Minister, was put back in office and it seemed that his firm hand did indeed manage to assuage the internal unrest, restore stability and create fresh momentum. The exchange rate became fairly constant at one US dollar to 9 zloty. Fritz thought that as long as the US dollar retained its value things should work out for

Poland.[141] Also in May, Rudy earned his diploma and, on his father's advice, decided to immigrate to the USA since the situation in Germany was so hopeless. Heddy therefore decided to learn English and began working on it with all her might. Happily, Kola returned from his summer at the rest cure looking much more mature and with new energy.

Fritz had a hard time finding work until well into September. There was not even enough money to celebrate their silver wedding anniversary on September 1 in style. In fact, they went out of their way to avoid any fuss and were able to escape for the day for a good lunch at a fine hotel. It was during the lunch that they ran into the chief accountant of a company called Cotonniere, who introduced him to his new boss, Director Herbert, a Frenchman. Fritz was promptly summoned to Cotonniere where he spent several days fixing a defective kettle, conducting heating tests, and checking control instruments. Immediately after that, another company decided to purchase a steam engine. Fritz was hired to be the intermediary and subsequently supervised the engine's installation. Then a textile plant, whose business was beginning to flourish, hired him to oversee the installation of some machines, and he spent an entire week at the factory. Before the end of the month he had two other consultations; he felt things were beginning to look up again.

Toward the end of September, Gerda brought Miska to Lodz to stay with her grandparents for a month while she returned to Janiszow to hand over the business of running the household. In October, after a year and one half alone in Janiszow, Gerda returned to Lodz for good and Kola began

---

[141] He noted that the zloty had stabilized against the dollar and that in 1938, the time of this writing, the dollar was worth about 5.25 zloty.

confirmation classes. Then, during the Christmas season Kola had another convulsive fainting spell. The doctor assured Fritz that it was entirely caused by his growing too fast for his heart. He prescribed some medicine and a few days later he had another fainting spell, and then no more.

Rudy wanted to get married soon, so that he and Heddy could start to build a new life for themselves in the USA where people were currently enjoying postwar prosperity. Of course, Heddy was planning to go with him, but the authorities started to get difficult. Since everyone wanted to leave bloodied Europe for America, the USA had set up immigration quotas for each European country. Heddy had an Estonian passport, a country that had been granted quotas for only 5-6 people. "In view of this seemingly insurmountable obstacle, Robert Kilian hatched one of his grandiose plans," wrote Fritz. Heddy should go to Canada and from there be smuggled into the US by a bunch of drunken Canadian excursionists. First, she should go to Quebec or Montreal as a household help for one of Papa Kilian's friends. Heddy agreed to the scheme. Papa Kilian obtained the immigration guidelines from the Canadian consulate, which of course specified that the applicant must have a valid passport from his/her native country. Heddy's native country was Poland and her Estonian passport was issued in Warsaw. "That was too hard for an Anglo brain to grasp," wrote Fritz. But she was an Estonian citizen so they said that her passport should be issued in Estonia. So Fritz wrote to the Estonians, first in Warsaw and then through them, to Tallinn. The answer was always the same; Heddy's passport had been legally issued by the Estonian Embassy in Warsaw who confirmed that it was valid all over the world. There was no such thing as a special passport for Canada. Once again Fritz tried to explain the situation as clearly as possible in writing. He sent his letter to Oskar in Tallinn and asked him to bring the matter before the Department of the Exterior, while Papa Kilian went, once more, to the Canadian consulate. Both offices remained adamant and that was that.

As the year ended the Maehles' financial situation had improved considerably. In the first half of the year they often had no more than 10 zloty left at the end of each month; in the second half they often had 600 zloty left.

1927

The bad times of 1924-1926 seemed to be over. Fritz was providing weekly service to the Cotonniere plant. The plant manager seemed to rely on him extensively, and he often spent twelve-hour days at the plant, which had become a major mill. And there always seemed to be more work for Fritz, from fixing boilers, to enlarging equipment to accommodate increased demand. He also obtained several more good clients during the course of the year, and although his earnings varied from month to month, he was making good money. The company that had made him the plant supervisor turned it into a permanent position.[142] Both he and Maria felt more relaxed-they were over the worst of it. In fact, Fritz felt so well that he quit smoking. However, his weight jumped considerably.

Kola was confirmed that Easter and Heddy went to Berlin to visit her future in-laws. From there she went to Dita's[143] where she stayed for two

---

[142] A plant supervisor provided oversight and was not a full time position.
[143] Dita Wermisher was Heddy's best friend in Berlin. She was also a musician who studied at the same school with Heddy. She came to America to visit us in Cleveland with Heddy sometime in the early 1970s. We liked her very much.. She once said, "When a German says

months. When she returned to Lodz, she brought Robert Kilian's fur coat to Fritz for which he paid Robert 500 marks. Finally, the whole issue of how Heddy should get to America was resolved. Heddy and Rudy must get married in Berlin. But even if she were to obtain a German passport, it would be no guarantee that she could get to America, since the US immigration quotas were severely cut for Germans. In any case, Rudy returned to Europe in late September. Heddy returned to Germany to meet him in Bremen where the ship landed and the wedding was set for October 20. Maria left for Berlin on October 18 to arrange a small wedding celebration in a restaurant, and after the wedding, Heddy and Rudy went to Switzerland for their honeymoon. Maria was very angry at her sister, firstly because they did not respond to the couple's engagement announcement and had called Rudy a "Jewish brat,"[144] and secondly because they had still paid nothing for Mama Jurgensen's funeral even though Hanna had agreed to split the cost 50/50. So Maria booked into a hotel and did not invite them to the wedding. Hanna was deeply distraught and begged Maria to forgive them. Maria felt obliged to make peace and went to visit them for ten days. Later Bodo paid Heddy what they owed the family for the funeral.

'I didn't know what was going on in WWII,' don't believe it; we knew. The issue was, what could we do about it? We were afraid, even of our own children." Dita died in the late 1990s and I was in correspondence for a while with her son who lived in Munich.

[144] This is the only reference to Rudy's ethnicity. And apparently, despite the several negative Jewish references in the memoirs, it did not seem to matter to the Maehles. Rudy's mother was a Jew, although he was raised as a Lutheran, which was Robert's religion. His mother, Dina was born Dina Dora Lowenburg to Alexander Ruben Lowenburg and Leah Helen Adler in Moisling, Germany, Nov. 1867. Her birth was recorded in the synagogue in Luebeck, Germany. Luebeck was an imperial city and capital of the Hanseatic League. On and off, from the 18th C., Jews were not permitted to live within the city so they settled in Moisling, a nearby village. See Luebeck (Jewish virtual Library.org.)

In summary, expenses for that year were very high with the wedding, trips back and forth between Lodz and Berlin, and Heddy's dowry. Fritz thanked heaven for the good fortune that allowed him to increase his income so considerably.

1928

The year began auspiciously. Never before had Fritz had so much independently contracted work. He wrote that he was very well off.[145] He even had a telephone installed in his home so that he could cope with all the business he was doing. In the spring he had the house refurbished, including new ceiling reinforcements, the walls repainted, the bathroom redone, the stoves overhauled, the gazebo and windows repaired and painted. The factory only paid for the painting and the stove work; Fritz paid for the rest. In April, Janusz Dobriski was promoted to the rank of captain that gave him an increase in his salary. As Fritz now had more money, in May he began to think of a trip to Estonia and Dago.

Meanwhile all during the spring Heddy and Rudy had been living amid boxes and out of suitcases in a furnished rental apartment in Berlin. They were trying with all possible means to obtain permission for Heddy to immigrate to the USA, all to no avail. Papa Kilian was getting furious and even began to think that Rudy no longer wanted to return there. In the end, some contact of his managed to get Heddy shifted into the Dutch quota, which was unfilled; the immigration permission arrived in mid-May and they cast off from Bremen on May 21, arriving in New York on June 1.

---

[145] Nevertheless, by then he was 57 years old and still had no savings what so ever.

Practically at the same time Gerda became gravely ill and was admitted to the Red Cross hospital of Lodz on June 2. When she visited Lodz in October 1926, she was feeling great. But then came the winter of 1926/27 and she, being a headstrong and pretty young woman, decided she needed to "live a little." She danced nights away at casino balls during the carnival season. Fritz implored her to mind her health. He still kept in mind the doctors who warned her at the time of her wedding, that in view of her bronchial condition, she had better not get pregnant for some time, or if she did, at least take very good care of herself. Except for an occasional cough, she showed no signs of ill health in 1927. But whenever Fritz pressed her about the coughing she seemed unconcerned.

Then in February 1928, she came down with the flu. But because Miska, then almost three, was also ill she neglected her own problem. Instead of staying in bed and simply asking Maria to help out, she got up prematurely and drove the child to see several doctors and so forth. Barely able to walk she also had to play tennis. "Fritz wrote, "Nobody could reason with her. She did as she pleased, almost as though she meant to do herself in. Or did she just plain refuse to believe that she was ill?" She even took a trip to Przyglow, a small town not far from Lodz. No sooner had she arrived there, she began vomiting and with a high fever, had to turn around and come back to Lodz. After three weeks in the hospital she seemed much improved. Her mucus and other secretions were examined daily but not a single x-ray was taken. "Perhaps," he mused, "x-rays could have saved her." The doctors described her condition as serious but by no means hopeless. Janusz drove to Warsaw to obtain authorization to send her on a cure for people with lung problems to a military sanatorium near the Romanian border. The trip was arranged and the date fixed.

On June 24, Kola and Fritz departed for Riga where they stayed with an old friend, Oskar Fischer, for two days. Fritz showed Kola the places of his student days and arranged a get-together in the postwar home of the Rubonen Club with his closest student buddies-Fischer, Buschmann, Habermann, and Reicher. The contrast between the present place and the former highly elegant old club was depressing. They also went to the beach. Fritz was disappointed that he had not been able to see his friend Feldwig about the inheritance for which Fritz served as executor, because Feldwig had just undergone surgery.

Their next stop was Tallinn where they arrived on June 29. They stayed with Oskar for four days to visit relatives and sightsee. As the news from Lodz continued to be positive, on the evening of July 3, they traveled to Hermann's home on the island of Osel, just south of Dago. The same day at 6 PM, Gerda died; she was just 22 years old. But in the early morning a storm had destroyed the connecting telegraph lines and they did not receive the telegram until much later. On July 5, Oskar finally telephoned with the news that Gerda was extremely ill (apparently he was not aware that she had died) and would Fritz please come home. He and Kola hastily collected their belongings and sped by car through the entire length of Osel then to Hapsal where they learned the dreadful news from Ewald's wife. Fritz broke down; he was overcome with grief. But they immediately continued on to Tallinn. When they arrived the only train for Riga had already left. The next one would not leave for 24 hours so they could not leave until the following evening. They reached Riga on the morning of July 7. Gerda's funeral was held on that afternoon in Lodz!

They arrived back home at 10 AM on the following day to find the house in a sad state. Maria was sick in bed and was just beginning to come around. Julie was undone and Janusz had lost his head. Fritz's trip had cost a great deal of money and brought the family nothing but grief. Poor Maria had to cope with the blow all by herself and she had collapsed. "Surely much of this could have been avoided if the physicians had been more honest with us. Obviously they knew that she was terminally ill with TB," he wrote. Then Fritz found a letter from Heddy, which had gone unanswered in all the turmoil. In it, she excitedly described her arrival in the USA. She, of course, had no idea of her sister's death, or that she had even been seriously ill. Fritz wrote, "It feels strange to think that the first letter from home that she will receive in the new land must bring this dreadful news."

Toward the end of July Maria had sufficiently recovered to get away from the depressing atmosphere at home, so she and Julie traveled to Mittersill, a town in southeastern Austria. Hanna and Bodo, who were on an automobile excursion with sister Hedwig from Estonia, joined them there for a few days. They stayed until the end of August and then travelled via Salzburg and Munich to Berlin, where they stayed for five days with Hanna before returning to Lodz. Upon Maria's return Wanda Warrikoff showed up to present her condolences, and after six years of silence the families were back on good terms. After Gerda's death, Janusz suddenly saw a chance to rent a really nice four room apartment where he could even take in his mentally declining brother, for which he was paid 300 zloty per month from his brother's large inheritance. This distressed the Maehles, as they thought about Gerda and how she had to work and fret to make do with a two-room abode.

During the last four months of the year Fritz's business slowed down. One plant hired a permanent engineer and in another he had completed his contract to install some machines. But although his income diminished quite a bit, his earnings for the entire year were quite good. He lamented that with travels and illnesses, it was all too quickly spent. One of Fritz's major concerns was the sale of Feldweg's estate and mortgage bonds. The news about his health was sounding worse and worse. After his surgery during the summer, he developed some kind of thrombosis that led to a brain hemorrhage with the usual consequences: cognitive impairment, partial loss of speech and so forth. The situation troubled Fritz. Feldweg had given Fritz power of attorney over his estate, which would expire with his death. Fritz would have dropped the matter but as the responsibility had given him nothing but headaches, he felt he owed it to Feldweg to act in his best interest. Feldweg was a Pole and a registered Polish citizen in the eyes of the state. Should he die before the matter of his estate was settled, his children would, of course, be the rightful heirs. But there was a problem: his children were already registered as Latvian citizens and inheritance matters for foreigners were subject to all sorts of requirements, restrictions and approvals. His property therefore had to be sold while he was still living. Oskar Fischer bought the mortgage bonds himself and then helped Fritz approach the Jewish community to sell the balance of the estate. Finally a Mr. J. Glatter purchased the property for $14,000, and Fritz was relieved of the entire affair.

The question of citizenship also resurfaced. A few hours before Fritz departed for Riga on June 24, he happened to run into old Mr. Greenwood who urged him once again to apply for the position of plant manager at Podnarski, saying that the top executive there, a good friend of his, was currently looking for a qualified man. The truth was that Fritz had made very good money over the first half of the year, perhaps more than he could have earned as a plant manager, and he rather enjoyed his independence. Had it been a serious proposal, he doubted that he would have pursued the matter. But with the ticket to Riga in his pocket, he was off the hook for the moment. So he simply assured Mr. Greenwood that they would discuss it when he returned to Lodz. Nonetheless, it kept upsetting him to think that in case he were indeed seriously interested, his status as foreigner would surely become such an obstacle that he would have to drop the whole idea anyway. It was the third time he had been offered a position, which the cursed citizenship question made it impossible for him to accept. It upset him even more during the last part of the year when his business went flat and his income fell sharply. As they were once more on good terms with the Warrikoffs and Hugo was about to be granted Polish citizenship, he thought of getting his citizenship question straightened out too. But, there was another problem. If he became a Polish citizen, Kola would have to serve in the Polish army.

As it happened, the mood at Kola's school was vociferously pro-German and the students lapped it up.[146] In addition, Kola was hoping that Rudy or Uncle Bodo could help him move "into the big world," and he knew that being a reservist in the Polish military would stand in his way. Kola wanted to hold on to his Estonian citizenship. Maria and Fritz felt they could not force him to change; the matter was too serious. The law held that if they acquired Polish citizenship all the children under 18 would automatically become Polish citizens also. So they

---

[146] The children always went to German schools, as did Fritz.

remained Estonian citizens. At the same time they asked Hanna and Bodo to help find a job for Kola when he finished high school. Perhaps he could make up his own mind concerning citizenship after further studies. Meanwhile, he had a very good education and could make a good living with it; many boys, in fact, never went further in their studies.[147] But Bodo's reply was discouraging-"extraordinarily difficult at this time." Meanwhile Rudy and Heddy were welcomed to Syracuse with open arms by Uncle Fred.[148] Fred's wife Mary, unfortunately, had developed a pathological dislike for Heddy.[149] Rudy landed a job at the Franklin Works in Syracuse and the newlyweds were busy furnishing their own home. Heddy wrote she was fine but homesick. And so the year ended sadly though relatively peacefully.

1929 & 1930

1929 marked the beginning of so devastating a world crisis that it paralyzed all business and social life. Fritz's contracts begin to expire and were not renewed. His only solid long-term contract at Barcunski's, where he had been employed for nine years and which had always paid punctually, was terminated. Although he had several other contracts, which continued throughout the year, they were not renewed. And no other new ones were available. The family simply could not live on his remaining income. Finally they decided to take in boarders to make up for some of the losses. They set aside several rooms

---

[147] Kola actually finished his studies in business management in Belgium.
[148] Uncle Fred was Robert's youngest brother. Apparently his parents had died because he lived with Robert in his youth and was like an older (about 10 years) brother to Rudy. He immigrated to the US after he finished high school. In Syracuse he started a ball bearing company (Kilian Manufacturing Co.) and became very successful.
[149] A few years later she committed suicide and Fred married Aunt Irene, his secretary, who was very close to our family.

facing the garden, which they had completely redecorated, and the first boarders came in September. Maria even crotched tablecloths which she sent to Heddy to sell in America; needless to say, it was not a flourishing business.

They were also very concerned about Kola's future. In April Bodo and Hanna visited and Bodo made it clear that he could not be counted on to help with regard to eventual employment, citizenship or anything else for Kola. In May Fritz was required, as a foreigner in Poland, to submit his Estonian citizenship and so the issue was settled; Kola was an Estonian. The family was beginning to seriously feel the strain of the hard years they had suffered. Fritz noted that he was almost 60 years old and was feeling more and more hopeless. Not only was he loosing income, but he also had no savings. And Maria, who had been upbeat through the worst of times, had become a mere shadow of herself since Gerda's death. Her optimism was gone. Things were not going well for Janusz either. He had sole responsibility for five-year-old Miska. Unfortunately, his brother died and he was no longer eligible for the monthly income he had received for his upkeep. He had to give up his expensive apartment and move back into a two room flat.

With the coming year, life only further deteriorated. Business had almost ground to a halt and to make matters worse, their boarder left in January and the apartment was vacant for two months. And the two male boarders who replaced the family gave the Maehles nothing but aggravation. In Fritz's words, "They caused a great deal of trouble for they turned the garden and their apartment into a 'public house' (a pub or tavern) and we were unable to get rid of them." So while Fritz was still able to hold things together with the several consulting contracts that remained, the apartment rent, and Julie's rent, the picture was bleak. Things were not looking good for Julie either. At one point she thought that the company where she was employed was about to go under and she would lose her job, although in the end they did not and she kept it. By late September the Maehles let their last servant go, and Maria had to do all of the housework herself with the assistance of an occasional cleaning woman.

In May Kola graduated from the German gymnasium, but his future weighed heavily on his parents. Fritz simply did not have the money to send him to university and to let him begin advanced studies (in what field?) in the vague hope that the situation would eventually improve. The only choice was to let him do his year of military service in Estonia. Until then he would stay in Lodz, take driving lessons so that he would at least have a driver's license. "Surely," Fritz thought, "every young person would sooner or later have to know how to drive." In addition he would take typing classes and continue his English lessons, which he had been doing with his father for some time. Fritz had been corresponding with the authorities back in Estonia since May and as a result, Kola left on September 1, for Reval where he had to report for service. But his military duty only began at the end of October so he stayed with Uncle Oskar for almost two months.

1931

The crisis had taken on global proportions. Unemployment grew by the millions everywhere. Most plants were operating only two or three days a week. Fritz was earning almost nothing. And the cost of living was very high. Nevertheless, the year began under a good omen. Fritz obtained two consulting jobs and, although short term, they paid some of the bills. In March Feldweg died and Fritz was relieved to have been so diligent in settling his estate.

Shortly before Easter the Maehles received an "urgent" invitation from Bodo and Hanna to visit them in Berlin.[150] Even though they could ill afford it, they went and stayed for about ten days, leaving Julie in charge of their home in Lodz. During that time they got to know Rudy's parents, which made the entire trip worthwhile. Upon their return Fritz found a number of consultations waiting for him. He was still in demand. But the prospects were dim for Kola. What would he do when his military service was over? Fritz had no money for his studies; he could barely scrape up enough money for his trip to Estonia. His future worried him day and night. Then as if from nowhere, a company with which he had been doing consulting had an opening for a permanent engineer. Fritz knew that he was more than well qualified for the job. Indeed, he noted that the engineer who left had always relied on Fritz's consultation and then taken the credit for the work that Fritz did. But Fritz also knew that there were younger Polish men who were qualified for the job and at a lower salary than Fritz required. So he decided to interview the top administrators on their thinking regarding the company's future direction. The decision paid off. They hired him as their permanent plant engineer for his asking salary. It was a half time position, which suited Fritz perfectly since he would have sufficient time to pursue his independent jobs elsewhere. On July 1, Fritz reported to Kola that he had moved into a new position. In August Fritz rented the apartment to a nice young childless Jewish couple. Up until this time Fritz had spent mornings helping Maria around the house but since this would no longer be possible, Maria hired a cleaning lady two days a week. A ton of worries were taken off his chest!

---

[150] The urgency of the invitation was never explained.

It had always been Kola's wish to attend business school in Antwerp with Fredi Romer. Fredi was already in his first year, while Kola was completing his military service. Now Kola's dream could come true. Fritz urged Kola to learn French immediately and get himself to Antwerp as quickly as possible after the end of his military year. At the same time Fritz contacted the Estonian Consulate for Kola's release from Estonian citizenship; Fritz knew from personal experience how many obstacles a foreign national had to overcome. Sadly, Julie finally lost her job and went to Posen to find employment. In November she left Lodz permanently. Meanwhile, Kola had finished his military service and went to Germany to visit Bodo and Hanna and friends of his. In October he left for Antwerp and university. Shortly before Christmas he informed his parents that he had passed the trimester exams with flying colors. Fritz was elated that he was able to pay for his education.

In October Janusz Dobriski married again. It never occurred to the Maehles that this marriage would cause them tremendous grief and bad blood. Janusz had sent them a wedding announcement and had also come to see them in person before the wedding; he promised that his new wife would visit them soon after the wedding. The Maehles had responded with a congratulatory telegram to the couple on their big day. They awaited her visit but she never came. Janusz himself never visited again after the wedding. Miska, of course, continued to live with her father and she was well cared for by her nanny, the good old Wodoracka, who occasionally brought her to visit her grandparents. These visits prompted Janusz to write the Maehles letters complaining that Miska always returned rebellious after her visits with them. It became obvious that he was trying to break off their relationship with her.

This grieved them deeply because they loved their granddaughter, but especially because Maria had promised Gerda on her deathbed to do her best to be like a mother to Miska.

1932

The year began with a worsening situation throughout Europe. Although he retained enough contracts to get by, Fritz continued to lose them as businesses went under or had to cut back to the bare bones. The weather that winter was extraordinarily cold (-18° C); many people died, including several of the Maehles' friends. In February, Fritz too, became ill with what appeared to be the flu and by April there was blood in his urine. The doctor ordered him to bed for several days.

Around the same time the Maehles became embroiled in a huge row with Janusz, which ended with a complete break between the two families. Fritz learned from Wodoracka that Miska was very ill with the flu. At the time Fritz was bedridden himself. Julie had just come to visit from Posen where she worked, so he and Julie talked Maria into dropping in to see Miska. Janusz and his wife were not home when Maria arrived but returned soon after. Mrs. Dobriski became so nasty that Maria was forced to leave. According to Wodoracka, who incidentally was owed two years salary, Janusz was so embarrassed by his wife's behavior that they came to blows. However, she convinced him that Maria was at fault and that he should completely break off relations with the grandparents. A letter from Janusz followed soon after the visit doing just that. And by mid-May they let Wodoracka go, and the Maehles contact with their eight-year-old granddaughter was completely severed.

Kola finished his school year in late June with flying colors and returned home via Berlin for the summer. The elder Kilians, Robert and Dina, spent the summer in the USA. At that time Rudy was then employed by Sealright in Fulton, N.Y. and his prospects appeared to be excellent. Heddy, they learned, had bad boils and was undergoing hormone treatments. Fritz, Maria and Kola spent several weeks vacationing with friends at the sea, and by the end of August Fritz and Maria were redoing the apartment for new tenants. Kola left for Antwerp at the end of September and Julie came for a visit and to pick up all her things once and for all. The new tenants moved in at the same time. The arrangement the Maehles had made was that they would live in the garden apartment themselves, and the tenants, named Wunderlich, would occupy the rest of the house. This arrangement required some degree of cohabitation, which proved to be surprisingly harmonious and pleasant. One wrinkle in the plan was that Heinzel, who owned the house, had folded and the company was purchased in a public auction. Fritz knew that he would soon be forced to vacate the house.

The trouble with Janusz was not over because he had let the Maehles keep some of his furniture in storage and was now obliged to send for it. And then on December 3, a totally unexpected surprise: Miska was brought by her stepmother to live with the Maehles. Janusz had been suspended from his office; his salary was frozen; he was arrested and she could not possibly afford to support the child. They took it as an act of providence; they had their granddaughter back. On December 11, Waclaw, another of Janusz's brothers paid the Maehles a visit and was shocked to hear of Janusz and his wife's behavior. He immediately went to the jail and properly "chewed out" his brother. During the month of December, Waclaw helped out with all the legal authorities regarding obtaining authorization to adopt Miska. So despite the mishaps and stresses of the year, Fritz had managed to make enough money to cover expenses and Miska was with them. They ended the year with joy.

1933

In January Karl Hoffrichter died. His death was a great blow because Hoffrichter was one of Fritz's most lucrative and stable contracts. The enterprise was becoming more and more tense. All the factory workers went on strike for a month. In March all company officials, including Fritz, were given notice, effective June; he had already lost his other stable contract when Heinzel folded in January. What was to become of him, a 62-year-old man with a son who hadn't finished his education, a wife and a grandchild to support?

Kola finished his second year at university and, although he had signed up for a three-year course, the last year was a specialization for Belgian natives, and he decided not to take it. He felt he had the crucial first two years under his belt, and he wanted to join a group of other students on an excursion to Paris. Although Fritz didn't have the money to send him, he then learned that he would receive 2,000 zloty in severance pay from Heinzel, so he gave Kola his blessing to go and enjoy himself.

In April, the Jews of Lodz staged a demonstration against the German Gymnasium in retaliation for Hitler's repression of the Jews in Germany. Things were becoming tense. Then out of the blue, the municipal power plant offered Fritz an unexpected bonus for his services the previous year on the new installations he had supervised. Around the same time Fritz was able to sell the family piano, so he felt a little more able to cope financially with whatever the year would bring. But what the year would bring was yet another ten percent salary reduction with Hoffrichter, who had only occasional work for him. He was now getting less than 23 percent of what he made when he started with them.

Under Fritz and Maria's loving care, Miska was beginning to recover from her life with a stepmother who felt nothing but hatred for the child and for the memory of Gerda — a hatred so intense that she ripped every photo of Gerda off the walls and burned them in the oven in Miska's presence. Then one day, Miska's father showed up, contrite and trembling, and begging to be forgiven for all the awful things he and his wife had done. The Maehles' reaction was cool, reserved and matter of fact. After all, it was he who broke off the intimate family relationship, something he acknowledged was irreparable. But somehow, he wanted to be friends again. Then he told the family that behind his back, a bunch of sergeants and bureaucrats in his division had been wheeling and dealing, selling army supplies on the black market and committing all sorts of fraud. He assured them that the case was going to court and he did not know if he would be discharged from his military. In the end he received three months jail sentence. But first off, he had to pay for whatever harm had been done and all of his assets were currently confiscated. In early May, Fritz summoned him and demanded that he take Miska out of her Polish elementary school where she was running wild and untutored, so that they could send her to Rothert, "a proper German Lutheran school." Reluctantly, he complied. But before Rothert would accept her, she had to be re-baptized. Her only baptism had been an emergency one immediately after her birth. These emergency baptisms only counted if the person received last rites, that is, was near death. So Miska was baptized in a Lutheran Church and was no longer a Catholic.

In the summer the family rented a villa in the country with some friends. It was a relaxing and fun experience for everyone except Fritz, who had to walk three kilometers every day to catch the streetcar for work. Fortunately, he had the month of July off. They returned to Lodz in mid-August. Kola passed all of his final exams very well except for law, where a professor was giving him such trouble that he had to take a make-up exam in the fall. He spent a brief holiday with the elder Kilians at their summer villa before starting his internship in August with SABAT, a Belgium shipping company. In late summer the Maehles were forced to give up the house they had just spent a great deal to fix up. Apparently, they had an altercation with the landlord who wanted them to remove some bushes from the garden and give up the washhouse.[151] After much arguing, the landlord returned all the money they had spent to have the place fixed up and they moved to another place, which was horribly run down. Again they had to do a major fix-up.

In October Kola passed the makeup exam and graduated cum laude. Nevertheless, he had additional courses that he had to take regarding training for his work. He also had to obtain a work permit. But because he was working full time in Brussels on his internship, he could not attend the lectures and training sessions. So the director of the business academy urged him to obtain both a

---

[151] In those days all upper class homes had separate washhouses where the laundry was done. A washerwoman would come weekly to wash, dry and iron the laundry. The washhouse had a large and very hot furnace for heating the wash water. Laundry was hung inside the washhouse so that it dried very quickly. It was a very unpleasant place to work and my mother told me that washerwomen had swollen red hands and huge muscular arms.

residence and work permit. In mid-December he went to Hamburg, hoping to persuade his business friends at SABAT to give him a contract as their overseas agent. Certain steps were taken that caused the Maehles new worries. Rudy too, had been having trouble with Sealright in Fulton. In the USA, the time of prosperity was suddenly over. And a crisis of enormous proportions was spreading. Rudy lost his job at Sealright. The family moved to Syracuse and in June to Baldwinsville where Rudy entered into a partnership with another man to build a paper-processing machine.[152] Of course, Maehles' financial worries rose again. New contracts were not coming in and Hoffrichter was in jeopardy and was getting a bad name in the town. At the same time, Miska's upkeep and education had increased considerably. Fritz had to cut down on the monthly amount that he was sending Kola who was making some money on his own. Last but not least, Bernhard von Dahm, Hedwig's husband died and, although still titled, all his money was gone.

1934

Compared to previous years and especially to 1932, 1934 looked like it was going to be far more difficult. Conditions at Hoffrichter were going from bad to worse. By mid-year everyone in town considered the firm bankrupt. Also, Kola had not yet obtained his residency permit and it looked like he would never get it. He was forced to spend a year in limbo, ready to leave in a moment's notice. And in the USA, the partnership with Rudy did not augur well. In mid-January Hanna and Hedwig suddenly appeared by car. The joy was great, of course, and spending some time with Maria was doing Hedwig a lot of good after Bernhard's death. But she had a very

---

[152] I never heard about this partnership.

bad cold due to the fact that Hanna drove with the window opened, despite the frigid weather. Hanna informed them that she and Bodo had purchased a large printing company from a Jew who had to liquidate his business, now that Hitler had assumed power. In May the elder Kilians came to visit the Maehles for four days. "Probably," Fritz wrote, "because it was easier for them to divest themselves of holdings they had in Czechoslovakia so that they could send money to Rudy to straighten out his partnership dealings."

Fritz's financial situation scarcely improved during the spring. He received a small contract with Hoffrichter but a potential contract he had been hoping for never materialized. The company could not get any credit for the project and he had not been paid by them for three months. Nobody trusted them anymore. In October, Fritz was let go and his remaining contract was cancelled. The only bright spot on his finances that year was a bonus installment from the power plant job. "We are fast becoming paupers," Fritz wrote.

In March, Miska came down with a serious case of mumps and, as she needed rest, the family took a place in the country for the month of July while Kola spent a few days with the Kilians. Barely back in Lodz from the country, Fritz received word from Kola that his request for residency permits as an overseas agent for the company in Hamburg had been denied. Once again, a big fuss ensued. His friends initiated steps on his behalf for an appeal and the elder Kilians urged him to ask for an audience with the king of Belgium himself. But everyone in Belgium cautioned him that it would be unwise. Robert Kilian was furious with Kola for not heeding his advice. For the time being Kola's expulsion from Belgium was delayed and hopefully would eventually be cancelled. Although he tried, he could not get a visa to visit Lodz for Christmas. And Dobriski continued to ask that Miska visit him and his wife. This felt to Fritz like more trouble from the stepmother and he adamantly refused to send the girl.

1935

The year began with more firings at one of Fritz's plants, which translated into an additional salary reduction for him. He was only making about half of his salary of 1931. In his own division, he had to lay off eight men, all with critical functions; yet, management expected the work to continue without interruption. And at home, the tax collectors demanded payment of taxes that had already been paid. Kola was offered a raise, but the residency requirement was a problem. One colleague suggested he marry a Belgium woman thus giving him legal residency. Kola thought the idea outlandish and he soon received his notice. He had to leave the country by May 28.

The senior Kilians and Maehles had been corresponding regularly and in one letter Fritz indicated that Miska was thinking of moving to South Africa one day. Robert Kilian got very excited. South Africa was where he made his fortune! He had many contacts and many plans. First, Kola, being unemployed, should embark for Johannesburg. Robert Kilian would pay for his passage. Being of German extraction, Kilian felt he would have no problem there.[153] He could work for one of Kilian's associates. But after exchanging a few urgent airmail letters, Robert calmed down. Apparently, his associates did not think the idea was a very good one. But on behalf of Kola he was able to get some interest

---

[153] Of course, Kola was not of German extraction but it seems to have been assumed.

from one friend named Tomaselli. Fritz was requested to obtain all sorts of documents for Kola that had to be certified at the consulate, all this costing time and money. Meanwhile, the Kilians decided to go to the USA. So Maria made a bunch of woolen clothing for children in America for the Kilians to take. They departed in May, which meant that the Africa plans were delayed.

There were more complication; Kola was running into more problems. He had intended to head straight home after a short stop in Berlin, but because he was an Estonian national, the Polish consul in Brussels denied him an entry visa to Poland. In the end he obtained one from the consular in Antwerp, who was also a graduate of the Antwerp business school and therefore willing to make an exception for an "old ASCA alum." Kola immediately left for Berlin where he was to receive a reply from Tomaselli. But when he arrived, Hanna had come up with an idea of her own; Kola should join Bodo's business and drop the South Africa plans. Although she was wildly excited about the idea, Bodo was less so. He was worried about Kola's Estonian citizenship-and for good reason. Bodo had frequent dealings with the German War Department. Until the matters were resolved, Kola stayed with Hanna and Bodo and worked in Bodo's firm in return for room and board and some pocket money.[154]

While Kola was waiting in Berlin for Tomaselli's reply, the long awaited letter came to Fritz. Tomaselli advised against Kola's coming in no uncertain terms. He warned that obtaining an entry visa would be

---

[154] There is no information on what sort of business Bodo was in. We do know that he had dealings with the National Socialists who by then were running the country. Whether he was a Nazi sympathizer or not is not reported. However, given the environment in Germany at the time and what Fritz has written about him, it would be hard to imagine that he was not.

extremely difficult which turned out to be true, as Kola was eventually denied a visa. They were only being granted to Jews. The question then became- "what next?" Fritz felt extraordinarily burdened and was in a constant state of anxiety. Hanna was begging Maria to come to Berlin to "talk things over." Finally, as the Maehles did not want to leave any stone unturned and didn't want to have self-reproaches later, Maria went to Berlin. Fritz stayed in Lodz to face new challenges. Maria had only been gone a few weeks when he received a call from Miska's camp that she had an inflammation of the renal pelvis and he should come and get her.[155] He left by car immediately, brought her home and wrote to Maria in Berlin. Maria rushed home utterly exhausted only to find out that Miska only had a cold, albeit a very bad one. Apparently she had contracted it because the "newfangled belief in roughing it to toughen oneself up; for instance, by sitting on soggy grass or around nightly campfires in the rain." Maria also brought the news that Bodo absolutely would not have any part of Hanna's idea to bring Kola into the business. However, Bodo had a friend, a certain Dr. Ernst, who was a big cheese in the National Socialist movement especially when it came to expatriates. He had promised that he would most certainly get Kola an overseas position as an agent of one or several large German international corporations. Fritz felt he was just the right kind of wheeler-dealer they needed. He was hopeful.

Finally the long summer passed and Kola arrived in Lodz in September-utterly frustrated. All his plans had been dashed. His Aunt Hanna's behavior was totally erratic and the great Dr. Ernst's

---

[155] The renal pelvis is the center of the kidney where urine collects and is funneled to the urethra, which makes this a pretty hokey diagnosis for a camp's medical staff.

had accomplished absolutely nothing. And last but not least, he'd completely run out of money. He was despondent-nothing but a charity case! He dropped all plans to work in Germany and resolutely mailed job applications to various enterprises headquartered in Gdynia (a Polish town on the Baltic) always listing his director at SABAT as a reference. Then, as so often happens in life, when things can't possibly get worse, something utterly unexpected occurs that gives the situation a kick in the right direction. A week after his arrival, Kola drove to Gdynia to see for himself if there really were opportunities. When he returned two days later he was practically hired! All he needed was a work permit required of "foreigners" and within a few days, a confidential letter from the firm in question assured him that, according to reliable sources in high places, the permit would be forthcoming.

Kola left Lodz in the last week of October to assume his duties at Bothert & Kibaczycki. An application for the work permit was submitted in December and a six-month permit materialized instantly, indicating that a permanent solution to the permit problem would require Polish citizenship; Fritz immediately wrote to Oskar in Reval to find out how the Estonians would react if Kola were to switch citizenship, considering that he was in the Estonian military reserves. By Christmas Fritz received assurances that the Estonian authorities expected it to create absolutely no difficulties. What a relief for Maria and Fritz! And as an added surprise, toward the end of the year Heddy informed them that she expected to deliver her first baby the next year. She was very excited, as was the rest of the family. So despite the fact that Fritz's income for the year had landed the family at the very bottom of the heap, they enjoyed Christmas in a relatively hopeful mood.

1936

The family's financial situation continued to deteriorate. They had to let their maid go, leaving only a cleaning woman who came in two days a week.[156] Maria decided to consolidate space and rearranged their rooms. Miska was given the big back room as a combined living room and bedroom. Fritz and Maria moved into another room, which then doubled as bedroom and study for both of them, and the front room became a living-dining room combination. Then in February, Miska was hospitalized with appendicitis. She had to have surgery, at a relatively low cost because of Fritz's connections. The hospitalization was followed by a weeklong recuperation at the Reybers' country home. And on April 1, Fritz's contract monitoring the turbines at Muller's was cancelled, leaving the family's situation near disaster. To make matters worse, in May an exchange embargo was put into effect, meaning that it became illegal to exchange Polish zloty for other kinds of currency.

Meanwhile, on Oskar's favorable news from Reval, Kola had applied for his discharge from the Estonian military service. In early January, he came to visit the family for a few days. Maria was bedridden with a severe case of angina. Kola informed the family that he had grown very fond of his landlord's adopted daughter, a Polish girl named Tatjana Chomya. Since the relationship had become serious, he asked his parents advice. Fritz wrote, that he thought that, at

---

[156] The servant situation with the family probably seems strange to today's reader but in those days ladies of the house did not do their own cleaning, washing, ironing etc. Furthermore, these chores were much more tedious than they are today. All clothes, as we've already noted, were washed by hand. The laundress even made her own soap. Then things were hung to dry and ironed with irons that were heated on coal stoves. Vacuum cleaners came to Poland late and even electricity was at a minimum. So, Fritz's reference to loosing help was a serious matte for them.

25 years of age, he was a bit young for a serious commitment, especially since his career prospects were only half-baked and the citizenship and work permit questions were still unresolved; he advised him not to rush things, for relying only on hope and a few vague promises of gainful employment would be irresponsible. However, he would not want to stand in his way. Obviously, they were less than thrilled by the situation.

So Fritz continued the tedious task of getting Kola's papers in order, running endlessly to bureaucracies to obtain his birth and christening certificates, and the official form proving that he had resided with the Maehles, and so on. In late March Oskar wrote that Kola's request for a discharge had been granted, which cleared the way for his engagement. By Easter Kola was officially discharged from the Estonian service. He immediately applied for Polish citizenship. And on April 27, a cable arrived from Rudy announcing the birth of a baby daughter; mother and child were doing fine and their joy was immense as were the Maehles.

By mid-May Kola's problems seem to have come to an end. He had received a permanent position and was no longer in the Estonian Military. Fritz was relieved beyond words. But Kola was hell-bent on getting married; the wedding took place on June 16. All sorts of family matters among the Chistals (Tatjana's adoptive parents) dictated the wedding date, which meant that the Maehles could not be present since Fritz could not leave the factory and Miska was still in school. Fortunately, the Reybers were able to attend and represent the family. Ten days after the wedding Maria and Miska arrived to visit the Chistals. Miska had been invited to spend the summer with them. But Kola's far too hasty wedding plans were not well thought out vis á vis the family. For example, the boarding house where Kola and Tatjana were living had no room for Maria and Miska, who had to find lodging elsewhere. And an extended stay for Miska didn't seem like a very good idea either, as both Kola and Tatjana had to work from 9 to 5, and Miska would have had to spend her days alone. So Maria put her into Rothert summer camp and returned home.

In late August Fritz had his usual summer vacation so he was able to have the stove in one room (remember, no central heating, just coal or wood stoves) moved. The dirty job was barely done when a postcard arrived from Heddy announcing that she intended to come for a visit toward the end of the month.[157] Their joy was beyond description. She arrived in Lodz on September 3, at 6 AM. Fritz picked her up by car. A few days later Julie arrived from Posen and in mid-September Kola and Tatjana arrived. The family was at last complete again. They had a family picture taken and discussed future plans. As Fritz could no longer afford to pay for Miska's school tuition, clothes, and other expenses, Kola took over the tuition. Heddy offered to send a monthly contribution to defray the cost of clothes, schoolbooks and such. Tatjana, as the family was to find out later, was already pregnant. As a result she was irritable and nervous and rather difficult to communicate with. Heddy left on September 24, Kola on the 26th and Julie moved in with her siblings in Lodz. The days were gone in a wink.

By the end of October Tatjana gave notice. Fritz anticipated that by January Kola and she would have only half of their regular income to survive. And, they were expecting a child. While Kola was still sending some money for Miska's tuition, Fritz knew

---

[157] Her baby, Gerda, was just four months old when she left. Gerda was left with a nanny known as Baba (her name was Barbara Kundred) who stayed with the family until Gerda was about four years old.

that it would not last long. In early November Fritz received a letter that Oskar had had a stroke; his speech was impaired and his right side was partially paralyzed. Fritz took it very hard. One small glimmer of hope came when Hoffrichter, where Fritz was again under contract, sent him his monthly paycheck on time for the first time in years.[158] Fritz took this to mean that business was slowly improving. In mid-December the Maehles received a letter from London from the elder Kilians that they had left Berlin. Fritz presumed that Kilian could no longer hide his foreign investments from the Germans and feared getting in trouble for non-declaration.[159] The year ended with a nice Christmas party at a friend's home and New Year's with Hanna and Bodo who came for the holidays, the Wunderlichs, and Julie, who were also in Lodz for the holidays.

1937

The Maehles serious financial straits continued. Hanna sent whatever information she could garner about the Jurgensens but there was very little interaction with Hedwig. Oskar, much diminished by his stroke, nevertheless returned to work in mid-January but had great trouble writing. And then in mid-February, Oskar wrote a letter to Fritz showing how his handwriting had improved. Also in February, Fritz's old friend Messer (from school) died. The elder Kilians, who were still in England, were trying to go to the USA to be with Rudy and Heddy. But the best news was the birth of Kola's son, Waldemar, called Valdi, on March 21.

---

[158] The company continued under new ownership and apparently still sought Fritz's services.
[159] It could also have been because Dena was Jewish and Robert knew that she would not be safe in Germany as Hitler's anti-Semitic policies had become all consuming.

In late winter Fritz was asked to go to Tschechensbochau to inspect a new steam kettle. It was a good kettle and Hoffrichter needed it badly. It was finally purchased in late April, complete with all its accessories. During the interim the person selling the kettle stripped it down to the basics. After endless foot dragging and haggling, the purchase was resolved, more or less to Hoffrichter's satisfaction in August. Work improved a little during the spring with a few more contracts. Also in April Fritz was asked to deal with another kettle problem, this time at Haebler's, whose license had been withdrawn when the inspectors found their kettle in dire need of repair. It looked like it could be a very big contract for Fritz, but it all ended with a decision to have the plant connected to the public power by mid-October, which made the kettle completely superfluous, at least for the time being.

In the spring, Heddy and her little daughter[160] joined Rudy in Middletown, Ohio, where he was mounting all sorts of machinery but having trouble with his new company, Sousa. She could only stay for a short time as the senior Kilians were planning a visit to Syracuse from England, and she had to receive them. In late July, after having sent Miska to Julie's in Zakopane, Fritz and Maria moved two floors up to a new bright apartment. Once Hoffrichter's kettle was functioning without constant prodding from Fritz, he and Maria joined Miska in Zakopane for two weeks.

In September there was much hemming and hawing over Miska's school and the Maehles decided to let her father pay for it. This made him feel that he was in charge again, and he tried to force Miska to

---

[160] Fritz never referred to Heddy's daughter by name. Perhaps it was because she was named after his own daughter and it was painful for him to say it.

pay a visit to his wife, which resulted in fresh trouble, aggravation and paperwork. Because Fritz was upset by the run-in with Dobriski and because he had great concerns that one of his consultations might be withdrawn, not to mention the fact that he should already have been sent into retirement with a pension of 160 zloty, he decided to inform Heddy and Kola of his precarious situation. Kola replied solicitously; Heddy did not reply at all. To give an idea of how tight times were for the Maehles, Fritz wrote that money from monitoring the engines at Seidel, one of his consultations, enabled him to buy his first new summer suit in years. Despite their miserable income, Fritz was relieved to see how well Maria managed the household, and so far they had had enough to eat. However, they could no longer pay for Miska's school expenses. Fritz was reluctant to advise Kola further of the financial problems even though Maria thought he should. But when Gerda got married, Kola was just a 13-year-old child; he belonged to a younger generation. Heddy and Julie, on the other hand, were Gerda's contemporaries, and therefore he felt it should be incumbent on Heddy to take care of her late sister's orphaned child, considering that the grandparents had been caring for her since she was a small child. Heddy had promised to do so but the matter rested there. Rudy simply did not make enough money by American standards. But Kola was not making very much either; he wasn't even settled yet.

Fritz's health continued to deteriorate. He had been on an iodine diet, followed by some European "cure" to strengthen his heart, which didn't seem to agree with him. Perhaps, he suggested, the occasional cigarettes that he smoked didn't help either. And he was very stressed with the Hoffrichter kettle problems. In any case, he felt awful. Maria finally dragged him to a doctor who prescribed homeopathic pills, to no avail. He continued to vomit frequently. Then in late October, Munchberg von Boroszyn (what a name!) returned from taking a cure for his stomach and recommended some stomach tea along with some salts. Fritz followed Munchberg's advice and by year's end he seemed to feel better.

But their situation was very depressing. Firtz applied for emeritus standing so that he could get something from his insurance company in case he lost his job at Hoffrichter's. And Haebler looked like it was in bad shape too. They rarely had enough money to pay him his monthly retainer. Technically, however, Fritz noted that his specialty in the field had kept him very busy considering the times. He had consultations at Hoffrichter, Haebler, Muller and Seidel as well as Gaede in Kalish. Fritz wrote, "I thank God that as I'm about to turn 67, I'm still able to hold my place in my chosen profession!" And then in mid-December, Hoffrichter's electrification contract with the central public power that Fritz had been pushing for two months was signed, translating into a large amount of work for Fritz in the coming year. "Little by little, everything would work itself out," Fritz thought. His only prayer was that God grant Maria and him to live out their remaining years in serenity and peace, and with means enough to cover their basic needs so that they could rest from their labors without being a burden to their children or a nuisance to the world. He was confident that God would turn their dire situation around, for up until then He had helped them always.

Chapter XI:
World War II[161]

1938

The year began with a visit from Kola. Apparently he was having some domestic problems, which seemed to involve his parents' attitude toward Tatjana. After some correspondence following his visit, they were able to settle the dispute and all was well, except for Kola's work. He had applied for a position in Rio de Janeiro but nothing came of it. Finally in June, he found a new position in a company named Bergtrans, thus relieving the family's anxiety somewhat. But other disturbing news continued. Fritz heard from his three remaining brothers. Oskar was forced out of his position and was in Dorpat for some medical tests; Ewald had asthma attacks; and Hermann had thrombosis and almost died of a blood clot.[162]

---

[161] Kola's narrative ended at this point. All we have are Fritz's dated notes, a series of events and dribbles of information, meant to jog his memory. As we know from his Introduction, he completed his narrative in 1938, early May to be specific. Because of the brevity of the notes and the fact that I lack Kola's personal knowledge of these times, it is impossible to give them the flavor of a narrative. There are no opinions or thoughts expressed by Fritz or anyone else, only facts. I have summarized his notes as best I can. I've left out some of the comments about friends' deaths, and such events, which have no meaning for us. I have also elaborated on some of his scant references to Hitler and the war.

[162] Fritz's brother Rudolf died in 1925.

Maria's youngest sister, Hedwig, wrote that Hanna and Bodo were getting divorced in June. Bodo remarried a month later. Good news arrived in July by telegram from Rudy announcing the birth of Frederic Rudolph, and by the end of the summer the Maehles' newly remodeled apartment was finished. Hanna came for a weeklong visit in September, and in November Heddy wrote that Papa Kilian had undergone surgery for retinal detachment in both eyes in New York City. The surgery failed and he was blind for the rest of his life.

Over the course of the year Fritz's work continued to dry up. There were strikes at several plants in Lodz which, added to the major changes in operations and the tension throughout Europe, were having severe consequences on his consulting business. Fritz had been waiting for his retirement pension, which finally began coming in June, two years after he turned 65. And although he managed to eke out an existence and hold on to some of the contracts for a little longer, it was the beginning of the end.

But worst of all, 1938 marked the beginning of WWII, and the beginning of the end of the Maehles' existence, as they knew it. In mid-March Fritz was on a train to Krakow with an engineer from one of his few remaining consultations exactly when Hitler occupied Austria. In May the situation became tense in Czechoslovakia and the Sudetenland. In September Hitler gave a major speech on Czechoslovakia and German rights. In response Czechoslovakia ceded her territory with 50% or more Germans to Germany. In October she evacuated the Sudeten. Chamberlain went to see Hitler in the same month and returned to London with the Munich Agreement. His "Peace in our Times" speech was meant to assuage the fears of the British people that Hitler had no designs on the rest of Europe. Fears were not assuaged in Britain or anywhere else. That Christmas, for the first time in many years, the Maehles had no tree. They sat glued to the radio. They had a quiet New Years Eve with the Wunderlichs and Hanna, who came for a week's visit and left on January 5 at 1 AM.

1939

January began with air raid drills, blackouts etc. Poland had long anticipated war would break out with Germany and on January 5, Hitler told the Polish Foreign Minister that Poland's Danzig area would always remain German. On January 26, Fritz was forced to remain at Hoffrichter until 9 PM because of an air raid; the following day there was another air raid drill. Life was becoming very tense again. Kola was a bright spot with a brief visit in late February while enroute to Kattowitz, a town near Lodz. The day after he left there were anti-Polish student uprisings and demonstrations in Danzig, with signs such as "Poles and dogs not admitted." The Czech crisis was worsening; Hitler had entered Slovakia. On March 16, the Czech territories of Moravia and Bohemia became German protectorates and on March 19, a triumphant Hitler returned to Berlin. Tension was heightening in Poland and war preparations were increasing. There was great agitation in Britain over the Czech situation, and there was great unrest in the Memel[163] region, which demanded to be incorporated into the empire of Greater Germany. On March 22, Kola was conscripted into the German army and was assigned to do secretarial duty in the commissioner's office. And on the same day, Hitler entered Memel. He returned to Germany two days later.

---

[163] German for Klaipeda, a city and seaport area on the Baltic in western Lithuania.

German baiting began early in the year at the Hoffrichter factory against the German administrative staff. Although Germany reacted semi-officially, it continued unabated. On March 25, Mussolini gave his famous speech in support of Hitler. It also appeared that he had designs on Albania. Madrid capitulated on March 28, and all Spain went to Franco. On March 31, since Hitler had brought up the Memel corridor and Danzig issues, Beck, the Polish foreign minister became concerned about those areas and went to London, where there was a lot of talk about far-reaching plans to blockade Germany. On April 1, Hitler gave a big speech in Wilhelmshaven, blaming Britain and other European countries for WWI. He renounced the Munich pact of September 1938, and expounded on England's suspicions, mistrust, and aggressive hostility towards Germany, implying for no good reason a war against Germany by Britain was taken for granted in that country.[164]

On April 14, Roosevelt sent a sensational message to Hitler and Mussolini expressing awareness that Europeans were living in fear of war and requesting that Hitler give assurances that Germany will not invade some 21 countries that he listed. He offered the US as an intermediary in securing a peaceful settlement.[165] Fritz found that notion idiotic. Mussolini delivered another speech on April 28, brushing off Roosevelt. But both he and Hitler retained friendly appearances toward England, although Hitler voided Germany's treaty with Poland and the agreement with Chamberlain. Political tensions were mounting in Poland. Fear of war continued to grow. Germany was claiming East

---

[164] See www.Avalon.law.yale.edu/subject_menus/bibkmenu.asp
[165] See Franklin Roosevelt, Letter to the Chancellor of the German Riech, April 14, 1939 on the Internet.

Prussia, Danzig and all the territories beyond Berlin. England declared itself willing to accept a non-aggression pact with Germany, and Hitler and Mussolini formed a military alliance on May 8. At the same time, Henderson, representing the USA, was lobbying German Foreign Minister Ribbentrip for a peaceful solution.

On the personal side, Fritz was suffering from extreme stomach problems with constipation, extreme stomach acid, and vomiting. One doctor diagnosed him with a hernia but when he went to be fitted for a support corset, it was determined that he did not have one, which Fritz also thought. Another doctor gave him carbon treatments, tranquilizers and other medicines but his indigestion, vomiting and stomach cramps continued unabated. Oskar wrote that he was feeling pretty well, considering he had had a stroke. Fritz continued to work for Hoffrichter who finally paid him, although Haebler, another consultation, still had not. Fritz was also negotiating with Hoffrichter for a leave of absence. Another big demonstration against the German administration took place in the factory courtyard one day while Fritz was in the factory. The Jews were predicting war was imminent.

Kathe Wunderlich and her mother, Irma came to stay with the Maehles in May to prepare for Kathe's wedding. Then on June 3, Julie arrived from Zakopane to announce that her engagement to Kola Warrikoff would become official in three days. Her fiancé arrived three weeks later and was truly giddy around Julie. They were married on July 8. The celebration was gala and for a few hours, the Maehles forgot about the tensions that surrounded them. Several days later Kola suggested that Tatjana and Valdi come to Lodz to be a bit more out of the line of fire. At the same time the German administrators at

Hoffrichter were dismissed. Fritz was beginning to feel pressure to resign from Hoffrichter also.

In late July Fritz and Maria went to visit Kola and his family, who asked if they could come to Lodz later in the summer. They then went to Danzig and a two-day sail aboard the ship *Teneriffe* where, on July 28, they celebrated Maria's birthday with splendid coffee and cake. Following their return, Maria left for Posen to be at Kathe's wedding, which coincided with some of Hoffrichter's friends' 50th wedding anniversary celebration. All the dismissed Germans from the company attended. In August Miska had surgery for polyps, and Tatjana and Valdi arrived for the summer.

On August 21, a bombshell! Ribbentrop went to Moscow to conclude a pact between Hitler and Stalin, something that Fritz had anticipated at the time of Julie's wedding in early July. The pact was signed two days later. Kola telephoned a few days later to say that tensions were at fever pitch at Bergtrams; an underground bunker was being built at the factory, and he would be leaving soon. He wanted Tatjana and Valdi to stay in Lodz. On August 29, the family received their last letter from Heddy before war broke out. Meanwhile, Maria was having eye problems. The treatment-leeches for bloodletting!

On September 1, Germany invaded Poland marking the start of WWII. Bombs were falling; air raids remained in effect all day and night. Hoffrichter offered 200 zloty per day for people to come in and seal windows so that not a ray of light could get out at night. A week later the plant was closed down, and as they had run out of money, it was not known when, if ever, it would be reopened. On September 4, the Haebler factory was set on fire and a warehouse of another of Fritz's factories was burned out. Fritz was on call day and night.

Sheer panic had seized Lodz and on September 6, although it was not being bombarded, the city was evacuated. Pandemonium ensued! General chaos! No more police! Not enough money, food or work! And the thunder of cannons all night long! All the young people left for Warsaw, ostensibly to straighten things out-only to return the following day. Here Fritz wrote, "This will all change dramatically as soon as the eastern lands (such as Galicia) that formerly belonged to Germany are at last reintegrated into the modern German Empire." He also noted that the people there had long been secretly listening to German propaganda broadcasts and were sympathetic to Germany.

The Germans occupied Lodz on September 8, and it was annexed to the Reich in November. On September 10, Tatjana, Valdi, Maria and Gerda Maria[166] left to stay with Mrs. Habe. The Germans were occupying Lodz while the Polish were attempting to reoccupy it. On September 13, Hitler drove through Lodz as the German army continued to advance. There were droves of airplanes flying overhead toward Kutno (a nearby city) where a battle had been raging for several days. Gdingen (where Kola lived) had already fallen and 60,000 prisoners had been taken in a nearby town. Fritz had not heard from Kola for some time and was very worried.

Germans had already been billeted in Hoffrichter's, so Fritz asked one of the officers to see about providing a new pump, as the old was not working. The pump was obtained, but it worked so slowly that there was almost no water to operate the machines. And on September 18, Fritz was almost

---

[166] This is the first mention of Gerda Maria and neither Hilde nor I have any idea who she was. Hilde thought she might have been a cousin, which I doubt. It may also be Miska's given name, which is logical as Fritz was writing about a small family group and Miska is often a Russian nickname.

arrested, accused of sabotaging the pump. However, he managed to get it working, again, and, again.

By mid-September there was no money in Lodz. Workers were not being paid and understandably, were very upset about this situation. So they helped themselves to merchandise instead. On September 17, they learned that the Russians had invaded along the entire Polish-Russian border. Poptaski[167] declared that this was the end; Fritz concurred. They were both wrong. On September 21, Kutno fell; about 50,000 prisoners were taken although that figure climbed to 170,000 by the following day. The war seemed to be over except for Modlin and Warsaw. Chamberlain and Daladier, the Prime Minister of France, stubbornly wanted to continue fighting.

By September 27, Hoffrichter's was in operation again and spinning resumed; the Germans were on top again in Poland. The following day, Warsaw fell. And the next day, despite the German presence, the factory closed again; everyone was fired. On October 3, the Maehles heard from Kola who was still in Gdingen with his firm liquidating things. Meanwhile, Tatjana was trying to get to Gdingen, as Kola had been able to obtain a certificate stating that she was an ethnic German.[168] Her efforts were unsuccessful, as all trains had been confiscated for military transport. On October 7, Hitler made another speech and a renewed peace offer, which Chamberlain turned down. By this time Fritz's stomach problems had returned. He was vomiting three times a day. He felt so wobbly that he had to go home to bed.

---

[167] He was probably some Polish official; Fritz did not say any more about him.
[168] She was actually Polish but apparently they thought that they would be safer as Germans.

On October 14, German U boats sank the British Ship, the Royal Oak, causing a worldwide sensation. On the same day, Fritz's brother Ewald died in Reval. In Lodz, there was severe panic buying for fear of currency exchange problems. Maria became very nervous. Tatjana was unhappy because she could not get to Gdingen and Fritz continued to vomit. Inflation was rampant; there was no coal and the autumn weather was dreadful with incessant rain. On October 23, the Maehles lost their maid and on the 24th Tatjana tried again for the umpteenth time to go to Gdingen. Finally, she was successful.

On October 26 a transport of Balts from Reval and Riga arrived in Gdingen, including Oskar and his family. Miska's father came to visit the Maehles, and Hanna wrote that she too wanted to visit. Miska left her Polish school, which she had returned to and returned to Rothert. Her father was displeased but could do nothing about it so he simply ranted and cursed. Fritz's health continued to deteriorate. The vomiting seemed to be incessant. Food also became scarce. Life was deteriorating.

On November 7, Kola wrote that he would soon be drafted into the SA, a branch of the SS for foreigners. The town of Wattegau near Gdingen was annexed by the Reich. Lodz too, was soon annexed by the Reich. There was a large German population in the city and it was renamed Litzmannstadt after the German general who captured it in WWI. About 34% of the Lodz population of 665,000 was Jewish and it was at this time that the Lodz ghetto was established.[169] On November 8, Hitler gave his

---

[169] It was completed in Feb. 1940. About 160,000 Lodz Jews and 38,000 from Luxembourg, Germany, Austria, and gypsies were imprisoned in the ghetto. 70,000 Lodz Jews were deported to work for the Germans. The total number of survivors of the Lodz Jewish community, which in 1939 exceeded 220,000, has been estimated at only 5,000-7,000. Today only a few hundred Jews live in Lodz.

famous speech at the Hofbrauhaus in Munich where an attempt was made on his life. Nine people died and 60 were injured.

In Lodz, coal and potatoes were very scarce. Then in late November Fritz finally got some potatoes, which he hid in a vacant room. And on the 25th he registered with the Workers' Front and his heating was turned on for the first time. The family could take baths once again. On the 30th they heard from Kola that he was in Warsaw and had been inducted into the German army. Fritz's vomiting increased; he spent many days in bed; he began vomiting during the night. On days he was not in bed, he had to lie down every afternoon. On December 10, Kola and Julie Warrikoff paid Fritz a belated birthday visit. And on December 13, Oskar died. Only Fritz and Hermann remained.

Allart notified Fritz that they would like to have him working there again but the vomiting continued and he was too weak. Things were getting very uncomfortable for foreign people living in Poland. Insofar as the Maehles were Estonian citizens with Estonian passports, they realized that they could be deported at any time. With few choices, and Germany gaining on Poland, Fritz wrote to Hermann requesting proof of ancestry. He needed an "Aryan certificate" so that he and his family could claim German heritage or face deportation from Poland. Hanna wrote that she planned to visit over the holidays. The vomiting continued; sometimes it was pink, indicating blood. Kola arrived at 3 AM on December 31, to wish his parents a Happy New Year and they chatted the whole morning away.

1940

Fritz's health continued to deteriorate. He had blood in his urine and stools. He became so weak that he could barely walk around the block. He spent many days in bed and the vomiting continued relentlessly. He lost considerable weight, down to 120 pounds at one point. No matter what he ate, he threw it up. He could barely get out of bed. On January 11, he went to see his doctor who thought that he had a clogged artery in his belly and prescribed iodine, garlic and magnesium. On January 23, he fainted; the doctor was called. He prescribed styptic medicine to stop the bleeding. The following day another doctor came and prescribed vitamin shots. His condition did not improve, and he was hospitalized in early February for three week, where he gained some weight and strength back. Word of his illness began to spread and many friends came to visit him quite regularly.

The winter happened to be very cold with temperatures ranging from -4° to -21° C, mostly in the -15° to -18°. As if things couldn't get worse, the pipes burst in their home, and they were without water for almost a month in freezing winter weather. And coal, which could only be obtained on the black market, was very hard to come by. Maria spent much time seeking it out.

As Fritz had been terminated from Hoffrichter's, the family was running out of money. Fritz had applied for social security and was waiting for his vacation pay from the previous year at Hoffrichter's. He was also pursuing other positions, some of which looked promising, including several brief consultations with both factories and the Lodz city. But there was very little money to live on. Maria went to an employment office to seek a housekeeper job and in January she obtained one, working for a Dr. Knorre.[170]

---

[170] It is unknown how long this job lasted.

Kola, who had been alerted to Fritz's health, had come from Warsaw to assist the family.[171] He was able to get two months of his father's pension pay. In fact, he seems to have been Fritz's legs in pursuing both job opportunities and the ancestry certificates. Hermann's genealogical documents had arrived but Kola felt they were not adequate. Fritz wrote back to Hermann for more, which he sent. Then in March, Hanna's genealogical data arrived and they were finally able to sort out and file the Jurgensen side of the family histories which fascinated them. Kola went around to various offices trying to obtain the necessary documents. A few weeks later Miska obtained her German nationality card. During this time, Kola also read Fritz's memoirs.

Fritz began to feel a little better. Kola returned to Warsaw in early March, planning to return for Easter. However, he could not as he himself was in the hospital. Fritz began to gain weight and the vomiting subsided somewhat. He was, however, too ill to keep many appointments for both jobs and job interviews. On March 13, Germany and Finland signed a peace treaty and on the 18th Hitler and Mussolini met. In late March the first sign of life arrived from Heddy via the Hamburg-American route.[172] The Red Cross, alerted by Heddy, came to visit. They wanted to see how the family was doing. Somehow, Heddy was able to send 200 marks, which arrived a few days later.[173]

On April 9, Germany invaded Denmark and Norway, and on the same day, Fritz was told that a job he was pursuing was virtually his. Two weeks

---

[171] This was to be Kola's last visit; it lasted about 6 weeks.
[172] No explanation was given.
[173] There was virtually no communication between the USA and Europe during WWII. People depended on the Red Cross and then only for emergencies.

later a letter arrived from the central office in Berlin telling him that they were sending someone else to take charge and the job fell through. On April 16, the family received a cable that Heddy sent to Hanna about being unable to find her parents. Fritz wrote, "It was the first storm signal." Hanna asked what she should reply; she had 25 letters given to her to reply. After much family consultation the cable was written. It must be noted that, although the US was not yet in the war, all such communication was read by both sides of the Atlantic and obtuseness was thought to be the best approach. On April 25, the Maehles obtained their Aryan Certificates. Unfortunately, Fritz's health was so poor that he often had to cancel his appointments with his few existing consultations. He nevertheless continued to pursue new positions, some of which seemed quite encouraging.

On May 2, the British were driven out of Norway, and on May 10 Germany invaded Belgium, Holland and Luxembourg. At this time Fritz was feeling better, gaining weight and working. Then on the 16th the landlord demanded rent payment and Fritz learned that friends of his had been deported. On the 28th the Belgium army capitulated and the following day, May 29, Fritz obtained a fine new consulting position. He wrote he was ready to assume it on the following Monday morning. He also heard from the municipal welfare bureau requesting an interview with him regarding financial assistance and payments for several of the other consulting positions arrived.

On the 31st Fritz wrote that the Battle of Flanders ended and the British had fled back to their island. This was his last entry. Fritz's illness was terminal. He died on June 17, 1941 in Lodz. The medicines he took and the doctors he saw did not seem to be very effective. Of course, medical knowledge was seriously wanting in those days, and especially in areas, which were not in the mainstream of medical advances. He seemed to have had a strong heart. But the war, we know, was raging around him and life was marginal at best. Perhaps he finally did have stomach cancer.

My mother used to say he died of a broken heart. That may be true.

Epilogue

We have no written record of what happened to the Maehles after the last entry in Fritz's calendar in May 1940. Following the German invasion of Poland and the occupation of Lodz, the country became devastated. We can only imagine what the family, consisting of Maria, Fritz, who was probably very ill, and Miska, went through. In addition to the ground war, everything was scarce, including food, heat, electricity, and medical care.

From mid-1940 through mid-1941, Germany and Russia negotiated a huge evacuation of Estonians to the east. According to a treaty between Germany and Estonia in 1939, persons who were entered in lists of German Cultural Autonomy Administration or who had certificates from the Estonian Ministry of the Interior (which the Maehles' had) were allowed to leave with their families. They were allowed to take with them, duty free, furniture, tools of their trade, some money and jewelry. Ethnic Estonians who claimed German ancestry, which Maria apparently had, and Baltic Germans received permission to leave country. After Fritz's death, Maria and Miska left Poland probably in early 1943. They settled in a small town in southwestern Germany, Oberndorf-on-the-Neckar (Neckar is a river). According to Heddy, who received a few messages via the Red Cross, they had very little to eat and were cold and hungry much of the time. In fact, this is what prompted her Care Package project, which lasted the duration of the war.

Meanwhile, able-bodied men with Baltic roots who had been drafted into Waffen SS military units for foreign nationals were sent to European countries under German occupation and to the Soviet front. Kola was sent to Russia. Since he had given up his Estonian passport several years before in an effort to obtain employment in Germany or Belgium, he was considered a German national by the Germans and the Poles, due to the passport that Fritz had acquired in the late 1930s. And, in fact, he had a strong German identification. As a boy of 13 in 1924, he had transferred from a Polish to a German school and, according to Hilde, was a member of a German youth movement. As already noted, when the war broke out, he was working in the Polish city of Gdingen and when it became occupied by the Germans in 1939, he was drafted. According to Hilde, the men were given a choice — Poland or Germany. Those who opted for Poland were "taken away." Kola opted for Germany and was sent to the Russian front. Kola became a Captain in the artillery and also served as an interpreter. Germany suffered major losses. Again Hilde explained, Kola's unit was surrounded but some men managed to escape. They headed back to Germany where they were captured by the Allies. Kola was sent to a POW camp where he was "deNazified." The process included interviews, a questionnaire regarding his background, how he came to join the army and so forth.

He was released in 1946. He did not want to go back to Poland as it was behind the Iron Curtain. He then tried unsuccessfully to bring his wife, Tatjana, to Germany. She refused, stating that she wanted to stay in Russia with her son Valdi, who was about ten years old at the time. Because she was Catholic, she would not grant Kola a divorce. Five years later, he was finally able to obtain one on the grounds of desertion. In 1952, he married Hilde, whom he met after the war in 1946, when they were both translators for the American Military in Germany.

There was virtually no communication between the USA and Europe during WWII. People depended on the Red Cross and then only for emergencies. Heddy was devastated. She did not know what was happening to her family or even where they were. But during the entire length of the war with Germany, she sent weekly CARE packages to a town in Luxembourg. She was limited by the number of packages she could send each week and the contents were strictly specified by CARE. She raised money for the effort through bake sales and needlework bazaars sponsored by the ladies of the First Presbyterian Church in Baldwinsville. Several of the other churches also joined in the effort and it became a village mission. A room in our house was set up like a store. Every week women would come over and pack boxes. When no one was around Zoe, my best friend, and I loved to play store in the room. After the war Heddy was made an honorary citizen of the Luxembourg town. She received a key to the city, a citation and German cookies at Christmas for years after. I still have one of the tin boxes that the cookies came in.

After the war, in 1948, Maria came to the USA and lived with us for about a year until she and Grandmother Kilian shared half of a two family house around the corner from us. In 1956, Kola and Hilde came to Canada where they settled in Stratford, Ontario; Hilde still lives there. In those days it was very difficult to get an American visa; everybody wanted to come here and one had to have sponsors and a job waiting. With the assistance of my Uncle Fred Kilian, who was a manufacturer of ball bearings, Kola obtained employment with a

Canadian firm, Fisher Bearing Co. Maria moved to Stratford to live with the Maehles soon after they settled down. Maria died May 5, 1965. Kola died May 17, 1972.

Miska went to Canada with her husband sometime in the 1960s. I met them once. I only recall that she was a tired, frail looking person. She took her own life May 5, 1965. Judging from what we knew about her life, it must have been extremely hard. Her daughter, Angelie, whom I also met, still lives in Toronto. Valdi became a physician while he was still in the Soviet Union. After his mother died, he immigrated to Canada with his wife Maria. She died quite a few years ago. They had no children. Valdi lives in Toronto and is still practicing medicine.

Heddy and Rudy remained in Baldwinsville, where Fred and I were raised. The marriage, which seems to have started our quite well, was very rocky. Rudy had become an angry and bitter person. They divorced in 1956. He had suffered many business failures, lost a great deal of money and became impossible to live with — for all of us. Estranged from his family, Rudy moved away, remarried, and settled in Nevada. He died in October 1965. Heddy had a great sense of freedom after the divorce. She was a highly regarded musician. For a while, she taught master classes at Syracuse University. She was the choir director in the Presbyterian Church in Baldwinsville for about 25-30 years, and a very popular piano and voice teacher, her main source of income. After her death on September 28, 1987, a voice and piano scholarship for high school students was established her name by the New York State Music Teachers Association, a group with which she was quite active. It continues to flourish today. After the divorce she traveled extensively with Bill Hanley, 25 years her junior, and a long term student and companion.

Heddy lived a very rocky life. She lived through a violent war when she was a teenager, observing lifeless bodies being transported in caissons in front of her home, sleeping on straw in the basement, and never having enough to eat. Then came the Bolshevik revolution. As a student in Berlin during the Depression, she experienced the highest inflation in the world. We don't know what she thought the USA would be like. But it certainly wasn't what she expected, shifting around from job-to-job through upstate New York and Ohio, and then settling in a town of 5,000 people. She was an intellectual who spoke many languages, a classical musician, and an independent soul who, at the same time was passive and demurring to others wishes. This was most evident with Rudy who brutally dominated her. But she made the most of it by surrounding herself with a group of people with her interests and intellect. Every Sunday night she held a soirée in our home, where six to eight people came for a light supper, conversation and music. Through them she escaped to another place with gracious and interesting friends for a few hours every week.

Most intergenerational studies reveal family cycles through bad and good times and they seem, over time, to survive and even flourish. The Maehle family does not end here. Heddy and Kola's children grew up to enjoy wonderful lives and families. Kola and Hilde had three children, Joan, Michael, and Irene. Michael is not married. He lives in Toronto and the girls live in Stratford near Hilde. Fred married Barbara Larson and had three children, Fritz, Kristen, and Kate. I, who married Donald Freedheim, also had three; Amy, Julie and Sara. Fritz's great-great grandchildren today number fourteen. They know very little about their forefathers, their joys and their sorrows. Having lived their lives in comfort and security it is hoped that these memoirs will bring some understanding about part of their heritage and help them to appreciate their lives all the more.

Appendix A:
The Island of Dago

Frederick Maehle[174]

Dago, now called Hiiumaa, is basically square. It is about 940 square km with a population of 15,000 or 15 people per sq km. The neighboring island of Osel (now called Saaremaa) is three times as large. Geologically, there are many steep cliffs running into the sea and the ground is very stony. The northwest coast of Dago is especially steep and very dangerous with rough and rocky cliffs reaching deep into the sea. A lighthouse sits on top of the NW corner of the island to warn ships of the treachery, but many a ship has ended its journey in disaster. Some shores are sandy with dunes and others are clay. Some beaches are covered with large sharp stones and pebbles so that one cannot swim, walk, or land a boat on them. In other places there are beautiful sandy swimming beaches, and in some places, where the seaweed and plankton have been deposited by the current over the years, we find the healthiest sea-mud known for its healing minerals. There are moors and swamps towards the middle of the Island.

---

[174] This section is 85 pages in the German MS. Hilde only translated the first five or so thus giving an overview of the island when Fritz was a youth. I have further edited her translation. I also left it in the first person present as he wrote it.

The Island is also covered with huge blocks of granite, deposited by glaciers during the Scandinavian Ice Age. Close to the village of Heiler, one can also find meteorites the size of houses. The soil is barely a few inches deep in some places, resulting in birch and fir forests desperately clinging to chalk rubble. The advantage to this is that with such ground, fine roads can be made by cutting down tree and rolling them into place. The largest creek is the Kertell Creek. Parallel to this surface creek is an underground creek which runs right through the village of Kertell where I was born. It surfaces as a beautiful crystal clear spring.

The climate is as rough as the sea around it, which is very deep. The cold current coming from the north hits Dago quite suddenly. As children we often witnessed the water temperature in the morning falling from 22° C to a mere 6.24° C (72-43 degrees Fahrenheit) by the next day. Summer days were always on the cool side. During the nights of midsummer one could read a newspaper in the streets at midnight. In winter heavy frost would only appear after the sea was frozen over. Then temperatures dropped to as low as -25 ° C (-13 degrees Fahrenheit). The sea seldom froze at the western and northwestern sides of the Island since strong currents and high seas prevented ice from forming. But the sea between Osel and the mainland was solidly frozen every year. Indeed, the ice was so strong that goods were carried across by horses pulling wagons on sleds (called sledges or sleds depending on size and number of horses) usually with several wagons in a group.

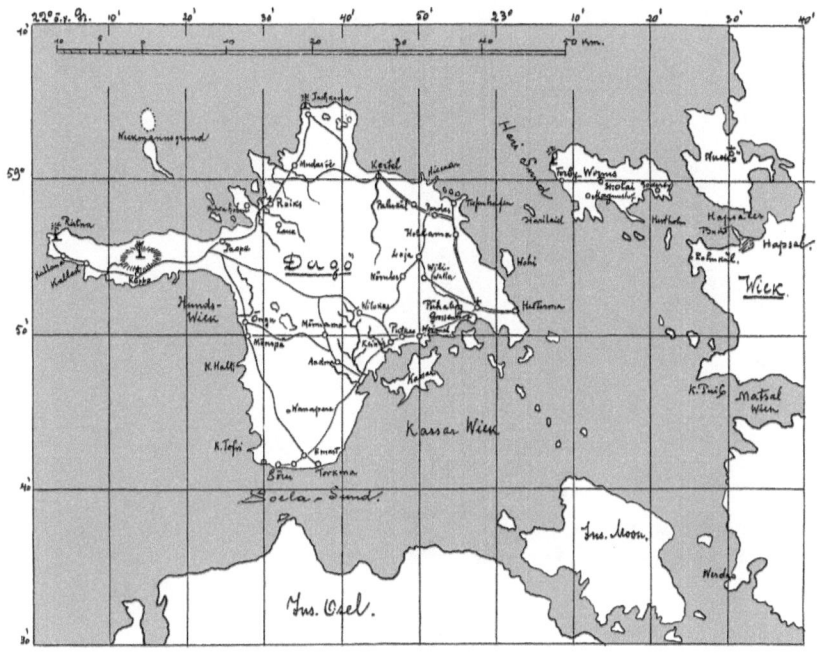

Map of the Island of Dago

Appendix B:
A Brief History of Estonia

It is interesting to speculate on the origins of the Maehle family prior to the 17th Century.[175] We can almost be certain that they were peasants or indentured servants on an Estonian island. They also may have been on the mainland and brought to either Osel or Dago by an estate owner. We do know that they were indigenous Estonians, who sometimes intermarried with Swedes who settled in the Baltic and on Dago. We base that on stories told to Fritz by his Swedish grandmother about his forefathers, even before they were given full names. Fritz also refers to church records of births, evidence that from the mid 17th Century they were serfs on the island of Dago, indentured to a large estate, Keinis, owned by a German aristocratic family that had emigrated from it's native land and for many generations owned estates on Dago and the Baltic mainland. Indeed, as Fritz noted, his ancestors had never been away from their village, which belonged to the Keinis Estate. Unfortunately, most of those records are lost. There are only a few from the 19th Century which are attached to Fritz's manuscript.

---

[175] Other than what is in Fritz's journal, we know nothing of Maria's origins except that her roots were Swedish and possibly German, and she was born in Riga.

Only a few of the first 85 pages of Fritz's memoirs, which deal with Estonian history and geography, have been translated. There are very few texts in English devoted to the subject. A thesis by Edgar V. Saks provides some interesting and credible insights. Much of his text deals with comparisons of names of places, words, and their various spellings over periods of time. But he also uses considerable archaeological evidence, and a great resource-ancient maps and texts.[176] Another text by Anatol Lieven summarizes an early history dating from 3500 BCE. The following information is taken from these books. Insofar as our interest is in the island of Dago, we will concentrate on both this island and Osel or Osilia (the earliest name), the larger one directly to the south of Dago.

Aestii is an ancient name for the people indigenous to the land now named Estonia. Their tribes, widely scattered, extended from the Bay of Finland to the Vistula River, now in Germany. Excavations in Kunda in Northern Estonia have yielded numerous items of daily living such as stone axes, arrow heads, weights, chisels to cut ice, bone tools, amber ornaments and even a carved relief of a man, dating from the Stone Age period around 7500-5500 BCE. This Finno-Ugric civilization developed on Northern Estonian rivers and lakes and spread east to other Finno-Urgic tribes of North Russia and Finland around 6650 BCE. In addition to Kunda, there were other Stone Age dwelling places including

---

[176] Saks's thesis analyzes the linguistic roots of Estonian language which the author concludes clearly shows that the Estonian people were members of the Finno-Ugric tribes and the first settlers in the area now known as the Baltic States. Through tracing place names and words in ancient texts, he documents the early history of the Estonians, once called Aestii, Finns, Cronians, Livonians and Churds — all members of the same racial and linguistic groups, known as the Finno-Urgic.

Undva on the island of Osilia,[177] and Dago, then called Dagaithi. Through barter, trade in flint, and amber, their culture appears to have spread out to other Stone Age tribes towards Poland, Galicia (Prussia), and Novgorod (Russia). Archaeological studies have shown that their religions beliefs were that the soul passes to small figures, which resemble the living man and are usually made of amber. This practice continued for several thousand years until about 1200 AD. In the 2nd millennium BCE, a new race appeared called the Battle-Ax culture. These Germanic-Nomadic tribes, ancestors of the Celts, were few in number in this area and were soon absorbed into the Finno-Urgic tribes.

Evidence of an Early Bronze Age appears in Estonia in 1500 BCE lasting until 500 BCE. Bronze, copper and tin were imported from central Europe, as these metals were not available in the Eastern Baltic area. Some of the common archaeological finds are leaf shaped swords, bi-conical urns containing ashes of their dead, stone hill graves 18-19 feet in diameter and 3-15 feet high, all reflecting a rather advanced society.[178] The oldest Estonian stone hill graves, dating from the 1st Century BCE have been found on the north coast of Dago. The Osilia settlement, Asva Castle, is a typical example of a Bronze Age settlement. Earth constructed on the top of a hill, it is dated to the 8th Century BCE and was continuously inhabited until the birth of Christ. Others castle settlements on the mainland near Riga and Reval show need for fortifications. A map compiled by a Soviet archaeologist shows 71 of the

---

[177] Osel in German, and Saaremaa in modern Estonian. This island is the one located just south of Dago.
[178] Recordings by Danish monks in 1220 AD of graves adjacent to existing villages show uninterrupted continuous settlement for 2500-3000 years. Also found were gold and silver jewelry from the 10-13th Centuries and Arabic coins from the 9th Century.

oldest settlements from Neolithic times into the 2nd millennium BCE. The fortified settlements are an evolution of these Stone Age settlements. Slavic tribes began penetrating the area in the 5th Century AD but disintegrated into wars among themselves by the 9th Century. [179]

Amber, unique to the Baltic, played a very important part in the life of the Estonian and other Baltic people since ancient times and thus became an important source of evidence of the ancient population. The oldest documented evidence comes from an Assyrian cuneiform tablet. Written in Akkadian, the old commercial language of Mesopotamia, it indicates that amber was obtained from an area in northern Europe. Amber is the only jewelry mentioned by Homer in the Odyssey.[180] Amber jewelry was also found by Heinrich Schliemann in his excavations of Mycenae. In fact, in addition, true Baltic amber (chemically verified) has been found in ancient Babylon, Assyria, and the Hittite empires. Thus, although there is no direct evidence of trading with the Baltic, the Baltic is the only source of amber. The discovery of gold coins of Alexander the Great (4th C. BCE) on the island of Osilia is further supporting evidence that trading relations existed in very early times.[181]

Herodotus (5th Century BCE) provides the first written record of the Finno-Ugrian people populating the northern Baltic, north above Finland, and the eastern Baltic into Russia. He describes them using various tribal names, which linguists trace to Finno-Ugric. [182] The Roman consul Tacitus (55-118 AD) was

---

[179] Saks, p. 57
[180] Ibid. p. 22
[181] Ibid, p.23
[182] Ibid, chapter III

the first to describe the nation of Aestii that ruled the Baltic on the east coast, and "which," he said, "used cudgels as weapons, are physically strong, religion and customs same as Swedes, wear masks of boars as cult emblems, cultivate grain, ransack the sea and collect amber which they trade unfinished, having no use for it themselves.[183] According to the Roman historian, Pliny the Elder (23-79 AD), Pytheas of Massilia, a Greek navigator and geographer, undertook a voyage to Britain in 320 BCE.[184] He visited all the coasts of Europe bordering the ocean and then went north and east, visiting the Baltic islands, including Osilia where the aforementioned Alexander the Great coins were found.[185] There is evidence that Ptolomy, the Greek astronomer and geographer (c.100-175 AD) was fully aware of the national characteristics of Aestii and close relatives of other Finno-Ugrians.[186]

A few medieval historical records and sagas specify that Estonians were occupying land north of the Vistula River. Even Dagaithi (Dago) and Aistland, are referenced.[187] One example is in a 7th C. Anglo Saxon poem, *Widsith*, written approximately 375AD. It is the song of a wandering minstrel (bard) but the substance of the poem comes from the 4th and 6th Centuries, known as the Heroic Age. *Widsith* records that he was with the Vikings, and states that the "Caelic (meaning Chuds), an Estonian tribe, ruled the Finns." The minstrel continues, "And I was with (the Goth) Eormanric, all the time; then the king of

---

[183] Ibid, p.25
[184] Historians actually credit him with discovering the British Isles.
[185] Saks p. 38
[186] Ibid. p. 42
[187] Ibid. p. 32

the Goths[188] treated me wellfull. Often there was dit (did) not fail (the Aestii fought valiantly) when the army of the Goths with their strong swords hat (had) to defend their ancient domain against the people of the Aetla (Aestii) by the Vistula wood."[189]

During the Middle Ages (6th C to 15th C) there was a great deal of sea traffic from Europe, especially by the Norse Vikings of the Scandinavian countries. In Sweden and the island of Gotland (an island close to Sweden and now part of it) they were organized into bands. Using small ships they crossed the Baltic, plundering and sometimes settling. The tribes on the eastern side of the Baltic were similar in structure and purpose although not as well armed as the Scandinavian Vikings since they lacked iron to make weapons. Nevertheless, considerable information from the 5th-7th Centuries shows that Estonia, whose population in the 1st Century AD was comparable with that of Sweden, was a serious adversary of the Swedes and Danes. Osilia Vikings amassed such a fleet that they attacked Sweden with small fast ships of 30 men each. It is therefore interesting that the warlike inhabitants of Osilia, who, in 570-600 AD, possessed such a mighty fleet that they were able to attack Sweden, voluntarily gave permission to the Gothlanders to settle on Dago. The Swedish Vikings however, did not make significant inroads and evidence suggests that the Aestii tribes began to organize and come together.[190] Records show that Waldia, the castle on Osilia, was

---

[188] Germanic people who settled the area between the Elbe and Vistula rivers. They were warlike Vikings who invaded the Roman Empire in the early Christian era.
[189] Saks p.50
[190] For example, on the mainland, in 1219 AD, the Danish King Waldemar II, took the harbor castle of Lyndanes (Reval) with a huge fleet of 1500 ships. But the warriors of Vizlav, Duke of Rugen, overthrew the Danish with a surprise attack in the night. Saks, 85

inhabited by an Estonian chief in 1241-55. There were also numerous references to Dago itself, which has a very ancient history with the oldest graves dating from the beginning of the Common Era. Dago seems to have belonged to Osilia who used it for cattle breeding and lumbering. It was sparsely settled, even by the end of the 12th C. when records show that there were several Osilia harbors and warriors garrisoned there. [191]

By the 13th Century, the Baltic people were a loose confederation of tribes with many kings, united into a federated state; at that time they entered into a mutual non-aggression pact with Gotland (and island in the Baltic Sea off the coast of Sweden). The advent of the new Christian religion brought Germanic and Scandinavian crusaders into the Baltic area.[192] They saw the Baltic as a fertile area, rich in land and woods and, most importantly, accessible to the Baltic Sea. The Teutonic Knights founded the city of Riga, while the Danes again invaded northern Estonia and founded Reval. Armed and fortified trading posts were established and in 1242 the famous Alexander Nevsky, Prince of Moscow, defeated the Teutonic Knights on the ice of Lake Peipus. In 1343 the Estonians rebelled against the German and Danish but were crushed in 1345. As a result, the Danish king sold Reval and the surrounding area to Teutonic Knights. German cultural influence began at this time and continued through World War I and beyond.[193]

---

[191] Ibid. p. 56-7; and 98.
[192] Manning, pp .4-6
[193] Ibid.

Russia continued to devastate the Baltic States until 1583, when Russia was defeated by the Swedes.[194] Estonia was divided between the Swedes (northern) and the Poles (southern) and the Teutonic Order was finished. But in 1629 Sweden took southern Estonia from Poland, only to lose all of Estonia in 1710 when Peter the Great conquered the Baltic States. In 1721 the Russian Monarchy guaranteed the privileges and local authority to the Baltic German nobility who had become the backbone of the Russian civil service. To be German was to rise to the top. Business leaders and high society spoke German only. In fact, Estonians who learned it strove to lose their accents and reflect a pure German, as if born to it. This is not to say that the Scandinavians, the Danes, and especially the Swedes, did not have an influence on the Estonian people. Many people well into the late 19th and early 20th Centuries only spoke Swedish. And many estate owners were of Swedish descent. That is, they acquired the land when Sweden ruled Estonia and continued to hold it into the 20th Century when the Soviets took over everything. The first Jews arrived in the Baltic States in the 14th Century and seem to have lived in relative peace, working as tradesmen and merchants. But a growing anti-Semitism is reflected in the role that the Baltic States played as participants in the Holocaust. By the end of the 19th Century, under Czar Alexander III there was a major shift in orientation, with an intense Russification effort, which had a profound effect on the 20th Century political shifting.

---

[194] This and the following data are taken from Anatol Lieven's *The Baltic Revolution*. See also Toivo U. Raun for and excellent Estonian History.

Estonia, the other Baltic States and Poland remained in Russia hands until the end of World War I when, in 1920 they became independent republics for the first time. In 1939 the Soviet Union forced the Baltic States to sign defense cooperation agreements under which Soviet troops were stationed on their soil. This was followed by Hitler's order to evacuate Baltic German people from the Baltic States. In June 1940, the Soviet Union invaded the Baltic States and in August they were annexed to the Soviet Union. Repression and major confiscation of property began immediately. In August 1941, Germany captured the city of Tallinn resulting in a complete withdrawal of Soviet troops. Germany recruited local auxiliary police and SS units from the local populous.[195] In 1944, the Soviet Army once again threatened the Baltic States and tens of thousands of Balts joined German forces to defend their homes. The Baltic States remained under Soviet control until 1991, when they regained independence and were admitted to the United Nations.

This brief history should give a little insight into the struggles of the Estonian people. Primitive, illiterate tribes with only sporadic connections to the civilized world through trading first, then plundering and finally wars, they are a people who, until the 20th Century, never governed themselves. The majority of the people were peasants and even elementary school education was only made available outside of the large cities in the late 19th Century. Even their intelligentsia and nobility, Germans and Swedes, who never gave up their national identity, were beholden to the current rulers. The first book in the Estonian language was not published until the 16th

---

[195] These were the special foreign nationals SA units who were conscripted into the German army.

Century, the first Bible in the 18th Century, and the first newspaper the 19th Century.

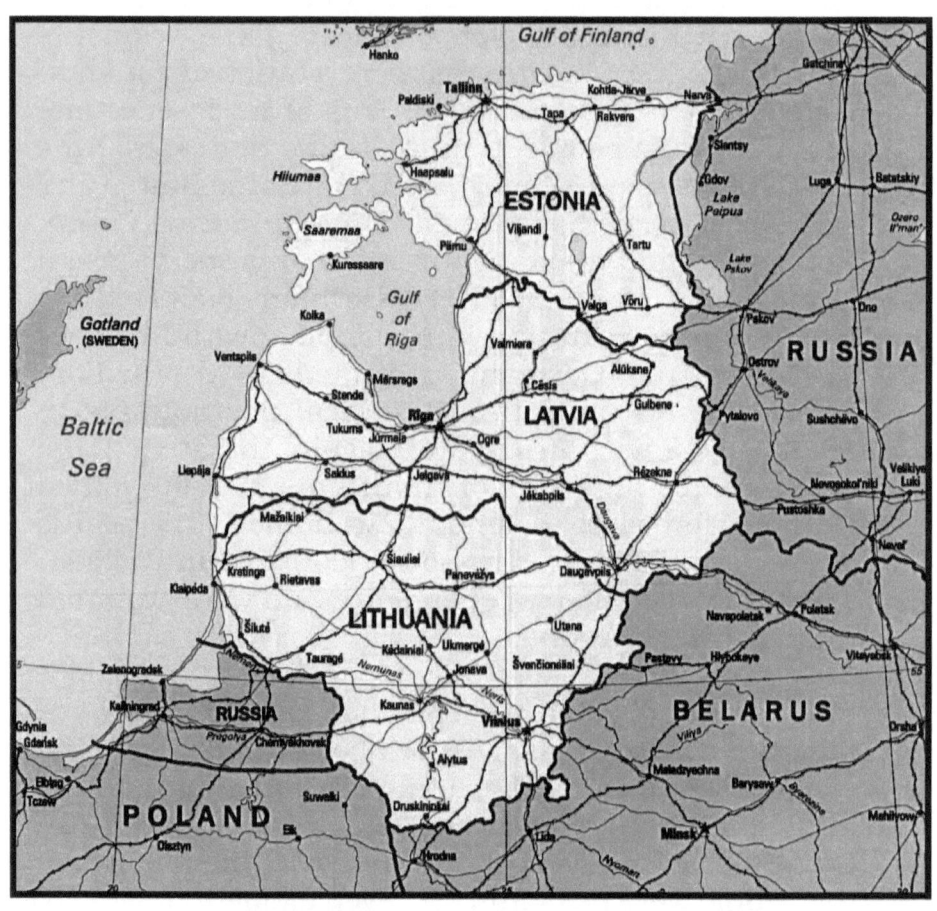

Map of the Baltic States

Photos

Maria about 1900

Grandmother Jurgensen — 1910

Julie, Gerda, Heddy
(with au per in back)

Grandfather Jurgensen — 1910

Rothert School for Girls

Rothert students:
Heddy — Front row second from left
Gerda — Front row far right
Julie — Second row third from left (with long braid)

Heddy, Kola, Oscar, Maria, Gerda

Skating, Grandfather's factory in background

Beach house in Latvia

Maria and children at beach house

Heddy as a boy in school play

Gerda, Oscar, Heddy, Maria, Kola

Heddy, Maria, Kola, Fritz — 1921

Heddy and Julie — 1925

Home in Lodz — 1920s

References

Books

Kerby, David. *Baltic World 1772-1993: Europe's Northerner Periphery in an Age of Change.* London: Longman, 1995.

Lieven, Anatol. *The Baltic Revolution.* New Haven and London: Yale Univ. Press, 1993.

Manning, Clarence. *The Forgotten Republics.* New York: Philosophical Library, 1952.

Page, Stanley W. *The Formation of the Baltic States.* Cambridge: Harvard Univ. Press, 1959.

Raun, Toivo V. *Estonia and the Estonians,* 2nd ed. Stanford CA: Hoover Institution Press, 2001.

Saks, Edgar V. *Aestii, An Analysis of Ancient European Civilization, Part I.* Montreal-Heidelberg: Verlag, 1960.

Articles

Helmreich, E C. Return of the Baltic Germans. *The American Political Science Review*, 1942, Vol. 36, No. 4 (Aug.) pp.711-716.

About The Author

Gerda Kilian Freedheim was raised in Upstate New York and earned her undergraduate degree at Simmons College (now Simmons University) in Boston. Later she earned Masters Degrees in Social Work (Administration) at Case Western Reserve University (CWRU) and in Business Administration at Cleveland State University. For twenty years, she was an Associate Director at the Federation for Community Planning in Cleveland and then Director of Policy & Planning at the Mid-America Consulting Group, as well as Adjunct Instructor at the School of Applied Social Sciences at CWRU. She is the author of several publications on human rights and social service delivery systems. She has been honored in Who's Who in American Women and Leadership Cleveland.

She is married to Donald K. Freedheim, Professor Emeritus in Psychology at CWRU. They have three daughters and six grandchildren. She and her husband are retired and live in Arlington, Virginia.

www.ingramcontent.com/pod-product-compliance
Lightning Source LLC
Chambersburg PA
CBHW030509080526
44586CB00011B/119